COMPARATIVE
ECONOMIC
S·Y·S·T·E·M·S

COMPARATIVE

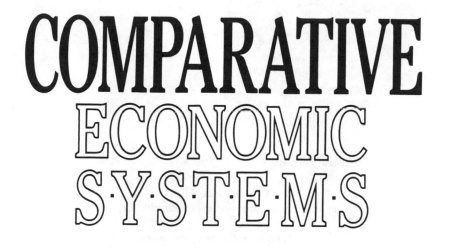

ECONOMIC
SYSTEMS

Richard L. Carson

M. E. Sharpe, Inc.
Armonk, New York
London, England

Library of Congress Cataloging-in-Publication Data

Carson, Richard L.
Comparative economic systems / Richard L. Carson.
p.   cm.
Includes bibliographical references.
ISBN 0-87332-583-4
ISBN 0-87332-580-X P (Vol. I)
ISBN 0-87332-581-8 P (Vol. II)
ISBN 0-87332-582-6 P (Vol. III)
ISBN 0-87332-680-6 (3 volume paper set)
1. Comparative economics. I. Title.
HB90.C37   1989   89-10888
330–dc20
CIP

Printed in the United States of America

The paper used in this publication meets the minimum requirements of
American National Standard for Information Sciences—
Permanence of Paper for Printed Library Materials,
ANSI Z 39.48-1984.

∞

ED (IIIp)   10   9   8   7   6   5   4   3

To those who have struggled for reform
in China, Eastern Europe, and the Soviet Union.

—— CONTENTS ——

Comparative Economic Systems is being published simultaneously in one clothbound edition, which includes the complete text, and three paperback editions, one for each major part. The complete table of contents and the complete index are included in the clothbound edition and in each of the paperback editions.

FIGURES

TABLES

PREFACE

This book is mainly an effort to understand contemporary economic systems, using an approach based on property rights plus elements from standard supply, demand, and cost analysis. The basic framework is developed within the first four chapters. More space is devoted to socialism than to capitalism in the early chapters, since the majority of readers are likely to be less familiar with and/or more curious about the former. Over the course of the book, however, this deficit is largely made up, so that space is more or less evenly divided between the two. There are analyses of several modern economies as well as of historical topics of interest. The political dimension of an economic system is developed, and the compatibility of different economic and political organizations is examined briefly. I also discuss the impact of sociocultural factors on economic organization and development when these are particularly important (as in the case of Japan), although my focus is on economic causes and consequences.

I view the traditional Soviet-type economy as a system based on disequilibrium and more precisely on shortage, a notion which I attribute to the well-known Hungarian economist, Janos Kornai. Portions of the first two chapters develop the properties of this system and pave the way for later discussion and analysis of socialist reforms, especially in chapter 5. In-depth treatment of the current reform movement includes careful consideration of the causes of reform, as well as the reasons for the failure of past reforms and the barriers to successful reform, plus progress reports and examination of the relationship between political and economic reform. The 1980s have been an exciting time to study comparative systems, and the revitalization of socialist reforms has been a major reason for this. Yet the traditional Soviet-type economy has demonstrated staying power again and again in the face of reform efforts, and while there is a growing feeling that its days are numbered in most places, the pace and exact direction of change remain treacherous to forecast. Reform and counterreform will continue to produce tension and surprise in these societies for years to come.

The 1980s have also witnessed efforts to redefine the economic role of government in capitalist market economies. Chapter 1 gives reasons for the expansion of this role since World War II, as well as efficiency arguments for and against widespread social insurance, now the largest category of public-sector outlays. In addition, it introduces the idea of national planning in a market economy and identifies common denominators with Soviet-style planning.

Nowadays, authors sometimes use the term "industrial policy" to describe a type or an aspect of planning. The last section in chapter 2 shows how this can be a tool for coping with market failure, although later discussion makes it clear that industrial policy has sometimes in practice held back structural change, thereby reducing growth and raising unemployment. I also give extensive treatment to two modern economies (Japan and Sweden), which are often cited as models and within which the government's policy role has been substantial, but which contrast in many ways as well. This includes Swedish labor market policy—attractive to socialist reformers as a way to combine full employment with flexibility in production in response to shifts in demand and cost—and the system of (limited) lifetime employment in Japan. Historical topics include National Socialism in Germany plus an analysis of the causes of Hitler's rise to power, including the role of the "debt crisis" growing out of World War I and the reparations levied on Germany in the Treaty of Versailles.

In addition, current "insider-outsider" explanations of unemployment and rigid wages in capitalist countries are outlined and contrasted with the Marxian explanation of unemployment. This is done mainly in chapter 3, which also gives the basic elements of Marx's theory of the evolution of capitalism and analyzes several precapitalist economies in the context of a theory of history based primarily on the writings of Marx and Engels, but also on those of modern economic historians. Although Marx devoted most of his energies to a critique of capitalism, Marx and Engels had more to say about the nature of the socialist system that they foresaw than is sometimes realized, and they did experience a leap of the "future into the present" (the Paris Commune) during their lifetimes. A socialist system meeting their requirements would not be a traditional Soviet-type economy. As is explained in chapter 4, however, efforts to implement the former would probably lead either to the latter or to some form of market socialism, under the pressure of a continuing need to resolve conflicts over resource allocation. ("Socialism" within the Marx-Engels historical evolution occurs when resources are still scarce.)

I intend this work to appeal to a variety of readers in terms of background and interests. It should be accessible to anyone who has completed a standard one-year course in principles of economics, but I have also found this material to be interesting to graduate students (not only in economics) and believe it will be useful and interesting as well to specialists and businessmen dealing with one or more of the countries covered here.

I view the study of comparative systems primarily as a study of systems alternative to one's own and also as a study of phenomena not readily encountered in other branches of economics. In such a context, "model" aspects are important, but exclusion of a specific economy from coverage does not necessarily imply any judgment on my part as to its importance or significance. Space and my own competence are both limited!

Special thanks are due to Gwen McBride, without whose help I never would have been able to get this manuscript in shape for publication, as well as to several others who did portions of the word processing along the way—notably, Norma Rankin, Charlotte Burba, and Ginette Harte. Special thanks also to Susan Klement of Information Resources in Toronto, who compiled the index on very short notice and against an extremely tight deadline. Finally, I would thank students and colleagues who have given me moral support. I have always found my students' enthusiasm for this subject a source of strength.

Richard L. Carson
Ottawa, Canada
December 1989

PART III

CAPITALIST ALTERNATIVES

12

THE JAPANESE ECONOMY: POSTWAR ADJUSTMENT

A quarter of a century ago, all the factories along the Tokyo Bay shore were destroyed, and although the water in the bay was perfectly clear, the people were cut off from the supply of jobs and food. People wanted food and an income, regardless of what happened to the water in Tokyo Bay. Today, storehouses all over Japan are overflowing with rice. Countless companies are looking for employees, while job hunters have decreased. In spite of this, the people are not satisfied. They are crying out for a return of clear water and fresh air. . . .

—Y. Ojimi, 1972
(Former Vice-Minister
of International Trade and Industry)

12-1. Introduction

The two major external shocks to the post–World War II Japanese economy have come from the Korean War during the early 1950s and the energy crisis of 1973–74. The Korean War found Japanese firms—whose products were not yet competitive on world markets—ideally placed to fill orders for the United States and South Korean armed forces, and special U.S. procurement demand caused the economy to boom. Instead of dying out at war's end, this boom triggered the most remarkable sustained expansion of income and output the world has ever seen, which lasted until the energy crisis. Between 1952, when Japan regained its independence after a seven-year United States occupation, and 1986, real GNP per capita rose to over 7.5 times its original value. In terms of purchasing power, it was more than 70 percent of the U.S. level in 1985 and above the average of all West European

Common Market nations. It exceeded per capita GNP in Australia, France, Italy, Austria, Belgium, Holland, and the United Kingdom, despite being only half that of the U.K. as recently as 1958.

Broadly speaking, Japan achieved record economic growth without increasing inequality of incomes. During the period of the economic miracle (1952–73), income distribution remained more equal than those of most Western nations.[1] In this sense, the gains from growth were widely shared, although the rise in living standards lagged behind increases in output. Moreover, Japan's success has always been vulnerable to a lack of natural resources. Although the average Japanese uses just over one-third of the energy consumed by an average American, Japan must import more than 80 percent of its total energy needs. This includes nearly all its oil, and it is also the world's largest importer of coal. After initial panic, it recovered quickly from the first energy crisis, but growth was permanently lowered. The crisis also speeded a change in priorities that had already begun, as a consequence of environmental problems plus growing dependence on imported fuel and raw materials.

Thus, rapid industrialization during the 1950s and 1960s had left Japan with the world's worst cases of pollution and congestion. (A Japanese banker, assigned to Manhattan during the mid-1970s, noted how glad he was to get away from the noise and congestion.) Police directing traffic in Tokyo have been nearly asphyxiated by photochemical smog, and smog has caused planes to be diverted from Tokyo airport. Japan has had more victims of pollution-caused cadmium poisoning than any other country, and in 1972, danger of mercury poisoning forced the government to advise people to cut their consumption of fish (which provided nearly half the protein for an average Japanese). Japan has the world's highest density of industrial production, and Japanese firms have dumped many pollutants into rivers, streams, and the surrounding sea. Although environmental safeguards have been strengthened, these are still among the world's most polluted waters. The smog has killed some of Tokyo's famous cherry trees and, in nearby Kawasaki, it appears to have killed some people.

Over 60 percent of Japanese industrial production is concentrated in three great urban regions, within which almost 45 percent of her population lives (and two of which are among the world's fifteen largest metropolitan areas). These are Tokyo-Yokahama, Nagoya, and Kyoto-Osaka-Kobe, which together form a megalopolis (called Tokaido), stretching along the central and southern Pacific coast of Honshu, the main island of the Japanese archipelago. The crowding of economic activity plus a heavy commitment of usable land to agriculture, has caused land prices to soar, until urban housing has become far beyond the reach of most workers. Many employees receive housing allowances or virtually free housing from their employers or from the government. Even so, Japanese commute longer distances to work under worse conditions than do either West Europeans or North Americans. In the early 1980s, the average price of a dwelling was 10 times average disposable income in the cities and 4.5 times in the country as a whole. By 1986, Tokyo real estate prices were 10 times as high as in New York.[2] These ratios have been rising.

By the early 1970s, other limits to growth had begun to appear. The wellspring of excess labor supply was drying up (although it has since been renewed by a growth slowdown following the energy crisis). Good factory sites were becoming nearly impossible to find, and community protests were blocking some construction—especially of electric power-generating and petrochemical plants—and forcing factories to switch to less polluting, but more expensive fuels. Lawsuits against firms causing environmental disruption were rising, and the courts were starting to award large damage claims. Japan has about 85,000 certified victims of environmental pollution. In addition, if the growth rates of the late 1960s and early 1970s had continued, Japan would have been importing as much raw material as the rest of the world combined by 1990, plus half the world's crude oil output. International political pressures would not have allowed this to happen.

Ordinary Japanese paid for growth in other ways. The quality and availability of housing, public works and other social overhead capital are still relatively low, for example. Housing space per resident has been rising, but remains meager, and quality lags ten to twenty years behind West European standards. As late as 1973, average government social security benefits totalled around $80 per month. Although these benefits have since gone up, a worker not receiving additional income during his "retirement" years is in dire straits, and he will not catch up with his counterparts in West European welfare states until well into the twenty-first century. Other social welfare benefits, as percentages of GNP, were also lower than in most developed countries as of 1985.

By contrast, the share of GNP going to investment in machinery and equipment has been over twice as high as in the developed West. Until the late 1970s, the relatively small percentage of public investment consisted mainly of harbors, roads, bridges, railways, preparation of industrial sites, and other "business-propping" construction that raised the yield on private investment. Social overhead capital was neglected. Thus, Japan consciously chose priorities differing from those of most Western countries and from those of socialist nations as well, although like the latter, it has emphasized high rates of investment to promote rapid development of key industries. It has also been spared large defense expenditures, at some price in terms of political dependence on the United States.

The Japanese formula has been to lavish the savings of its populace on modern growth industries—iron and steel, metals, machinery, motor vehicles, chemicals, electronics, and computers—where each yen invested has quickly produced relatively large additions to output and income. Higher incomes have produced higher savings to restart the cycle. By and large, Japan has chosen investment projects wisely and has systematically moved on to new areas after past ventures had begun to bear fruit. After building up basic industries—steel, electric power, machinery and machine tools, shipbuilding, inorganic chemicals, and others—it proceeded to expand the markets (notably autos, engineering, and electronics) for their products. In the process, it kept savings away from housing and social amenity capital, where the short-term growth return on investment is low. Moreover, since it has had to import nearly all its raw materials and energy requirements—which accounts for the high priority of shipbuilding—it has also had to expand exports rapidly. Japanese success on world markets has aroused the hostility of other nations, whose producers have found it difficult to sell their own manufactures successfully in Japan.

The crowning success of Japan's growth strategy came in the years just prior to the energy crisis. Over 1965–73, labor productivity nearly trebled, and per capita GNP more than doubled. Yet, it was in the same period that the costs of growth became fully apparent, assuring a major change in priorities. On the one hand, this change is reflected in Japan's move into high-technology industries—such as microelectronics, plant automation, and precision instruments—which are nonpolluting and energy extensive, but in which international competition is fierce. On the other, it is mirrored in the dramatic expansion of public investment and housing construction. In 1960, Japan completed only 5 houses per 1,000 inhabitants and trailed all developed nations in this regard. But since 1970, it has completed 13–14 houses per 1,000 residents, as an annual average, to lead the world. Japan's percentage of home ownership (over 60 percent) is second highest in the world after the United States.

If we are to understand Japan at a crossroads, we must probe the nature of its present economic system. First, however, to orient ourselves, we note that Japan is a 2,000-mile-long island archipelago lying off the eastern coast of Asia at about the same latitude as the United States. To the north and west lies the Sea of Japan, and, beyond this, the Soviet Union and Korea. Japan comprises four main islands— Hokkaido, Honshu, Shikoku, and Kyushu, from north to south, and about 4,000 smaller islands. Nearly 80 percent of the population and 85 percent of the economic activity are on Honshu, where all the main cities are found. Japan is slightly smaller (about 145,900 square miles) than California and almost exactly the same size as the Canadian province of Newfoundland and Labrador. Thus, it is one of the most densely populated countries in the world.

In addition, nearly three-fourths of its land is mountainous, and two-thirds is covered by forests. Only 14 percent is cultivated, and Japan has the world's most densely populated rural areas, where over 27 million people still live. (Urban densities are similar to the United States.) For political reasons, the Japanese government has followed a policy of rural overpopulation, helping to perpetuate a system of tiny private farms. In 1984, about 17 percent of the population still lived in "farm households," although just 15 percent of these were farming full time. At three acres, average farm size was smallest in the world and about the same as in 1950, although the farm population has shrunk from about 45 percent of the total.[3] The main crop is rice, as it has been for centuries, and Japan produces a surplus, thanks to a subsidy program that keeps the price paid to farmers around five times the world market level. Farm price supports also boost the value of land kept in agriculture, thereby restricting the supply available for residential and commercial use, which raises the cost of housing and office space. The average per capita income of farm families is above the national average, although less than a fifth of this comes from agriculture.

Japan's climate ranges from subtropical on Okinawa, which is south of the four main islands, to cool on Hokkaido (much like the Canadian Maritimes). The climate is favorable to intensive farming, but the small size of farms keeps value added per worker there at around a fourth of the level in manufacturing, even with farm price supports. Japan imports about 30 percent of its food requirements, making it the leading net importer of food among OECD nations, even though domestic production is protected by a maze of official and unofficial import barriers. To become self-sufficient in food production would be impossible, another reason why Japan must export manufactured goods. (Indeed, the growing cost of present levels of farm protection suggests that they cannot be maintained.)

Japan probably has the world's most homogeneous population, in part, the consequence of an absolute prohibition of immigration. The only sizable ethnic minority is the Koreans, who constitute less than one percent of the inhabitants. However, the descendants of former outcasts, known as *burakumin*, form an exploited group, constituting another two percent. Major religions are Buddhism and Shintoism, the latter indigenous to Japan and based on legends and rituals of prehistoric Japanese. Under it, the Emperor of Japan, the symbol of the state, claimed to be divine until Japan's defeat in World War II. In the latter nineteenth century, the Meiji government recognized Shintoism as the official state religion and used it in harnessing patriotic and nationalistic feelings to the promotion of economic development. The latter had not previously been a goal of government, although Japanese culture has been highly developed for at least 1,200 years. Japan's literacy rate approaches 100 percent, and its people are among the world's best educated.

Politically, Japan is a parliamentary democracy operating under universal suffrage and a Constitution written and imposed by United States occupation authorities in 1947, which places ultimate sovereignty with the voters. Ironically, much of this Constitution is strongly supported by left-wing parties, who especially applaud its provision that "land, sea, and air forces, as well as other war potential, will never be maintained. The right of belligerency of the state will not be recognized." Article 9 of the Constitution, from which this clause is taken, was interpreted until 1987 to imply that Japan should not spend more than one percent of its GNP on defense. This released more funds for investment, which increased growth.

Japan is also a unitary state, in contrast to the federal governments of the United States, Canada, and West Germany. The Japanese central government is more powerful vis-à-vis the 47 prefectures (regional governments) and 3,250-odd local governments than would be possible in a federal system. This power is reinforced by making lower government levels financially dependent on the center. The Japanese Parliament or Diet has two houses. The lower chamber, or House of

Representatives, consists of 512 members, elected from 130 election districts for, at most, four years. The upper chamber, or House of Councillors, consists of 252 members, half of whom are elected every three years.[4] Over 70 percent of eligible voters usually cast their ballots in elections for the House of Representatives.

The two main political parties are the Liberal Democrats and the Socialists, the former having ruled continuously since 1947.[5] The Liberal-Democratic party (LDP) is, in fact, conservative and maintains close ties with businessmen and farmers. The Socialists form the principal opposition, while the center is held by the smaller Clean Government party (Komeito), with Buddhist links, and the Social Democrats. The Communists on the far left are increasingly isolated. Members of the LDP work closely with business interests, and both maintain a continuing dialogue with the civil service bureaucracy. Most Japanese civil servants "retire" before their sixtieth birthday, which means that they must find another job. The best of them step directly into executive posts in private firms—with whom they will have cultivated relations over many years—or else become successful politicians.

Executive power in Japan is vested in a cabinet headed by the Prime Minister, who must be a member of the Diet and is appointed by the Emperor on Parliament's recommendation. In practice, he will be leader of the LDP. The Prime Minister appoints and removes the rest of his cabinet, a majority of whom must be Diet members. The government usually changes when the Prime Minister retires or loses the support of his own party, an event made more probable by the fact that the LDP is a coalition of competing factions. Each faction has its leader, and it is from the group of leaders of the five major factions that the Prime Minister is usually chosen. Of the two Diet chambers, the House of Representatives is the more important. Its confidence alone is required to keep the cabinet in office. When the LDP lost control of the upper house in the July 1989 elections, it maintained control of the executive branch. Bills become law after passage by a simple majority of both chambers. However, should the House of Councillors fail to pass a bill, this "veto" may be overcome by a two-thirds approval of the House of Representatives. Not too much should be made of this because no Japanese government is likely to ride roughshod over a large opposition minority very often. Japanese decision making strives for consensus, and the LDP is usually unwilling to take responsibility for decisions reached without compromise.[6]

Moreover, with one major exception, the Diet has been less important than the government bureaucracy—especially the Ministries of Finance (MOF) and of International Trade and Industry (MITI), where economic matters are concerned. The cabinet and the Diet "decide only the broadest outlines of policy, leaving implementation entirely to permanent administrators. The higher civil servants are 'permanent politicians' who effectively control the administrative machinery. . . ."[7] There is practically no turnover of higher level civil servants, except through retirement, and civil servants have latitude in formulating, as well as in implementing government policy. Over 90 percent of all legislation is government sponsored and prepared by the bureaucracy. Even private members' bills are usually drafted with ministerial help. However, leading LDP politicians, known as *zoku* (or "tribe"), must also endorse policy initiatives and constitute the exception indicated above. *Zoku* politicians become specialists in key policy areas (trade, taxation, information processing, agriculture, etc.) corresponding to areas of responsibility of the various ministries, with which they develop close ties. They serve on LDP committees covering these areas and collectively belong to the LDP's Policy Affairs Research Council, which must approve policy changes.

Thus, MITI and MOF do not always get what they want, nor do business interests. But Japan's bureaucrats have always had a strong sense of élitism, strengthened by Confucianism, which taught that government officials were superior to the masses. By law, such officials are public servants, and the Confucian ethic has eroded since World War II. But MITI and MOF are also widely perceived to have played a key role in Japan's postwar economic success. For this reason, élitism persists, and the Finance Ministry is still the first occupational choice of the best university graduates, followed by MITI and the Bank of Japan. The upper echelons of the civil service, along with leading businessmen and LDP politicians, essentially form the coalition that has led Japan since the end of the postwar occupation, but a few other special interests have also influenced policy in a fundamental way. These include farmers, who receive higher protection from imports than in any developed Western country except Switzerland, and small shopkeepers, who have been able to limit chain-store competition and preserve Japan's fragmented distribution system, which acts as an effective barrier to imports.

The viability of Japan's leadership coalition depends on the LDP's ability to win one election after another—a phenomenon that facilitates economic planning by lengthening the time horizons of public officials.[8] Continued rule by the LDP has rested on the votes of farmers and small businessmen, aided by the fact that a rural vote is worth up to three times that of a city dweller in electing members to the House of Representatives. Rural districts account for the majority of seats in the Diet, and most rural seats go to the LDP, even though Liberal Democrats from different factions often run against each other in these areas. The LDP consistently polls over 60 percent of the rural vote vs. around 30 percent in the cities.[9]

Today's electoral districts still approximate those drawn up in 1946–47, when the rural population was at an all-time high, as demobilized soldiers, repatriates from Japan's former colonies, and workers whose factories had been bombed out took refuge in the villages close to the food supply. Since 1950, the farm labor force has continually shrunk, although huge farm subsidies have limited migration to the cities. Japan's farmers have always been conservative, and government subsidies plus restrictions on agricultural imports have preserved their votes for the LDP, albeit at high cost. Total explicit plus implicit subsidies for agriculture come to 75–80 percent of gross farm output, exceeding value added in agriculture.[10] Because of a thorough-going land reform under the United States occupation régime after World War II, most peasants are small proprietors. This reform produced the proliferation of tiny farms, which government agricultural policies have since helped to maintain.

12-2. Social and Economic Consequences of the Postwar Occupation

We may view the post-World War II Japanese economy as a synthesis of the prewar system and of the one that arose during the United States occupation. When the occupation began in 1945, the economy lay in ruins. Perhaps a fourth of national wealth was destroyed during the war.[11] Around half of the built-up area of the 66 cities attacked from the air had been demolished. Some 20–25 million people had lost their homes, on top of which came a net population increase of 5 million, due to repatriation from territories formerly occupied by Japan and demobilization. About 30 percent of Japan's industrial capacity, 80 percent of shipping, and 30 percent of thermal power-generating capacity were gone, along with nearly all colonial assets, which had been worth around $20 billion. About 3 million Japanese died in the war, and hundreds of thousands were maimed. The average consumption standard of those left alive was around the level of 1890, and average caloric intake was below what had been considered minimal before the war.[12]

Moreover, while there was an enormous serviceable capacity to make arms and munitions, relative to peacetime needs, this could not be converted quickly to light industrial uses. The capacity of light industry was not adequate, either to supply the needs of the people or to fully employ them. During the final months of the war, many city residents were dispersed to the countryside, as bombing turned Japan's cities into infernos, and most had to stay there because of food shortages in urban areas. Repatriated soldiers and overseas residents also thronged into the villages, and farm employment reached an all-time high. Because of this, plus the relatively small damage to the rural capital stock and the postwar land reform, farm production recovered more rapidly than industrial output. (The latter did not regain its 1941 level until 1953, whereas agriculture surpassed its previous peak in 1950.)

The United States occupation authorities (SCAP) did not start with the primary goal of helping Japan to recover from the war. As in Germany, the occupation authorities were originally indifferent or hostile to restoring prewar production levels. On this basis, we may divide the occupation into two subperiods, with the first evolving into the second in early 1949. By then, U.S. aid to Japan was over $1.3 million per day, much of it necessary to prevent famine and extreme hardship. At the same time, the U.S.-sponsored Nationalist régime was well on its way to defeat in the Chinese civil war. It was becoming clearer from week to week that if the United States was to maintain its Asian profile, this would have to be bulwarked by a strong Japan, not itself dominated by a left-wing party.

Thus, the U.S. became enthusiastic about Japan's recovery rather suddenly in 1949. At SCAP's initiative, an Economic Stabilization Board—forerunner of the present Economic Planning Agency—was established to draw up the Rehabilitation Plan of 1949–53. Before then, the attitude was one of punishment and reform, designed, in principle, to ensure that Japan would never again make war on the West. In practice, the motives guiding SCAP and its U.S. advisers were a mixture of idealistic egalitarianism, laissez faire economics, and respect for the potential international competitiveness of Japanese industry—although, in retrospect, the latter was underestimated.

At first, the United States planned to demand a crushing reparations burden. According to the Pauley recommendations of December 1945, Japan would have lost most of its heavy industry and received little or no U.S. aid. If followed, the Pauley report would probably have raised unemployment, as well as the number of famine-related deaths, and might even have provoked an armed uprising against the occupation. Fortunately, this did not happen. While the aircraft and munitions industries suffered dismantling, reparations consisted mainly of Japan's overseas assets plus sums that it later negotiated with the Asian victims of its World War II aggression. The latter were modest relative to Japan's growing ability to pay.

Uncertainty about reparations and permitted levels of production did help to delay Japan's recovery. But the Pauley-recommended constraints on heavy industry were transformed into constraints on the military establishment and defense industries, written into the Japanese Constitution of 1947, which was approved by SCAP. These freed Japan's savings for the development of iron and steel, electricity-generating, chemicals, shipbuilding, electronics, motor vehicles, metalworking, machinery, and other industries that Pauley would have restricted. Production of all these goods grew at a record pace after 1953 and soon became competitive with the products of Western industries.

With oversimplification, we may say that the punishment and reform phase of the occupation made fundamental changes in Japan's economy, at some immediate cost in terms of recovery from the war, while the economic rehabilitation phase sparked rapid growth but did not make basic changes, with one or two exceptions. The four basic reforms of 1946–49 were probably too left-of-center to have been carried out by a popularly elected government. They equalized the distribution of wealth and made Japanese society more stable and cohesive. In the long run, they probably made a positive contribution to the economic miracle. They were as follows:

(a) Japan received a new Constitution with ultimate authority based on popular sovereignty. The earlier Constitution of 1889 had put ultimate authority in the hands of the Emperor, who was declared divine. On January 1, 1946, the Emperor renounced his claim to divinity and was described in the 1947 Constitution as the "symbol of the state and of the unity of the people" rather than as the formal head of state. Moreover, women received the right to vote for the first time in the April 1946 elections, and 38 of them were elected to the Diet. The civil code was rewritten to express equality between the sexes, and all children received inheritance rights, in place of the former practice of primogeniture. (In agriculture, this ensured that the average size of farms would remain small.) Compulsory school attendance rose from 6 to 9 years, and education was to stress democratic values.

(b) In labor relations, SCAP tried to establish a strong union movement capable of exercising countervailing power against management. A Ministry of Labor was created in 1947, and laws covering all aspects of labor relations and standards, modeled on New Deal legislation in the United States, were passed by the Diet. Whereas in early 1946 there existed just 1,179 unions with a membership of 900,000, by June 1949 there were almost 35,000 unions with over 6.5 million members. These were all enterprise unions—with membership confined to a single company's employees—and this is still the character of the Japanese union movement. The rights to organize, to bargain collectively and, in most sectors, to strike, were firmly established in law. However, when left-wing unionists became militant, SCAP reversed itself and sought to curb the unions. This brought it into conflict with the socialist government, ensuring the latter's departure from power.[13]

(c) SCAP's most far-reaching reform was probably its massive redistribution of land to the tiller. The land reform was passed by the Diet in 1946 and carried out over 1947–50. It virtually wiped out absentee ownership of farmland and farm tenancy, which fell from 46 percent of land under cultivation in 1945 to 10 percent in 1950. (It is now under 6 percent.) About a third of Japan's farmland was redistributed, largely by transferring ownership from absentee landlords to those who worked the soil. Rates on remaining tenant holdings were fixed at levels far below the income from the land. Tenants received security of tenure and protection against arbitrary changes in rental contracts, and an extremely low ceiling (one hectare or approximately 2.5 acres) was placed on the amount of farmland that one person could lease. Another low ceiling, usually 3 hectares, was placed on the amount of land that any owner could cultivate.

Land over these ceilings was taken by the government, under compulsory purchase, and resold to landless or to land-poor peasants. Those receiving land were forbidden to sell it for thirty years, except with special permission. Usually, the state paid a price for the land that was close to fair value in 1945. But general inflation over 1945–50, pushed the price of rice to more than forty times its previous level, which caused a similar increase in the price of land. The practical effect of the land reform was therefore to confiscate the land and to give it to the poorest rural families. Only in 1965 did the state finally offer partial compensation to landlords "for cooperating in the land reform."

In fact, the Japanese carried out the reform enthusiastically, viewing it as an extension of their own wartime policy toward the countryside. The reasons for this enthusiasm were partly political and partly economic. About 1.8 million landlords were forced to sell an average of 2.7 acres each, but 4.3 million peasants representing 70 percent of all farm households received land. Moreover, the landlords had largely lost their economic function. They no longer launched local industries or sought to improve the technology of farming, and relations between them and the working peasants were semifeudal. After World War II, there was a risk that the peasants would become revolutionary. The land reform helped to turn potential revolutionaries into solidly conservative voters, who are largely responsible for continuous Liberal-Democratic party rule. The LDP followed the land reform with infusions of capital into agriculture, farm price supports, and subsidies to lure industry into villages and towns. These wiped out real-income differences between urban and rural areas, which were on the order of 2-to-1 or more (in favor of the cities) before the war.

(d) Finally, SCAP set out to destroy the centers of power in industry. An "extraordinary tax program" passed in the fall of 1946 placed confiscatory levies on the top 2 percent of the Japanese income distribution. This category consisted almost entirely of families with ownership claims on the financial and industrial conglomerates known as *zaibatsu*, which had dominated the pre–World War II Japanese economy. The extraordinary tax program consisted of two main parts—a tax on capital, with rates rising to 90 percent of assessed valuation at the top of the income distribution (comprising mainly the wealthiest *zaibatsu* families) and a war indemnity tax that cancelled 85 percent of the government's huge war debt. The real burden of the capital levy was severe for wealthy families, but it was lower in practice than on paper, mainly because it did not have to be paid until a year after assessment, amid annual inflation of 150 percent.

SCAP's deconcentration program also included a U.S.-style antimonopoly law, passed in April 1947, and a Fair Trade Commission (FTC) was set up in June 1947 to enforce this. The main goal was to dissolve the *zaibatsu* and other concentrations of industrial power in pre–World War II Japan and to prevent them from rising again. The three largest *zaibatsu*—Mitsui, Mitsubishi, and Sumitomo, in order of prewar size and power—were special targets for deconcentration, even though they had often opposed the military during the 1930s. These *zaibatsu* were family controlled through holding companies (although by 1939, the family heads no longer ran the business on a day-to-day basis). They were semifeudal in their structure and internal relationships, and their banks and trading companies occupied central positions of power, both within each conglomerate and in the economy as a whole. The occupation authorities considered these features antidemocratic and moved against the *zaibatsu* and other power centers—first by dispersing the wealth and authority of the *zaibatsu* families, and second by dissolving their ties with affiliated enterprises, as well as by breaking up large companies into smaller ones. The extraordinary tax program played an important role with respect to the first objective.

SCAP also designated 57 members of 11 families as "*zaibatsu*." Their assets were frozen, and they were removed from their official positions and forbidden to participate in their businesses for 10 years. About 220 additional corporate executives were purged from *zaibatsu* firms, and 2,500 executives and large shareholders were purged from other large companies as punishment for their wartime activities. All holding companies were dissolved and outlawed, which effectively destroyed the main ties binding the *zaibatsu* empires. Some 1,250 additional companies and financial institutions were ordered to divest their shares in other firms, although half failed to do so because of inadequate enforcement. Finally, the 57 *zaibatsu* family members had to transfer all their remaining securities to a Holding Company Liquidation Commission (HCLC), which also acquired the stocks divested by the holding companies and the 1,250 other firms just mentioned. The *zaibatsu* families were paid with government bonds, whose real value soon fell by 95 percent, owing to the rampant inflation. Thus, most of their wealth was effectively confiscated. After the occupation, they received partial compensation, but never regained their prewar wealth or power, even within their own concerns.

The HCLC sold the 166 million shares it received to employees of the affected firms, to private investors, and to the general public. Despite the traditional reluctance of Japanese to invest in securities, a fairly wide distribution was achieved. However, a far greater number of shares was paid in to the Finance Ministry, because of the extraordinary tax program or by firms trying to finance reconstruction. The government also resold these shares to the public, but this time the main buyers were financial institutions, notably the former *zaibatsu* banks, who were getting into position to reconstitute their industrial empires. Ownership of these institutions was dispersed, however. For example, the number of stockholders of the six leading banks grew from 2,511 in 1945 to 181,000 in 1949.

On balance, the deconcentration program was not as successful as that to disperse wealth and authority, and neither worked as well as SCAP and its advisers had originally hoped. Regarding deconcentration, Corwin Edwards, the program's mastermind, wrote that "The most drastic dissolution was that of the Mitsui and Mitsubishi trading companies [which had handled about 70 percent of Japanese foreign trade]. . . . After liquidation they were replaced by more than 300 separate firms."[14] The trading companies had been responsible for Japan's penetration of world markets—although their activities were often resented at home—and none of the successor companies had the facilities or financial strength to carry on in their stead. The splintering of trading companies especially hurt Mitsui, since Mitsui Bussan was the largest and most powerful and had played a crucial role in the operations of that *zaibatsu.*

The HCLC split up 27 other large companies and ordered all cartel-like associations dissolved, although 296 nonfinancial enterprises suggested by SCAP for possible dissolution remained intact. With the major exception of Mitsui, large banks also escaped the axe—partly because SCAP did not get around to them before the cold war began and U.S. policy changed. However, the *zaibatsu* companies and banks were forced to discontinue their official ties, by selling their respective holdings in one another and by adopting new names that were quite different from their old *zaibatsu* names. SCAP also eliminated the interlocking directorships involving the banks and former *zaibatsu* affiliates and placed strict limits on the amount of stock that one institution could hold in another.

The new Anti-Monopoly Law was designed to preserve the competitive conditions that dissolution was supposed to have created. Holding companies were permanently outlawed. According to Professor Edwards, this law also "placed drastic curbs upon mergers, stock acquisitions and holding of debentures, and interlocking corporate offices. [Its] provisions were designed not only to prevent direct impairments of competition, but also to place obstacles to the re-establishment of powerful conglomerates like the *zaibatsu*."[15] At the time, it was clear to many Japanese, even outside the business world, that deconcentration was tearing Japan's economic fabric apart, and delaying recovery. Enterprises were "splintered into uneconomic units, severed from customary sources of finance, and cut off from sources of raw materials," as well as from markets.[16] Many Japanese civil servants who had to carry out the dissolution were far from enthusiastic.

The occupation authorities apparently agreed that dissolution was delaying recovery, because when the cold war began and the tax burden of American aid to Japan became too much of a political liability, the deconcentration program was halted. Although the successor companies and financial institutions of the *zaibatsu* were prevented from official, formal cooperation, they could and did cooperate informally.[17] The personnel running these firms were still loyal to their former umbrella organizations. Purged executives functioned as "advisers," until they were eventually allowed to rejoin their companies. Soon after the end of the occupation, most former *zaibatsu* companies went back to their old names and trade marks. According to Cohen, "in the five years following the end of the occupation, the [deconcentration] process was reversed. Restrictions and laws were eased, companies merged to form larger, more effective units, old financial relationships were re-established, and the traditional Japanese tendency to integration, monopoly, cartels, quotas, allocations, administered prices, and restrictive business practices began to re-emerge."[18] The Anti-Monopoly Law was weakened through amendment and application to allow depression and rationalization cartels and many special exemptions.

Not long after the Occupation, the big *zaibatsu* reconstituted themselves. Today, these groups are known as *keiretsu*, and their combined importance is not far below prewar days, although their ownership is more diffuse, their leadership is more collective, their organization is less formal and less centralized, and most of them have less internal cohesion. As its sole act of major bank dissolution, SCAP split the Dai-Ichi Bank off from the Mitsui Bank, leaving the latter too small to satisfy the financial needs of other Mitsui firms. Some former Mitsui companies refused to rejoin the group or (as in the case of Toshiba, Toyota, and Oji Paper) did not rejoin until after 1970. Thus, Mitsui never regained its prewar position, allowing Mitsubishi to become Japan's strongest *keiretsu* during the postwar era. In 1971, the Dai-Ichi Bank merged with the Nippon Kangyo Bank to become the nucleus of the Dai-Ichi Kangyo Bank group, presently Japan's largest *keiretsu*. The postwar purges allowed junior executives to be promoted, and many of these "third-grade executives," as they were sometimes called, proved to be first-rate. The infusion of new blood made Japanese industry more dynamic and aggressive, just when these qualities were especially important.

As part of the Dodge Deflation, that separated the punishment and reform from the rehabilitation phase of the occupation, the government introduced large increases in personal and corporate income taxes and also in inheritance taxes. These helped to preserve the more equal income distribution brought about by the land reform, extraordinary tax program, and *zaibatsu* dissolution. Once the surge of rapid growth was underway, moreover, tax revenues at existing rates were always greater than projected public spending until the energy crisis. As a result, the government enjoyed the luxury of tax cuts in nearly every year until 1977.

The Dodge Deflation created the financial stability necessary for the postwar economic miracle. Before February 1949, Japan's finances were a shambles. The first price explosion took place over the last half of 1945, as the economy collapsed. It was a long-delayed consequence of the huge sums of money printed to help finance recovery from the Great Depression, then the military buildup, and, finally, World War II. During the war, tax revenues covered less than a fourth of government spending, and in 1946, this coverage shrunk to 11 percent. To reduce the monetary overhang, the government carried out a currency reform in early 1946, exchanging new money for old and greatly reducing the money supply. At the same time, it put a quasi freeze on bank deposits and subsequently levied the extraordinary tax program.

The currency reform and special tax program each halted rampant inflation for a few months, although considerable purchasing power remained from the war years (when it had been effectively frozen by wartime controls). In addition, both the real base of income and output on which taxes could be levied and the government's own tax-collecting machinery remained deficient. Tax evasion and black marketeering were rife. Yet, the requirements of reconstruction were overwhelming, and the effect of the war indemnity tax on industry and finance was potentially devastating. Faced with this, the government continued to create money at a rapid rate, causing prices to soar to five times their average 1946 level and 220 times their average 1936 level by mid-1949. This was its only honorable choice. Virtually all new money took the form of subsidies or loans to firms involved in reconstruction. In February 1947, the Reconstruction Finance Bank was founded as a channel for loans to help rebuild the economy. Over the next two years, it supplied about 70 percent of all corporate fixed investment, ultimately getting its funds from expansion of the money supply. Thus, it played a big role in the price explosion, although it is unclear how else the reconstruction and reequipment of basic industries could have been achieved.

Nevertheless, a more conservative approach to finance would eventually become necessary. In 1949, Joseph Dodge, a Detroit banker, instituted a nine-point stabilization program designed to lay the groundwork for economic progress, which had become popular in United States government circles as a way to make Japan self-supporting. (Without nearly $1 billion in U.S. aid over 1948–49 and another $1.1 billion over 1950–51, Japan would have faced famine, although real national income by 1949 was 45 percent above 1946.) The deflationary medicine featured a tax increase that produced a ''super balanced'' budget, in which revenues covered all spending, retired a fourth of the national debt (greatly reduced in real terms by the preceding inflation), and even provided some savings for reconstruction. Afterward, the central government religiously balanced its budget until fiscal 1965.

As well, the Dodge Deflation established a uniform exchange rate for the yen, at 360 to the U.S. dollar. After the war, the Occupation authorities had set an official rate of 15 yen per dollar, subsequently corrected to 20–25 yen by the black market. Inflation then destroyed much of the yen's value, and just before the deflation, multiple rates varying between 100 and 900 per dollar were in effect, depending on the purpose of the exchange. The deflation also curtailed lending by the Reconstruction Finance Bank, which caused it to close, and established a counterpart fund similar to those set up in European countries receiving Marshall Plan aid. As shipments of goods in the form of aid flowed into Japan, the government created sums of money equal to the value of goods received and deposited these into the fund, which was used to finance investment and to retire government debt. Thus, to reduce the impact of the deflation on industry, the government made loans from the counterpart fund that would formerly have been made from the Reconstruction Finance Bank. It also abolished the excess profits tax and allowed businesses to overvalue their assets, thereby granting liberal depreciation allowances, which reduced profits taxes further.

The Dodge Deflation had a favorable long-run impact on Japan, although at an immediate cost in terms of higher unemployment, reduced living standards, stagnating output, and a rise in small business failures due to the sudden drop in demand. But it is hard to know what would have happened had not the Korean War begun in June 1950, just as American aid was winding down. Japanese industry found itself with a near monopoly in supplying United States and South Korean armed forces, and the resulting ''special procurement'' demand stimulated the economy at a critical time in its recovery. Over 1951–60, demand stemming from the Korean War and subsequent military occupation financed exports equal to 20 percent of total Japanese imports, and other exports did not cover imports until 1965. But the profits earned were not wasted. By reinvesting them in key industries, Japan generated record growth and developed export competitiveness.

Finally, a basic change took place in the structure of the economy, partly during World War II and partly during the occupation period. Before the war, Japanese industry financed its investment first from internal sources, second from selling shares, and only third from bank loans. The Bank of Japan had less leverage over investment, production, and distribution than did the central banks of most Western countries. However, the number of commercial banks declined during the war, and the Bank of Japan increased its control over them. Subsequently, the government became almost the sole supplier of investment funds—ultimately generated by creation of new money—partly because the programs of dissolution and deconcentration dispersed wealth and disrupted normal channels of finance and partly because of the enormous requirements of reconstruction. The war indemnity tax alone came to more than the entire value of all industrial assets and fell most heavily on heavy industries and large financial institutions. There could be no question of allowing widespread bankruptcies in these sectors, and the government therefore financed what amounted to a massive rescue operation.

Thus, bank loans became the major direct source of the funds industry needed, both for investment and for working capital. Business firms went deeply into debt to the commercial banks, whose own debt to the Bank of Japan also grew. When the Dodge Deflation put the Reconstruction Finance Bank out of business, the role of the commercial banks in financing reconstruction rose dramatically. Since they did not have nearly enough resources for this task, they had to increase their own borrowing from the Bank of Japan, which resulted in further creation of new money.

In this way, a centralized system of finance came into being, partly as a consequence of SCAP's efforts to disperse wealth and to fragment the economy into something approaching perfect competition. By destroying or drying up existing channels of finance, the occupation authorities forced the entire system to depend on one ultimate source—the government. For many years, banks were the main source of investment finance in Japan, and firms were "overborrowed" from the commercial banks, which borrowed regularly from the Bank of Japan (and still do). This became one channel, among several, through which the government could influence the nature and direction of investment.

Notes

1. However, trends in the distribution of income have been divergent and complex. See Hiromatsu Ishi, "Effects of Japanese Income Taxation on the Distribution of Income and Wealth in Japan," *Hitotsubashi Journal of Economics*, June 1980; and Malcolm Sawyer, "Income Distribution in OECD Countries," *OECD Economic Outlook, Occasional Studies* (Paris: OECD, July 1976).

2. See OECD, *Economic Survey of Japan*, 1984–85 (Paris: OECD, 1985), p. 46, and Sam Nakagama, "Turning Japan into an Importing Nation," *New York Times*, April 19, 1987, Section 3, p. 2.

3. Over 40 percent of all farms are under 0.5 hectares and almost 70 percent are under 1 hectare (= 2.47 acres) in size. Nearly all farmers belong to one or more cooperative associations, which supply them with marketing, purchasing, credit, warehousing, insurance, and production guidance. Although virtually all farmland is privately owned, these associations determine what outputs Japanese farmers will produce and what inputs they will use. Sometimes, Japanese agriculture is also described as farming by the three chans (or *sanchan* farming): *kaachan* (mama), *baachan* (grandma), and *jiichan* (grandpa).

4. One hundred members of the House of Councillors are elected at large from the country as a whole, while the remainder are elected by district.

5. In fact, the Liberal-Democratic party was founded in 1955. Before that, the Liberals and Democrats, as separate parties, effectively controlled the government.

6. A major exception was passage of the United States-Japan Treaty of Mutual Cooperation and Security—in effect a defense pact between Japan and the United States.

This was opposed by leftists, who wanted a neutral Japan, and by many others. An unprecedented 17,300 petitions with 1.9 million names were gathered against the Treaty, and a majority of Japanese appeared to be opposed. The Treaty was nevertheless pushed through during an extraordinary session of the House of Representatives at 12:17 a.m. on May 20, 1960. By this time, only 233 Liberal Democrats remained in the House (whose total membership was then 467), all Socialists having been ejected by the police for staging a sit-in against the proceedings. The treaty has since been renewed, and the Socialists now support it. (Only the Communists remain opposed.)

7. Chitoshi Yanaga, *Big Business in Japanese Politics* (New Haven: Yale University Press, 1968), p. 106.

8. The LDP hold on power appeared to be in danger after the 1976 Lockheed scandal. The U.S. Lockheed Aircraft Corp. had paid $10 million in bribes to Japanese companies and prominent individuals, in order to overcome informal barriers to selling its products in Japan. About $5 million found its way to leading civil servants and LDP politicians, some of whom are still in office. A major beneficiary was former Prime Minister Kakuei Tanaka, who had been relieved of the leadership in a separate 1975 income tax evasion scandal. Tanaka was arrested, but reelected to his Diet seat in 1976. (He has controlled the flow of patronage and other political spoils to his home district.) While no longer officially an LDP member, Tanaka leads its strongest faction and remains in the Diet despite his conviction in 1983 on charges stemming from the Lockheed affair. However, a stroke in February 1985 may have ended his role in Japanese politics—in particular, as reputed "Kingmaker" of the LDP. The subsequent Recruit scandal of 1989 could still play a major role in causing the LDP to lose control of government.

9. Local governments are often dominated by Socialists or Communists.

10. See Yoshikazu Kano, "Japan's Agriculture: It can Be Revitalized," *Japanese Economic Studies*, Spring 1985, especially pp. 37–39, and *OECD Survey of Japan, 1985* (Paris: OECD, 1985), p. 64. Besides price supports, the government has promoted mechanization and structural changes in Japanese farming, along with more rational organization and land use. In particular, the "Paddy Field Reorientation Program," adopted in 1978, has succeeded in reducing land devoted to rice, in which Japan has a strong comparative disadvantage, by nearly 25 percent. Government rice stockpiles have therefore been falling, and the price to consumers is now about the same as the price paid to producers (although both are far above the world market price). In addition, prices of fertilizers, irrigation water, small tractors, rice transplanters, and other farm inputs are kept down by subsidies, and agricultural land rents were fixed at extremely low levels after the 1945–50 land reform. Despite tiny farm size, Japanese agriculture uses more mechanical power, chemical fertilizer, and insecticides per hectare than does any other country. It has one of the world's highest yields per acre, and Japan is closer to having maximum potential per-acre yields than any other country. (However, the productivities of labor and capital are both low.)

11. Alternatively, destruction came to five times that caused by the Great Earthquake of 1923.

12. J. B. Cohen, *Japan's Postwar Economy* (Bloomington: Indiana University Press, 1958), p. 14. Cohen is a major source for this section.

13. In July 1948, civil servants lost the right to strike and to bargain collectively. Thus, there were limits to SCAP's reforming zeal, especially after the cold war began.

14. Corwin Edwards, *Trade Regulations Overseas: The National Laws* (Dobbs Ferry, N.Y.: Oceana, 1966), p. 658.

15. Ibid., p. 661.

16. Cohen, *Japan's Postwar Economy*, p. 196.

17. G. C. Allen recounts a visit to the head office of a former *zaibatsu* bank after dissolution. He noticed that many other firms from the same former *zaibatsu* had their offices in the building. "We are now, of course, entirely separate," he was told, "but it is convenient

446 COMPARATIVE ECONOMIC SYSTEMS

to be able to visit our former associates so easily." G. C. Allen, *Japan's Economic Expansion* (London: Oxford University Press, 1965) p. 185n.

18. Cohen, *Japan's Postwar Economy*, p. 196.

Questions for Review, Discussion, Examination

1. What limits to growth were starting to appear in Japan by the early 1970s? What were some of the costs of growth?

Why has Japanese growth aroused some hostility in other nations?

2. How is Japanese agriculture organized? Would you describe it as efficient? How great is the cost of protecting it and what costs does this protection impose on other Japanese? Why has this protection been continued for so long?

Are there any direct or indirect benefits of this protection? (*Hint*: Are time horizons of public officials in Japan long or short? Why?)

3. Did the United States occupation of Japan begin with the goal of promoting recovery and economic growth? Explain. How did recommended constraints on Japan's heavy industry become constraints that permitted this industry to grow later on?

4. What basic reforms in Japanese society did the occupation bring? How did land reform help (apparently) to equalize the distribution of wealth?

*5. How did SCAP attempt to deal with the financial-industrial conglomerates known as *zaibatsu*, which had dominated Japan's prewar economy?

Ideally, dissolution and deconcentration were supposed to move the Japanese economy closer to perfect competition, thereby increasing efficiency. Is this what happened? Why wasn't deconcentration carried out completely?

6. Briefly describe the Dodge Deflation. Why was inflation rampant before the deflation and how did the deflation help to establish a foundation for future growth, albeit at short-run cost?

What unrelated event then launched the economic miracle?

*7. How did occupation and reconstruction alter the method of investment finance in Japan? Why did this happen?

* = more difficult.

13

THE JAPANESE ECONOMY: BASIC FRAMEWORK AND SYSTEMS

Even if my company goes bankrupt because of the rate at which I expand my plant, the plant itself will remain to be used for the development of Japanese industry. So I will take the risk.

—S. Honda

. . . what is important . . . is whether a corporation has a clear sense of social responsibility. TDK's responsibility is . . . to contribute to the world's culture and industry through creation. Each of our workers is fully committed to this ideal and is doing his work under his own initiative. This may be the closest thing to the secret of our company's success.

—Fukujiro Sono
(President of TDK Electronics)

13-1. Underlying Social Framework of the Japanese Economy

In Japan, to a greater extent than in the West, the functioning of the economy stems from the nature of human relations. Contracts are usually vague, without long lists of clauses guaranteeing protection for each party, because what counts is not the specifics of a particular agreement, but rather the entire relationship between the contracting parties. It follows that people are careful about entering into agreements. Personal relationships, once established, are longer lasting, less casual, and more deeply rooted in mutual loyalty and trust than in the West. Even the purchase of a small consumer durable carries with it a greater commitment to quality and to after-sale service. Within relationships, adaptability by each party serves as a partial substitute for mobility, in the sense of downgrading or terminating one relationship and starting another.

From an economic standpoint, we may view trust and loyalty as intangible forms of capital. Individuals build trust by helping each other and by not taking advantage of or behaving opportunistically toward one another.[1] In the process, they "save" and "invest," in the sense of foregoing short-term gains in order to improve the prospects for and the benefits from longer term cooperation. In Japan, small investments in trust or loyalty may yield smaller returns than in more open Western societies. In a densely populated, resource-poor environment, where incomes have historically been low, Japanese are naturally competitive. Relatively large investments are needed to develop personal relationships, but when potential gains from long-term cooperation are large enough and sufficient commitments are forthcoming, the return on such investment can be high. During the nineteenth-century drive to industrialize, Japanese capitalism successfully coopted the feudal value structure, whose key element was loyalty.

Thus, the impersonal, anonymous market of Western economics textbooks is alien to Japanese culture. American firms, wanting to establish their products in Japan, have often been frustrated by what seems to be a cumbersome, obsolete distribution system, with much fragmentation and overlapping and many middlemen, that would not move their goods. But one reason for their lack of success has been a failure to build the necessary network of personal ties (or to find a competent Japanese to do this for them). Individuals may not be as alienated from the production and distribution of goods and services as in the West, but the Japanese system is also abuse-prone, as the 1976 Lockheed and 1989 Recruit scandals have emphasized.

The first and most basic feature of Japan's economy is therefore the broader social framework within which it is embedded. Chitoshi Yanaga says that "the social structure [of Japan] is held together by a network of criss-crossing loyalties, obligations, and commitments of a highly personal nature." The worst punishment most Japanese can imagine is ostracism—especially by one's fellow workers—and a group can correspondingly impose its performance standards on its members. There are two basic kinds of social relationships, vertical and horizontal, respectively linking individuals with unequal and approximately equal status. Of these, the vertical is the more basic, binding together superiors and subordinates of all types: teacher-student, master-apprentice, leader-follower, employer-employee, senior-junior, foreman-worker, and so on.

In a market transaction, the seller must accept a lower status position vis-à-vis the buyer in most instances. In a bargaining situation, the buyer can usually dictate the terms of the agreement—subject to remaining above the seller's reservation price—although he is under a moral obligation not to take too much advantage of the seller. As a rule, negotiations will lead to a better deal for the buyer than they would under comparable conditions in a Western country. Japanese exporters tend to assume the lower status of a seller, and they are also willing to accept short-term losses in exchange for long-term gains based on long-term relations in the importing country. By contrast, "if an American seller takes his [normal] bargaining behavior to Japan, the negotiations are apt to end abruptly. The American seller expects to be treated as an equal, [but] the Japanese buyer is likely to view this rather brash behavior in a lower status seller as inappropriate and lacking in respect."2

In any social situation, Japanese are only comfortable when status distinctions are clearly understood by everyone involved. An especially strong vertical relationship is called *oyabun-kobun*, literally "parent-child," which evokes the broader image of Japanese society as a network of family-type relations. For example, a Japanese employer once described how he led his family and his employees to the safety of a river bank during a fire-bombing raid on Tokyo in World War II and stayed all night with them. By implication, his responsibility toward the two groups was similar. Vertical, family-type relations would also bind a professor and his leading students at a university, a senior bureaucrat and his subordinates, a department head in virtually any organization and the people working under him, and a schoolteacher and his pupils.

Thus, it would be normal for a Japanese teacher to visit his pupils in their homes and to spend many hours giving individual guidance, in matters pertaining to life as well as to school subjects. If a pupil got into trouble, the teacher, as well as the parents, would be called to account. If a large Japanese firm were to hire an employee upon graduation for "life," it would ask his teachers to guarantee his conduct and character.3 If such an employee were later to quit his job—an unusual move—the former employee would be obliged to explain his actions to anyone who had given a guarantee on his behalf (and who would probably suffer loss of face). In short, a Japanese teacher must take a total interest in the lives of his students, and a superior on the job must do the same, at least with his immediate subordinates. To quote Yanaga again:

> The concept of *giri-ninjo* (moral obligation and human sentiment) is of paramount importance. Moral obligation . . . generates personal loyalty and determines the behavior of individuals in business, politics or any sphere of activity. A Japanese can argue for the rule of law as emphatically or as convincingly as an American or a Briton . . . yet on serious reflection, he is likely to convince himself that human and personal considerations should take precedence over issues, policies, and even principles, which are . . . impersonal.4

Japanese are more likely than Westerners to settle disputes informally. One indication of this is the relatively small number of lawyers—less than 5 percent of the U.S. level or 15 percent of the number in the United Kingdom, on a per capita basis.

When asked his job, a Japanese employed by a large firm will usually not say that he is an accountant, a machinist, or a truck driver. Instead, he will say that he works for Mitsubishi, Hitachi, Sony, Nissan, Sanyo, etc. His basic responsibilities are apt to be vaguely defined, although with an emphasis on loyalty to his firm. In choosing an employer, he will decide on the basis of prestige, how well the enterprise suits his personality, beliefs, and goals, its long-range vision, the personalities of its work force, and other social criteria that count for as much as pay and working conditions, narrowly defined. Except among older workers, job changing has historically been lower than in virtually any Western country, although only a minority of Japanese actually become lifetime employees. Low turnover is partly compensated by switching from one product line or department to another within firms. Japanese enterprises practice more extensive job rotation and train both their white- and blue-collar employees more broadly than do even progressive Western firms. This is one reason for their efficiency. Moreover, just as a firm in hiring an employee receives a stronger guarantee against his or her quitting than would be the case in North America, so an employee receives an implicit guarantee that he is more likely to be kept on or looked after when the company faces hard times. Such guarantees, buttressed by government subsidies, held Japan's unemployment rate to half or less of what it otherwise would have been, in the period after the first energy crisis.

Internally, Japanese firms are organized as hierarchies of groups, and the need for harmony tends to make decision making more participatory at each level. On the production floor, workers have some input into everyday decisions and are expected to improvise and otherwise take initiatives in overcoming minor difficulties. In some cases, they have greater power to control the flow of goods-in-process to their work stations and greater power to stop production for quality control reasons than do their counterparts in most Western countries. Such property rights require profit sharing to reward employees for enterprise success, plus strong team spirit backed by social pressures and capped by the possibility of ostracism, to prevent free riding. Workers are also encouraged to make suggestions and rewarded when their proposals are adopted. This happens on a regular basis.

As a rule, major initiatives and new ideas come directly from middle managers and work their way upward. Superiors rarely order subordinates around, and it has been said that a manager over forty should never win an argument with a junior. Instead, Japanese managers lead in fatherly fashion, allowing subordinates to take the initiative, which they shape and channel through suggestions, hints, selective encouragement and support, etc., so that top management effectively controls the direction and performance of the enterprise. Because of the correlation between rank and age, a superior usually knows that those under him cannot be promoted past him (which would require him to retire or resign). They pose no threat to him, and he can promote their careers, knowing that he is thereby helping his own.

Before a decision can be taken, informal but elaborate consultation is necessary with everyone affected, a procedure known as *nemawashi* (literally, "cultivating the root"). Each person consulted has a chance to give suggestions, and many will make at least a small contribution to the final outcome. Japanese executives commonly work ten hours a day or more, spending much of this time in meetings and consultation, from which they derive most of their job-related satisfaction and fulfillment. As a rule, individual Japanese are reluctant to commit the organizations they represent or to take initiatives that will lead to commitments. Instead, they rely on decision making by compromise and consensus that will preserve harmony as far as possible. This does not stop Japanese firms from seizing profit opportunities quickly, because time lost in taking decisions is made up in implementation. Once a decision has been reached, everyone lines up behind it. By contrast, a failure to consult those affected before taking a decision—as in the building of the Narita airport near Tokyo—is potentially disastrous.

Within the enterprise, distinguishing characteristics between managers and workers are suppressed. All employees, from highest to lowest, wear the company uniform or dress similarly, except where job requirements rule this out. Managers and workers eat in the same cafeteria, and both white- and blue-collar employees belong to the same company-wide union. It is not uncommon for white-collar employees to be rotated temporarily into blue-collar jobs, since everyone connected with the firm is supposed to understand its entire production process and the way in which jobs in various departments relate to this. More generally, managers are supposed to relate to their workers, and pay differences have historically depended as much on seniority as on productivity or kind of work performed. When a worker is transferred to a job with a lower rating, the union places limits on the extent to which his earnings can be cut.

Horizontal ties stem largely from kinship, marriage, and shared experiences, such as coming from the same village or neighborhood, playing on a team or going to school together, belonging to the same club, being born in the same year, being university classmates, working for the same firm, fighting for the same ideal, and so on. Japanese society is cliquish, partly because individual Japanese are unable to directly confront disagreement. Prizing harmony above all else, they seek close relations based on common beliefs, values, goals, or experiences. Within cliques (or *batsu*), relations are informal to the point of intimacy, and an atmosphere of deep mutual trust and camaraderie prevails. Between cliques, relations are more formal and at arm's length. While cooperation is the rule within a clique or organization, different cliques compete fiercely with one another.

The extended family is a type of clique (called *keibatsu*) as is a firm. Cliques (called *gakubatsu*) are also based on university and school ties. In both factory and school

> there emerges a pattern of empathy and responsibility within an accepted hierarchy . . . a community, [in the] sense that all are bound together by common feelings, common experience, and well-understood objectives . . . [Thus,] teachers and students dig fishponds together; they plant flowers together. Teachers watch over the school at night, instead of watchmen; and students sweep up and wash up . . . as a result of which no maintenance men are employed."[5]

Prior to World War II, Japan was controlled by three cliques—the military (*gumbatsu*), the bureaucracy (*kambatsu*), and the financial-industrial (*zaibatsu*). The power that was temporarily dissipated when the *zaibatsu* were dissolved has been reconstituted in the hands of newer, more decentralized business groups, the *keiretsu.* In the political arena, the influence of big business is now largely exercised through *zaikai,* a clique of business leaders. The coalition that has governed Japan since World War II consists of top business leaders, bureaucrats, and Liberal-Democratic party members, a kind of clique of cliques.

Japanese society as a whole may still be thought of as an extended family whose father-figure is the Emperor. Japanese tend to feel culturally distant from all foreigners, probably because of the centuries of isolation before Perry's "black ships" sailed into Tokyo Bay. Many scholars, especially Marxians, have decried human relations in Japan, calling them "paternalistic," "backward," and "feudal." Marxians are especially wont to insist that paternalistic ties stemming from "Emperor worship" suppress class consciousness among Japanese workers. Sociological studies reveal an acceptance of company goals by employees, who sometimes refer to their places of work almost as they would to their own homes. Relations between foremen and rank-and-file workers, and between senior and junior executives are generally close, and company employees form clubs for leisure-time activities from which outsiders are barred. Employee beliefs about working conditions and wage distribution tend to be unrelated to rank or status within a company, and many firms practice profit sharing among their employees.[6]

But to regard Japanese labor relations as artificial or backward and the division of a "capitalist" society into hostile propertied and laboring classes as natural may reflect a Western cultural bias. Large Japanese enterprises depart both from Marxian and from conventional Western textbook models. In doing so, they have achieved a level of efficiency that is the envy of both East and West.

13-2. Nature of the Economic System

The Japanese economy is basically a market economy, in contrast to the command or administratively planned economies of Eastern Europe, the USSR, China, and Cuba. The Japanese government does not directly manage the industrial sector from above the level of the enterprise, although it does use a variety of levers to steer the system along perceived lines of national advantage, and it plays a major role in collecting and disseminating information. In this sense, Japan is a market-planned economy. Private ownership also prevails over most of the material means of production and distribution. However, private ownership in Japan, especially where large firms are concerned, is not the same as private ownership in North America. "Outside" Japanese stockholders are virtually powerless vis-à-vis management, and all members of a Japanese board of directors are insiders, close to management.[7] Managerial decision-making horizons in Japan appear to be among the longest in the world because managers are not under pressure to produce large short-term profits. Instead, they identify with long-term company fortunes because of strong vertical and horizontal ties, nourished by lifetime employment plus an expectation of continuing family association with the enterprise or industrial group.

The management of a Japanese corporation is also more subject to government influence than would be the case in North America, and managements of companies belonging to one of the *keiretsu* will be influenced by managements of other firms in the same industrial group. Until recently, moreover, a glance at the balance sheet of a Japanese corporation would have given a North American auditor heart failure. By the standards he was used to, the firm should have gone out of business long ago, because of its burden of debt and illiquidity. In the United States, about 60 percent of the capital of a typical corporation has been financed by selling stock or reinvesting retained earnings. At most, 25 percent would be financed by bank loans. In Japan, the percentage of self-financed investment has been rising, but as of 1980, borrowing had paid for about two-thirds of the capital of most large firms and for 55–60 percent of the capital of the entire manufacturing sector. Among trading companies, the share of borrowed funds has been greater still.

Over most of the postwar era, Japanese business has been "overborrowed"—a condition that arose in the decade after World War II, when many firms contracted huge loans, first to reconstruct, and then to launch the long expansion that would come to be called the economic miracle.[8] Japanese corporations also became illiquid, by North American standards, although their average return on investment has been roughly the same as in the United States. Prior to the 1973–74 energy crisis, it was common to see statements like "Japanese firms are in debt up to their executive suites." But while formally true, this observation overlooks the close ties between banks and firms. In Japan, a bank loan is often not an arm's length transaction. Earlier, we noted that the *zaibatsu* dominated Japanese industry before World War II. When a Mitsui firm borrowed from the Mitsui Bank, the loan really came from an internal rather than from an external source. To a lesser extent, the same thing is true today—especially if the two belong to the same *keiretsu*, but in some cases even otherwise. (For example, three leading independent firms— Honda, Sony, and Matsushita—have close ties, respectively, with the Mitsubishi, Mitsui, and Sumitomo Banks.) Banks often own stock in companies to which they lend. In fact, private financial institutions own over a third of all shares, by value, issued by Japanese corporations. This exceeds the combined holdings of individuals.

Within a *keiretsu*, 10 percent to 30 percent of the shares of any given firm will typically be owned by other group firms, including the group's main bank, which will also hold a somewhat larger share of a representative group firm's debt. This debt is, in part, a substitute for equity, which is limited by a clause in the Anti-Monopoly Law forbidding a bank to hold more than 10 percent of the shares of any single company. In terms of residual claimancy, it also resembles equity to a degree. Thus, a group bank will go to extreme lengths, when necessary, to help out firms in the same *keiretsu* family during a financial squeeze. In return, the bank captures part of the profit earned by companies in its group through such devices as charging higher average interest rates of group firms than of outside borrowers. It also exercises some influence over investment decisions within the group.

Since the mid-1970s, enterprises have relied more on internal funds to finance investment, and banks have devoted more of their resources (although not always by choice) to financing the central government's budget deficit. Corporate liquidity, including business holdings of short-term government bonds, has been higher than during the 1950s and 1960s. Indications are that these conditions will persist over the long term. During the 1980s, domestic demand for loanable funds had been far lower, as a share of GNP, than over 1946–80. Thus, Japanese capital has been flowing abroad in record volume, and Japan is now the world's leading creditor nation.

13-3. The Financial System

Japanese financial institutions divide naturally into five conventional categories. At the apex of the financial structure we find the central bank, the Bank of Japan, which is often viewed as a policy-implementing arm for the Ministry of Finance.[9] Second are the commercial banks—including thirteen city banks, sixty-four regional banks, three private long-term credit banks, the Bank of Tokyo (specializing in foreign exchange), seven trust banks, and seventy-six foreign bank branches, as of end-1984. Before the Second World War, two of the long-term credit banks—the Hypothec Bank and the Industrial Bank of Japan—were closely controlled by the government and became prime movers of economic development. After the war, SCAP cut these ties, and the banks remain formally independent of the state. The Industrial Bank lends mainly to big business, while the Hypothec Bank lends largely to small- and medium-sized firms. In recent years, the long-term credit banks have made some short-term loans, while the other commercial banks have made some contractually long-term loans (and have always made *de facto* long-term loans), reducing differences within this category. The ten largest Japanese banks, in terms of deposits, are also the ten largest banks in the world.

Third, we have financial institutions specializing in loans to small business, agriculture, forestry, and fisheries. These include various specialized credit cooperatives and associations, as well as the 69 *sogo* (mutual savings and loan) banks and the 456 *shinkin* (mutual credit association) banks, which are the main source of finance for many small- and medium-sized firms. Fourth are the government financial institutions, including the Japan Development Bank, which we could also list as a fourth long-term credit bank. It is the successor to the Reconstruction Finance Corporation and, role-wise, to the prewar Industrial Bank of Japan. A second government bank, the Export-Import Bank of Japan, finances exports on a deferred-payments basis and also lends to companies and to governments that import Japanese products and technology. Finally, there are a number of special-purpose finance corporations for housing, small business, agriculture, forestry and fisheries, and other areas which receive government assistance on a continuing basis. Government lenders get most of their funds from the Finance Ministry's Trust Fund Bureau, into which flow postal savings from the 23,000 post offices throughout the country, as well as obligatory contributions to government pension programs. Postal savings account for more than a fifth of all household financial assets, excluding cash.

Aside from foreign bank branches, most Japanese commercial banks are divided into two basic categories—city banks and regional banks. The city banks are the heart of the system. They conduct business all over the country and have, on average, assets eight to nine times as great as the assets of an average regional bank. Over half of all city bank loans to the private sector since World War II have gone to large firms, from which these banks have also received well over half their short-term deposits and over a third of their time deposits. By contrast, regional banks lend mainly to small- and medium-sized companies, and a much larger percentage of their total deposits comes from individuals. The city banks accounted for over half of all outstanding bank loans as of end-1984 vs. over 30 percent for the regional banks and more than 18 percent for the four long-term credit banks (including the Japan Development Bank).

A major difference between the city and regional banks has been the former's habitual state of overloan to industry—and, more recently, to the central government—the counterpart of the latter's indebtedness. City banks have been short of funds for lending and in debt themselves to the Bank of Japan. The regional banks are never able to borrow from the central bank and usually have a surplus of deposits over loans. Because of a comparative lack of good lending opportunities and some government restrictions on their lending, they are usually liquid. By contrast, until a new Bank Law was passed in 1982, a single city bank loan was sometimes as high as 80 percent of its net worth. Many city bank loans are legally short term, but, in practice, are extended indefinitely. A bank will rarely call in a loan to a good customer.[10]

Because of their relative excess supply of deposits, the regional banks, along with the trust banks, the credit cooperatives and associations, and others lend large sums to the city banks on the call-loan and discount markets. Over most of the postwar era, these have been the only markets for loanable funds in Japan where interest rates were set by supply and demand. As a result, these rates have been quite volatile. When money has been tight, they have ranged 50 percent or more above the bank rate, at which the Bank of Japan lends to the city banks.

Indeed, call-money loans, made for a few days or even overnight, have often commanded higher rates than long-term industrial or government bonds. Thus, it has been attractive for regional banks to lend here and on the discount market, and this siphons money away from small- and medium-sized firms during periods of tight monetary policy. City banks have borrowed on these markets during credit squeezes—apparently at interest rates above those at which they have lent to their best corporate customers, although this is not certain, since every loan carries a "compensating balance" requirement.[11] In any event, each bank knows that failure of a major client would probably bring it down as well, and no bank would allow a firm within the same *keiretsu* to fail, without prior group approval.

For our purposes (and to summarize), the Japanese financial system has had four key features over the postwar era. First, the economy still relies heavily on banks to move funds from net savers (householders) to net borrowers (business firms and government). Up to 1975, banks supplied around 60 percent of all funds obtained through financial markets vs. 10 percent from stocks and bonds, 20 percent from government financial institutions, and 10 percent from nonbank financial intermediaries. Genuine bond markets were nearly nonexistent because of government restrictions on bond issue, and the equity base of Japanese business has been small. Second, the government kept nearly all interest rates, on both deposits and loans, below levels that banks would have set on their own. Within the banking system, one group, the city banks, has been overloaned and short of funds. They continually borrow from the Bank of Japan at low interest rates, but in limited quantities, and from the regional banks at higher rates. Until the late 1970s, the latter were virtually the only interest rates set by supply and demand. The free interest-rate sector is now much larger and growing, but most savers still faced deposit rates below market equilibrium levels, as late as early 1987. Although government regulation has kept down both deposit and lending rates, it has also widened the spread between them, which has increased bank profitability. The third feature is that credit has been rationed, in an environment where below-equilibrium interest rates have produced an excess demand for loanable funds. Finally, the state itself controls postal savings, which are quite popular in Japan, along with public financial institutions that rely on postal savings as their main source of loanable funds.

13-4. Financial Leverage of the Government

A. *The System Until the Early 1980s*

Even today, the Japanese government retains part of the financial leverage over economic activity which it established during the postwar occupation and reconstruction. It has used this leverage to influence both the pace and direction of economic growth, in an environment where loanable funds were almost perpetually in short supply until the early 1980s. In particular, large firms have often borrowed more than half their investment needs from the city banks, who have been persistent borrowers, in turn, from the Bank of Japan. The size of city bank debt to the central bank has been small—usually less than 3 percent of the former's loans and discounts. However, this is also the cheapest source of borrowing for the city banks, and it has therefore been of crucial importance to them at the margin. We recall that they generally have more lending opportunities than they can finance from their own deposits. Consequently, they must finance their overlending by borrowing from the Bank of Japan—at low interest rates, but in limited quantities—and from other financial institutions on the call-loan and discount markets, in unlimited quantities, but at much higher rates. By cutting one bank's borrowing quota, relative to the quotas of rival banks, the Bank of Japan could cause it to lose both profits and market share.[12]

Quantitative restrictions on the lending of government banks—and especially on Bank of Japan lending to the city banks—have been the major macroeconomic policy tool in Japan. That is to say, they are the major means of restraining spending, when this is deemed necessary to avoid excessive balance-of-payments deficits or inflation, since periodic restraint has been the main goal of macro policy. Fiscal policy (or variations in public spending and taxes) has been relatively unimportant. When the city banks come to the Bank of Japan's discount window for loans, BOJ will advise them on their own portfolio and lending behavior. This is called "window guidance" (*madaguchi shido*). In particular, the central bank will limit the volume of net increase in each bank's loans, and back this up with restrictions on city bank borrowing from itself.[13] In periods of tight money, there will also be direct and indirect restrictions on other types of loans.

Thus, the government has controlled aggregate demand by controlling the volume of credit available to private and public borrowers. Indirectly, this is also a control over the money supply, since money is created by government borrowing from the central bank or via Bank of Japan loans to the city banks. BOJ may also change the money supply by altering bank reserve requirements—although this is a relatively minor policy tool—and by open market operations. Thus, when it wants to tighten monetary policy (or reduce the growth rate of the money supply), it will typically reduce the growth of its own lending to city banks and increase its sales of short-term government securities. This lowers security prices and absorbs part of the money that would otherwise be lent on the call-loan market. The supply curve of call loans therefore shifts to the left, causing the call-loan interest rate to rise, and making it more expensive for city banks to borrow there. For regional banks, the rise in call-loan rates and the fall in securities prices makes lending to their own business customers less attractive. Loan volumes of other financial institutions have been directly restrained by quotas, and the state largely dictated the volume, composition, and timing of new bond issues, both public and private, until the early 1980s.

More generally, the government has used its leverage to influence the direction as well as the volume of lending, and in this way, the direction, as well as the pace of economic development. Here, its main goal is still to ensure ready access to finance for priority industries, keeping in mind that priorities are set in close consultation with private business. The government provides part of the necessary finance through tax forgiveness, subsidies, and accelerated depreciation (which is, in effect, a loan at zero interest). But it also influences the direction of lending on organized financial markets. Once MITI, the Finance Ministry, and leading businessmen have decided to promote an industry, the government is able to mobilize large amounts of investment credit and working capital for it almost overnight. This is part of the secret of Japan's successful penetration of foreign markets. Thus, Japanese entry into the U.S. semiconductor market in the latter 1970s led to complaints by American firms before the United States International Trade Commission that Japanese companies had an unfair advantage because they could borrow twenty times as much and rely on government guarantees of repayment.

Some of this credit will normally come from public lenders, notably the Japan Development Bank and the Export-Import Bank, which draw their funds from the Finance Ministry's Trust Fund Bureau. The latter has deposits greater than half the deposits of all banks, since it is the destination of postal savings and pension contributions, both of which have grown rapidly in recent years. (Postal savings have benefited from tax advantages, and there are over twice as many postal savings outlets as bank branches.) However, most of this money is earmarked for public corporations, like the Japan National Railways, as well as housing, small business, public investment, and environmental improvement, in which Japan has become a world leader. Industrial borrowing from public lenders is now less than 20 percent of that from private financial institutions, and government borrowing from these institutions has also been falling, as part of Japan's fiscal restraint in the wake of large budget deficits. While public lenders are a cutting edge in promoting the growth of priority sectors, government influence has extended beyond these to the behavior of private lenders as well.

As indicated above, the state has controlled the volume of loanable funds through a system of formal and informal quotas and put downward pressure on interest rates, creating excess demand. In early 1980, for example, many city banks had requests for three times the loan volume that they were able to honor. Interest rates have also been rigid. During periods of tight money, the shortage of loanable funds rises—together with the number of turned-down, cut-short, and postponed borrowers—as a partial substitute for cutting demand by raising interest rates. Except on the call-loan and discount markets, rates have either been negotiated by the government (as in the case of public borrowing) or tied to the bank rate at which the central bank lends to the city banks. They have generally remained below maximum rates that private borrowers are willing to pay.[14] Ultimately, the government can suppress interest rates because of its bargaining strength, but government regulation has also increased bank profits, as noted earlier, by reducing competition between financial intermediaries and allowing the spread between deposit and lending rates to widen.

With below-equilibrium interest rates and an excess demand for loanable funds, criteria other than price must enter to help determine who will have access to credit. Here, government plays a role, although aside from appropriating a large share of loanable funds to cover its own deficits since 1975, it does not usually command private banks to lend according to its priorities. The effect of its policies, however, is to exclude part of the demand for credit from the market, and the part remaining includes those industries whose growth it wishes to promote. First to be excluded are households, which have been virtually unable to borrow except to finance the purchase or major renovation of a home. More than 90 percent of consumer credit is for this purpose, and even here, a down payment of 30 percent or more must be made from one's own savings.

Traditionally, city banks divide their business customers into large and small borrowers, and their large borrowers into main borrowers and others.[15] As money grows tighter, first the nonprincipal large borrowers and then the small clients are cut back, and new clients are not accepted, as a rule. In general, the treatment of a borrower will depend on the strength of his long-term ties with the bank, as well as his size and business prospects. Often, city bank priorities in rationing credit will harmonize with those of the government, and BOJ will be aware of any potential for conflict, since it keeps comprehensive records of city bank lending by industry and region. When necessary, the central bank does indicate its preferences, and the city banks will be aware of state priorities, in any event, because of ongoing consultation between business and government. For example, in 1980, banks were told to favor projects related to energy production and conservation. In 1974, they were asked to favor housing, and earlier they had been advised to show a preference for heavy industry, autos, and chemicals.

Moreover, by giving tax rebates or subsidies on high-priority investments and by protecting the firms involved from import competition, the government raises the expected profitability on these investments and reduces the risk involved in bank loans that help to finance them. As well, there are often explicit or implicit guarantees that, if loans for government-promoted projects go sour, the lender will be at least partly reimbursed.[16] Such guarantees act as collateral, and imply further state absorption of investment risk. In these ways, the Japanese government has redirected the pattern of private lending, although it has often eased the private sector in a direction that it also wanted to go. It is equally a strength of the system that some firms have been able to prosper and grow without official blessing—and even in defiance of official views—eventually shaping government priorities to their own achievements, instead of vice versa.

To summarize, Japan's postwar expansion has been financed mainly by savings of domestic households and business firms, although creation of money, in the form of Bank of Japan loans to the city banks, has been important at the margin. This has helped put BOJ in a position to set and enforce quotas on other kinds of loans. Control over the aggregate volume of credit is the government's main means of controlling aggregate demand. The state also influences the direction of economic development through differential taxes and subsidies plus its leverage over the composition of investment loans. The percentage of loan-financed investment was higher in Japan over 1945–80 than in any Western country. In effect, households have been large net savers, while business and, lately, government have been large net borrowers, and financial institutions, especially banks, have played the intermediary role. The government has influenced the allocation of loans, both through public lenders and through city banks and the bond market, in an environment where interest rates were generally below equilibrium levels prior to 1981. In the process, the state has absorbed some of the risk of high-priority investment. Finally, the government has also isolated Japanese from foreign financial markets, by regulating international capital flows into and out of the country.

B. Deregulation

Japan's regulated financial system helped to generate the domestic savings on which its economic miracle depended and to channel these toward firms with growth and export potential. Because of their low access to credit, households have had to save in advance of major outlays for durable goods, as well as for weddings and other ceremonial occasions. The underdeveloped social welfare system has forced them to save for old age. Household savings have run 12–13 percent of GNP or more, and until the energy crisis, business was the main user of these funds. In addition, Japan realized higher growth per million yen invested over 1954–84 than virtually any other nation.

However, Western nations (especially the United States) have long objected to the isolation of Japanese from foreign financial markets. They have wanted better access to securities and loanable funds markets, to direct investment in Japan, and even to acquisitions of Japanese enterprises by their own nationals, banks, and business firms, as reciprocity for Japanese access abroad. (Because of their narrow equity base, moreover, Japanese corporations are potentially vulnerable to takeovers.) As a result of such measures, foreign governments would expect the demand for yen from abroad to rise, increasing its value in terms of Western currencies and making Japanese exports more expensive. Similarly, free domestic interest rates would be higher than controlled rates. With a freer flow of foreign capital into Japan, higher interest rates would also help to push up the yen's value. Foreign pressure on Japan to deregulate its financial system has therefore been growing since the late 1960s. During the 1980s, it has been successful, partly because domestic pressures have worked in the same direction. Deregulation has five basic components: Internationalization of the Yen; Liberalization of Interest Rates; Expansion of Capital Markets; Lowering of Barriers to Competition Between Different Kinds of Financial Institutions; and Relaxation of Controls on Foreign Banks in Japan.

Thus, the volume and variety of stocks and bonds has expanded and access to these markets has widened. The number of foreign-owned firms operating in Japan has increased manyfold, and a few foreign takeovers of Japanese firms have occurred—although they have only been allowed when this appeared to be in the long-run interests of the employees affected. (There are still *de facto* barriers to foreign capital inflows.) New savings deposits (certificates of deposit and, later, money-market certificates) have been created with decontrolled interest rates. To date, minimum requirements on savings volume place these instruments beyond the reach of most households, but such barriers are falling. Eventually (perhaps by the early 1990s), the majority of Japanese will have access to savings accounts with interest rates set by supply and demand. As early as 1981, Toyota was able to earn over half its profit from portfolio management.

Domestic pressures toward deregulation are rooted in the energy crisis. As in the West, it permanently lowered economic growth and raised the government's budget deficit, which increased the difficulty of simultaneously financing this deficit and controlling inflation. In the process, it reduced the power of the state to control interest rates and savings options. At first, inflation shot up in Japan, as the consumer price index jumped by 70 percent over 1973–76. The resulting destruction of accumulated savings magnified the impact of this on the general population, increasing resentment toward the low ceilings on deposit interest rates. To get inflation under control, the Finance Ministry began massive sales of government bonds in 1975. Over 1973–83, net government debt expanded to more than 10 times its original low level, and new bond issues grew to 5.6 times the volume of 1973. Before the energy crisis, the government had used its leverage to force financial institutions (mainly banks) to buy its bonds at high prices, or low interest yields. To make this requirement palatable, the Bank of Japan originally promised to buy back each bond one year after issue, at which time it either expanded the money supply by the bond's repurchase value or issued a replacement bond. Once the energy crisis had caused the government budget deficit to soar, therefore, BOJ was in danger of permanently losing control over the money supply. Yet, the optimal monetary policy appeared to be restrictive, so that limited demand at home would force Japanese firms to intensify their efforts to export.

To reestablish control over money-supply expansion, BOJ weakened its repurchase guarantee and began to price bonds so that their yields were more attractive to banks, relative to other lending opportunities. Banks were (and are) still obliged to hold more bonds than they would have chosen to buy on their own, but the market for *Gensaki* (bonds with repurchase guarantee) within the private sector also expanded. Here, interest rates became more attractive to savers than those on savings accounts. The minimum purchase requirement of 100 million yen excluded households from the demand side of this market, but many business firms found *Gensaki* purchases better than keeping money in bank deposits. As a result, BOJ has not generally had to honor its repurchase guarantee. However, because they were losing business to securities companies, which are licensed to trade in *Gensaki*, banks asked the Finance Ministry to allow them to issue a competitive security. In 1979, the first certificates of deposit appeared, with decontrolled interest rates. Since then, the free interest-rate sector has expanded, while the sector with regulated rates has shrunk. Yet, Japanese interest rates were generally lower in the mid-1980s than they were in 1973, and they have continued to be lower than interest rates in Western nations as well.

Deregulation of interest rates has coincided with decreasing inflation plus a long-term decline in the demand for loanable funds, relative to GNP. These factors have kept interest rates from rising. We recall that households have been the major net savers in Japan, financing much of the investment that made the economic miracle possible, and then the massive budget deficits of the 1970s. But since 1981, government's financing requirements have absorbed a smaller share of GNP than before, while net business demand has been around 3 percent of GNP vs. 8 percent before the energy crisis. With slower growth, business investment takes a smaller share of national income, and with higher accumulated profits, firms are better able to finance given investment levels from their own funds. As late as early 1988, much household demand for credit was still excluded from official markets. Consequently, the weight of domestic supply is now holding down interest rates in Japan. Loanable funds have become buyers' markets, as far as business customers are concerned, instead of sellers' markets, as over most of the postwar era to 1981.

As of 1988, Japan has run balance-of-payments surpluses continuously since 1980, which have coincided with surpluses of domestic saving over domestic requirements for financing investment plus the budget deficit. Together, these surpluses have produced record investment and lending overseas, which have helped to hold down interest rates in the United States and other Western countries. Over 1985–87, for example, Japanese buyers reportedly took about a third of all new debt issued by the U.S. federal government, and Japanese have become heavily involved in other kinds of loans, as well as in the purchase of real estate, equities, and capital assets in the United States. Japan has passed the United Kingdom to become the world's number one creditor nation and is second behind the United States in economic aid to developing countries. Deregulation has not yet produced an upward surge of interest rates in Japan, although it has reduced the spread between average lending and deposit rates. During the 1980s, this spread has been lower for Japanese banks than for the banks of any Western nation, because of both lower unit costs and smaller profit margins. (In each case, Japanese levels are 30–40 percent of those in the U.S., West Germany, or the U.K.) Eventually, the lower profit margins will squeeze some Japanese banks, and a few may not survive as independent entities. In addition, as more households receive full social insurance coverage and as consumer access to credit improves, net household saving may fall enough to begin putting upward pressure on lending rates in Japan.

13-5. Industrial Structure

A. *Competition and* keiretsu

Many Japanese industries are oligopolistic, in the sense that 75 percent or more of domestic sales are accounted for by the industry's four or five leading firms. In 1980, the 100 largest nonfinancial enterprises owned more than 21 percent of all nonfinancial business assets, although this was down from about 26 percent in 1967. The 100 largest manufacturing corporations accounted for about 30 percent of all sales by manufacturing corporations, although this was a smaller share than in the United States, the United Kingdom, or West Germany. Nevertheless, the period since the late 1960s has witnessed an explosion of mergers, in Japan as in the West, and Japanese producers still enjoy considerable protection from import competition. The government's farm policies—especially its price supports, which are largely maintained through import quotas—also keep many food prices far above world levels. Finally, there are a number of formal and informal agreements to restrict supply and raise price, which are often concocted with MITI's tacit approval or even encouragement. Japan's Fair Trade Commission (FTC), charged with enforcing the Anti-Monopoly Law, calculated that 17 percent of national income was produced in "extensively regulated" sectors in 1980. These are industries where the government restricts the number of producers and exercises some control over output, investment, and pricing.[17]

Yet, when all is said and done, only 27 percent of Japanese national income was produced under conditions of oligopoly in 1970, while 65 percent originated in at least approximately competitive industries, and 13 percent was produced by public enterprises that, in principle, are not profit oriented.[18] The many mergers over 1970–85 appear to have created a slight increase in industrial concentration—although the trend is ambiguous—but without altering these results dramatically. For manufacturing alone, the oligopoly share was higher, at 35 percent, and it was higher still in heavy and chemical industries, where economies of scale are greatest. Yet, aside from the extensive subcontracting that is a feature of industrial dualism in Japan, the competitive sector does not appear to be overly dependent on the oligopoly sector, although the high concentration in basic industries—such as iron and steel, petroleum, coal, and transport equipment—makes it impossible to be sure.

The above measures fail to take account of cartels and other collusive agreements between firms, which are often supported unofficially by the government. The Lockheed and Recruit scandals have also drawn attention to the widespread system of bribes and "goodwill" payments by firms to politicians and government officials. Many of these seek to establish, preserve, or get around barriers to competition and would not be present in an environment that remained free of such barriers. However, there are factors as well which tend to promote competitive behavior on the domestic market. In this connection, let us look at the enterprise groups known as *keiretsu*.[19]

When Japan embarked on its industrial revolution in the latter half of the nineteenth century, there had been no preceding accumulation of profits in private hands (as there had been, for example, in England and Holland during the commercial revolution). Yet, capital formation in modern industry required vast sums of money. Thus, a way was needed of combining the savings of thousands of small savers, mainly rural landowners, and of channelling them to investment projects in industry, where prospective returns were high. The question of collateral was crucial here. These projects were often risky, and the borrower would frequently lack security for a loan, other than the project itself. But to allow investments to be used as collateral for the loans that financed them required banks to protect themselves by acquiring a good knowledge of borrowing firms and of their investments—and, in the final analysis, to get involved in owning and managing these enterprises. Hence, the emergence of close ties between banks and firms that is the hallmark of finance capitalism.

This system arose in Japan, as in countries on the continent of Europe that were also late comers to industrial development and where growth of industry was initially financed by savings generated in agriculture. It allowed banks to assume greater risk burdens and, thus, to provide a secure harbor for savings, while advancing large amounts of industrial capital. The Japanese version of finance capitalism rested on the *zaibatsu*. Each of these conglomerates included a bank and a trading company, as well as several enterprises, each of which normally operated in a different branch of industry. The conglomerate was controlled through a holding company, which held shares in member firms. After World War II, holding companies were outlawed and the *zaibatsu* dissolved, as described earlier. Following the U.S. occupation, however, several prewar *zaibatsu* regrouped themselves into new financial-industrial clusters called *keiretsu*.

The *keiretsu* include the revitalized Big Three of Mitsubishi, Mitsui, and Sumitomo plus the three bank groups—Dai-Ichi Kangyo, Fuji (or Fuyo), and Sanwa. Together, the assets of the core companies of all six groups came to about 15 percent of the total assets of industry in 1980, which rises to 25 percent if we add the assets of more loosely affiliated companies. In this respect, they are not far below their prewar eminence.[20] However, because holding companies are illegal, the *keiretsu* must be coordinated through the group bank and trading company, interlocking corporate directorates, intercorporate stockholding, joint investment ventures, presidents' clubs (where managers of member firms meet, usually once a month or more), and various informal channels. Several of these avenues are also constrained by the Anti-Monopoly Law.

Today's *keiretsu* are more loosely organized and more decentralized than the prewar *zaibatsu*. They are held together by mutual benefits from cooperation, rather than by a strong central power. Thus, they help group banks and trading companies to diversify their risks and group firms to gain access to a secure and stable source of credit, as well as to share technical information and experience. Moreover, the *keiretsu* are often able to influence government policy making and are still agents for carrying out policies, although not to the extent of prewar days. Yet, the firms, the bank, and the trading company always do a large business outside the group. Group coordination is probably highest in the case of Mitsubishi, the most powerful *keiretsu*, and lowest in the case of Dai-Ichi Kangyo, also the largest *keiretsu* in terms of assets, employees, and sales. (However, Dai-Ichi Kangyo includes remnants of two smaller prewar *zaibatsu*, Kawasaki and Furukawa, within which attachment to the former group is stronger.)

More generally, company identification with the group appears to be fairly strong in four of the *keiretsu* (Mitsubishi, Mitsui, Sumitomo, Fuyo), which have become strong rivals. By nature, Japanese are conscious of status and naturally tend to rank firms in an industry, largely according to market share. Managers and even ordinary workers derive prestige from belonging to the company that is first in sales, and enterprises will therefore compete for market shares, even to the detriment of profitability. The *keiretsu* help to support this competition, and they compete as well in trying to establish themselves in new product lines. Because of their eagerness to promote production where growth potential is greatest, the *keiretsu* tend to increase the mobility of capital and, to a lesser extent, of labor across industrial and regional boundaries.

The *keiretsu* also have the financial strength and connections to overcome most entry barriers. When the Ministry of International Trade and Industry (MITI) tries to set up a cartel, the companies least likely to go along are *keiretsu* members or relatively strong dynamic and independent firms, such as Sony, Matsushita, and Honda. Thus, while Japanese industry has several characteristics of oligopoly, it is now more competitive than in prewar days and probably more competitive as well than the industrial sectors of most Western countries.

B. The Role of the Trading Companies

Japanese industry is unique in relying on general trading companies (*sogo shosha*), which have few counterparts in the West, although the British East India Company gives us an historical example. Trading companies specialize in buying and selling. Historically, Japanese manufacturers have focused more narrowly on production than have their counterparts in North America or Western Europe, turning the bulk of their sales and purchasing operations over to trading companies, much as a Western firm routinely turns to a bank for finance. Thus, Japan has a separate industry made up of companies specializing in buying and selling, just as most countries have separate financial industries.

Most of the *keiretsu* have their own trading companies, which play leading roles within them. The largest, Mitsubishi Shoji, owns stock in many other Mitsubishi enterprises, and 35 percent of its shares are owned within the group. In 1980, it handled about 12 percent of Japan's foreign trade—a share that has since declined—including 15 percent of its oil imports, and a comparable volume of domestic trade. More than 10 percent of its transactions now involve only third countries. In the process, it deals in 25,000 different types of goods—everything "from missiles to instant noodles." Mitsui Bussan, the prewar leader of this industry, is now close behind Mitsubishi, followed by C. Itoh (Dai-Ichi Kangyo Group), Marubeni (Fuyo Group), and Sumitomo Shoji.

However, we should not think of trading companies simply as marketing and purchasing arms of *keiretsu*. There are more than 5,000 trading firms in all—most of which are specialized by product line—and the vast majority of these do not belong to an industrial group. Nine companies dominate the industry, accounting for about half of Japan's foreign trade plus a fifth of the domestic wholesale trade. The term, *general* trading company, is usually reserved for those Big Nine, because of the wide variety of goods that they handle and because they operate all over the world. Most general traders are affiliated with a *keiretsu*, but they also serve many outside enterprises. In 1980, less than 10 percent of Mitsubishi Shoji's sales and under 20 percent of its purchases, for example, were on behalf of other Mitsubishi firms. Increasingly, *keiretsu*-affiliated industrial firms buy and sell on their own.

A general trading company will provide many services for its customers beyond buying and selling, narrowly understood, for it specializes in knowing markets at home and all over the world. It is especially good at gathering information about products, supplies, and potential buyers, and the intelligence services of the top companies are legendary. In 1971, Mitsubishi learned before the Japanese government that the U.S. dollar would be devalued. Mitsui reported the movement of the Russian Baltic Fleet toward the war zone in the 1904–1905 Russo-Japanese War, enabling the Japanese Navy to score the decisive victory. A general trading company will often research the market for a new product, provide technical advice and financing for the producer, and arrange for storage, transportation, and insurance. It will put its own trademark on the product of a small, unknown manufacturer and take responsibility for service after the sale. According to one author, "the trading company employs many thousands of staff [including] highly qualified scientists, engineers, and economists. They are scattered all over the world, speak the local language, and provide better research, inspection and servicing than even a very large manufacturer could do for itself."[21] Trading companies spend large sums training their employees, many of whom do not become really effective until years after they are hired.

Arguably, big trading companies provide more services to small- and medium-sized producers than to large ones. Their existence allows many small manufacturers to export who could not otherwise reach foreign markets. Trading companies also supply warehouse space, which is costly in land-scarce Japan, as well as insurance and transportation. They absorb risks for small producers, taking advantage of their size and diversity and the opportunities which come their way because of their role as information centers. In particular, they absorb risks related to changes in exchange rates, and they lend to small businesses on both long and short term.

Each of the general trading companies also has close ties with one or more city banks from whom it often borrows. It then utilizes its own knowledge of the small-firms sector to lend to enterprises whose goods it is willing to sell or for whom it has decided to become a supplier. Postwar Japan has gone through several financial squeezes when money has been difficult to borrow. It is the small firms which are hardest hit when credit is tight, and trading companies often finance their best small-firm customers through such a period by buying stock in them, as well as by granting them loans. If a small enterprise goes under anyway, the trading company may help to reorganize it and take advantage of the low price of its assets to acquire a controlling interest.

The general trading companies have outstanding loans amounting to around 10 percent of the total loan volume of all privately owned Japanese banks. The same companies are the recipients of 5 percent to 10 percent of all bank loans. In effect, the trading companies are also financial intermediaries who borrow from banks at the prime lending rate, and then relend most of the funds they have borrowed to their clients. As a rule, trading companies know the financial condition of small firms better than do banks, and the former can therefore lend larger amounts to this sector at lower rates. The Big Nine are also the largest shareholders in close to 1,500 Japanese companies, although it is doubtful that they control this many. Nevertheless, the FTC has charged that the largest of them may have become *de facto* holding companies.

Economists say that there are often external benefits from learning about new markets and starting operations in them. Contacts made and knowledge gained from selling automobiles in North America or Western Europe, for example, can help to sell machine tools, tractors, or other consumer durables. But we should then ask why comparatively few trading companies exist outside Japan, since the marketing and purchasing roles could be specialized in any economy. The disadvantage of a large trading company is that, since it handles so many goods, it cannot devote as much attention to any one as a manufacturer would want. Nor does it always have enough detailed knowledge about individual markets or sources of supply.

When we weigh the costs and benefits of specializing the buying and selling function, therefore, we find that these depend on cross-product externalities in marketing, as well as on special liabilities or advantages that manufacturing firms might have in gaining access to markets. In feudal Japan, there were large merchant houses long before there was large-scale production. When the Industrial Revolution began, it made sense not to burden the nascent manufacturing sector with marketing and procurement, which were therefore specialized in the trading companies. The latter, in turn, have always worked closely with government agencies (principally MITI since World War II). To a degree, trading companies are also a creature of Japan's dual industrial structure, since the access to markets, finance, and sources of supply that they provide are most valuable to small firms. Likewise, trading companies are skilled in the art of human relations in a country where this is critical for successful consummation of transactions. Japan's high population density makes land scarce, storage costs high, and puts a premium on better use of storage space, which larger firms handling larger volumes of different kinds of goods with compensating seasonal demand or supply fluctuations are able to obtain.

Yet, trading company services have been most crucial in foreign trade, where these enterprises have continued to be instruments of national policy. Since Japan is culturally distant from all other nations, foreign markets have been hard for Japanese manufacturing firms to penetrate until quite recently. Japan must import essential raw materials and food to maintain its living standard (to some extent, even to survive), and it needs access to up-to-date technology, as well as to specialized equipment from abroad, in order to maintain export competitiveness. Thus, it has made sense to specialize the handling of trade-related tasks within trading companies, which can attract those Japanese with an orientation toward foreign languages, markets, and cultural contacts. The main function of these enterprises has been to scour the world for the raw materials, technology, and export markets essential to Japan's survival and prosperity. Earlier, we noted that Japan's wholesale and retail distribution networks often seem an impenetrable maze to foreign producers, and the trading companies have been accused of restricting the access of foreign manufacturers to domestic markets. The Japanese are also famous for blocking imports with product standards, bureaucratic red tape, and other unofficial barriers. But where high-priority imports are concerned, the barriers dissolve like magic, and the trading companies steer goods past all distributional hurdles with apparent ease.

In recent years, manufacturing enterprises have come to do more of their own marketing. By 1984, the general trading companies' share of Japanese exports had fallen below one-third (vs. half of all imports). The *sogo shosha* are not much involved in marketing of consumer electronics, autos, or other products which have shown rapid export growth since the energy crisis. By the early 1980s, Japanese businessmen were speaking of the "winter of *sogo shosha.*" Reports of their demise have proved to be exaggerated but, to remain viable, they have had to diversify into manufacturing and mining, often in foreign countries and frequently in joint ventures with foreign firms. The latter need the marketing, supply, organizational, and informational capacities of the big traders, about a third of whose investment has gone outside Japan since the mid-1970s. From the Japanese viewpoint, these investments help to leapfrog trade barriers in host countries by establishing factories there—which are often allowed to import some inputs from Japan, provided they also export. The trading companies have also helped to relocate labor-intensive production in developing nations, and they have recently invested heavily in high-technology industries within Japan itself—including electronics, information processing, and biotechnology.

However, the main reason for foreign investment by the *sogo shosha* has been to ensure supplies of energy and raw materials for Japan. For example, Sumitomo Shoji has gone into ocean development and petroleum exploration on a joint-venture basis with other countries. Mitsubishi has launched three liquefied natural gas projects—in Brunei, Alaska, and Malaysia—and Nissho Iwai is involved in three others. Mitsubishi has also helped to build a petrochemical complex in Saudi Arabia, which began operations in late 1985. Typically, part of the payment for this venture will be delivery of 200,000–250,000 barrels of oil per day to Japan, providing up to 6 percent of domestic consumption. The risk involved in such ventures is indicated by the subsequent fall of oil prices and by Mitsui's experience with a similar project in Iran. The latter has yet to begin operating, despite an investment of over $4 billion, but the Japanese government will absorb most of the loss on this venture.

C. Industrial Dualism

Finally, Japanese industry remains dualistic, to an extent more characteristic of a developing than of a developed nation. Industry can still be divided into a sector consisting of large, modern, capital-intensive enterprises, within which the skill mix of the labor force, labor productivity, and wages are relatively high, vs. a sector with much smaller firms using labor-intensive technologies. Small firms also tend to use disproportionately large numbers of young people, who are starting out in the labor market, and older workers, who have retired from their formal careers between the ages of 55 and 60, but who cannot afford to stop working. Traditionally, this sector has served as an employment sponge, absorbing workers who find it hard to get work in larger firms.

Even outside agriculture, about 20 percent of Japan's labor force still consists of self-employed and family workers. Most of these are in the small-firms sector, and they account for just under 15 percent of the manufacturing labor force plus 20 percent of all workers in the service sector and a third of those in retail and wholesale trade. Altogether, 35–40 percent of the industrial labor force works in enterprises with no more than 30 employees vs. 12–15 percent in companies employing over 1,000. Within the latter, capital and value added per worker are at least three times as high as in the former. Although the difference in average profitability is smaller, the dispersion of profitability from one firm to another is higher among small enterprises, so that the extremes of success and failure are more frequently encountered there.

The small-firms sector is varied in other ways. Many small companies operate in the growing service industries, while others turn out luxury goods, highly specialized machinery, or products for local markets. Many do artisan work, and still others produce manufactures in which scale economies are not important—especially in the food, clothing, textile, and leather-goods industries, but also in some areas of high technology. Even today, small enterprises often perform just one stage of a multiprocess production chain. They buy inputs from other small producers and sell their outputs to still others, one stage downstream in the production flow. A trading company is likely to finance such an operation and to play a role in organizing and coordinating it. However, the basic phenomenon predates the rise of the *sogo shosha* and may owe its existence to the earlier-mentioned status ranking of buyer over seller. The ability of the buyer to make his deal, subject to taking the seller's circumstances into account and in combination with a relatively high level of trust between the two, limits the transactions costs associated with a vertical chain of independent companies.

Over half of all small- and medium-sized companies in manufacturing work as subcontractors for large enterprises, on whom they are apt to be highly dependent. These subcontractors employ a fourth of the manufacturing labor force, and are often referred to as "child" companies (*ko-kaisha*). A typical large firm (with over 1,000 employees) has 80 to 90 subcontractors and is twice as dependent on subcontracting (in terms of share of value added in the final product) as would be normal in North America or Western Europe. A subcontractor may even rent space in a factory of the firm for which it does most or all of its business, although a tendency has now arisen for subcontractors to take business from more than one parent company. Whether he works for several parents or just one, the subcontractor will perform relatively labor-intensive, less skilled operations, including maintenance, repair, and janitorial services. Often, a subcontractor will buy his raw materials from the parent to whom he sells his output. He will frequently work with used machinery, which he may also rent or buy from the parent. Thus, the parent is usually able to squeeze his subcontractors. In the event of a downturn in demand, subcontractors will have to lay off employees or even go bankrupt before the parent reduces its own permanent work force, although the parent will go to some lengths to avoid this, and the usual relationship between the two is one of long duration.

As a rule, small firms also pay higher borrowing costs than do larger companies. Moreover, they have lower access to credit and receive fewer tax breaks for investment, research, and development. When money becomes tight, the small firms bear the brunt of liquidity shortage. A parent firm will shift a portion of its own illiquidity onto its subcontractors—for example, by paying its debts to them, not with money, but with IOUs called "childbirth bills," that can be cashed only in nine months' time.

Why is the small-firms sector so large in Japan and, in particular, why do large companies subcontract operations that they would do for themselves in the West? Subcontracting is, in part, an outgrowth of the Japanese system of labor relations, to be examined shortly, which limits large enterprises in laying off their own employees. When the demand for their products falls, they sometimes lay off workers, in effect, by reducing their demand for services provided by subcontractors. The parent firm may then take over some previously subcontracted work or reallocate it among fewer "children." A second reason for the large small-firms sector is the strategy of economic development followed by Japan, especially over the century after 1880, when modern economic growth began. It has concentrated investment funds on a relatively small number of industries and enterprises, as of any given point in time, whose products were considered crucial to further development or which were expected to benefit from significant increases in demand. Instead of spreading funds evenly over the economy, they have been lavished on such key areas where potential gains from adoption of new technology, including scale and experience economies, were believed to be high. Meanwhile, other industries and enterprises were relatively starved for credit. The firms with best access to investment funds have also enjoyed best access to foreign technology, by and large, whose use has required relatively capital-intensive production facilities.

Although it has often been exploited, small-scale industry has also supplied needed flexibility. For over a century, economic development has motivated the introduction of mass-production technologies requiring large doses of capital per unit of labor. To achieve acceptable quantity and quality in many industries, Japan has had to adopt this approach. Yet the overall labor-to-capital endowment has exceeded the maximum usable in modern industry. Population growth has overcrowded the land, causing migration to the cities plus underemployment of farm labor. Large-scale, capital-intensive industry could not absorb most of this surplus, which consequently had to find jobs in the small-firms sector. Since many small companies use second-hand equipment, they also help to raise the average service life of industrial capital.[22]

By the first energy crisis, there were signs that the dualistic nature of the Japanese economy might disappear. Because it had invested over 30 percent of GNP in every year between 1959 and 1973, Japan's overall capital-to-labor ratio had risen by 1973 to more than 3.5 times the level of 1952. The expanding economy was starting to create a severe labor shortage, and growth of labor costs in small firms was much greater than in large ones. Over 1950–63, the latter showed no net change, as productivity and wage increases cancelled. But in an average small firm, labor costs rose by two-thirds. By the mid-1960s, small enterprises were already obliged to offer higher wages to workers under 30, although big companies continued to give better employment guarantees, fringe benefits, and on-the-job training. The practice began of shifting more and more subcontracting and other labor-intensive work out of Japan to Taiwan, South Korea, and other Asian developing nations. This continues, but the effect of the energy crisis was to reduce growth and to end the overall labor shortage. During the 1980s, unemployment has reached its highest level since the mid-1950s, and the small-firms sector has resumed its traditional role of shock absorber and employment sponge. In 1984, average pay in cottage-level firms, with fewer than 5 employees, was under half that in large companies with 500 employees or more. Average pay in enterprises with 5 to 29 employees ran 60 percent of that in large firms.

13-6. Labor Relations

A. *"Lifetime" Commitment and Seniority-Based Wages*

The dualistic nature of the Japanese economy and the social web of vertical and horizontal ties described earlier are reflected in Japan's system of labor relations. In large firms only, this system has rested on three main pillars over most of the postwar era—*sushin koyo*, or lifetime commitment; *nenko* or seniority-based wages; and company-based unions. All firms, whether large or small, consider themselves families of a sort. Traditionally, a small proprietor would be expected to find suitable husbands for his female employees and to otherwise look after his work force. However, small- and medium-sized firms are usually not financially strong or secure enough to guarantee permanent employment. Neither are most of them unionized, and the wages they pay are more closely determined by market forces, so that the seniority effect is less.

Lifetime commitment means that a worker is hired—or "adopted" into the organization family—not for life, but until retirement, which usually comes early in Japan, between the ages of 55 and 60. The probability of even a temporary layoff before then is low. An employer commits himself never to fire a lifetime employee unless the alternative is financial ruin, although workers usually have general rights to employment rather than specific rights to specific jobs. The government will support the system with subsidies, as during the recession of 1974–76, and may even help to reorganize a bankrupt firm or to find a merger partner, so that lifetime employees can be kept on. The lifetime guarantee is not embodied in any written document. But an employer who breaks the rules, as they are commonly understood, faces government harassment, public ill will, loss of employee morale, union pressure, and future recruiting difficulties. The lifetime employee who quits will rarely be able to find such a good job again—a new employer would inevitably enquire about and take a dim view of such a departure—and he will lose his accumulated seniority.

Although they are implicit, the courts have also upheld employment guarantees, and not only where *sushin koyo* is concerned. No Japanese enterprise can discharge workers unless it is in serious financial straits.[23] The moral obligation binding employer and employee nearly always runs deeper in Japan than in the West, although it is especially strong in the case of the lifetime employee. When such a person suffers occupational injury or disability, his employer must take care of him and provide for his family. (Women rarely achieve lifetime employment status.) Large firms maintain health care and medical clinics for their regular workers— along with recreational, social, and cultural facilities and vacation retreats. They also provide housing or housing allowances, as well as allowances for dependents, for commuting to work, and often, for other expenses.

Employers have a strong incentive to invest in training their lifetime employees. Large companies pay semiannual bonuses, averaging over a fourth of current wages or salaries, to their permanent employees as a way of sharing the return on this investment.[24] Both wages and bonuses vary more flexibly with profits over the business cycle than do industrial wages in most Western countries. Moreover, wage differences between industries and firms are greater in Japan, whereas intrafirm wage and salary differentials are lower, despite pay differences based on seniority—a phenomenon made possible by the lower mobility of labor in Japan. The earnings of all employees are more closely linked to company performance, and in this sense, Japanese enterprises practice a greater degree of profit sharing than do their counterparts in the West.

The employer also receives a lifetime commitment from his employees. Workers promise to be loyal achievers and, indeed, to devote their lives to the enterprise. Japanese managers in large firms tend to supervise more subordinates, and the chain of command between top management and production workers is correspondingly shorter than in the West. Traditionally, lifetime employees have been hired directly out of school and only after passing examinations, interviews, and extensive probing into their backgrounds, values, beliefs, family connections, and so on. Then, they must survive a probationary period of up to a year, by proving that they are both good workers and good prospective members of the enterprise family. The employer obtains a series of pledges from the worker's relatives, former teachers, and others, that make it unlikely he will leave before retirement. As a rule, the lifetime employee does not resist technological change or the hiring of temporary or subcontract labor, because these pose no threat to him. On the contrary, they can raise his earnings by improving the performance of his company.

Over most of the post-World War II era, lifetime employees have received *nenko* (or seniority-based) wages. In 1974, for instance, wages and salaries, averaged across all manufacturing employees aged 45 to 54, were 25 percent greater than for those aged 25 to 29. For nonproduction employees (mainly white-collar workers), the difference was close to 70 percent, despite the overstaffing of Japanese companies at the middle management level. Among large firms, these ratios were much greater. By contrast, in Britain, France, West Germany, and Italy, workers aged 45 to 54 earned about the same or less, on average, than those aged 25 to 29. From another perspective, the earnings profile, by age, of Japanese blue-collar workers in large companies (over 1,000 employees) was similar to that of white-collar workers (averaged over all but the smallest companies) in Western Europe. The age-earnings profile of Japanese white-collar workers showed even larger seniority differentials up to age 55.[25]

Nenko wages reflect the investment made by firms in training their workers— training which covers a wider variety of jobs and is broader than a Western worker is likely to receive. During the early years of his employment, the employee pays for his training by accepting relatively low wages. Because of this and because the employer can capture a return on his investment later, Japan has a lower rate of youth unemployment than virtually any Western country. On average, the training period of white-collar employees is longer and costlier than for blue-collar workers. Afterward, employees share in the return on this investment with the employer, through higher wages and profit-linked bonuses. While the influence of seniority on earnings has been high, the individual's performance also counts, and better performance means faster promotion. Indeed because there is no schedule of standardized pay rates attached to particular jobs—and because each worker has only a general right to employment—a lifetime employee knows to the day he retires that his performance will affect his future income and status. This reinforces his moral commitment to the firm.

To sum up, Japanese employers tend to be stronger and more paternalistic vis-à-vis their workers than are employers in the West. But more importantly, the underlying philosophy stresses the harmony of interests between employers and employees, rather than the inherent conflict between them. Managers accept an obligation to take care of their employees in a general way and to insure them against disability or sickness. The large company invests heavily in training its regular employees and provides them with housing, family allowances, and lei-sure-time activities. Relations between superior and subordinate are personal and informal. Managers often wear the same company uniform and eat in the same cafeteria as their workers. Executive salaries are smaller multiples of average blue-collar earnings than in most developed Western countries.

Managers also consult with workers, through their union representatives, on a range of issues of mutual interest—including transfer of personnel between distant work places, working conditions, company housing, production scheduling, technological change, and productivity. At the industry level, various joint councils discuss pollution and congestion and other economic policy issues. Informal contacts are also numerous, and much consultation takes place on company time at company expense. Work rotation is frequent and extensive. "Within a workshop, it is not rare to see transfers among all positions occur daily or every few weeks. . . . Furthermore, transfers between workshops that have a limited technical association . . . are quite widely recognized, in Japan, as temporary work assignments."[26]

Widespread work rotation is part of the broader job training mentioned above and includes white-collar participation in blue-collar labor, such as engineers doing repair work and sales staff taking part in production, usually on a temporary basis. One effect of this is to ratify the divorce of an individual's wage or salary from the particular job he is doing as of any moment. Another is to buttress security against layoffs, since the broadly-trained worker can more easily move to a new type of job when his old one disappears. But widespread work rotation and broadly-based job training also give Japanese companies an organizational advantage over their Western rivals. Employees are more adaptable and can be used where they are most urgently needed on a given day, even if they are normally doing a different type of work. The enterprise can therefore respond more flexibly to temporary problems and to shifts in product demand. Moreover, all employees in a Japanese factory must have a physical understanding of its production process. This makes coordination of the firm easier and reduces the likelihood that sales or design staff will create costly production problems that cannot be justified on the basis of higher revenues.

Workshop meetings are frequent in a Japanese plant, and workers are both expected to show initiative and rewarded for doing so. As noted earlier, Japanese workers in large companies apparently find work more enriching and rewarding than do their Western counterparts. Japanese employees identify more easily with their products and companies, to which they are deeply committed. But in the final analysis, Japanese managers still have more power to direct and allot the work than do Western managers, provided they carry out elaborate consultation before major decisions. This includes power to decide questions of work rotation.

B. Background of the Lifetime Employment System

Critics of *sushin koyo* charge that the relations between employer and employee that it promotes are a paternalistic relic of feudalism.[27] In appearance, lifetime employment could easily be part of Japan's successful adaptation of the feudal value structure to promote rapid industrial growth. However, while the roots of *sushin koyo* are traceable to merchant houses of the Tokugawa era, the practice did not really begin until World War I. It became prevalent among large firms only after World War II, mainly as a response to union demands for job security amid the widespread unemployment and underemployment then prevailing. Originally, lifetime employment developed from efforts to overcome a paternalistic guild system of supplying industrial labor. During the nineteenth century, industry had to recruit labor directly from agriculture. Many workers were young, unmarried women, badly exploited by their employers, who did not usually keep working after marriage. Others were men, who often moved back and forth between factory and farm and from one industrial work place to another.

In an effort to stabilize their work forces, employers made contracts with middlemen called *oyakata*. The latter became responsible for supplying industrial labor and for setting wage rates. To do this, they built up their own cliques of followers, formed through their contacts in rural villages. These followers, called *kokata*, developed strong *oyabun-kobun* (i.e., "parent-child") relationships with their *oyakata,* and horizontal relations also developed at both levels. The *oyakata* were usually skilled workmen with more technical expertise and practical experience than company managers, who were normally university graduates. Neither did the latter have good ties in rural areas and, at first, they could not do without the *oyakata.* However, management was dissatisfied with this system because the *oyakata* and their *batsu* frequently moved from one factory to another. The *oyakata* were generally independent, and they naturally sought to maximize their own incomes and status. It was also they, and not the employers, who commanded the loyalty of the workers, and at times they caused chaos by disrupting a firm's labor supply. In addition, "as industrialization spread, the *oyakata* were increasingly incapable of transmitting the necessary knowledge and skills required for increased production, complex machinery (usually imported from abroad), diverse products, and new types of raw materials."[28]

Lifetime employment was the price paid by large companies to co-opt and then to replace the *oyakata-kokata* system. Managers began by offering individual *oyakata* high wages, guaranteed lifetime employment, and considerable status. In some cases, the *oyakata* and their *batsu* were allowed to form unions, and in other firms, company unions were established. At first, the work remained organized around the *oyakata,* who were now kept within a single enterprise. But gradually, the companies undermined the *oyakata* in two ways. In the political arena, they lobbied government to expand secondary education as a way of raising the supply of skilled workers and foremen. By improving their ties with the educational system, large companies were eventually able to recruit right out of school. They also organized their own vocational training programs staffed by instructors loyal to the company. New recruits eventually had to demonstrate company loyalty during harsh apprenticeship programs.

In this way, loyalty to the *oyakata* was replaced by loyalty to a company. Nevertheless, Japanese foremen, the successors to the *oyakata,* are still required to maintain highly personal ties with their workers. As a rule, foremen are promoted from the ranks and represent the highest level a lifetime blue-collar worker can hope to achieve. (Company loyalty also plays an important role in their selection.) During World War II, the government tied employees to their work places in the name of the war effort. After the war, SCAP greatly strengthened the union movement, which pushed to expand the lifetime employment system in order to increase job security.

C. The Percentage of Lifetime Employees

Today, while the lifetime employment system covers most public sector employees, it applies to only a minority in the private sector and probably to no more than one-third of all industrial blue-collar workers. Lifetime employment is rare in firms with fewer than 100 employees and by no means the rule in companies with 100 to 1,000. It is only in big enterprises that most workers are guaranteed *sushin koyo*. Moreover, besides their permanent employees, large firms hire many "temporary" workers, often a fifth or more of total employment. They hire only as many permanent employees as they expect to need through the depths of a recession. Temporary employees have short-term labor contracts, but can expect to be regularly rehired, except in recessions, when they may be laid off, in effect. Neither do they belong to the company union, nor are they entitled to as many fringe benefits as permanent employees.

In addition, we have seen that large companies hire many subcontractors, a number of whom operate right inside the parent firm's plant. This is a survival of the *oyakata* system, but since the parent companies could do much of the work themselves, it is equally another way of hiring workers without giving them lifetime status or benefits. Traditionally, it has also been a way of hiring low-wage labor. Even large enterprises may therefore have an effective minority of lifetime employees, who are the ones considered most crucial to the firm's success. At most factories and construction sites, regular workers with lifetime status are distinguishable by some element of their dress from temporary and subcontract labor. Since the earnings of the lifetime élite depend on company performance, they also share to some extent in the profits earned from the labor of these relatively disadvantaged workers. It is this, together with the job protection afforded the lifetime élite, that makes the unions happy to allow their companies to employ temporary and subcontract labor. But most of the latter earn higher pay than they would if the company did not take them on. The system probably generates more employment and output than it would if differentiation in wages, fringe benefits, working conditions, and employment guarantees were not allowed, in which case temporary and subcontract workers would be worse off still.

From one standpoint, labor relations in Japan do remind us of those in the West. In both Europe and North America, the most exploited segment of the labor force consists mainly of immigrants, some of whom are illegally in the host country and therefore virtually without bargaining power. Even legal immigrant or "guest" workers are normally first to be fired when demand falls off and last to be rehired when it picks up again. They perform the most menial chores and suffer discrimination in wages, fringe benefits, and working conditions, when they do work similar to that performed by natives. The latter, buttressed by strong unions, can often share with employers in the profits generated by the immigrant sector, as well as by any native workers who may be targets of discrimination on racial, ethnic, religious, or other grounds. There is no evidence that discrimination in Japan is any greater, and it is probably mitigated by the moral commitment of Japanese employers and the ethnic homogeneity of Japanese workers, as well as by the virtual absence of foreign or immigrant labor.

In this context, it is usually company policy to go to some lengths even to avoid layoffs of temporary and subcontract workers. This includes taking up the production of new goods as an alternative to layoffs, and a number of Japanese enterprises have quite different output profiles today than they had twenty to thirty years ago. Pressures on firms to adapt to changes in supply and demand in ways that minimize layoffs are greater than in most Western countries. In January, 1976, for example, during the post–energy crisis recession, the Economic Planning Agency surveyed firms of all sizes and found that over half felt they were carrying surplus labor. Among large enterprises, this percentage was close to 65 percent, but it was around 45 percent even among small firms. Most of the Employment Adjustment Subsidy, designed to prevent layoffs during this period, was paid to small enterprises.

Subsidies aside, Japanese labor costs still vary over the business cycle and are not necessarily less flexible than those in Western countries. Japanese employment contracts effectively trade wage flexibility for job security. Thus, employment fluctuations are smaller in Japan; in particular, fewer workers are laid off in recessions. Flexibility is achieved instead by varying earnings and hours worked, as a substitute for employment variations.[29]

D. The Erosion of Nenko (Seniority-Based) Wages

Because of a falling birthrate and an aging population, seniority wage differentials have declined in Japan, and one author even argues that the *nenko* wage system has disappeared.[30] However, such a conclusion seems premature. The comparative surplus of older workers did cause seniority to lose some of its value over the 1970s, but part of this has been regained during the 1980s. Among male university graduates, a "typical" 55-year-old earned about 4.2 times as much as a 22-year-old starting out in 1971. By 1981, this differential had fallen to less than 3.6 times, but it recovered to nearly 4 times by 1984. A similar evolution occurred among high school graduates, although here, the seniority differential is only about half as great.[31] A disturbing sign was a rise in the number of surplus white-collar workers aged 45 and older (known as *madogiwa zoku* or "tribe by the window")—who benefit from *sushin koyo*, but no longer perform much useful work for their employers—possibly to two million or more by the mid-1980s.[32]

The tendency for Japanese to stay in school longer and for more people to try for white-collar jobs has also reduced pay differentials based on education. At present, junior high school graduates, the traditional source of blue-collar labor, are in excess demand because the supply has virtually dried up; 95 percent of all students now try to finish senior high school.[33] More and more senior high school graduates have had to accept blue-collar jobs, to the accompaniment of some tension and frustration of ambition (and loss of face). Japan presently uses more industrial robots than the rest of the world combined, partly to develop a leadership in this technology, but partly as well to remain competitive in key industries, despite a growing shortage of skilled and experienced blue-collar workers. The percentage of college-age population attending university has also exploded, from 10 percent in 1960 to about 40 percent by the mid-1980s, and the average pay difference between senior high school and college graduates has fallen below 15 percent as a career average.

Because they have found it harder and harder to recruit potential blue-collar workers out of school, big companies have recently become more willing to offer better wages, working conditions, job security, and fringe benefits to workers who change firms. Traditionally, these mid-career (*chuto*) recruits are not considered members of the enterprise family—although this is changing—and they have endured a variety of forms of discrimination, including more limited advancement opportunities. Some observers also argue that, as the labor force becomes more urbanized and cosmopolitan, it will seek to change jobs more often, thereby eroding the familistic nature of Japanese firms. Today, there is a tendency for young people to try several jobs before settling on permanent employment, more often than did their parents, and to find greater difficulty adapting to work-place discipline. This is especially true of those unable to obtain employment with large companies.

E. Japanese Labor Unions

Just under 30 percent of all Japanese employees belong to labor unions, including 78 percent of workers in the public sector, where unions are most militant, but where collective bargaining rights are also limited. Most unionized employees in the private sector work in large companies, and the percentage of unionized enterprises falls rapidly with firm size. Thus, there is a strong overlap between unionized workers and the élite which enjoys lifetime status. Ninety percent of Japanese unions are organized on an enterprise basis—one union for each company—and both white- and blue-collar workers belong to the same company-wide union. Since unions have some bargaining power, this aspect of labor relations reinforces discrimination in wages, employment guarantees, and working conditions in favor of the lifetime élite vis-à-vis other Japanese workers. However, the fact that all company workers belong to the same union, which does not necessarily identify with any craft or industry, also permits the Japanese enterprise to be a more adaptable organization.

At best, most Japanese unions have rather loose national affiliations. Nevertheless, the national organizations, which are usually confederations of company locals, have tried to develop some economic clout. At the initiative of *Sohyo* (the

General Council of Trade Unions), the largest and most militant national organization, Japanese unions began the annual ritual of a spring wage offensive (*Shunto*) in 1955. This is a nationwide effort to negotiate higher wages, and since 1961, it has been the centerpiece of national union activity. The basic idea is to press demands for a uniform percentage wage increase across all industries and the public service sector each year, and to support this campaign by coordinated strikes against selected industries and firms.

Most strikes occur in Japan in connection with *Shunto*, and the most devastating are likely to take place in public transportation, whose militant union is affiliated with *Sohyo*.[34] Since company-level wage negotiations usually occur in the spring, the union movement will make its demands known before the end of the preceding year. This forces the Japan Employers' Confederation (*Nikkeiren*) to respond, and nationwide bargaining of a sort takes place in Tokyo amid publicity and government pressure. However, the single percentage increase agreed to there does not bind any employer or enterprise union in the company-level negotiations. Therefore, during the company-level bargaining sessions, the unions try to collaborate in a "joint struggle" campaign with strikes at companies considered vulnerable to union demands. The campaign is bolstered by general political appeals designed to serve as a catalyst for "working-class solidarity."

The success of *Shunto* in raising wages is uncertain, although both employers and company union officials say that their own wage settlements are based on the outcome of the nationwide bargaining plus or minus amounts reflecting the circumstances of individual enterprises. But company-level bargaining is still the most important. Surveys by the Ministry of Labor suggest that the influence of enterprise profitability on wages has increased since the energy crisis first raised the rate of unemployment in 1975 and threatened layoffs in several industries (most of which did not actually occur).[35] The influence of *Shunto* has declined in this interval, and wage differences between firms are probably as great now as at any time since 1950.

Neither has *Shunto* been able to weaken the "enterprise consciousness" of workers, which remains far stronger than class consciousness. Many company unions do not belong to a national labor organization, and the latter are loose alliances that do not control their affiliates. When company-level bargaining occurs, unions and employers do not normally consider themselves in confrontation, and an "all-in-the-same boat" mentality often prevails. Japanese workers are frequently unaware of their formal rights to grieve under collective agreements, and most complaints are settled informally. Rarely will a dispute go to third-party settlement (arbitration, mediation, conciliation), since both union and management tend to regard this as unwarranted outside interference in the enterprise "family." However, frequent and informal consultation does take place between labor and management on issues of interest to both parties.

Japanese workers are also reluctant to press their claims against management. The key officials of an enterprise union are likely to be important employees of the company as well. When Japanese workers go out on strike (generally in connection with *Shunto*) they rarely stay out for more than a day, and that mainly to show seriousness of intent. Later, they are likely to make up the lost time. During the 1970s, Japan lost far fewer days per 1,000 employees to industrial disputes than did most Western nations, although more than West Germany, Austria, Norway, or Sweden. This situation persisted into the mid-1980s. (For example, Japan lost 12 days per 1,000 employees in 1983 vs. 393 in Canada, 171 in the U.S., 0.18 in Austria, 1.7 in West Germany, 83.7 in France, about 820 in Italy, about 165 in the United Kingdom, 9.5 in Sweden, and 3.5 in Norway.) The European countries with better records than Japan all have elaborate, formal institutions and procedures for consultation between labor and management and for settling disputes peacefully. Maintaining labor peace is therefore costlier. Western nations also have higher absentee rates than Japan, where most of the industrial labor force still works more than a five-day week, and most employees take less than half the total vacation time to which they are formally entitled. Thus, although West Germany lost just over five working days per 1,000 employees in 1980 vs. twenty in Japan, the average Japanese employee put in 25 percent more hours than his West German counterpart and was paid by the month rather than the hour.

Since the most meaningful collective bargaining occurs at the company level, top national leaders of the union movement are politically active and often run for office through left-wing parties. *Sohyo* supports the Japan Socialist party, which is rather to the left of West European socialists, while the more moderate *Domei* (Japanese Confederation of Labor), whose affiliates are mainly in the private sector, supports the Social Democratic party, with an orientation similar to West European Social Democrats. (However, this is a weak party, with under 10 percent of the popular vote.) Union contributions and votes are crucial to each of these parties, but the political orientation of national union leaders has also tended to isolate them from daily concerns of rank-and-file. Because the Japanese left-wing is weak at the polls, unions do not receive many tangible benefits from the political sphere.

F. Older Workers and Retirement in Japan

When a Japanese worker "retires" from his formal career between the ages of 55 and 60, with at least 20 years' consecutive service for a single firm, he can expect his employer to give him a lump-sum retirement allowance equalling two to four years' basic pay, depending on his length of service and the size of his company. He does *not* receive a pension from the enterprise in addition to this, although some firms are now willing to substitute a small pension for the lump sum. Retirement benefits are used "to start a small business, to acquire a farm, to settle debts, including those contracted for the children's education or the marriage of a daughter, to purchase a home to replace the [subsidized] company housing, [and] to support children who may, in turn, provide a home for the retired worker. . . ."[36]

Besides this, most employees are, in principle, entitled to state pensions from annuity funds, to which both employers and employees contribute. Japan was the first Asian country to establish a comprehensive social insurance system. However, it is equally true that, until recently, most state pensions were far below living costs, and most Japanese received no pension at all. In 1973, state pensions in Japan came to just 1.8 percent of gross domestic product vs. 9.1 percent in West Germany, 6.8 percent in France, 4.4 percent in the United States, and 2.4 percent in Canada. (The OECD and Common Market geometric averages were, respectively, 4 percent and 4.9 percent.) Japan was also at the bottom of the list in terms of public expenditure on health care, family allowances, and other social benefits. To an extent, employer obligations made up for this, although the bulk of these went to regular employees of large firms and their families.

Consequently, well into the post-World War II era, Japan continued to rely heavily on the extended family system—in which a working couple or husband helps to support the older generations. However, as in other countries, this institution has been giving way to the nuclear family, and anxieties about old age have been rising. Recent surveys reveal financial apprehensions to be uppermost in the minds of Japanese contemplating their retirement years. Nevertheless, government pensions have been improving; their ratio to GNP was over 6.5 percent in 1984. Most employees are now covered by public pension programs, but benefit levels are not expected to become adequate to fully support most of the elderly. The Employees' Pension Plan, more generous than the national pension plan, is financed by a payroll tax on regular male employees in all enterprises. Together, with fees to cover public health insurance, it results in a levy of about 16 percent on monthly pay, including bonuses, which is shared equally between employer and employee, as of early 1986.[37] Beneficiaries under this plan are also those most likely to receive retirement allowances from their companies, although these have been declining, as a percentage of pay, and may eventually disappear.

Like most developed Western nations, Japan faces problems of financing pension programs because the population is aging and the ratio of contributors to beneficiaries is falling dramatically.[38] In Japan, the problem is complicated by a traditional retirement age of 55, whereas the employees' pension does not begin until age 60 and the national pension (the other main program) starts only at age 65. To lower these ages would probably bankrupt the respective programs or else increase the government deficit. The alternative is to raise the enterprise retirement age, and efforts here have met with moderate success, although less than 5 percent of all companies with compulsory retirement systems were willing to go beyond age 60 in 1984. Yet, over 75 percent of all Japanese males continue to work after age 55, and more than 40 percent work beyond age 65—a higher percentage than in any Western country—mainly because they need the money to live on.[39] In 1982, public pensions provided 43.3 percent of the income of households headed by a male over 65 or a female over 60 vs. 43.6 percent from work and 8.2 percent from property.

For workers aged 55 and older, the ratio of job applications to vacancies has been greater than 5-to-1 continuously since 1975. The majority of firms have disobeyed a 1977 law requiring them to hire workers in this age category until they constitute at least 6 percent of staff. Consequently, many older workers go through a prolonged period of job search. Most are eventually reemployed, although at lower wages and often at less desirable work. As a rule former lifetime employees fare better than others. They often do the same kind of work as before, although as temporary employees for the same company or as employees of a subcontractor or of another firm in the same *keiretsu*. In 1984, highest monthly wages in the private sector were earned by those aged 45 to 49. Younger workers received less, because of the *nenko* wage effect, but older workers got less as well, and earnings generally declined after age 50. This "reverse *nenko*" wage effect has been a persistent feature of the earnings profiles of Japanese workers.

Notes

1. See Ronald Wintrobe and Albert Breton, "Organizational Structure and Productivity," *American Economic Review*, June 1986. The discussion below also relies on Chitoshi Yanaga, *Big Business in Japanese Politics* (New Haven: Yale University Press, 1968), ch. 1. The first quote below is from Yanaga, p. 9.

2. John L. Graham, "A Hidden Cause of America's Trade Deficit with Japan," *Columbia Journal of World Business*, Fall 1981, p. 9. Graham is the source for this paragraph.

3. A "lifetime" employee in Japan is an employee hired directly from school, with the expectation that he will stay with the company until he "retires," usually between the ages of 55 and 60, at which time he is likely to change firms rather than quit work. We shall return to this topic. The classic discussion in English of Japanese labor relations is J. C. Abegglen, *Management and the Worker: The Japanese Solution* (Tokyo: Kodansha International, 1973).

4. Yanaga, *Big Business in Japanese Politics*, pp. 9–10.

5. Nathan Glazer, "Social and Cultural Factors in Japanese Economic Growth," in Hugh Patrick, Henry Rosovsky, eds., *Asia's New Giant: How the Japanese Economy Works* (Washington, D.C.: Brookings, 1976), p. 842.

6. For examples of sociological studies of Japanese firms, see Robert Cole, *Japanese Blue Collar: The Changing Tradition* (Berkeley: University of California, 1971); Abegglen, *Management and the Worker*; and Glazer, "Social and Cultural Factors." The Marxian view is given in Jon Halliday, *A Political History of Japanese Capitalism* (New York: Pantheon Books, 1975).

7. When outside shareholders try to be difficult, they usually encounter the *sokaiya*, or professional stockholders hired as enforcers by management to ensure that the annual shareholders' meeting always runs smoothly. *Sokaiya* have even been known to use violence to this end.

8. For example, "In June 1951, Toray introduced nylon technology from DuPont. While Toray's capital was only .75 billion yen at that time, DuPont requested an immediate advance of . . . 1.08 billion yen for Toray's annual royalty payment . . . Tashiro [Toray's president] got over this difficulty by making the payment in installments. In November 1950, Nishiyama announced a new plan for an integrated steel mill, which could produce 500,000 tons of crude steel a year, at a cost of . . . 27.275 billion yen. . . . His company, with a capital of .5 billion yen at that time, was no more than an open-hearth furnace steelmaker. . . . When Honda Motors' capital was still 60 million yen in the early 1950s, it imported the most advanced equipment for 400 million yen. . . ." These firms could only meet such expenses by massive borrowing. See Hideichiro Nakamura, "Japan, Incorporated and Postwar Democracy," *Japanese Economic Studies*, Spring–Summer 1978. See, as well, R. Caves and M. Uekusa,

"Industrial Organization," in Patrick and Rosovsky, *Asia's New Giant*, especially pp. 479–504.

9. The Bank of Japan has an executive board, comprising a governor, a vice-governor, and various directors and advisers, plus a seven-member policy board, including the governor, one representative of the Finance Ministry (MOF), one representative of the Economic Planning Agency (EPA), and four members appointed by the cabinet (with Diet approval), representing the city banks, the regional banks, industry, and agriculture, respectively. The MOF and EPA representatives have no votes on policy decisions, but MOF does have strong legal powers to supervise and constrain the actions of the bank's policy board. Nevertheless, a strong governor can win some independence for the bank.

10. See L. C. Thurow, R. Engle, L. D'Andrea, R. Hartman, and C. Pigott, *Foreign Experience with Monetary Policies to Promote Economic and Social Priority Programs*, staff report of the Committee on Banking and Currency of the U.S. House of Representatives (Washington, D.C.: U.S. Government Printing Office, May 1972), p. 79. The discussion below borrows from this study, as well as from The Bank of Japan, *The Japanese Financial System* (Tokyo: Bank of Japan, 1978); H. Eguchi and K. Hamada, "Bank Behavior under Constraints: Credit Rationing and Monetary Mechanism in Japan," *Japanese Economic Studies*, Winter 1977–78; Shoichi Royama, "The Japanese Financial System: Past, Present, and Future," *Japanese Economic Studies*, Winter 1983–84; and Juro Teranishi, "Economic Growth and Regulation of Financial Markets: Japanese Experience during Postwar High Growth Period," *Hitotsubashi Journal of Economics*, December 1986.

11. In effect, the borrower must keep part of the loan—usually 20–25 percent—on deposit with the bank in a noninterest-bearing account. Suppose a firm borrows 10 million yen at 5 percent with a 25 percent compensating balance requirement. Then, it may use only 7.5 million yen, but must still pay annual interest of 5 percent x 10 million = 500,000 yen, which is 6 2/3 percent of 7.5 million. The effective interest rate (6 2/3 percent) is the actual rate divided by one minus the compensating balance requirement. The figures below on Japanese financial markets come from Royama, "The Japanese Financial System."

12. See Eguchi and Hamada, "Bank Behavior under Constraints." There are formal credit limits (*kashidashi gendogaku*) on the borrowing of each city bank from the Bank of Japan. But a bank is rarely allowed to go to this ceiling. Instead, lower, more informal, and more frequently changed limits are imposed, which are almost always binding.

13. The Bank of Japan also puts ceilings on the lending of regional banks and other financial institutions, including their lending on the call-loan market. The direct leverage of the central bank over these institutions is far less than over the city banks, because other financial institutions hardly ever borrow at the discount window. Yet, the latter have generally complied with their loan ceilings. Ultimately, the government has a myriad of ways to punish "uncooperative" banks, since banking is a regulated industry and government agencies can influence bank business dealings through many avenues.

14. Even though contractual interest rates are well below equilibrium, effective rates could remain near equilibrium because of the compensating balance requirement (note 11). For example, a firm borrowing at 7 percent, with a 30 percent compensating balance requirement, pays an effective rate of 10 percent. If credit grows tighter, the contractual rate could stay at 7 percent, while the required compensating balance was raised to 50 percent, increasing the true borrowing cost to 14 percent.

In practice, the reverse happens. As money grows tighter, the compensating balance tends to fall, and effective interest rates go down, increasing the excess demand for loanable funds. The benefit to a bank from raising its compensating balance requirement lies in its ability to use the higher balances as reserve backing for increased lending, but strict controls by BOJ have denied city banks these increases during periods of tight money. See the Bank of Japan, Economic Research Department, "Recent Developments in Corporate Financing," Special Paper No. 85, Tokyo, February 1980, p. 6n.

15. See Bunji Kure, "Window Guidance of the Bank of Japan," *Japanese Economic Studies*, Winter 1977–78, pp. 65–66.

16. For example, the government will absorb most, though not all, of Mitsui's loss on its Iranian petrochemical project. (See below.)

17. The discussion below and above relies on Ken'ichi Imai, "Japan's Industrial Organization," *Japanese Economic Studies*, Spring–Summer 1978, as well as the OECD's *Annual Reports on Competition Policy*, 1980, No. 2, pp. 67–70; 1981, No. 2, pp. 39–44; and 1983, No. 2, pp. 56–57 (Paris: OECD).

18. Imai, "Japan's Industrial Organization," pp. 19–26. Let us define the six-firm concentration ratio as the share of an industry's sales accounted for by the six largest firms. The three-, four-, twelve-, etc., firm concentration ratios are defined in the same way. Then, an industry is considered an oligopoly if the 6-firm concentration ratio is over 50 percent or if the 12-firm ratio is over 75 percent. Otherwise, it is considered to be competitive, unless it is a publicly owned monopoly.

On the other hand, the *ownership* concentration of Japanese industry is high. See, e.g., K. Yamamura, "Structure is Policy," in I. Frank, ed., *The Japanese Economy in International Perspective* (Baltimore: Johns Hopkins, 1975).

19. The following historical works by G. C. Allen are relevant here: (a) "The Concentration of Economic Control in Japan," *Economic Journal*, June 1937; (b) *A Short Economic History of Modern Japan* (London: Allen & Unwin, 1972).

20. Upon dissolution, the Big Four *zaibatsu* controlled a fourth of all business assets. For further discussion of the *keiretsu*, see Tadao Kiyonari and Hideichiro Nakamura, "Establishment of the Big Business System," *Japanese Economic Studies*, Fall 1977.

21. K. Bieda, *The Structure and Operation of the Japanese Economy* (New York: Wiley, 1970), p. 203.

22. As a rule, both large and small Japanese firms are able to write off many of their assets quickly for tax purposes. (Japan practices widespread accelerated depreciation.) This makes them willing to replace their capital equipment more frequently as a means of reducing taxes. But a machine may still have years of useful life left when a large company has almost entirely depreciated it and is ready to get rid of it. Thus, if it is not too specialized or difficult to modify, it can go on functioning in a small firm, where it is depreciated again. The data below on average earnings come from the *Oriental Economist*, March 1985, p. 40.

23. The Labor Standards Law allows temporary layoffs ("vacations") at 60 percent or more of normal wages, but even this is usually avoided by management, if at all possible. Although a laid-off employee may know that he will return, he suffers anxiety because his expendability has been demonstrated. See Katsumi Yakabe, *Labor Relations in Japan* (Tokyo: International Society for Educational Information, 1974), pp. 10–11.

24. See M. Hashimoto, "Bonus Payments, On-the-Job Training, and Lifetime Employment in Japan," *Journal of Political Economy*, October 1979.

25. See Yoko Sano, "Seniority-Based Wages in Japan—A Survey," *Japanese Economic Studies*, Spring 1977, and Kazuo Koike, "Blue Collar Proficiency is Key to Japan's Success." *Oriental Economist*, August 1981.

26. Kazuo Koike, "Japan's Industrial Relations: Characteristics and Problems," *Japanese Economic Studies*, Fall 1978, p. 44.

27. The discussion below borrows from Solomon Levine, "Labor Markets and Collective Bargaining in Japan," in W. W. Lockwood, ed., *The State and Economic Enterprise in Japan* (Princeton: Princeton University Press, 1965), especially pp. 641–67.

28. Ibid., p. 643.

29. See Haruo Shimada, "The Japanese Labor Market After the Oil Crisis: A Factual Report," parts I and II, in *Keio Economic Studies*, Nos. 1 and 2, 1977. See as well the OECD *Economic Survey of Japan*, 1981 (Paris: OECD, 1981), pp. 44–61.

30. See Ryohei Magota, "The End of the Seniority-Related (*Nenko*) Wage System," *Japanese Economic Studies*, Spring 1979.

31. See "Wages on a Minor Rise," *Oriental Economist*, February 1982, pp. 8–9. Also, "Growth of Average Pays Mark Time," *Oriental Economist*, July 1985, p. 55; and "Model Wages by Ages and Industries," *Oriental Economist*, January 1985, p. 41.

32. These employees are usually assigned office space near a window.

33. See, e.g., Magota, "The End of the Seniority-Related Wage System," p. 87, Table 2. Only 46,000 junior high school graduates were hired in 1980 vs. 415,000 in 1960. There were almost three times as many vacancies as applications. About 490,000 senior high school graduates were hired in the same year with a vacancy-to-applicant ratio of just under two. The overall vacancy-to-applicant ratio was 0.75; for all applicants aged twenty-four and under, it was 1.4.

34. The most militant and radical unions are in the public sector, notably the transport workers and teachers. But even here, good relations prevail between foremen and workers and between teachers and students or parents.

35. See OECD, *Economic Survey of Japan*, 1981, p. 58.

36. Paul Fisher, "Major Social Security Issues: Japan, 1972," *Social Security Bulletin*, March 1973, pp. 30–31. See, as well, Angus Simmons, "Recent Social Security Developments in Japan," *Social Security Bulletin*, October 1978.

37. This compares, e.g., with an 18.2 percent payroll tax to cover pensions alone in Sweden, as of 1980. The other main pension program is the National Pension Plan, which includes anyone not covered by other programs. There are also special plans for civil servants, seamen, farm workers, schoolteachers, and other groups. Two-thirds of the people insured under the National Pension Program are women—a third of whom are dependents of wage earners covered by the Employees' Pension Program.

38. The number of contributors per beneficiary of the Employees' Pension Plan is expected to fall from around 25 in 1980 to 4 after 2000. For the national plan, which covers about the same number of people, the ratio will fall from 8.5-to-1 to 4-to-1.

39. Magota, "The End of the Seniority-Related Wage System," pp. 89–111. Nearly all corporations with more than 300 employees have compulsory retirement. Between 1970 and 1984, the percentage of these firms requiring "retirement" at age 55 or younger fell from over 70 to about 27. The percentage allowing retirement at age 60 or later rose from 23 to 55, although most of these set it right at 60. See "55 percent of Corporations Adopt Compulsory Retirement Age of 60 Years," *Oriental Economist*, September 1985, p. 38. Regarding income sources of the elderly, see OECD, *Economic Survey of Japan, 1985* (Paris: OECD, 1985), pp. 45, 83.

Questions for Review, Discussion, Examination

*1. "The impersonal, anonymous market of Western economics textbooks is alien to Japanese culture." Why is this? In what sense are personal relationships in Japan less casual than in the West?

Briefly describe the two basic kinds of social relationships in Japan.

2. Historically, how have Japanese firms compensated for low employee turnover, in terms of shifting labor into occupations where its value of marginal product is relatively high? Why do Japanese firms practice a high degree of job rotation?

3. What is *nemawashi*? Why is it important in the Japanese decision-making context? Recalling section 2-2, why do you believe Japanese firms practice a relatively high degree of internal profit sharing?

4. "Outside" shareholders of a Japanese firm are nearly powerless, unless they

486   COMPARATIVE ECONOMIC SYSTEMS

represent a major bank or trading company or other firm in the same *keiretsu*. Western economic theory would suggest that outside shareholders will pressure management to adopt longer decision-making horizons because owners wish to maximize the value of their equity, which reflects the present value of expected future profits.

Yet, Japanese managerial decision-making horizons appear to be relatively long. What accounts for this? Explain briefly. In practice, do outside shareholders in Western countries pressure management to adopt longer time horizons?

5. What are major differences between city and regional banks in Japan? Which is most apt to be lender and which borrower on the call-loan and discount markets? Why?

What can you say about interest rates on the call-loan and discount markets? How can these rates rise above the discount (or bank) rate?

6. What has been the major tool of macroeconomic policy in Japan? Explain what is meant by *madaguchi shido*.

*7. Why have controls over the volume of bank lending been part of the Japanese government's effort to keep down interest rates on loans? (In answering, please take the compensating balance requirement into account.)

8. If government pressure has reduced most interest rates over most of the postwar era, how did government regulation also help to increase bank profits? As deposit rates have been low, why have Japanese households been such large net savers?

9. What are the basic components of financial deregulation in Japan? Describe each briefly. Why is Japan deregulating? (Indicate the pressures which have worked in this direction.)

10. Deregulation of financial markets in Japan has generally been carried out with no major upward pressure on interest rates. If rates are now decontrolled (to a greater extent than before the energy crisis), why do Japanese interest rates remain low? Does this have anything to do with Japanese overseas investment?

11. Is the domestic Japanese market competitive? Discuss briefly.

*12. Sometimes the Japanese economy is described as an example of "finance capitalism"—that is, of an economic system based on close links between banks and business firms. These ties also arose in Sweden near the end of the nineteenth century and have been prominent in Germany as well.

Explain why such a close relationship arose. What problems of economic development did it help to solve? What is the nature of this relationship and why is it associated with countries that were comparative late comers to the process of industrialization? Compare and contrast the specific form of finance capitalism in Japan before World War II with the form Japanese finance capitalism takes today.

13. What are the general trading companies (*sogo shosha*)? Historically, what role did they play in the Japanese economy and what role do they play today? Why are they important to the small-firms sector? Why have they been more prominent in Japan than in Western countries?

14. How has the role of the Japanese trading companies been changing in recent years? Why has it changed? Why have some Japanese spoken of the "winter of *sogo shosha*"?

*15. A feature of Japanese industrial structure is pronounced dualism. One might argue that a similar dualism exists in Japanese labor relations.

(a) Describe each type of dualism. Are there any links between the two? Why did industrial dualism arise? How do large firms compare with small, in terms of wages, profits, and capital intensity?

(b) How is labor treated in large firms and in small firms during an economic recession? (Are any jobs transferred between the two sectors? Who is most likely to lose his job? Explain carefully.)

16. How extensive is subcontracting in Japan? What is often the nature of the link between a subcontractor and its "parent"?

17. What are the three pillars of Japanese labor relations in large firms? What are the differences with small firms? Is labor a fixed cost in Japan?

How do Japanese labor relations relate, more generally, to human relations in Japan?

18. What aspects of Japanese labor relations help to promote efficiency and growth? Explain.

*19. Why have large Japanese firms invested so heavily in vocational training? How does this relate to *nenko* wages? How does it relate to work rotation?

20. In what ways does the union structure in Japan help to promote efficiency and growth? Why do Japanese unions allow the employment of temporary and subcontract labor, generally without protest? Do unions also help to promote inequality in Japan? Explain carefully.

21. What is *Shunto*? Do you believe it increases wages and benefits in Japan? Why or why not?

How strong is the class consciousness of Japanese workers? How are grievances usually settled?

22. What is retirement like for a lifetime worker in Japan? Does he have a good pension to rely on as soon as he stops working? (Why must "he" be used in this question?) What is the "reverse *nenko*" wage effect?

* = more difficult.

14

THE JAPANESE ECONOMY: GOVERNMENT GUIDANCE

When people speak of "economic planning" in Japan, they usually have in mind the national economic plan prepared by the Economic Planning Agency once every two or three years. Yet, in my view, these national plans are not . . . as important as they appear at first. . . . In recent years especially, the national economic plan is becoming less and less relevant to actual economic policy.

This does not mean . . . that the Japanese economy is run without much government planning. The . . . government intervenes widely in individual sectors, industries, or regions, and there is much planning on industrial as well as regional bases. Many of the plans in individual fields appear to be quite effective in channelling resources into particular industries or regions.

—Ryutaro Komiya

The government is the captain and *zaikai* is the compass of the ship.

—Former Prime Minister Ikeda

14-1. Formal Economic Planning

We classify Japan as a mixed economy because the government has tried to steer it along lines of national advantage, indicating which industries and regions have priority in economic development. Thus, Japan has tried to combine planning with the market, hoping to get the best of each. The state does not usually impose production targets covering either the short or the long run. But it does look several years into the future, and it has a variety of incentives to influence the direction and pace of economic growth. The government has also maintained distribution priorities favoring farmers, low-income wage earners, and people who derive most of their income from property (the latter, in principle, to encourage entrepreneur-ship). Since the early postwar days, however, Japan has largely been spared the costly struggles over distribution that have preoccupied several Western nations.

To supervise the construction of formal plans, Japan has an Economic Planning Agency (EPA) whose Director-General is a cabinet member. The EPA dates from 1957 under its present name and from 1946 under others. To cover the period 1956–81, it prepared eight medium-term plans, each of which was originally intended to run from five to ten years.[1] Formally, the EPA is the Secretariat of the Economic Deliberation Council, one of the Prime Minister's advisory bodies, and a plan takes shape after he asks that body to draw one up. However, the members of this council serve part-time and largely on an honorary basis. They are mainly well-known businessmen and retired government officials, along with a few academics, labor representatives, farmers, and consumer advocates. The council has about two hundred subcommittees that meet occasionally, whose membership composition tends to be similar to that of the council and also part-time.

Thus, most of the work of plan construction necessarily falls on the EPA, which also brings in representatives of government ministries and agencies when their jurisdictions are affected, since these agencies can veto any proposals in their own areas. A typical plan contains forecasts—relating to output, income, prices, pro-duction in particular industries and regions, the balance of payments, shifts of the labor force, public spending, social welfare, pollution, etc. It also discusses the evolution of government priorities, but usually avoids or remains vague on espe-cially contentious issues. Moreover, the plan's targets are purely indicative. The EPA has no administrative or legal power to impose controls or goals; such authority is vested in the cabinet and the ministries. Quantitatively, its forecasts have generally been wide of the mark, making most plans obsolete before they have run their course. (This is why eight different plans covered just twenty-five years.) The first five plans dramatically underestimated Japan's economic growth, while the sixth, seventh, and eighth plans overestimated it, due to their failure, first to foresee the energy crisis and then to fully take its effects into account.

This is not to say that EPA's plans have had no impact. The agency has gathered and processed large amounts of information to facilitate the dialogue between different components of government and business. Its plans have "predicted more or less correctly the directions of change in industrial structure, the industrial distribution of the labor force, and the composition of exports, but almost always underestimated the extent of such changes."[2] They may also have had important announcement effects, especially the famous income-doubling plan for 1961–70. This plan forecast a doubling of Japanese national income, a feat virtually unprec-edented in the history of any nation beyond the developing stage. To achieve such a goal, income and output would have had to grow at an average 7.2 percent per year. When the plan first appeared, the EPA was criticized for being too optimistic.

In fact, the forecasts were too pessimistic. GNP growth for the entire decade averaged more than 10 percent per year, and national income grew to over 2.5 times its original level, one of the most remarkable decades of growth ever recorded by any nation. To retain perspective, we should note that, in 1960, Japan was not fully readmitted to the world community of nations. (It did not join the United Nations until 1956.) Before the war, GNP had never grown by as much as 7 percent for more than a handful of years in succession. Many economists felt that the EPA was underestimating the balance-of-payments constraint on growth, and left-wing Japanese were sure that a crisis of capitalism was just around the corner. Thus, journalists, social commentators, economists, and left-wing politicians criticized all the early plans—and notably the plan for doubling of national income—as being too optimistic.

Nevertheless, Japanese businessmen were aware that the first plan had predicted an average 5 percent growth rate for 1956–60 vs. a realized 9 percent, and that the second had foreseen growth rates over 1958–60 of 5 percent to 6 percent vs. realizations of 14 percent to 15 percent. These businessmen were ready to take the targets of the income-doubling plan as minima, somehow guaranteed by the government.[3] Japanese companies stepped up their investment programs, fearing to lose their shares of expanding markets or to be left out altogether from new ones. This investment fueled demand and expectations even further, helping to create the record growth. But aside from the announcement effect, the impact of formal planning on the Japanese economy appears to be minor. To the question, "Are government policies largely formulated in the context of the EPA's medium-term plans?" the answer appears to be, "Largely, no." This leads us to a more informal, but also more important kind of planning, in terms of its practical consequences.

14-2. Industrial Policy

One author notes that Japan has three interrelated parts to its planning process: national economic planning, regional economic planning, and industrial policy. "However, the last has had so much real force that the first two have become the residuals of industrial policy and their most successful aspects have been related to industrialization."[4] By "industrial policy," we mean programs to promote the growth, efficiency, prosperity, or, occasionally, the orderly decline of specific industries. More often than not, the underlying motive has been export expansion.

In this context, there are about two hundred advisory councils—like the Economic Deliberation Council, except that they report to cabinet ministers instead of to the Prime Minister—that do long-range planning. Most of these report to the Minister for International Trade and Industry, including an Industrial Structure Deliberation Council and councils for the promotion of electronic data processing, petroleum, machinery, mining, and other industries. Each council covers a narrower territory than the Economic Deliberation Council, but partly for this reason, the advisory councils are usually more influential. In particular, the Industrial Structure Council has played a major role in shaping Japan's industrial growth strategy. The various council reports are also used by the ministries in their own planning.

Likewise, there are over one hundred major industry associations that engage in long-range planning. These also act as funnels for information flowing between business and government, help to organize the transfer of foreign technology to Japan (including inspection tours of advanced companies abroad), and represent their industries in formal and informal negotiations with the government. Specifically, each association bargains with a government counterpart, called a coordination (or *genkyoku*) bureau—the state agency with primary responsibility for the industry in question. Most *genkyoku* bureaus belong to MITI, and are divided, in turn, into divisions in charge of more narrowly defined industries.

Industry associations and *genkyoku* bureaus constantly negotiate policies, programs, and means of execution. It is here that major government policies affecting the growth of industry first take shape. However, when they emerge, industrial programs are often inconsistent with one another, and overly ambitious, given the economy's capabilities, the government's commitments to other programs, and the balance-of-payments or government budget constraint. Thus, a dialogue ensues, involving MITI, MOF, and other ministries, as well as the advisory councils and the EPA—the latter in the role of coordinator, as well as information gatherer, processor, and supplier. Eventually, a consensus of sorts emerges between these elements and industry representatives. In the dialogue, each *genkyoku* bureau usually acts as a spokesman for its industry. Later, the industry association will have the task of persuading reluctant firms to go along with government policy. Komiya identifies five different types of industrial policy—development of a new industry, modernization, control of excessive investment, assistance to declining industries (such as coal, textiles, and aluminum smelting), and planned shipbuilding, which suffered a dramatic decline over 1976–79, after having earlier served as one of Japan's most spectacular postwar growth industries.[5] Some specific programs would be hard to classify.

When a program emerges from a *genkyoku* bureau, it must still get approval from the Finance Ministry, which contains the Bureau of Budget. In this context, "the veto power of the Ministry of Finance over inducements to industry based on government funding and tax concessions is formidable."[6] Then, it must be passed by the Diet, implying a need for approval by the LDP's Policy Affairs Research Council. If there is a question of violating the Anti-Monopoly Law, the Fair Trade Commission may also be a hurdle. Moreover, MITI and MOF control most instruments for implementing policies, including taxes and subsidies.

One might say that Japan has an informal planning structure—headed by MITI, MOF, peak business associations, and leading LDP politicians—which has been effective. Among the private associations, the loose structure of top business executives called *zaikai* has been especially influential, partly because it has been able to resolve disagreements internally and maintain solidarity toward the government and other private organizations. *Zaikai* dates from a meeting of business leaders the day after Japan's formal surrender to the World War II allies, which focused on ways of reunifying the country, rebuilding basic industries, and dealing with the occupation authorities soon to arrive. It embraces four peak businessmen's organizations—the Federation of Economic Organizations (*Keidanren*), the Committee for Economic Development, the Federation of Employers' Associations (*Nikkeiren*), and the Chamber of Commerce and Industry. Of these, *Keidanren*, the top coordinating body of big business, is most important; its chairman is widely viewed as the head of *zaikai's* "invisible government." Senior government officials often attend meetings of *Keidanren's* executive, and the Federation maintains its own internal structure of committees, including a committee on industrial policy, to study and make recommendations on policy questions. Other government agencies, notably the "economic" ministries—such as Agriculture, Forestry, and Fisheries; Transportation; Construction; and Health and Welfare—plus the cabinet and *zoku* (or leading LDP) politicians share top planning roles.

In fact, however, business leaders propose and help to formulate many of the policies that they end up executing. Industry associations and *genkyoku* bureaus play a liaison role between industry and government, and there are informal discussions and negotiations between businessmen and government officials all the time—in bowling alleys, restaurants, on the golf course, and in tea houses, which play an important role in the shaping and altering of government priorities. According to one author, "What began [after World War II] as an *ad hoc* and practical response to immediate needs for industrialization and increased foreign-exchange earnings has gradually become an explicit policy of changing industrial structure and comparative advantage to upgrade the economy."[7]

The array of forms and institutions to facilitate government-business interaction reflects the importance of business in the goal-forming process, but equally the need by Japanese for harmony. Without compromise and consensus, there is little hope of getting the cooperation between government agencies, industry associations, and firms that is necessary to execute policies efficiently. However, we have already seen that government relies on more than voluntary compliance to achieve its goals, and we therefore turn to the implementation of government policy.

14-3. Administrative Controls

In principle, MITI approval is necessary for all new production facilities and additions to production capacity. While such approval is often given routinely, the government has used this means to stop expansion in industries where excess capacity was already believed to exist or where future comparative advantage was expected to be less than at present. In addition, the state has sometimes prevented firms from locating in areas where industrial concentration, congestion, and pollution were already too high. Historically, it has also controlled import quotas. Until recently, MITI could set formal ceilings on the amounts of fuel, raw materials, components, parts, machinery, tools, and other goods that firms were allowed to buy abroad. Perhaps its most important single authority was its right to decide which companies could purchase know-how in the form of patents, and from which foreign sources. It still exercises this power formally in a few cases and is believed to do so informally in others.

Thus, between 1950 and 1978, Japanese buyers made 32,000 contracts to import technology from the United States at a total cost of $9 billion—far less than the cost of developing this technology.[8] In many cases, the foreign supplier had to bargain with MITI, in effect, as the agent of the Japanese buyer. MITI participated directly in royalty negotiations, often playing potential foreign suppliers against each other or dealing with small or financially weak foreign companies. This allowed it to bring leverage to bear on foreign patent holders, as a means of getting the best possible deal on technologies that Japan wanted to copy and to adapt for its own use.

Once the technology was in Japan, MITI promoted its diffusion, subject to such restrictions as the foreign supplier was able to enforce and to domestic rivalry, which makes Japanese firms (like any others in a competitive environment) reluctant to share technical knowledge. However, Japan has had a tradition of sharing such information, which is still intact, although it has eroded since World War II.[9] (For example, industry associations still publish costs, prices, and technical data of individual enterprises.) MITI's role allowed Japanese companies to pay low royalties for imported technology until 1968, when foreign pressure forced the government to reduce its control over the acquisition process. This caused royalty payments to rise, but even in the 1980s, Japan has been able to acquire some technology at bargain prices. Historically, Japanese firms have exploited technology efficiently, although they have not originated as many major breakthroughs as we might expect, given the size of the manufacturing sector. In part, this has resulted from the lack of protection for industrial secrets. Since the mid-1970s, however, Japan has turned this comparative dearth of innovation around. Over 1976–83, according to one study, Japan outperformed all other nations in developing new products and processes.

A major factor in Japan's efficient exploitation of technology has also been the high quality standards of its industrial enterprises, which MITI and other government agencies have helped to promote. Thus, MITI carries out elaborate audits, not only of products, but also of production processes, and works closely with firms to improve performance. MITI's Industrial Engineering Bureau requires reliability tests on parts and components and makes test results readily available to Japanese firms. Finally, the government sponsors quality competitions and awards prestigious prizes, such as the all-Japan Quality Award (although the Deming Prize, Japan's best-known quality award, is not government sponsored).

MITI has used its leverage to acquire and disseminate foreign technology in other ways, including the "First unit imported, but following units home produced" policy. For instance, "when an electric power company built a power station and installed several units of generators, the government requested the power company, as a condition of the issue of an import license for the first unit, to request the [exporter] to give a patent and know-how license to some Japanese maker to produce the second and following units.''[10] In some cases, MITI has used import licenses to promote the realization of scale economies. For example, in collaboration with the petrochemicals industry, it refused to authorize plants for production of ethylene without a capacity of at least 300,000 tons per year or polyethylene plants without at least 30,000 tons capacity. Control over imports of raw materials and technology was its main means of enforcement.

Indeed, MITI's broad control over imports—until Japan was forced by foreign pressure to liberalize its foreign trade and payments, beginning in the late 1960s—gave it enormous leverage and enabled it to regulate all aspects of an industry, including the extent of competition within it. In the case of petrochemicals, MITI slowed the entry of firms into the industry to ensure that existing companies remained profitable as demand expanded. It promoted the auto industry during the 1950s over opposition from the Ministries of Finance and Transportation, which wanted Japan to rely on the United States for motor vehicles. Beginning in the early part of that decade, it gave the industry comprehensive protection from import competition through a variety of tariff and nontariff barriers, including higher taxes on cars above compact size, which were made abroad (especially in the United States), but scarcely at all in Japan. MITI also got the industry several low-cost loans from the Japan Development Bank, along with accelerated depreciation and other subsidies, at a time when its technological level was twenty years behind the international standard.[11]

In 1984, after more than a decade of slow, reluctant liberalization, Japan retained formal import quotas on just twenty-seven product categories, most of which were farm goods and none of which were major industrial items. Japan had the lowest average tariff rate among industrial nations. Yet, per capita imports of manufactured goods were also among the lowest of industrial countries, and manufactures were an even smaller share of total imports than during the 1960s. In 1982, imports accounted for just over 6 percent of Japanese consumption of manufactures vs. 8.5 percent in the U.S., 23 percent in France, 26.5 percent in Britain, and 31 percent in West Germany. This is partly because MITI was able to suppress imports with unofficial barriers, which preserved most of the large Japanese market for domestic firms.

Informal barriers include bureaucratic red tape in testing and inspecting imported goods, exclusion of imports failing to meet a variety of questionable product standards, the willingness of general trading companies (who control over half of Japan's imports) to limit their handling of manufactured imports, and the fragmented, highly personalized domestic distribution system, which is difficult for foreigners to penetrate. Before Japanese firms actually produce a good embodying new or advanced technology, however, the Japanese market is more accessible to foreigners.[12]

Domestically, MITI has been the main protagonist in promoting mergers and cartels and in weakening Japan's Anti-Monopoly Law and price competition. It has sponsored a number of special laws at different points in time, designed to promote industries believed to have good growth potential. Such promotion has included protection from foreign competition, restrictions on the number of Japanese producers, low-cost loans, accelerated depreciation, and even formation of cartels.[13] MITI has also sponsored laws to ease the adjustment of declining industries—likewise via subsidies, cartels, and protection from foreign competition. However, it usually subsidizes withdrawal and dismantling of production capacity that is no longer cost effective, rather than its continuing operation at a loss.

In the case of a rising industry, MITI's aim is to give firms time to gain production experience with new technologies and to reach a scale that will allow them to compete on the world market. MITI is more worried about inefficiency due to small size, lack of experience, or excessive competition—which may eliminate companies before they have a chance to make an important growth or export contribution—than it is about inefficiency stemming from the exercise of monopoly power. In the case of a declining industry, MITI's aim is to forestall bankruptcies among large firms, to achieve an orderly withdrawal of capacity, and to reduce financial hardships for the companies directly involved, as well as for their employees. However, while it emphasizes orderly marketing, access to supplies, and transition, the effect of MITI's intervention is usually to reduce the number of competitors in an industry.

Thus, for many years, it was MITI's practice to allocate key imports to firms on the basis of production capacity and, to a limited degree, this is still done unofficially, although informal quotas are harder for MITI to enforce and control. For example, a sugar refinery with a capacity of 100,000 metric tons per year would be allowed twice as much raw sugar and fuel from abroad as a refinery with a 50,000-ton-per-year capacity. Similar formulas have been applied to iron and steel mills, chemical plants, paper mills, cement factories, aluminum smelters, and others. These allocations have tended to prevent firms from entering such an industry, unless they could persuade MITI to grant them quotas, but the practice has also led to a competitive scramble among established producers to increase capacity in order to raise their claims to imports. The prospect of a cartel tends to have the same effect, since it will assign production and import quotas to member companies on the basis of existing capacity or market share.

But while the result has been to raise investment within the industries in question, it has also been to create excess capacity within these same industries. Here, MITI has worked at cross purposes with itself. On the one hand, it has allocated import quotas in a way that raised the incentive to invest, and its known enthusiasm for cartel formation has had the same effect, when cartels were anticipated. Yet the primary purpose of a cartel is to restrict output and investment, so as to prop up prices. Thus, MITI has promoted investment that led to excess capacity and then promoted cartels to restrict investment in the same industries. (Often, however, these have not been too effective.) Whenever an official cartel is formed, Japan's Anti-Monopoly Law requires a government agency, usually MITI, to participate. A MITI representative therefore sits on the steering committee that manages the cartel, providing a convenient avenue for MITI to monitor and to influence the arrangement. Consequently, we may suspect that MITI has sometimes used its leverage and the prospect of a cartel to produce the excessive investment that became the grounds for cartel formation.

However, this activity has been made more difficult by the liberalization of international trade and payments, which has forced Japan to abandon most formal import quotas. Today, nearly all official cartels are export cartels, cartels organized under the Environmental Sanitation Act, or cartels organized under the Medium and Small Enterprise Organization Act. Over half are in the latter category. They often make the economy more competitive, by enabling small firms to realize scale economies and to stand up to larger rivals. Similarly, over 70 percent of all mergers involve only small- or medium-sized firms.[14] Export cartels arise because other nations now restrict their imports from Japan through formal or informal import quotas. (Japan uses the same methods.) These cartels help Japan to enforce the quotas it receives, as well as to realize such monopoly power as may result for the nation as a whole from the supply restrictions.

Outside agriculture, the main threat of domestic monopoly power over the past several years has probably come from unofficial or "clandestine" cartels, which usually have MITI's blessing and even its participation. As a rule, these are backed by import barriers, most of which are also unofficial. However, in a landmark decision, the Tokyo High Court ruled in September 1980 that such cartels violate Japan's Anti-Monopoly Law. Only cartels based on clear legal exemptions from this law are now themselves legal. Previously, the status of unofficial cartels before the law had been ill defined, and this type of situation is not unusual in Japan.

In fact, MITI and other Japanese government agencies do not normally enforce their guidelines by invoking legal sanctions or penalties. Instead, they rely on a strong form of moral suasion called "administrative guidance" (*gyosei shido*). This "is a vague word for discretionary advice, wishes, requests, or sometimes threatening orders given by government officials to private firms." Normally, such guidance is "not based on any clear-cut, well-defined stipulation in laws and ordinances, [although] there is usually a vague, comprehensive stipulation in the law that a certain government agency is responsible for the orderly condition of a certain field and [that it] may take appropriate measures" to ensure this.[15]

Examples of administrative guidance would be informal input, output, or investment quotas for firms in a particular industry, a suggestion that firms specialize more narrowly by product line (in order to realize scale economies), unofficial pressure on companies to merge or to stay out of an industry, a request to buy only from domestic suppliers, and so on. "Japanese firms accept such government officials' meddling . . . [because] in a society in which the central government has traditionally so wide a power over citizens, it does not pay, in the long run, to be openly opposed to government, or so most people think."[16] However, government interference is also tolerated, in part, because it appears to be successful, and MITI promotion of specialization in production and pooling of resources for collaboration in research and development does not necessarily inhibit (indeed, often enhances) future competition between cooperating enterprises. By nature, Japanese firms are fiercely competitive and without government restraint would often waste resources in excessive competition—in particular, failing to realize the economies of scale and experience with which MITI often seems preoccupied. Moreover, following the 1980 High Court ruling, administrative guidance based on vague stipulations, which results in supply restriction or price fixing is illegal, and MITI must now be more careful about leading businessmen to violate the Anti-Monopoly Law.

14-4. Financial Incentives and Controls

A. *Internal Incentives*

We may divide the state's financial incentives into two categories. Internally, the Finance Ministry gains leverage over the distribution of credit and subsidies among would-be investors through its control over monetary and fiscal policies and its authority over the Bank of Japan, the Japan Development Bank, the Trust Fund Special Account, and other government financial institutions. Externally, Japan achieves greater control over the composition of imports than do most Western nations, through import quotas and a variety of informal barriers to imports. In addition, until 1972, foreign currencies were rationed among would-be Japanese users through a centralized exchange control system, managed by the Bank of Japan. This system was formally abolished under pressure from Japan's trading partners, although some controls on the purchase of foreign currencies remained until 1981, and informal controls still persist.

With respect to subsidies and tax concessions for business firms, one author finds that "the array and effectiveness of aids and incentives used by government is dazzling. . . . [It is] surprising how flexible Japan's fiscal standards can be among various industries."[17] Tax concessions include tax-free reserves, accelerated depreciation—especially on machinery embodying new technology—and special incentives for exports, the latter now smaller than during the 1950s and 1960s. Until the energy crisis, rapid growth allowed the government to cut tax rates each year without running serious budget deficits. This made it easier to grant selective tax concessions and exemptions designed to promote growth in priority industries.

MOF also has some control over the allocation of public spending, which can often be viewed as a financial incentive in Japan

> because the government rarely invites an open, public [bidding on an investment project], but receives tenders only from those nominated by the government. This is common not only with the central government, but also with local governments and government enterprises, such as Japan National Railroads, Japan Telegram and Telephone Corporation, and Japan Highway Corporation.[18]

Recently, bidding has been opened up a bit, as part of deregulation, but is still restricted. Control over public utilities and transportation also puts the government in a position to influence regional industrial location and to effectively subsidize some industries through low rates for electric power, railway transport, and communications. The government also influences the allocation of loanable funds through the banking system, as we have seen, and can make it possible to raise more money for key investment projects more rapidly and at lower interest rates than would be possible in Western nations. Since 1975, the government has also borrowed huge sums to finance its own deficits, generally at interest rates significantly below those on government bonds in the West. At first, it kept interest rates below equilibrium, obliging the city banks to purchase bonds at high prices. Subsequently, it lost part of this leverage, as the public debt skyrocketed, but interest rates have remained low, owing to the reduced business demand for loans and the government's own fiscal restraint.

In this context, a striking feature of postwar Japan has been the high rate of household saving. It is now about 16 percent of disposable income, but until recently, it ran 18–20 percent or more, three times as high as in the United States and significantly above other Western nations. Household savings have varied from about a fourth to over half of total gross saving since 1952. They have made Japan's record growth possible by allowing up to a third of GNP to be invested, instead of the usual 15–25 percent or less in market economies. In part, the high rate of saving is due to thrift, but differences between Japanese and American households may result largely from differences in the budget constraints which they face. In Japan, the underdeveloped social insurance system has motivated saving to prepare for old age and to build up a reserve in the event of illness or accident. In addition, there has been almost no consumer credit, except for the purchase or major improvement of a home. The exclusion of most other consumer demand from loanable funds markets has helped to keep interest rates low, although household access to credit has been rising since 1985. Finally, until April 1988, the Japanese government encouraged small savers by allowing tax-free savings accounts—up to 6 million yen in bank accounts and another 6 million yen in postal savings.[19] In the United States, by contrast, consumer credit has been freely available and mortgage interest payments have been deductible from taxable income, but there has been no tax relief on savings accounts. A typical United States household also invests a larger percentage of its disposable income in housing and other durables than does a representative Japanese household, and this is a form of saving.

Japan's low interest rate policy has acted like a tax on household savings. Economists believe that the propensity to save varies directly with the interest rate, so that lower rates mean smaller voluntary savings. But the effect of changes in the interest rate on desired savings is likely to be weak. (A household saving toward a fixed goal, such as buying a car, may even save more when deposit rates fall, in order to offset the effect of lower interest earnings on its accumulation.[20]) On balance, any depressing effect of low interest rates on saving in Japan has probably been more than offset by tax relief on savings accounts and the low borrowing priority of households, which must consequently maintain a savings reserve against contingencies and build up their savings in advance of large outlays. Thus, the main effect of low interest rates has been to reduce household interest earnings and to transfer this return to business as an investment subsidy.

Traditionally, Japanese have also been wary of buying stocks and bonds, and the government has helped to preserve this attitude by restricting the variety and attractiveness of securities available to most households. As of September 1987, only 16 percent of household financial assets, excluding money, were in stocks and bonds. About 18 percent were in postal savings and another 37 percent were in bank savings accounts, while around 29 percent were in trusts and insurance. This is why the ability to influence the allocation of loans financed by the latter three sources has been a component of the government's ability to direct the economy.

B. External Incentives

Externally, the actions of MITI, MOF, and other government agencies have promoted and subsidized exports, while restricting imports. For many years, foreign currencies were formally rationed among would-be Japanese buyers—importers, tourists, firms wanting to invest abroad, and so on—with the generosity of an applicant's exchange quota depending on the priority attached to his use of funds. Highest priority has gone to imports of key raw materials, to food that cannot be produced in Japan, and to machinery and equipment embodying advanced technology. By contrast, there have been informal limits on imports of manufactured consumer goods and strict formal quotas on food imports that compete with domestic production. High-priority industries have received the most generous import quotas, and many of these same firms have also enjoyed the best access to low-cost loans, protection from foreign (and sometimes domestic) competition, accelerated depreciation, and other subsidies.

Japanese export promotion has been both direct and indirect. According to one author, "speculative investment in plant facilities was actively promoted during the period of the economic miracle by confidence on the part of entrepreneurs that output that could not be sold at home could always be sold abroad."[21] Indirect promotion has also included subsidies to adopt and to improve on imported technology, the results of which are directly and indirectly embodied into most of Japan's exports. Priority access to credit at low interest rates is, itself, a subsidy, and during the late 1970s, about 40 percent of Japanese exports still received additional assistance (vs. 15 percent in the U.S., 9 percent in West Germany, and 30 percent in France). From time to time, Western countries have also complained that Japan is "dumping" such exported goods as steel, television sets, microwave ovens, videocassette recorders, autos, ball bearings, and other manufactured durables into their domestic markets. By this they mean that Japanese goods are being sold in the West at prices below production costs or below their prices (exclusive of taxes) in Japan. But while Japanese producers have historically practiced price discrimination against domestic household consumers, there is less evidence that they persistently set export prices below average costs.

The incentive to dump is greater, the higher the percentage of a firm's costs that are fixed rather than variable in the short run. Dumping allows full utilization of production capacity, when domestic demand is depressed, thereby enabling fixed costs to be spread over a larger output. From another perspective, when fixed costs are high, average total cost will be falling over a substantial range of output, as in Figure 14.1. Marginal costs (SRMC) will then lie below average total cost (SRAC). However, the firm can profitably export at any price above SRMC. Suppose the company in Figure 14.1 is producing and selling one million color TV sets in Japan at a price equivalent to $1,000 in U.S. funds. Thus, it will take a loss if it produces only this many, since SRAC is greater than $1,000 above one million units. However, it can reduce its loss or even turn this into a profit by exporting another 1.5 million at a price of $400, even though its average cost exceeds $400 above 2.5 million units. It would then be dumping, in the sense that its domestic price and its average cost both exceed its export price.

Complaints about dumping have led to a number of formal and informal quotas on imports from Japan, to which the Japanese have reacted, in part, by farming out more production to Asian countries that do not yet have quotas. By and large, however, the Japanese export successfully because they are willing to price competitively and have achieved a cost or quality advantage, rather than because they sell below average cost. For example, output in tons per labor hour was nearly 1.7 times as great in Japanese as in U.S. steel mills in 1982, although wages and benefits were lower in Japan. Energy consumption per ton of steel produced was no more than two-thirds of the U.S. level. A Japanese auto worker was producing at least three times as many vehicles as his opposite number in France or Britain in 1980, and the time needed to build a small car, with fewer workers, was about half that in the United States.[22]

The claim that Japanese firms are more aggressive dumpers than their Western competitors (in the sense of setting export prices below unit costs) rests on one or both of two basic assumptions. First, the Japanese are often more willing to sacrifice short-term profit, in order to establish themselves in a market and then to expand their market share. When products are targeted for promotion, Japanese producers also receive more generous access to low-cost credit plus tax breaks to help them absorb temporary losses while establishing themselves in export markets. Second, Japanese companies are supposed to have higher ratios of fixed to variable costs, owing to their greater reliance on debt finance and their greater reluctance to lay workers off. But the former has declined considerably in recent years, and the latter is compensated by greater flexibility of wages and hours worked. Moreover, the compensating balance requirement, which is part of the real cost of a loan, tends to fall when credit is tight—essentially when domestic demand is depressed and the incentive to export is strongest. For these and other reasons, export-oriented

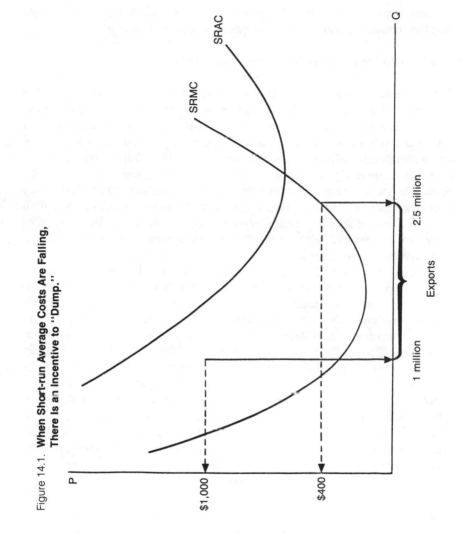

Figure 14.1. **When Short-run Average Costs Are Falling, There Is an Incentive to "Dump."**

Japanese firms do not necessarily operate with higher percentages of fixed costs than their counterparts in Western Europe or even North America.

14-5. Control over Foreign Trade and Capital Flows

Until the liberalization of import quotas, foreign exchange rationing, and foreign investment into and out of Japan, beginning in the late 1960s the Japanese government controlled international payments and imports more closely than did any other developed or semideveloped market economy, except Yugoslavia. Even after a liberalization of foreign currency controls over 1971–72, the state continued to monitor every foreign-exchange transaction made by Japanese banks, firms, and citizens, and to require approval for every significant purchase of foreign currency with yen. Japanese were forbidden to hold large foreign-currency deposits until 1980. Officials of socialist nations expressed admiration for Japan's system of controls, which seemed able to harness trade to the service of economic growth in a country without natural resources.

In addition, both foreign investment into Japan and investment abroad by Japanese were subject to case-by-case approval. The 1950 Law on Foreign Investment forbade foreign companies to obtain more than a 49 percent ownership of any Japanese enterprise, even when MITI's approval for a joint venture was forthcoming. Such approval usually depended on the ability of the venture to make Japan more self-sufficient in something, and even then, if MITI could get the technology through imports or licensing of Japanese firms, this was the preferred way. Prior to the mid-1970s, foreign companies dominated only the petroleum industry, with about 60 percent of the domestic market, and IBM Japan had about 30 percent of the market for data processing. In no other industry did foreign affiliates have as much as 20 percent of the Japanese market.[23] Quantitatively, the Japanese economic miracle therefore relied scarcely at all on foreign capital, and it was probably MITI's major coup to gain access to foreign technology, without having the "flag follow trade," except in a handful of cases (like IBM).

As part of trade liberalization, under foreign pressure and in response to the large balance-of-payments surpluses over 1969–72, the government made it easier for Japanese firms to invest abroad. Direct and portfolio investment overseas, which was running under $150 million per year during the late 1960s, skyrocketed to almost $2 billion in 1972, to more than $8.75 billion in 1979, and to well over $100 billion in 1987. (Part of this rise represents inflation plus an increase in the U.S. dollar price of the yen.) Japan has become the world's number one creditor nation, in the sense that the value of its overseas assets exceeds the value of its foreign liabilities by a greater margin than for any other country. The government's attitude toward Japanese investment abroad was still rather selective, at least prior to the huge balance-of-payments surplus of 1985. Some efforts have been discouraged, while outlays to ensure or to improve Japan's access to foreign energy supplies and resources have been promoted, along with those to increase goodwill in markets for Japanese exports. The latter has motivated construction of some production facilities within countries that are major export markets.

Foreign pressures plus the growing refusal by foreign companies to supply technology to Japanese firms without equity participation have also caused the constraint on foreign ownership in Japan to be liberalized. A major change came in 1980 when foreign direct investment into Japan began to be approved in principle. Prior to then, it was in principle disapproved, although exceptions were made, and the system grew more liberal over 1967–80. Today, foreigners may gain up to 100 percent ownership of firms operating in Japan, except in four industries— agriculture, forestry, and fishing; mining; leather and leather products; and petroleum, where the extent of Japanese ownership has been considered far too low. Nevertheless, a variety of bureaucratic roadblocks—including refusal to process applications—continues to restrict foreign direct investment into Japan, which remains at low (and in some years, even at negative) levels.[24] Foreign portfolio investment, which gives no decision-making role in Japanese firms to foreigners, did expand dramatically, from an average of $190 million over 1965–69, to nearly $11.9 billion in 1980, before falling back even more dramatically to become negative in 1984. Since then, it has oscillated wildly—e.g., from minus $6 billion in 1987 to plus $11 billion in the first quarter of 1988.

In practice, liberalization of trade flows is also less than it appears to be because of the informal barriers noted earlier, which have become more prominent over time as formal controls have receded. A major purpose of these barriers has been to conserve foreign exchange to buy fuel, raw materials, and food that cannot be produced in Japan. In 1984, imports in these three categories combined came to about 70 percent of total imports, by value, including a 44 percent share for mineral fuels, lubricants, and related materials vs. an average 20 percent during the ten years prior to the first energy crisis. Japan also continues to make some use of the "sole agent" system, whereby just one trading company or other buyer will import a given product. This allows it to exercise whatever buying power Japan as a whole may have on the world market. Nevertheless, liberalization of imports is continuing, partly because of renewed foreign pressure following Japan's record surpluses since 1984.

At end-1980 a new Foreign Exchange and Trade Control Law came into effect to replace the 1950 Law on Foreign Investment and the 1949 Foreign Exchange Control Law, which had legitimized government regulation of this area. In principle, most capital movements into and out of Japan were deregulated, although informal restrictions again remain. In particular, it seems unlikely that foreigners will ever be allowed to gain control of more than a handful of major Japanese companies. (Such takeovers will be allowed, moreover, only when they are in the long-term interests of employees of the firms being acquired.) A partial freeing of interest rates has taken place since 1980, and the present situation (early 1989) is one of coexistence between regulated and deregulated rates, with all rates scheduled to shift into the latter category by the early 1990s. Both foreign lending in

Japan and Japanese lending abroad expanded dramatically over 1980–87. Today, Japanese interest rates cannot fall too far below those in the United States or Western Europe without triggering large outflows of funds.

Capital flows are now freer than at any other time during the twentieth century. However, much of the large net outflow of funds since 1980 reflects a one-time adjustment of Japanese portfolios to include previously prohibited foreign assets plus the policy of recycling trade surpluses in ways that minimize their political cost to Japan, while developing new overseas markets and ensuring future supplies of raw materials and energy. The 1980 legislation also lifted several formal barriers to trade and to other current-account transactions, and the government has since undertaken to simplify regulations and procedures. Japan now has nearly the lowest tariffs in the world. In 1984, the combined shares of chemicals and all manufactured goods in Japanese imports was about 27 percent vs. 30 percent in 1973 (before the energy crisis) and 24.5 percent in 1979. But by 1987, this share had reached 44 percent, leaving just 56 percent for fuel, raw materials, and food. Japan's market is more open, although balance-of-payments surpluses have also remained at historically high levels.

14-6. Criticisms of the Government's Role

In the fall of 1976, a Detroit auto executive spent a week test-driving the new Honda Accord. His experience prompted him to promise that "You'll see cars like this from Detroit within five years, the Lord willing." At the time, Japanese cars were selling so quickly that they could not be shipped across the ocean fast enough, and dealers were selling the Accord at about 20 percent over suggested list price. Divine intervention did not occur, and by 1981, Japan had passed the United States to become the world's leading manufacturer of automobiles. Two years later, General Motors signed a joint-venture agreement with Toyota, in order to use the latter's technology in producing subcompact cars at a California plant.

Yet, in 1956, Japanese-made cars cost 40 percent more to produce than comparable foreign models, and the Japanese prime minister refused to ride in one, for fear it would break down. The industry could only survive under a thick blanket of MITI protection—the least important part of which was a 40 percent tariff on cars and a 30 percent tariff on trucks—that generated much criticism from other government agencies. The low product quality resulted partly because motor vehicle producers were forced to use Japanese steel, whose prognosis was equally bad. Some observers look at the rapid growth rate and vast improvement in product quality—for those who remember when Japanese goods were considered shoddy—and conclude that government guidance of the economy has been successful.

But there are also many economists with the opposite view, although government efforts to promote the collection, exchange, and spread of information generally win higher marks than its intervention in markets or in enterprise decision making. The critics note Japan's vast potential for economic growth in

1950, and give primary credit for realizing this to the Korean War stimulus, to the enthusiasm and innovativeness of private entrepreneurs, to the hard-working and docile labor force, to the absence of defense commitments, and to other factors external to the government's role. One version argues that if "the general environment was favorable for enterprise, it was . . . the entrepreneurs who seized the opportunities. Companies such as Sony, Honda, and Matsushita, founded by brilliant innovators and managers, are widely known outside Japan, but there were many others [in a variety of industries] whose executives acted as catalysts and pathfinders in the expansion of Japanese industry. It is not credible that these talented men could have been closely guided and directed by a cadre of civil servants . . . or that their vision and skills could have been adequately exploited within a tightly-managed, essentially bureaucratic system.''[25]

According to this view, government's contribution to economic development may have been positive. But it did not extend much beyond creating a climate of private investor confidence; assisting private enterprise with complementary public investments; providing a large volume of easy credit; restraining public spending (which freed resources for private investment); and using the state's bargaining power to cut the cost of foreign technology. As well, the formal planning process may have organized a useful information exchange, and there were many informal exchanges of technical information, in which government agencies were involved. These helped Japanese firms to share the benefits of each other's experience and, thus, to bring down costs and improve quality more quickly.

However, bureaucratic interference has also had its costs. A particular weakness of the system of government guidance, according to some critics, is a lack of coordination of separate regional and industrial policies. Each *genkyoku* bureau works closely with its particular industry, but above this level we find, not coordination, but "inter-agency rivalries, attempts at bureaucratic empire-building, and diffusion of responsibility.''[26] Government agencies often disagree in Japan, as elsewhere. For example, MITI clashes with the Fair Trade Commission over domestic competition policy and with MOF over protection of small- and medium-sized firms against foreign competition. Neither do we find any clear set of guidelines that could serve as a consistent, overall industrial policy framework, according to the critics, although the work of MITI's Industrial Policy Bureau and Industrial Structure Council could be said to have played this role.

Nevertheless, policies are often formulated by groups working in partial isolation from one another, and they sometimes work at cross purposes. The Liberal-Democratic party must respond to a variety of special interests, and the party itself is a coalition of competing factions. Consequently, prime ministers must shuffle their cabinets often to ensure that many politicians have access to portfolios, which tends to preclude bold initiatives, to reinforce cautious attitudes, and to help prevent the establishment of a consistent framework for policy making. In addition, over most of the postwar era, Japan's economy has operated close to its production potential. In such conditions, subsidizing the expansion of one group of industries and firms inevitably means slowing expansion elsewhere. Often, the state has assisted declining or marginal industries with below-average growth potential—such as agriculture, textiles, wearing apparel, and coal mining—or continued subsidies for too long, as in the case of shipbuilding, steel, and petrochemicals. At the same time, many individual enterprises and industries grew, prospered, and exported without extensive government attention.

In this context, administrators have made some famous gaffes in allocating import quotas and investment funds. We have seen that MITI blocked the application of Sony to import transistor technology—for which it had paid $25,000—on grounds that Sony lacked the ability to develop cost-effective uses for it. However, Sony went on to develop the transistor radio, and, subsequently, more sophisticated products which sold well on export markets, without much government help. The Japanese computer industry, which started with a huge technological lag vis-à-vis the United States, has been the object of intensive MITI promotion efforts since the mid-1960s. But Texas Instruments, an American firm whose technology Japan needed, refused to transfer this technology except via direct investment in Japan, which MITI would not then allow. This cost five to ten years in catch-up time.

More generally, Japan has followed a strategy of economic development known as "import substitution." The basic idea is to suppress imports with quotas, tariffs, exchange controls, and/or a variety of informal barriers. Instead of allowing imports to expand, Japan increases production of similar goods at home. Thus, most manufactures have been nearly impossible to import, except in limited quantities, while domestic output has multiplied manyfold. Many nations have tried import substitution, and most have been disillusioned with the results. Inefficient domestic industries have been created, which require long-term protection or subsidies to survive. Frequently, such a strategy raises a nation's dependence on imports, because the import-substituting industries themselves need inputs that must be imported. In this light, it now appears that Japan pushed domestic production of ships, aluminum, and some petrochemicals too far, but it is also hard to think of an industry that it could encourage without increasing its reliance on imported supplies. The industries being promoted have usually developed an export potential more than sufficient to pay for their imported inputs, in contrast to the experience of most countries that have pursued this strategy.

As a rule, economists frown on import substitution, calling instead for specialization according to comparative advantage. That is, each nation should produce those goods in which it has a cost advantage over other nations, as well as those which are too expensive to trade because of transport costs. The sole exception relates to infant industries in which a country can reasonably expect to have a future comparative advantage, once it has gained enough experience and expanded to a rate of output high enough to allow all scale economies to be realized. Protecting infant industries is consistent with comparative advantage—and one could justify much of Japan's import substitution in this way—provided the protection is not too great or kept on for too long. Unfortunately, protected industries usually acquire political power, which makes it hard to wean them, even after they have become adults. Several of Japan's heavy and chemical industries are candidates for this status.

14-7. Japan's Strategy of Economic Development

A. The Evolution of Industrial Priorities

While we cannot settle all issues raised by the above criticisms of government's role, we note that there are replies to most of them. In general, Japanese-style planning has been consistent with vigorous competition and entrepreneurship. In addition, industry-by-industry priorities have evolved systematically—from labor-intensive to physical-capital-intensive to knowledge- (or human capital) intensive production.[27] After World War II, Japan first reconstructed its textile industry, both because its exports had historically financed most of the imports essential to its growth—and it possessed a fund of accumulated knowledge and physical capital in this industry—and because the occupation authorities prevented Japan from promoting any sector that could add to its capacity to wage war. In 1955, textiles still accounted for 37 percent of Japan's exports, and subsidies were also being given to other labor-intensive sectors—including cameras, binoculars, sewing machines, and scientific instruments—as well as to agriculture, coal mining, and fishing.[28]

However, by the early 1950s, the highest development priority had shifted to basic heavy industries—steel, fertilizer, electric power, and shipbuilding—in which Japan was a marginal producer by world standards. Several of these industries got a shot in the arm from the special procurement demand associated with the Korean War, but Japan was still not expected to improve its competitiveness by much over the long run. These expectations proved wrong. Through a combination of doggedness and ingenuity, Japan became a world leader. For example, by building steel plants close to the sea and by bringing down the costs of ocean transport with its huge carriers, Japan was able to deliver fuel and iron ore to its factories at lower prices than many countries paid to exploit domestic resources.

Right behind development of the steel industry came promotion of steel-using industries—especially motor vehicles (whose output remained small until 1960)—but also electrical engineering, electronics, machinery, machine tools, and other metal products. Japan was successful in designing and producing high-quality, energy-efficient automobiles, which gave it a (partly unforeseen) export boost, once the energy crisis was underway. Subsidies also assisted inorganic chemicals, followed by organic chemicals during the 1960s—notably petrochemicals and derivative industries, such as plastics. Prior to the energy crisis, Japan did achieve a cost advantage in organic chemicals, partly because this industry was allowed to ignore most of the costs of its pollution.

By the early 1970s, priorities were shifting again, this time toward high technology and, especially, toward information-based industries. Residential construction was also growing rapidly, and a master plan had been drawn up for the regional dispersion of industry. During this decade, sophisticated machinery (including robots and aircraft), transport equipment, fabricated metal products, microelectronics, fiber optics, lasers, atomic energy, fish farming, ocean development, pollution control, solar energy, and integrated production facilities for export were all targeted for government aid. As noted earlier, Japan became a world leader in pollution-control technology, besides which it began to enforce the world's strictest environmental protection standards and introduced the world's most generous program of compensation for its 85,000 victims of environmental pollution.

As of 1986, however, only electronics and electrical machinery, among the high-technology industries, had made major contributions to Japanese exports. Within electronics, semiconductors have become a special target for domination. Japan is challenging the United States for world leadership, and Japanese firms have nearly pushed U.S. rivals out of some key markets, precipitating a major trade dispute between the two countries. Since the energy crisis, high-technology processes, with relatively modest energy and raw-materials requirements and comparatively high value-added per yen spent on imported inputs, have dramatically increased their share of industrial value added, while the share of raw-materials-intensive sectors has fallen from 40 percent to around 30 percent.[29] The technological sophistication of industry will continue to rise, along with social overhead and welfare spending, although this will remain an area in which Japan trails most developed Western nations.

As a rule, the government actively fosters no more than five to ten industries at a given time. Once an industry has matured, it is expected to survive on its own, although it may continue to have better-than-average access to credit and to enjoy effective export subsidies. Both the system and its priorities have remained flexible. One of the system's strengths is that it can offer guidance, based on collective wisdom, without suppressing initiative. Thus MITI held up Sony for just two years (1952–54). Once enough businessmen, banking officials, and/or government leaders are convinced of the advantages of entering an industry, the expansion of output is likely to be swift—as in the case of iron and steel, autos, home entertainment, and, most recently, semiconductors. (Once again, while decision making is slow and cumbersome, due to the need for consensus, subsequent implementation is often devastating.)

Moreover, the system is adaptable:

> For instance [in the early 1950s], Kawasaki Steel Corporation's proposal for a new integrated steel mill at a new location was completely at variance with the rationalization program put forth by other steel companies . . . Kawasaki advanced its project against the majority opinion held by MITI bureaucrats, steel industry leaders, and banks that since Japan lacked raw material resources, no up-to-date steel mill would have sufficient international competitive power and that Kawasaki's project would result in redundant capacity. . . . However, Kawasaki

started this project at its own expense . . . and obtained later approval from MITI, the Bank of Japan and the city banks, as well as the steel industry's agreement to the *fait accompli*.[30]

B. The Role of Comparative Advantage

The above strategy of evolution is the brainchild of no single government or business agency, although MITI has played a prominent role. Nevertheless, a rational pattern does emerge. A country specializing according to comparative advantage will produce goods that use relatively large amounts of inputs with which the nation in question is well endowed. Thus, Canada and the United States specialize in wheat production, which is land intensive, and in computers and information-processing equipment, which is physical- and human-capital intensive. India, by contrast, specializes in labor-intensive goods. In 1950, Japan's people were virtually its sole natural resource, and a policy of specializing according to comparative advantage therefore had to build on this. At first, Japan could best utilize its human resources in labor-intensive industries, where their diligence, patience, capacity for hard work, and ingenuity gave them an advantage over Western competitors. As noted earlier, there was also an accumulation of capital and experience here after the war.

But this was just the beginning. Japan's people were also thrifty, and the government had the means to mobilize savings, which were channelled into productive investment. This allowed Japan to shift its emphasis toward more capital-intensive heavy and chemical industries, which are basic to any major development effort. Reliance on trade for natural resources and mineral fuels plus a naval tradition dictated a strong merchant marine, and Japan quickly became the world's leading builder of ships, which also allowed it to bring down ocean freight rates. At the same time, Japanese have been generally well educated and ambitious, and Japan trebled its supply of technically-trained people during the 1950s. Rapid expansion in this area has continued and helped to pave the way for a shift toward knowledge-intensive or human-capital-intensive industries, beginning in the 1970s. The shift from labor-intensive toward physical-capital-intensive and then toward knowledge-intensive production is not unusual. What is remarkable is the speed of Japan's transition, as well as the high quality of product eventually achieved in each area.

Within this broad evolution, the government appears to have used both demand-side and supply-side criteria to help determine which industries to encourage. During an era of record economic growth in many parts of the world, it has tried to promote products whose price and income elasticities of demand were high, so that decreases in price and increases in world income would lead to even larger increases in quantity demanded. To achieve cost reductions that would permit price decreases, it has focused on production processes in which potential gains from importing new technology and from experience or scale economies were expected to be large. Since the energy crisis, Japan has also raised the share of domestic value added in industrial output and reduced the energy intensity of production and consumption. (The latter has raised the priority of knowledge-intensive industries, in which gains from accumulating experience with the relevant technologies are high.) Once established in a foreign market, Japanese firms have tried to reduce the price elasticity of demand for their products, in effect, by establishing a reputation for quality, reliability, and after-sale service.

To encourage the growth of priority sectors, the government has used three basic instruments. First, it has protected domestic manufacturers from foreign competition, thereby reserving most of Japan's large domestic market for them, one motive being to permit rapid realization of experience and scale economies. Second, it has increased the availability of low-cost finance via its leverage over financial markets and its tax-subsidy policies. Third, it has ensured the availability of raw materials, energy, information, and technology at reasonable prices (although subject to Japan's ability to procure these on the world market). Domestic producers have therefore received a variety of explicit and implicit subsidies, especially when trying to establish themselves in new lines of production. However, these have been given with a *quid pro quo*. The government has expected firms to develop an export potential, except in the cases of assistance to agriculture or to declining industries. Otherwise, the survival of current management has depended on performance, as measured by export expansion. Enterprises receiving technology from abroad, with the help of MITI or other government agencies, have also had to share this with rival producers, along with a variety of cost and technical data. During the 1950s and 1960s, one result was to preserve the traditional absence of protection for industrial secrets, thereby speeding technological diffusion at the cost of discouraging major innovations (although not necessarily minor ones) by Japanese enterprises.

The entire process worked well enough to make us forget that it could have collapsed long ago like a house of cards. If investors had been too cautious at the outset, if the weakness of labor unions and traditional worker attitudes had not fostered wage restraint, if government had not established the expectation that markets would grow, or if a few key sectors had failed to expand and become bottlenecks, subsidies might simply have expanded profits or increased wages, without stimulating a commensurate rise in output. If most firms had been unwilling to expand rapidly, those which sought to do so would have encountered difficulties in obtaining supplies at reasonable prices and with good quality, or in finding markets for their products. Thus, they would have taken losses, while those who played it safe by restricting supply would have prospered or at least survived, and the psychological effects of such a lesson could have devastated the government's growth ambition. The role of the city banks was also crucial, since they made the loans that fueled the economic miracle. Many of these were risky, and government guarantees often formed part of their collateral. Such guarantees were worth less during the late 1940s and early 1950s than they came to be, after rapid growth was established.

Once Japan's industrial initiative was mobilized, it had a large potential to draw on, and several constraints on growth operating in the West did not apply to it. Its people were well educated and achievement oriented; with the end of the Empire and the diminished status of its armed forces after World War II, the main achievement outlet became economic development. The existence of the dual economy meant that Japan had reserves of underutilized, but high quality labor that could be transferred to more productive jobs in modern industry, once the capital and technology were in place. Another benefit of backwardness was a backlog of technology that Japan could import and adapt to its needs. Finally as incomes rose, savings climbed even more rapidly, and there has been no large defense establishment to compete with investment for the use of this money.

As growth proceeded, Japan plausibly specialized according to comparative advantage via import substitution. The two were compatible, because Japan's comparative advantage kept changing as it accumulated physical and human capital. It repeatedly expanded industries in which technological improvements and gains from economies of scale and experience were substantial. The necessary investments involved considerable risk, but once expansion was achieved and experience gained, relative prices and costs were quite different from what they had been at the outset. Again and again, Japan achieved a cost or quality advantage, where previously it had not been competitive.[31] However, if government had not fueled investment demand with low interest rates and partial assumption of investment risk, it is far from obvious that the economy would have operated close to its production-possibility frontier.

The auto industry is the most obvious example of Japan's postwar success, but its experience with audio equipment is no less remarkable. Over 80 percent of the high-fidelity products sold in North America are made in Japan. Yet most of the inventions that launched the industry during the late 1940s and early 1950s originated in the United States. Many pioneering U.S. companies then went bankrupt, in an expanding market, or else gave up most production to become importing and marketing agents for Japanese firms, enabling the latter to sell under locally known brand names. The reason usually given for Japan's success in this competition is greater access to highly productive, but relatively low-wage skilled and semi-skilled labor and engineering talent. There is some truth to this claim, and the consumer electronics industry has a low natural resource requirement. Thus, it suits Japan's endowments.

But Japanese companies also had better access to low-cost funds for expansion of plant and equipment and for product development. Until the 1960s, large companies in the American radio, phonograph, and television industry saw little future in high fidelity and did not appreciate the technological advantage that this could provide for manufacture of related products, such as television sets and equipment. The entire consumer electronics industry, and much of producer electronics, is based on a small number of technological breakthroughs, whose mastery potentially leads to cost effectiveness in a wide range of products. Because prospective lenders in the United States failed to realize this during the 1950s, the small American firms engaged in high fidelity had no collateral against which to borrow the investment funds that expansion and large-scale product development required. By contrast, Japanese banks, businessmen, and (after initial hesitation) government officials were enthusiastic. Banks lent money, partly against the promise of future sales, and organized an exchange of technological information. Many Japanese producers went on to become world leaders in television and videotape recorders, as well as in audio.

It is still true, in Japan as in other countries, that subsidies were sometimes continued for too long or given for largely political reasons, notably in the case of agriculture. However, we should also separate assistance designed largely to maintain incomes or to ease adjustment burdens from aid intended to promote output expansion. A policy of adapting the economy to an ever-changing profile of industries in which the nation has a comparative advantage requires aid to sectors with growth potential, but also adjustment assistance to industries that have passed their peaks and face decline. Except for agriculture, whose votes the Liberal Democrats need to stay in power, Japanese industries have rarely been propped up artificially over long periods. The fact that a number of firms and industries made it on their own without extensive government help could be viewed as a compliment to administrative guidance. This aid sustained many firms now considered efficient, yet the bureaucracy did not smother initiative elsewhere.

Over time, Japanese industrial policy has also become less intervention intensive and more information intensive, in the specific sense of helping to produce and spread technical information, as well as to raise technological and quality standards. To a degree, this reflects the evolution toward more knowledge-intensive production, in which early access to improved technology and rapid accumulation of experience economies are more crucial than ever to export success. The government has also expanded its basic research and development role, as the technological backlog readily available to Japan for adoption from abroad has declined. In addition, the evolution of industrial policy reflects a reduced power of intervention, which has forced MITI and other government agencies to fashion new niches for themselves. This decline should not be overstated, however. Some kinds of intervention have expanded since the high-growth era—notably pollution control and the orderly withdrawal of capacity from depressed industries.

14-8. Toward the Future

At the outset of *Tokyo Joe*, a 1949 film with Humphrey Bogart and Sessue Hayakawa, there are Tokyo street scenes featuring a scarcity of private automobiles. When an American drops a few coins onto the pavement, beggars converge on them instantly. The Japanese economic miracle was unprecedented and unimagined in the years just after World War II, and it is sometimes useful to remind ourselves how far Japan has come. Unfortunately, Japan's future is again a subject for speculation. For it seems to have passed a watershed during the dozen or so years after 1974, as a result of the energy crisis; the appearance of intense competition from newly emerging industrial nations (such as South Korea and Taiwan); the pressures to decontrol imports, money-capital flows, and financial markets; soaring land prices and foreign-currency prices of the yen following deregulation; a succession of scandals involving government officials; and pent-up internal pressures, which have boosted spending on welfare and social overhead capital.

During the next twenty years or so, Japan will have to deal with at least three potential time bombs. First, its trading partners, especially the United States, are threatening higher trade barriers unless Japan goes further in opening its own markets to imports. Even then, it is likely to find it difficult to expand its current export volume, because of the steep rise in the value of the yen over 1986–87 plus intensified competition from newly industrializing nations, as well as restrictions on imports by trading partners. Although these may not end its string of balance-of-payments surpluses, they have reduced the number of export-related jobs in an era of labor-force expansion. Second, the aging of Japan's population will put further pressure on the welfare system and increase the need to raise the technological sophistication of production, in order to keep export industries competitive.

Finally, Japan has nearly the world's highest food and land prices, which reduce the real incomes of most urban dwellers, and Japanese consumers have usually paid higher prices than foreign buyers for products made in Japan. Recently, soaring real estate prices have made home ownership unaffordable for many middle-class Japanese, threatening a social and motivational crisis. High food and land prices result, in part, from suppression of food imports in order to protect domestic agriculture, which is mostly high cost. More generally, import barriers have drastically reduced the depressing effect on consumer prices of recent increases in the value of the yen. However, this rise has put pressure on Japanese exporters, thereby constraining wage increases and hiring, and causing some layoffs. In these ways, a higher yen has been harmful to urban dwellers. Tables 14.1 and 14.2 indicate why the ruling Liberal-Democratic party will nevertheless have to rely more and more on nonfarm votes in future elections, in order to stay in power. Despite subsidies, agriculture's shares of labor and value added have progressively declined, bringing a gradual erosion of rural voting power through periodic (although limited) reapportionment of election districts.

If efficiency considerations were all that mattered, Japan should lower the barriers to imports of farm produce and let domestic food prices fall closer to world market levels. This would also reduce the value of farmland—particularly, if the price of rice goes down—and cause more land to move into residential, commercial, and other nonagricultural uses. Land prices would then fall throughout Japan, and with them prices of all kinds of housing, office, and factory space. Real incomes of nonfarm families would rise, as a result of these price decreases. Many

Table 14.1

Evolution of the Breakdown of the Japanese Labor Force by Industry (in percentages)

Year	Agriculture/ forestry/ fishing	Mining and quarrying	Manufacturing	Construction	Transportation/ communications utilities	Trade and finance	Other (mainly services)
1952	45.2	1.5	17.4	4.4	4.7	13.8	13.1
1961	31.2	1.0	22.5	5.6	5.6	18.6	15.4
1974	13.1	0.3	27.2	8.8	6.9	24.1	19.6
1986	8.5	0.1	24.7	9.1	6.6	26.7	24.3

Source: Bank of Japan, Statistics Department, *Economic Statistics Annual,* 1961, 1976, and 1986 editions (Tokyo: Bank of Japan, 1962, 1977, 1987).

Table 14.2

Evolution of the Breakdown of Japanese Net Domestic Product by Sector of Origin (in percentages)

Year	Agriculture/ forestry/ fishing	Mining and quarrying	Manufacturing	Construction	Transportation/ communications utilities	Wholesale and retail trade	Finance	Other (mainly services)
1952	23.1	3.1	24.1	3.8	8.6	17.0	5.2	15.0
1961	14.0	1.4	30.0	5.8	9.5	16.1	8.9	14.2
1974	5.2	0.6	31.8	8.7	6.3	15.7	12.3	19.5
1985	2.8	0.3	28.5	7.0	8.5	14.2	13.8	24.9

Sources: Bank of Japan, Statistics Department, *Economic Statistics Annual,* 1961, 1976, and 1986 editions (Tokyo: Bank of Japan, 1962, 1977, 1987).

farm families would be hurt, but nearly all have major sources of income outside agriculture, and the average after-tax income of part-time farm families exceeds that of urban dwellers by 40 percent or more. (In addition, the government could cushion the blow by changing the form of agricultural subsidy—so that it does not boost the price of food or land—and by giving more encouragement to farmers to shift away from land-intensive crops.) Over time, this scenario does describe what is likely to occur, as the farm population dwindles and slowly loses its political clout. But we should not expect it to happen quickly.

In the meantime, Japan must reorient production toward domestic demand, since opportunities for increasing export volume will be restricted, and this process has already begun. The service sector will continue to expand, along with health care, and more resources are likely to go into infrastructure. For more than a century, however, Japan has made a living by importing raw materials and energy and adding value to these, in order to export finished products. The shift toward domestic demand requires a change of underlying attitudes and outlook plus a reworking of the basic consensus between business and government that cannot be achieved overnight. Nor will Japan ever be able to prosper without an efficient export sector. Over the longer run, this will have to become even more knowledge intensive, because of increased competition in product areas that it dominated in the 1960s and 1970s, plus a greater welfare burden and an aging work force, as well as the likelihood of higher energy prices in the 1990s.

A bright spot has been Japan's improved ability to innovate and even to outperform Western countries in this regard. It still tries to import the best technology from abroad, but it is also assuming a leading role in basic research and new product development. A 1979 MITI white paper on science and technology argued that the 1950s was a period of introducing foreign technology into Japan, while the 1960s was mainly a time of improving on basic technology that had already been adopted. The 1970s were seen as a period of transition to indigenous technology. The paper then proposes that an indigenous base for technological progress be fully established during the 1980s, so that Japan can enter the twenty-first century as "a nation of science and technology." Research and development spending has climbed to over 2.5 percent of GNP, placing Japan in the front ranks of industrial nations with respect to this measure. Further changes in property rights may also be desirable, which increase protection for industrial secrets in order to give domestic enterprises and inventors more incentive to innovate, although this would probably be at the cost of less rapid diffusion of technology. In addition, there should be easier access to finance for small- and medium-sized firms, who need a more favorable environment in which to get started and grow. These enterprises are a major source of innovation in most market economies, and they represent a promising avenue of employment expansion, since they create more jobs for a given investment than do large companies.

When we add the continuing pressures to liberalize international trade and payments, meet foreign competition, expand social overhead capital, raise social welfare spending, and reduce environmental disruption, we can see that economic and political life must continue to change over the next twenty years, perhaps profoundly. Although Japan's growth will be lower than in the past, an opportunity also exists to translate the recent rise in the value of the yen—the fruit of past increases in output and efficiency—into standard-of-living gains for ordinary Japanese. To do this, the government would have to further liberalize imports, especially of farm goods, while transferring resources out of sectors harmed by liberalization and promoting the growth of industries in which Japan has (or can achieve) a comparative advantage. This will be no easy task, and Japan's ability to carry it out may well determine whether future economic historians regard it as the success story of this century.

Notes

1. These are conveniently summarized by G. C. Allen on p. 38 of his *The Japanese Economy* (London: Weidenfeld and Nicholson, 1981).

2. Ryutaro Komiya, "Planning in Japan," in Morris Bornstein, ed., *Economic Planning: East and West* (Cambridge, Mass.: Ballinger, 1975), p. 193.

3. How is not entirely clear, although the government did provide a myriad of subsidies to priority sectors, as well as assurances about the availability of export markets. See G. C. Allen, *Japan's Economic Expansion* (London: Oxford University Press, 1965), ch. 3.

4. W. V. Rapp, "Japan: Its Industrial Policies and Corporate Behavior," *Columbia Journal of World Business*, Spring 1977.

5. Because of Japan's lack of natural resources, this industry has been of critical importance, and by the mid-1970s, Japan was building about half the world's ships. This was still true in 1984. However, shipbuilding the world over became one of the worst casualties of the energy crisis. In Japan, output fell by two-thirds between 1976 and 1979, before recovering somewhat (although 1984 output was still 37 percent below the 1976 level and 43 percent below the 1974 level). Government leaders and industry officials decided together which shipyards would be closed, and by March, 1980, a third of all capacity had been taken out of operation. No subsidies were paid to keep yards open, and most workers were relocated to new jobs. Prior to this sudden reversal, "Under Planned Shipbuilding, the government announces every year the total tonnage of each major type of ship . . . to be built . . . and selects qualified shipowners and shipbuilders from among the applicants. A certain percentage—recently 50 percent to 80 percent—of the total funds necessary for new ships is supplied by the Japan Development Bank under terms substantially more favorable than ordinary financing. More than two-thirds (in tonnage) of ocean-going ships now carrying the Japanese flag were built under Planned Shipbuilding" (Komiya, "Planning in Japan," p. 216).

6. E. J. Kaplan, *Japan: The Government-Business Relationship* (Washington, D.C.: U.S. Government Printing Office, 1972), p. 64. Komiya, however, is less impressed with MOF's power.

7. Rapp, "Japan: Its Industrial Policies," p. 40.

8. The United States has been the leading supplier of technology to Japan, followed by the United Kingdom and West Germany.

9. For a discussion of the sharing of technological know-how during the Meiji era, see G. R. Saxonhouse, "A Tale of Japanese Technological Diffusion in the Meiji Period," *Journal of Economic History*, March 1974. Regarding quality promotion in Japan, see D. A. Garvin, "Japanese Quality Management," *Columbia Journal of World Business*, Fall 1984. finally, see "Novel Technique Shows Japanese Outpace Americans in Innovation," *New York Times*, March 7, 1988, p. 1, regarding the study mentioned at the end of this paragraph.

10. R. Komiya, "Japan's Non-Tariff Barriers on Manufactures," paper presented to the Fourth Pacific Trade and Development Conference, Ottawa, Canada, October 1971.

11. See Kaplan, *Japan: The Government-Business Relationship*, especially pp. 103–106. MITI also used its control over imports of parts and technology to eliminate two Japanese firms from the industry, since it feared "excessive" competition. As well, it succeeded in transferring the manufacture of auto parts to Japan through an arrangement with foreign patent holders. MITI agreed to guarantee royalty payments for the use of foreign technology, provided patent holders would allow the transfer of 90 percent of parts manufacture to Japan within five years.

12. Most products must still undergo lengthy and stringent testing before they can be sold in Japan, although there was a major relaxation of this requirement in 1981. Grounds of exclusion are often questionable. For example, in 1983, Canada had been waiting nine years for the Japanese government to reclassify British Columbia softwood plywood as "safe for house construction," despite its widespread use as a building material in North America. Japanese inspectors claim that British Columbia apples contain coddling moths, which have not been a serious problem in Canada. Product standards often change. In 1976, when its own auto exports were booming, many foreign cars were excluded from Japan's home market because of failure to pass emissions control tests, which Japanese autos, except Honda, failed as well. For many years, any imported cosmetic that contained an ingredient not on a government list was held up for a year or more to be tested. The list was kept secret from foreign manufacturers. Items restricted on grounds they had military applications have included buttons, which, after all, are part of any uniform. And so on.

13. Basically, there are three kinds of legal cartels in Japan. A *depression* cartel can be formed when excess capacity appears and when, without collusion to restrict supply, a number of firms would have to set prices below average costs. In theory, such a cartel must not "unduly" harm the interests of customers or restrict entry into the industry (or keep firms from breaking the cartel agreement).

A *rationalization* cartel can be formed when there is a need to standardize production in order to realize mass production economies. If each company in an industry is producing a wide range of styles, shapes, sizes, and designs, a rationalization cartel may be permissible. It limits the number of models produced by each firm and assigns different ranges of sizes and designs to different companies, but is not supposed to restrict supply or control prices. If a rationalization cartel can solve an industry's problems, a depression cartel is, in principle, not permitted.

In recent years, there have been few depression or rationalization cartels, partly because the FTC must approve them, and its interest in combatting monopoly power is much greater than MITI's. Most *legal* cartels have been authorized under special laws, which is the third type referred to above. These include the Environmental Sanitation Act, the Medium and Small Enterprise Organization Act, the Export and Import Trading Act, and the Act on Extraordinary Measures for the Stabilization of Designated Depressed Industries. There have also been a number of unofficial cartels, which are illegal, but which appear to have at least implicit MITI approval. (Indeed, many were formed at MITI's initiative and, in most cases a MITI official is rumored to sit on the board of directors.)

14. Thus, the well-publicized 1969 merger between Yawata and Fuji, Japan's largest steel producers, was an exception to the rule. This fusion recreated the pre-World War II Nippon Iron and Steel Co., which had been broken up by SCAP. After the merger, it controlled 30 percent of domestic steel production, which violated a key FTC condition for merger approval. But since Nippon identifies closely with MITI—indeed, is controlled by ex-MITI officials—the FTC could not withstand the political pressure put on it. In the same year, it prevented a merger of the three largest paper companies, which would have led to a firm with over 60 percent of the domestic market. We should note, as well, that Japanese mergers are effectively fusions of two or more different family units that take years to

consummate. Within the newly created enterprise, each group of employees identifies with and continues to give its loyalty to the old firm, treating the other group as outsiders. For this reason, it takes longer to realize the potential advantages of mergers in Japan than in Western countries.

15. Komiya, "Japan's Non-Tariff Barriers on Manufactures," p. 20.

16. Ibid., pp. 20–21.

17. Kaplan, *Japan: The Government-Business Relationship*, p. 46.

18. Komiya, "Japan's Non-Tariff Barriers on Manufactures," p. 20.

19. In addition, over half the large, semiannual bonuses paid to lifetime employees are saved.

20. More generally, while the substitution effect of a higher interest rate acts to increase savings, the income effect usually acts to reduce them. The higher rate makes it costlier to consume now rather than to save. But the higher rate will also make someone with positive net savings wealthier, because any given volume of savings will buy more future consumption. On this account the individual will tend to consume more *both* in the future and in the present, which is to say that he will save less.

21. The author continues, "In this sense, Japan's economic miracle was export-oriented." See Leon Hollerman, "Foreign Trade in Japan's Economic Transition," in Isaiah Frank, ed., *The Japanese Economy in International Perspective* (Baltimore: Johns Hopkins Press, 1975), p. 176.

22. However, the sources and magnitude of the Japanese cost advantage over the U.S. in automobiles are in some dispute. See Melvyn Fuss and Leonard Waverman, "The Extent and Sources of Cost and Efficiency Differences Between U.S. and Japanese Motor Vehicle Producers," University of Toronto, Institute for Policy Analysis, International Economics Program, Working Paper OP 87–10, December 1987.

23. By far the largest single foreign affiliate is IBM Japan, followed by Nestlé of Japan, Mobil, and Shell. MITI has gone to great lengths to promote domestic competition for IBM and to limit its share of the Japanese market.

24. Rarely is an application rejected, but many are never acted on, especially when suggestions by the Japanese government to the applicant are not accepted. For a discussion of all aspects of foreign investment in Japan during the postwar era, see R. B. Ozaki, *The Control of Imports and Foreign Capital in Japan* (New York: Praeger, 1972), Part II.

25. Phillip Trezise and Yukio Suzuki, "Politics, Government, and Economic Growth," in Hugh Patrick and Henry Rosovsky, eds., *Asia's New Giant: How the Japanese Economy Works* (Washington, D.C.: Brookings, 1976), p. 810. A similar view is put forward by Komiya in "Planning in Japan." See, as well, Kozo Yamamura, *Economic Policy in Postwar Japan* (Berkeley: University of California Press, 1967) and "Structure is Behaviour." Finally, see Kotaro Suzumura and Masahiro Okuno-Fujiwara, "Industrial Policy in Japan: Overview and Evaluation," Australian National University, Centre for Economic Policy Research, Discussion paper no. 156, Canberra, January 1987.

26. Trezise and Suzuki, "Politics, Government and Economic Growth," p. 787.

27. The discussion below borrows from G. C. Allen, *A Short Economic History of Modern Japan* (London: Allen & Unwin, 1972), 2nd rev. ed., pp. 178–81, as well as Rapp, "Japan: Its Industrial Policies."

28. About 45 percent of the animal protein in the diet of an average Japanese comes from fish, and the efficient Japanese fishing fleet catches one of every seven fish caught in the world. Japan also leads the world in fishing output, with the USSR close behind, but this industry has not expanded since 1977, when coastal nations adopted a two-hundred-mile limit beyond their shores, within which they now exercise exclusive jurisdictions over fishing. Thus, the Japanese fleet was wholly or partly excluded from several traditional fishing grounds.

29. In its *Vision of International Trade and Industrial Policy for the 1980s*, MITI listed

eight areas of science and technology for promotion during the 1980s and beyond. These are energy-related technology; electrical technology; advanced materials technology; traffic technology; disaster-prevention technology; life science; space development, and ocean development.

30. Hideichiro Nakamura, "Establishment of the Big Business System," *Japanese Economic Studies*, Fall 1977, p. 79.

31. The Japanese term for this process is *Kaizen*, or continuing improvement. See Masaaki Imai, *Kaizen: The Key to Japan's Competitive Success* (New York: Random House, 1986).

Questions for Review, Discussion, Examination

1. Why do you think Japan has largely been spared costly struggles over distribution?

2. What have been the three basic components of planning in Japan? Which has been most important? Has formal planning under the Economic Planning Agency been of only marginal importance? Discuss briefly. How is planning used to compensate for market "failure"?

3. What are the components of Japan's informal planning structure? What role do industry associations and *genkyoku* bureaus play in plan formation? Why are negotiation and consultation so important in Japanese planning?

*4. Explain how MITI has promoted technological progress in Japan. Has this required a high degree of indigenous innovation? How have traditional property rights to information plus actions of the government and the banks promoted technological diffusion? What has been the cost of this, until recently?

5. Why did MITI have so much power to regulate industrial activity during the 1950s and 1960s? What has caused this power to decline since then? How, in particular, has MITI helped to promote industrial concentration and collusion?

6. What is "administrative guidance"? Why is it important in Japan?

*7. Indicate some of the selective subsidies and tax exemptions used by the Japanese government to promote growth and technological diffusion. What has been the *quid pro quo* for state support? Has the Japanese government been entrepreneurial in promoting growth?

Do such subsidies necessarily increase the growth of real GNP? When are they most likely to do this? (*Hint*: They will raise the growth of GNP when they increase the average social return on investment. When are they most likely to do this?)

*8. "The main effect of low interest rates [in Japan] has been to reduce household interest earnings and to transfer this return to business as an investment subsidy." Why has this, rather than reduction of savings and investment, been the main effect of the low interest rate policy?

9. Broadly speaking, how has the Japanese government sought to improve Japan's balance of trade?

Have incentives to "dump" been greater in Japan than in Western market economies? Discuss briefly.

10. Although Japan has now "liberalized" foreign trade and capital flows, there are suggestions that informal barriers have sometimes arisen to replace the discarded or reduced formal barriers. What indirect evidence is there of this?

*11. The organizational changes in the Japanese economy since the end of the postwar occupation in 1952 have apparently not been major ones. However, government priorities have changed, and some argue that they have evolved systematically.

What has been the basic strategy of economic development in Japan over the postwar era? How have priorities evolved? Has this evolution been consistent with comparative advantage? What have been some of the criteria used by government to determine which industries to promote?

12. Once rapid growth was underway in Japan—in part, owing to the Korean War demand stimulus—several factors helped to prolong and to increase it in Japan. What were some of these?

13. How has Japanese industrial policy changed over time? Why has it changed in this way?

14. Over the next twenty years or so, Japan faces three potential time bombs. Briefly explain what these are.

What are some of the changes that Japan must make to deal with pressing economic and social problems? Why?

*15. How are high land (or real estate) values related to farm price supports? Why have farm price supports been maintained at such high levels and why are pressures on government to reduce support levels growing?

16. Do you think there are lessons from Japan's experience with economic development applicable to other nations? Indicate what you think these lessons are or develop an argument to the effect that there are none.

* = more difficult.

Suggested Further Readings

Note: Japanese authors are translated in the journal, *Japanese Economic Studies*, and there are several Japanese economic journals published in English. The OECD Annual Economic Surveys of Japan also provide much useful information.

Abeggelen, J. C. *Management and the Worker: The Japanese Solution*. Tokyo: Kodansha International, 1973.
Abeggelen, J. C., and W. V. Rapp. "Japanese Managerial Behavior and 'Excessive Competition.' " *The Developing Economies* 8 (December 1970): 427–444.
Adams, T. F. M., and Iwao Hoshii. *A Financial History of the New Japan* (Tokyo: Kodansha International, 1972.
Allen, G. C. "The Concentration of Economic Control in Japan." *Economic Journal* 47 (June 1937): 271–286.
———. *Japan's Economic Expansion*. London: Oxford University Press, 1965.
———. *A Short Economic History of Modern Japan*. London: Allen & Unwin, 1972.
———. *The Japanese Economy*. London: Weidenfeld and Nicholson, 1981.

Bank of Japan. *The Japanese Financial System.* Tokyo: Bank of Japan, 1978.
Bieda, K. *The Structure and Operation of the Japanese Economy.* New York: Wiley, 1970.
Cohen, J. B. *Japan's Postwar Economy.* Bloomington: Indiana University Press, 1958.
Cole, Robert. *Japanese Blue Collar: The Changing Tradition.* Berkeley: University of California Press, 1971.
Daido, Eisuke. "Why Are They 'General Trading Firms'?" *Japanese Economic Studies* 4 (Summer 1976): 44–62.
Eguchi, Hidekazu, and Koichi Hamada. "Banking Behavior Under Constraints: Credit Rationing and Monetary Mechanism in Japan." *Japanese Economic Studies* 6 (Winter 1977–78): 3–41.
Fisher, Paul. "Major Social Security Issues: Japan, 1972." *Social Security Bulletin* 36 (March 1973): 26–38.
Frank, Isaiah, ed. *The Japanese Economy in International Perspective.* Baltimore: Johns Hopkins University Press, 1975.
Garvin, David A. "Japanese Quality Management." *Columbia Journal of World Business* 19 (Fall 1984): 3–12.
Graham, John L. "A Hidden Cause of America's Trade Deficit with Japan." *Columbia Journal of World Business* 16 (Fall 1981): 5–15.
Haitani, Kanji. *The Japanese Economic System.* Boston: D. C. Heath, 1976.
Hashimoto, Masanori. "Bonus Payments, On-the-Job Training, and Lifetime Employment in Japan." *Journal of Political Economy* 87 (October 1979): 1086–1104.
Hazama, Hiroshi. "Characteristics of Japanese-Style Management." *Japanese Economic Studies* 6 (Spring–Summer 1978): 110–173.
Ikeo, Kazuhito. "Japan's Financial System: A Micro Approach." *Japanese Economic Studies* 16 (Fall 1987): 50–77.
Imai, Ken'ichi. "The Corporate Network in Japan." *Japanese Economic Studies* 16 (Winter 1987–88): 3–37.
———. "Japan's Industrial Organization." *Japanese Economic Studies* 6 (Spring–Summer 1978): 3–67.
Imai, Masaaki. *Kaizen· The Key to Japan's Competitive Success.* New York: Random House, 1986.
Ishizaki, Tadao. "Is Japan's Income Distribution Equal? An International Comparison." *Japanese Economic Studies* 14 (Winter 1985–86): 30–55.
Junzo, Ishii. "Competitive Strategy of Japanese Business." *Japanese Economic Studies* 15 (Winter 1986–87): 3–48.
Kagono, Tadao, Ikujira Nonaka, Kiyonori Sakakibara, and Akihiro Okumura. "Strategic Adaptation to Environment: Japanese and U.S. Firms Compared." *Japanese Economic Studies* 12 (Winter 1983–84): 33–80.
Kano, Koshikazu. "Japanese Agriculture: It Can Be Revitalized." *Japanese Economic Studies* 11 (Spring 1985): 34–66.
Kaplan, Eugene. *Japan: The Government-Business Relationship.* Washington, D.C.: U.S. Government Printing Office, 1972.
Kawahito, Kyoshi. "Relative Profitability of the U.S. and Japanese Steel Industries." *Columbia Journal of World Business* 19 (Fall 1984): 13–17.
Kiyonari, Tadao, and Hideichiro Nakamura. "Establishment of the Big Business System." *Japanese Economic Studies* 6 (Fall 1977): 3–40.
Koike, Kazuo. "Japan's Industrial Relations: Characteristics and Problems." *Japanese Economic Studies* 7 (Fall 1978): 42–90.
———. "Blue-Collar Proficiency is Key to Japan's Success." *The Oriental Economist* 49 (August 1981): 6–10.
Komiya, Ryutaro. "Japan's Non-Tariff Barriers on Manufactures." Paper presented to the Fourth Pacific Trade and Development Conference, Ottawa, Canada (October 1971).

——. "Planning in Japan." In Bornstein Morris, ed. *Economic Planning: East and West*. Cambridge, Mass.: Ballinger, 1975, pp. 189–227.

——. "Industrial Policy in Japan." *Japanese Economic Studies* 14 (Summer 1986): 51–81.

Kure, Bunji. "Window Guidance of the Bank of Japan." *Japanese Economic Studies* 6 (Winter 1977–78): 42–70.

Lockwood, W. W., ed. *The State and Economic Enterprise in Japan*. Princeton: Princeton University Press, 1965.

Magota, Ryohei. "The End of the Seniority-Related (*Nenko*) Wage System." *Japanese Economic Studies* 7 (Spring 1979): 71–125.

Miyazaki, K. "Rapid Acceleration in Money and Capital Liberalization." *The Oriental Economist* 53 (May 1985): 4–11.

Mizuno, Asao. "Wage Flexibility and Employment Changes." *Japanese Economic Studies* 16 (Winter 1987–88): 38–73

Muramatsu, Kuramitsu. "The Effect of Wages on Employment in Japan." *Japanese Economic Studies* 15 (Spring 1987): 29–57.

Naito, S. "Victors and Losers in 'Free' Interest Rate Era." *The Oriental Economist*, 53 (November–December 1985): 20–33.

Nakamura, Hideichiro. "Japan, Incorporated and Postwar Democracy." *Japanese Economic Studies* 15 (Spring–Summer 1978): 68–109.

——. "The Challenge of Japanese Small Business." *Japanese Economic Studies* 15 (Fall 1986): 76–101.

Nakamura, Takafusa. "Japan's Giant Enterprises: Their Power and Influence." *Japanese Economic Studies* 12 (Summer 1984a): 50–90.

——. *The Postwar Japanese Economy: Its Development and Structure*. Tokyo: University of Tokyo Press, 1984b.

Ohkawa, Kazushi, and Henry Rosovsky. *Japanese Economic Growth*. Stanford, Calif.: Stanford University Press, 1973.

Ozaki, Robert S. *The Control of Imports and Foreign Capital in Japan*. New York: Praeger, 1972.

Patrick, Hugh, and Henry Rosovsky, eds. *Asia's New Giant: How the Japanese Economy Works*. Washington, D.C.: Brookings, 1976.

Pucik, Vladimir. "White Collar Human Resource Management: A Comparison of the U.S. and Japanese Automobile Industries." *Columbia Journal of World Business* 19 (Fall 1984): 87–94.

Rabino, Sam, and Elva Ellen Hubbard. "The Race of American and Japanese Personal Computer Manufacturers for Dominance of the U.S. Market." *Columbia Journal of World Business* 19 (Fall 1984): 18–31.

Rapp, William V. "Japan: Its Industrial Policies and Corporate Behavior." *Columbia Journal of World Business* 12 (Spring 1977): 38–48.

Royama, Shoichi. "The Japanese Financial System: Past, Present, and Future." *Japanese Economic Studies* 12 (Winter 1983–84): 3–32.

Sano, Yoko. "Seniority-Based Wages in Japan—A Survey." *Japanese Economic Studies* 5 (Spring 1977): 48–65.

Saxonhouse, Gary R. "A Tale of Technological Diffusion in the Meiji Period." *Journal of Economic History* 34 (March 1974): 149–165.

Shimada, Haruo, and Shunsaku Nishikawa. "An Analysis of Japanese Employment System and Youth Labor Market." *Keio Economic Studies* 16, 1–2 (1979): 1–16.

Shimokawa, Koichi. "Japan's *Keiretsu* System: The Case of the Automobile Industry." *Japanese Economic Studies* 13 (Summer 1985): 3–31.

Shinozuka, Eiko. "Employment Adjustment in Japanese Manufacturing." *Japanese Economic Studies* 15 (Spring 1987): 3–28.

Simmons, Angus. "Recent Social Security Developments in Japan." *Social Security Bul-*

letin 41 (October 1978): 26–30.

"Sogo Shosha in Revival." *The Oriental Economist* 53 (April 1985): 26–41.

Sumiya, Mikio. "Japanese Industrial Relations Revisited: A Discussion of the *Nenko* System." *Japanese Economic Studies* 5 (Spring 1977): 3–47.

Suzuki, Naohito. "Japanese-Style Management and its Transferability." *Japanese Economic Studies* 12 (Spring 1984): 64–79.

Tachi, Ryuichiro. "The Softization of the Japanese Economy." *Japanese Economic Studies* 13 (Spring 1985): 67–104.

Takamiya, Makoto. "Japanese Multinationals in Europe: Internal Operations and Their Public Policy Implications." *Columbia Journal of World Business* 16 (Summer 1981): 5–17.

Taya, K. "Auto Industry: A Never-Ending War." *The Oriental Economist* 53 (November–December 1985): 14–18.

Thurow, L. C., R. Engle, L. D'Andrea, R. Hartmann, and C. Pigott. *Foreign Experience with Monetary Policies to Promote Economic and Social Priority Programs.* Staff report of the Committee on Banking and Currency of the U.S. House of Representatives. Washington, D.C.: U.S. Government Printing Office May, 1972, pp. 63–139.

Tsurumi, Yoshi, and Hiroki Tsurumi. "Value-Added Maximizing Behavior of Japanese Firms and the Roles of Corporate Investment and Finance." *Columbia Journal of World Business* 20 (Spring 1985): 29–35.

Woronoff, Jon. *Japan's Commercial Empire.* Armonk, N.Y.: M. E. Sharpe, 1984.

———. "Fading Role of Entrepreneurs." *The Oriental Economist* 53 (June 1985): 35–37.

Yamamura, Kozo. *Economic Policy in Postwar Japan.* Berkeley: University of California Press, 1967.

Yakabe, K. *Labor Relations in Japan: Fundamental Characteristics.* Tokyo: Int'l Society for Educational Information, 1974.

Yanaga, Chitoshi. *Big Business in Japanese Politics.* New Haven: Yale University Press, 1968.

Yoshida, Satoru. "Japanese Financial Innovation." *Japanese Economic Studies* 15 (Summer 1987): 67–96.

Yoshikai, Masanori. "R. and D. and Technology Policy in Japan." *Japanese Economic Studies* 14 (Summer 1986): 3–50.

15

THE SWEDISH ECONOMY: BASIC FEATURES

15-1. Introduction: Basic Features of the Swedish Economy

Most people think of Sweden as the archetypal welfare state, and this reputation is well deserved. Every Swede enjoys social insurance protection against illness, old age, disability, unemployment, obsolescence of job skills, and virtually every other kind of economic misfortune. To pay for this, Sweden has the world's highest taxes, and government participation in the economy is considerable. But Sweden also has a tradition of entrepreneurship and a rate of new product development that is remarkable for such a small country. More than 80 percent of its material means of production are privately owned. Because it has long had low barriers to imports, it must export more than 40 percent of her industrial output and 30 percent of GNP to maintain the balance of payments. Thus, much of Swedish industry is competitive, despite the small domestic market, and efficient by world standards. The powerful Swedish labor unions have played a role in promoting this efficiency.

To some observers, Sweden seems schizophrenic. Virtually everyone is guaranteed a decent living standard, and steeply progressive taxes limit the accumulation of wealth. The extremes of poverty and affluence are largely avoided. However, this is superimposed on a competitive system where entrepreneurship and efficiency are highly prized. Even today, half or more of all blue-collar workers have substantial portions of their wages geared to piece rates, a fact that has horrified visiting labor leaders from other countries. Swedish managers have also had more authority to direct and to discipline labor than their counterparts in North

America or Western Europe, although this authority was eroded during the 1970s by the drive toward "democracy at the workplace." Beginning in that decade, efforts to build a union-based version of industrial democracy became one of the most explosive political issues of this century.

Some authors have labeled Sweden "socialist" in terms of distribution, but "capitalist" in term of production.[1] Perhaps it would be better to say today, as Marquis Childs did over 50 years ago, that Sweden represents a "middle way" between the extremes of collectivism and individualism. The essence of this middle way is a fusing of socialist concerns for equality and well-being with a capitalist emphasis on efficiency in production. Modern socialist nations do not try to achieve a just income distribution via progressive personal income taxes and subsidies to households with anything like the zeal displayed by Sweden. In addition, most socialist countries have practiced extreme forms of job protection that grant specific workers rights to specific kinds of jobs in specific firms. The threat to jobs in obsolete and potentially insolvent enterprises has held back progress in the Hungarian economic reform, for example. Sweden has long had low unemployment, but until the mid-1970s, job protection was mainly general. Every Swede had a right to work and to be retrained free of charge when necessary, but he or she usually had limited rights to a specific job, and this attitude is reaffirmed by the 1982 Agreement on Efficiency and Participation between labor and management.

It is still true that, when a firm is teetering on the brink of insolvency, the relevant labor union may make wage demands that force the company out of business. Historically, unions have opposed rescues of marginally efficient enterprises, maintaining that it is in the best interests of workers and of society for these firms to shut down, thereby releasing labor to more productive and better paying work. In contrast to unions in other countries, both East and West, the Swedish labor movement has promoted the elimination of low-productivity jobs, along with labor mobility, worker retraining, and Sweden's specialization on the world market according to comparative advantage. This has been made possible by the financial security of the welfare state and by Sweden's large investment in worker retraining. An active labor market policy seeks to combine job security with flexibility in production by promoting occupational and geographical mobility of labor. In this respect, it serves as a model for socialist reformers in Eastern Europe. Nevertheless, in the wake of the growth slowdown following the energy crisis, Swedish unions have moved toward more conventional attitudes on layoffs, plant closings, and specific job protection.

Similarly, to label Swedish industry "capitalist" overlooks the fact that today Swedish managers of privately owned firms generally have more restricted property rights than their counterparts in other Western nations. Swedish employers face the world's strongest labor unions and are, themselves, tightly organized to develop countervailing power, which requires some loss of independence by individual companies. Since the mid-1970s, several laws plus union pressure and the need to compete for labor with the expanding public sector have forced firms to pay growing attention to job safety, job enrichment, and the working environment. Sweden is a world leader in promoting occupational health and safety, in supporting disadvantaged workers, in some aspects of industrial democracy, and in the struggles to conserve energy and preserve the environment. In the 1988 election campaign, environmental issues came to the fore. Although Swedish unions have often favored compromises on environmental quality to create or preserve jobs, the head of the Metal Workers' union recently argued that some polluting factories should be closed, even if this caused unemployment to rise.

It has also become harder in recent years for Swedish managers to exercise their traditional decision-making rights. For example, employers must now give two to six months' notice—depending on the number of employees involved—to the county employment board before making production cutbacks that will require dismissals. As well, they must notify the relevant labor union and give one to six months' notice to each affected employee. (Likewise, an individual must give one month's written notice before quitting his job.) During the period of notice, a worker receives full wages, and he must be dismissed on "reasonable" grounds, as ultimately interpreted by a special labor court. Unless his contract specifically allows it, no worker can be laid off if the firm has jobs to offer. In addition, a 1976 law has altered management's traditional right to "direct and allot the work" in sweeping fashion, so that companies must codetermine work rules and job assignments with the unions. If the latter so request, codetermination rights must also be extended to investment, finance, marketing, and production, although such extensions have, in practice, been limited.

The government's powerful Labor Market Board, which implements labor market policies, also controls many fiscal policy instruments, as well as the allocation of building permits. It can often use its authority to induce a firm to change its employment practices in "socially desirable" ways, such as increasing its percentage of older or of teenage workers. It can require companies to hire a certain number of partially disabled workers, although it also gives subsidies to this end. Finally, Swedish firms now face some of the world's stiffest environmental regulations and are responding, in part, by developing world leadership in environmental technology.

The Social Democratic party, which has ruled Sweden since the Great Depression, except over 1976–82, has generally followed a policy of "functional socialism." Instead of nationalizing property, it has nationalized specific property rights. In the 1930s, a prominent Social Democrat said, "We shall not abolish the right of ownership, just make it meaningless." In fact, socialization has not gone this far, and Social Democratic governments have tried to promote efficiency and steady growth, as well as equity, a high quality of life, and most recently, union-based industrial democracy. Today, Sweden has one of the world's highest living standards.

It has also been a laboratory for socioeconomic change. During the 1970s, it followed a largely unexpected evolution, in which considerations of redistribution and industrial democracy tended to push aside those of efficiency, at what turns out to have been a bad time (the aftermath of the energy crisis). The public sector also expanded at the expense of Sweden's export industries, on which its livelihood depends. As a result, the "middle way" has been "on trial," as Childs recently put it, although a renewed emphasis on efficiency, profitability, and export expansion during the 1980s has brought a revival of optimism. The main features of the Swedish economy, as of 1988, are as follows:

(a) It is basically a market economy, but also one of the world's foremost welfare states, providing all manner of "womb to tomb" social insurance protection. Marginal tax rates on personal income are close to being highest in the world, despite a tax reform over 1983–85, and income redistribution remains a major concern of the central government.

(b) Private ownership prevails over most of the material means of production, although private property rights are in many ways restricted. Sweden also has one of the world's strongest union movements, which has achieved a measure of industrial democracy since the early 1970s.

(c) The weight and influence of the public sector in economic life have been growing since World War II, both to administer the expanding welfare state and to keep unemployment low. Government expenditure rose to two-thirds of GNP in 1982, before falling slightly, while current revenues of government (taxes plus social insurance fees) were close to 60 percent of GNP over 1983–85. Both ratios are highest in the world. More than half of government spending took the form of transfer payments—reflecting the welfare state, but also interest on the rising public debt—while most of the rest went for public consumption. The public sector's share of employment rose from 12 percent in 1965 to 38 percent in 1983, although many government employees are part-time workers. By contrast, industrial output showed a net decline over 1974–83, and the balance-of-payments current account registered nine deficits during this period, despite five devaluations of the Swedish crown. Sweden lost shares of nearly all important export markets, and there was general agreement by the late 1970s that the export sector had become too small, while the public sector had grown too large.

Spurred by a 16 percent devaluation in October 1982, plus restrictive policy at home, Sweden began the painful process of readjustment over 1983–84. Industrial output rose 16 percent between the first quarter of 1983 and the last quarter of 1984, but then stagnated again over the next two years. Balance-of-payments surpluses were finally achieved in 1984 and 1986, the latter at least partly because of a major decrease in oil prices. At the same time, unemployment fell from 3.5 percent of the labor force in 1983 to 1.9 percent in 1987, and the public-sector budget deficit, which was about 6.5 percent of GNP in 1982, had turned to surplus by 1987.

(d) Until the mid-1970s, the government used fiscal policy to successfully combat recessions, which were therefore less severe in Sweden, in terms of lost output and employment, than in most market economies. Until 1970, there were usually more job vacancies than unemployed, although the reverse has been more usual since then. Even so, unemployment averaged just over 2 percent for the 1970s, rising to 3.5 percent in 1983, before falling back, as noted above. Keeping unemployment low has been the government's top macroeconomic priority, but since 1970, it has had to rely heavily on its own expansion plus labor market measures to create new jobs. These measures include state-financed worker retraining, as well as subsidized and protected employment and make-work projects.

(e) The government also uses its weight to alter the composition of goods and services produced—mainly via social insurance, public spending on goods and services, and a variety of taxes and subsidies that encourage production in some industries and regions more than in others. In particular, state leverage over the allocation of credit, within a system of credit rationing, has increased the availability of finance for housing and public borrowing during most of the postwar period, although financial deregulation took place over 1978–86.

(f) We may call most of the measures under (d) and (e) *demand management* because they alter the level and composition of the nation's demand for goods and services. By contrast, active labor market policy seeks to adapt the supply of and demand for labor to one another in terms of skill mix and geographical location. It tries to promote worker mobility to regions and industries where labor's marginal product is relatively high, a necessary condition for combining high wages and full employment with competitiveness on world markets, especially in periods of rapid structural change. In recent years, expansion of the public sector and a proliferation of subsidies to declining industries and regions have had an offsetting effect on labor mobility and productivity. Along with high marginal tax rates on personal incomes, they have held back the movement of labor to firms whose export potential is greatest. To improve matters, the 1983–85 tax reform modestly raised income incentives for most workers, and relative expansion of the public sector has at last been halted. Restructuring of export industries, begun during the latter 1970s, has made progress, and most support for ailing firms has ended, allowing more public funds for promotion of growth and renewal.

(g) Government and government officials in Sweden are open in a way that makes a Watergate-type scandal there unlikely. At the same time, Swedish society is highly conformist and revolves around the activities of well-organized groups. Partly for these reasons, direct negotiation between major special interest groups (which are also lobbies or political pressure groups) plays an important role in economic and political life.

We shall examine (g) below and leave the others for later discussion. Writing in 1983, Nils Lundgren, chief economist at Sweden's second largest commercial bank, looked forward to a new era of industrial growth, following a decade of stagnation.[2] But he also saw three threats to successful reindustrialization. First was the risk of a wage explosion, following several devaluations of the Swedish crown and several years of low pay increases. (After a threefold rise of real industrial wages over 1950–76, there was virtually no net gain between 1976 and 1986, and after-tax real wages fell.) Second was the threat of continuing public sector expansion or support for declining industries, which could hold back the flow of resources into sectors with growth potential on world markets. Finally came the threat of employee investment funds, discussed in section 15-8, which were originally designed as a vehicle to take over most of Swedish industry and change the economic system in a fundamental way. Lundgren was optimistic that these hazards would be overcome and that Swedish industry could look forward to at least a decade of "reasonably successful" growth. At end-1986, Dr. Lundgren was more guarded, largely because of wage-cost and other inflationary pressures, along with falling growth, but his basic outlook was still optimistic.[3]

Before going further, we orient the reader by noting that, geographically, Sweden is a Scandinavian country sharing the Scandinavian peninsula with Norway. It is the fourth largest country in Europe, after the USSR, France, and Spain, and is about the same size as California (or somewhat larger than the Canadian province of Newfoundland and Labrador). It is nearly as far north as the Yukon or Alaska, but enjoys a temperate climate, thanks to the Gulf Stream. Sweden's population of 8.35 million is about one-third of California's and fifth from the bottom in Europe. Her population density is about 70 percent of that of the United States. Despite two waves of immigration in the 1960s, Sweden retains a fair degree of ethnic homogeneity. Today, immigration is tightly controlled, except from the Nordic area (Finland, Norway, Denmark, Iceland), within which labor from each Nordic nation may move freely. About 85 percent of all Swedes live south of a line approximately 100 miles north of Stockholm, in 40 percent of the country's land area. Most agriculture and industry are found here. The north contains most of the forest land, but is sparsely populated, with just 13 inhabitants per square mile. Yet, around 40 percent of Sweden's unemployment is in the north. Her population is about 70 percent urban, in the sense of living in cities and towns with more than 2,000 residents. Around 17 percent of all Swedes are 65 or over, one of the highest percentages of senior citizens in the world.

Sweden is also rich in natural resources, mainly forests, iron ore, iron pyrites, hydroelectric power sites, and several minerals. It lacks petroleum reserves, however, and must import nearly all its needs, as well as 75 percent of its total energy requirements. It hopes to reduce oil consumption by 40–45 percent over 1980–1990. In 1986, 53 percent of its electricity was hydropower, but this was down from 88 percent in 1955, and the best sites have either been harnessed or are protected on environmental grounds. Hence, much of the current emphasis is on nuclear power, which accounted for over 40 percent of electricity generated in 1986 and whose development and exploitation were ratified in a 1980 referendum. The same referendum decided to phase out atomic power stations over the very long run, however, and all are to shut down by 2010. The Chernobyl accident has reinforced these decisions. (Sweden received much of the fall-out from that disaster, and the world first learned of it from Sweden.)

Sweden is a parliamentary democracy with (since 1976) a single 349-seat Parliament known as the *Riksdag*. Of its members, 310 are directly elected in universal suffrage by geographical district, while 39 are appointed, in such a way that each political party's relative parliamentary strength closely approximates its relative vote total in the whole country. Each member of Parliament is expected to support his or her party's platform, and political party discipline is strong. However, minority government is made more likely by the ability of the executive branch to pass its proposals into law whenever a majority of the Riksdag does not vote against them. (A majority in favor is not required.) To avoid proliferation of political parties, none may hold seats in the Riksdag unless it gains at least 4 percent of the national vote or 12 percent within a particular constituency. General elections now take place every three years, in which candidates are elected to office at all three levels of government (national, county, and municipal). Voter turnout is usually over 90 percent of those eligible—mainly Swedish citizens, aged 18 years or older.

The central government tends to dominate the 23 county and 284 municipal governments, although a 1977 reform strengthened the latter and greatly reduced the detail in central government regulation of lower government levels. Further decentralization is taking place during the 1980s. Nevertheless, Sweden will continue to have a unitary system of government, in contrast to the federal systems of Yugoslavia, the United States, Canada, and West Germany, which grant greater financial independence and autonomy to regional authorities. Until 1975, Sweden was governed by the Constitution of 1809, when the monarch was dominant, and the spirit of that Constitution still prevails. The executive branch has inherited considerable power from the monarchy.

In one way, Sweden is more democratic than most other Western countries. This relates to the formal openness of government—sometimes dubbed the "principle of the goldfish bowl." The foundation of this openness is the Freedom of the Press Act, essentially dating from 1812 and now one of the three basic acts that form the Swedish Constitution. (These acts are basic in the sense that they can only be amended or repealed if Parliament votes to do this on two occasions separated by a general election.) According to the Freedom of the Press Act, all government documents must be made available to any citizen who wants to see them for any reason whatever, which need not be disclosed. There is a Secrecy Act which defines a narrow category of exceptions, including documents relating to national security and foreign policy. When authorities reject an application for a specific document, they must tell the applicant where he can appeal.

Information not specifically labelled secret by the Secrecy Act must be produced promptly, properly indexed for public inspection. Information cannot be withheld simply on grounds of inconvenience or because no decision has yet been reached on an issue. The press regularly exercises its right to learn about the "background of decisions: the complex of facts, arguments, interests, motives, on the basis of which an authority has decided or is going to decide."[4] Not only does any government employee have the right to provide the press with information not specifically excluded by the Secrecy Act, but it is a criminal offense for an official to try to discover the source of such a leak. The anonymity of journalists' information sources is fully protected by the Freedom of the Press Act.

Such openness affects the activities of political pressure groups representing business, labor, and other special interests. In Sweden, even more than in most Western-style democracies, these groups play a major role in social goal formation, and the spirit of compromise and consensus is strong. The Freedom of the Press Act reinforces the compromise nature of policy making by making it harder for government officials to deal in secret with representatives of some pressure groups while excluding others. The government also subsidizes organizations representing such economic interests as blue-collar workers, salaried employees, private businesses, consumers, and farmers. The result is a form of political corporatism in which the various communities of interest are forced to bargain with one another, in order to reach compromises that ultimately become part of government policy. The government promotes this process in some instances and keeps a low profile in others, intervening only when negotiations break down.

As well, it is usual for boards of enquiry, government commissions, special courts, and policy-implementing agencies to be made up of representatives of all the various interested parties. For example, the powerful Labor Market Board has 24 county offices, each headed by a county labor board. The latter are chaired by county governors and contain representatives of the Swedish Employers' Confederation (SAF), the country's dominant management organ; LO, the confederation of blue-collar labor unions; TCO and SACO, the white-collar union confederations, and, usually, one representative of female labor and one from agriculture. This arrangement is duplicated in the 24-member board at the top of the national organization. The big special interest groups—called "associations" in Sweden—are represented, in turn, on many government agencies and are brought into social goal formation in other ways that we shall indicate. Many members of Parliament represent specific associations, and delegates from two or more associations with conflicting interests will often find themselves side by side on the same board or panel.

For example, the Labor Court, the last resort for settling labor disputes, consists of three senior jurists (including the chairman and vice-chairman), two delegates from SAF, two from LO, and one from TCO. The Labor Market Council, a permanent labor-management forum for discussing and mediating labor disputes and problems, consists of three representatives from each of labor and management and is presided over by an impartial judge. While most of its decisions are nonbinding, its recommendations are usually accepted. Other joint labor-management efforts include the Joint Industrial Safety Council, the Joint Industrial Training Council, the Joint Female Labor Council, and the Joint Rationalization Council, which is charged with improving job satisfaction, job security, and labor productivity. None of these has enforcement power, but once again recommendations are usually accepted, partly because both sides are represented and have a fair opportunity to present their points of view.

There is also a joint council composed of members of LO and of the large Consumer Cooperative Chain, the Kooperativa Förbundet (KF), probably the foremost spokesman for consumers in the country, to discuss problems and policies of mutual interest. Finally, the special Market Court, charged with protecting consumer interests and applying the Restrictive Trade Practices Act (against abuse of monopoly power), consists of a tribunal with representatives from consumers, labor, and business, under an impartial chairman. It generally tries to eliminate abuses, first by negotiating with the parties involved. If it fails, it has only limited power to apply sanctions; nevertheless, its recommendations are usually accepted. In fact, Swedish competition policy is not based on criminal sanctions, for the most part. The Competition and Consumer Ombudsmen prosecute few cases. Most complaints are resolved by negotiating solutions without going to court, which is in the spirit of the Restrictive Trade Practices Act.[5]

The above examples could be multiplied to show that the major special interests in Sweden have learned to cooperate on a continuing basis, to settle their problems in many instances with a minimum of official government intervention, to act responsibly (since they clearly are responsible for agreements reached between them), and to educate their members and supporters on the constraints that must be accepted if efficient goal formation is to be possible. The result is considerable self-discipline, self-reliance, and self-policing by the various interest groups.[6]

Finally, we note that, thanks to more than a century of economic growth, Sweden has one of the world's highest levels of per capita income and output. Excluding the oil-rich Middle Eastern states, it ranks sixth in the world, behind the United States, Norway, Canada, Luxembourg, and Switzerland. In purchasing power, Swedish GNP per capita was about $12,300 U.S. in 1985, or a bit less than 75 percent of the U.S. level ($16,750).[7] Over 1952–85, it grew to 2.35 times its former size in real terms, or at an annual rate of 2.6 percent. This was near the median growth of OECD nations. (Because Sweden's population growth was below average, however, the rate of increase in GNP was below the OECD median.) Unfortunately, stagnation has been a problem in recent years, along with budget and balance-of-payments deficits. Real GNP per head rose by only 13 percent over the entire decade, 1976–85. Since 1976, Sweden has had one of the lowest growth rates in the OECD.

Sweden is still one of the world's most affluent societies. There are nearly two passenger cars and more than two dwellings for every five residents. Over 95 percent of all households own a TV set, while more than 90 percent own or have easy access to a refrigerator, a washing machine, and a vacuum cleaner. Sweden has one of the world's lowest infant mortalities, longest life expectancies, and highest rates of per capita energy and animal protein consumption. As a share of GNP, its public expenditure on education and health care are the highest in the world, and Sweden also contributes a higher percentage of its GNP in the form of official aid to developing nations than any other country except the Netherlands.

15-2. The Swedish System of Labor Relations

When writers refer to a "Swedish model," they usually have one or more of the following in mind: (1) Sweden's extensive welfare state; (2) its system of collective bargaining and labor relations, including the institutions for promoting cooperation between labor and management; and (3) its policies to promote prosperity, in combination with better economic opportunities and improved working and living environments. A key part of this model since World War II has been Sweden's system of wage determination. Over 1952–82, and again in 1986, central negotiations set the basic guidelines for determining most wages and salaries in the country. By Swedish law, a labor contract is signed between an industry association (usually belonging to SAF) on behalf of employers and a national union representing all blue- or all white-collar workers in an industry. The Swedish Constitution gives a collective bargaining monopoly to these bodies, and there are grievance procedures, as well as provision for mediation, should negotiations break down.

However, under centralized negotiations, industry-level bargaining has mainly decided how to apply the central agreement, covering the nation as a whole, where major issues are concerned. Local-level bargaining has been similarly circumscribed by the industry-wide as well as national agreement. Of the three, the central negotiations, usually every two or three years, have been most important, although the resulting agreement is presented to industry associations and to unions as a suggestion. Such "suggestions" are accepted, because the negotiating parties—notably, SAF on behalf of private employers and LO on behalf of blue-collar employees—have financial leverage over their memberships.

Until 1977, the central agreement was negotiated by LO and SAF. In making its own demands, TCO, the largest white-collar union confederation, followed the pattern set in the LO-SAF talks. But since 1977, white-collar representatives have been more actively involved, a reflection of their growing share of the labor force. Besides TCO, there is a second white-collar union confederation, SACO/SR, which organizes mainly professional people with university-level degrees. SACO/SR has about 270,000 members vs. 2.2 million in LO and 1.1 million in TCO.[8] Frequently, SACO/SR unions have not considered themselves bound by the centrally negotiated guidelines. LO has consistently followed a "solidaristic" policy of seeking to equalize earnings by asking higher percentage wage increases for less well-paid employees. This was its main reason for wanting centralized collective bargaining, which constrains unions representing better paid workers from negotiating the highest wage increases they can get. Thus, the incomes of SACO/SR members have generally risen more slowly than the national average since 1950, and the government has encouraged this tendency by subsidizing an expanded supply of university graduates. SACO/SR has been involved in a few sharp disputes—notably, the 1986 doctors' strike under the slogan, "An education should pay." At least one death may have resulted from this.

TCO and SACO/SR do not participate directly in collective bargaining. For this purpose, TCO unions are organized into three agencies—the Civil Servants' Section (TCO-S), the Federation of Salaried Local Government Employees (KTK), and the Private Salaried Staffs' Cartel (PTK). PTK includes six unions from TCO plus 14 from SACO/SR and one independent union—representing 560,000 employees in all, 90 percent of whom work for SAF-affiliated companies—which have joined forces to increase their bargaining strength (vis-à-vis LO as well as SAF). TCO-S and KTK negotiate, respectively, with the central and local government employers' associations, while PTK negotiates with SAF. SACO/SR public-sector unions are also organized into bargaining agencies for the local and national government sectors. After 1977, LO and PTK coordinated their negotiations with SAF.

The importance of the central negotiations is underscored by the fact that over 85 percent of all blue-collar workers belong to one of LO's twenty-four member unions, while over 75 percent of organizable white-collar workers belong to one of the twenty TCO unions. Employers must extend the terms of union contracts to nonunion workers. (The union shop is outlawed in Sweden, although the best unemployment insurance is tied to union membership, and there are strong social pressures to join.) For its part, SAF embraces 35 employers' associations with around 43,000 member firms, employing over 1.25 million people—60 percent of whom are LO members. Over 80 percent of these companies employ twenty-five workers or less, but most of Sweden's major manufacturing concerns are also included. Together, 160 large firms, each with more than 1,000 employees, employ 40 percent of the labor force encompassed by SAF.

Historically, SAF arose primarily as a strike-insurance society, and it retains that role. Thus, it pays a small sum per worker per day to each strike-bound company that is affiliated with a member association and in good standing. During some recent wildcat strikes, SAF has reimbursed affected companies fully, including compensation for lost profits. Firms threatened with union organization for the first time usually join employer associations affiliated with SAF, if they have not already done so. The national unions belonging to LO and to TCO also have substantial strike funds, but these can be used to compensate striking workers only if the walkout has been approved by the national union board. (Wildcat strikers do not receive strike pay.) As well, SAF, LO, and TCO each have major information and public relations programs. SAF's medical department collects statistics and does research on industrial illness and accidents, and SAF and LO collaborate on joint research projects. Together, they have founded the Labor Market Vocational Council to advance vocational education.

Nevertheless, their main function has been to negotiate the central collective agreements. In addition to pay guidelines, these usually include a social package of prescriptions about pensions, accident insurance, working hours, the working environment, and so forth. To assure central control, SAF can require each industry-level contract to be submitted to it for approval before signing, and a company paying wages above agreed-on levels can be fined. Affiliated firms must also respect its instructions on interpretation of agreements reached between it and LO, although there is normally room for further interpretation and detail at the industry-wide and local levels. Finally, firms must respect SAF policies on managerial issues and working conditions, unless these violate existing agreements. No affiliated firm or industry may order a lockout without SAF's consent, but a two-thirds majority of SAF's General Council can require a member to order a lockout.

Similarly, national unions affiliated with LO have adopted almost identical constitutions, requiring decisions on strikes and other industrial actions to be taken by the national union board which controls the purse strings of the locals. But a national union cannot order a strike involving more than 3 percent of its membership without LO's consent. The union cannot call a smaller strike if this is expected to cause a lockout involving over 3 percent of its members.

From an efficiency standpoint, the main potential advantage of centralized bargaining over industry-by-industry negotiations is that parties to the central negotiations cannot ignore the costs of "spillovers." Actions which raise wages and profits in one sector, at the expense of others or of the public, are less likely to be taken. When LO is unreasonable in its wage demands, for example, inflation invariably wipes out part of the resulting increase. Moreover, because of Sweden's exposed trading position, wage-cost inflation at home that exceeds wage-cost increases in nations whose industries compete with Sweden's on world markets will lead to domestic unemployment or to devaluation of the crown, which raises consumer prices further. Thus, LO and PTK have had to bargain in terms of real rather than of money earnings, which is to say that they have had to consider any erosion of workers' purchasing power resulting from the inflationary consequences of their own demands. In addition, while higher pollution levels may benefit one industry, much of the population affected by the pollution is likely to belong to LO, PTK, or SAF, or to have close relatives who do. This cost is not external to the central bargaining. The same is true, e.g., of relaxed safety standards for trucks, trains, air, or water traffic. Part of the cost will fall on other users of transport facilities, many of whom are represented at the negotiating table.

This contrasts with the usual collective bargaining on an industry-by-industry or craft-by-craft basis, where no representative of society as a whole is present. Then, one industry or union has an incentive to try to shift part of the costs of its gains onto others. For example, work stoppage in a major industry or profession can bring large parts of the economy to a halt, even though many who are affected are not parties to the dispute. Even a large union in a basic industry will find the impact of its wage demands on overall inflation to be small. By negotiating large wage increases, steel workers may raise the price of steel, but part of the cost of this will fall on third parties. The same is true of inflationary wage gains in any one industry, although not of inflationary increases in all industries together. However, when industry-by-industry negotiations prevail, no one bargains on behalf of all employers or all wage earners. The union that shows restraint in its wage demands is apt to fall behind, while its officers fail to win reelection.

In Sweden, the central wage talks have been mainly about how national income and output were going to be divided. With three qualifications, both sides have sought to make income and output as large as possible. This is why both LO and SAF promote the world's best developed and most expensive programs for retraining, relocating, and reemploying labor, following dismissals. It is also why LO cooperates extensively with management, agrees to productivity bonuses for most workers (although it prefers these to be based on the productivity of a work team rather than of an individual), helps to push inefficient firms into bankruptcy, and advocates free international trade. These policies have all tended to raise income, output, and, thus, wages, for any given wage share of national income.

The exceptions to the policy of national income and output maximization relate, first of all, to the quality of living and working environments. Both LO and TCO are willing to sacrifice production and income for a more humane work place (including more employee control over conditions of work, less stress and boredom, more job safety, and less alienation) and also for less pollution. However, this is consistent with efficiency when account is taken of the fact that individuals derive pain and pleasure in other ways than from consuming goods and services they buy in the market. The second exception relates to long-run vs. short-run effects of union bargaining power. If unions raise the current wage-and-salary share of national income, at the expense of profits and other property income, they may also reduce domestic investment, either by reducing investment yields or by reducing the pool of savings available to finance investment—since the percentage of labor income that is saved is usually lower than the savings share of property income.[9] This would trim the growth of capital, which would have a depressing effect on future real wages. To avoid such a result, the union movement would have to find a way of increasing savings out of labor income and of ensuring wise investment of these increases. LO has sponsored legislation to this end, as we shall see.

The final exception has been the policy of wage solidarity. Since the early 1950s, LO has tried to equalize wage differentials between industries, regions, and skills, and this complements its efforts to raise wages relative to property income and to executive salaries. Since 1970, Social Democratic governments have also sought to compress pay differentials within the public sector. Wage solidarity is part of the foundation of the Swedish union movement and the major reason why LO has favored centralized negotiations.

15-3. Wage Solidarity

Wage solidarity is sometimes described as "equal pay for equal work." LO believes that wages should not depend on the profitability of the company paying them. Neither should they depend on industry or geographic region. It is in pursuit of wage solidarity that LO has pushed marginal companies into bankruptcy or merger by sustaining wage demands these firms could not afford. Such "low-wage adjustments" have been a major area of dispute between LO and SAF. LO has not demanded complete wage equality, realizing that different training requirements, accident risks, working conditions, regional living costs, and other factors must cause wages to diverge to some degree. Yet, the thrust of its demands has been toward making average wage differences between industries less than average differences in productivity.

Wage solidarity has increasingly been interpreted in this way, at a cost of many failures among firms in textiles and other light industries. These companies could not cope simultaneously with low-wage adjustments and increased competition from developing countries, 90 percent of whose exports to Sweden enter duty-free. Today, Swedish textile and clothing workers are better paid, relative to textile and clothing workers in other countries, than are Swedish engineering workers, relative to their counterparts abroad—which goes a long way toward explaining the comparative success of these two industries in Sweden. More generally, the correlation between average productivity and average earnings per employee across Swedish industrial firms is low.[10] High wages are almost as likely to go hand-in-hand with low as with high productivity, and the same is true of low wages. At times, this has helped to promote Swedish exports by restraining labor costs in key export industries. However, in combination with the government's commitment to full employment, pursuit of wage solidarity during the 1970s helped to inflate Sweden's labor costs and to depress her exports in the aftermath of the first energy crisis, as we shall see.

The drive to equalize blue-collar wages between industries has enjoyed some success, especially over 1965–75. In 1959, there was a 30 percent spread between average wages paid in the highest and lowest industries. By 1964, the gap had only narrowed to 26 percent, but by 1975, it was down to 14 percent, and in 1981, it was under 12 percent, although the trend subsequently reversed itself marginally. There has also been success in raising blue-collar wages relative to executive salaries, and in reducing the dispersion of white-collar incomes. Finally, the average hourly earnings of female industrial workers rose from 69 percent of those of men in 1960 to 90 percent in 1981. A 1980 law forbids all forms of sex discrimination on the job. In particular, it mandates equal pay for equal work, as well as equal opportunities for men and women. (However, the former has tended to preclude the latter. Since men and women must be paid the same for doing the same jobs, they don't get the same jobs.)

Wage solidarity has been less successful in reducing wage differences between skills. This is due to a substantial "wage drift," or movement of wages above levels prescribed by the central negotiations, which therefore become wage *floors*. In effect, the labor market will not sustain the wage equalization that LO and SAF agree on. Specifically, an excess supply of less skilled labor and workers in the north of Sweden has usually gone hand-in-hand with an excess demand for skilled workers, especially in the southern and central parts of the country, at negotiated wage rates. Rather than try to impose wage ceilings on short-handed firms, SAF has usually allowed them to increase pay above centrally agreed-on levels, thereby undoing, in part, the negotiated wage equalization. In some years, this wage drift has equalled or exceeded negotiated wage increases.

Because of its commitment to full employment, the Swedish government has stimulated aggregate demand enough to remove most of the disemployment effects of the relatively large negotiated wage increases for less well paid employees. Unfortunately, this has also been enough to generate inflation, especially during the early and mid-1970s, which harmed Sweden's ability to export. As well, there have been selective employment policies (retraining, a variety of subsidies for households and firms, public-sector expansion) to provide temporary jobs for and/or to recycle workers who are disemployed because their services are priced out of the market.

LO remains committed to wage solidarity as the most visible sign of a more general solidarity believed to be the cement that binds the disparate elements of the union movement together. By actively seeking as much equalization as they can get, LO's leaders believe they are maximizing their support among union members, as well as following the dictates of their own consciences. Yet, many well-paid workers have chafed under wage solidarity. Their displeasure has sometimes burst forth in wildcat strikes, and they have been quite willing to take advantage of wage-drift opportunities.[11] The two largest private-sector unions in LO (including the relatively well paid Metalworkers) formally renounced wage solidarity in 1986. Efforts to break out by unions representing workers with above-average earnings thwarted the central negotiations in 1983 and 1987 and may have helped to bring this institution to an end. Future collective bargaining will be more decentralized by industry and even by region or company. Profit sharing and result-based pay schemes have also made the earnings of Swedish workers less uniform in recent years.

Thus, the 1980s witnessed less aggressive pursuit of wage solidarity than the 1970s, and less equalization was achieved. From one perspective, this is a result of the more restrictive fiscal policy since 1982, in the face of record budget and balance-of-payments deficits. The government has been less able to remove the disemployment effects of large wage increases by stimulating aggregate demand. Given the commitment to full employment, this has put the burden of earnings equalization more squarely on labor market policies, whose role we shall discuss in sections 16-2 and 16-6 below.

15-4. The Record of Labor Peace

SAF has opposed wage solidarity, on grounds that it is inflationary and that it reduces the incentive for workers to improve their skills and performance. In return for accepting the central wage talks, SAF received guarantees of labor peace. By North American standards, strikes and lockouts are rare in Sweden. According to a Swedish official, "There is a balance of power on the Swedish labor market comparable to that between the United States, the Soviet Union, and China . . . the effects of a major conflict would be devastating, [and] everyone concerned knows this."[12] Thus, when one firm associated with SAF is struck, SAF will usually order other companies to lock out workers belonging to the striking union. Union solidarity may then cause the strike to spread further. Nationwide solidarity on both sides of the labor market threatens to escalate any labor dispute into a national confrontation. This prospect has helped to foster restraint, which improves the prospects for labor peace. In 1983, for example, Sweden lost 9.5 working days per 1,000 employees to labor disputes, trailing only Austria, which lost 0.18 days, West Germany, which lost 1.7 days, and Norway, which lost 3.5 days. Otherwise, Japan lost 12 days; France, 83.7; the United Kingdom, about 165; the United States, 171; Canada, 393; and Italy, 820. Figures for the decade 1972–81 show a similar ranking.

As an offset, Sweden also has one of the world's highest rates of absenteeism from work—a consequence of comprehensive health insurance, including sick pay, as well as strong employee protection against dismissal and high marginal taxation of personal incomes. Swedish sick pay comes to 90 percent or more of basic earnings, and no medical excuse is required for the first week of illness. The effort to introduce two qualifying days of illness before health insurance would begin compensating a worker for loss of pay may have caused the defeat of the non-socialist parties in the 1982 elections.[13] On an average day, over 15 percent of the labor force is absent from work.

Sweden has an elaborate system to promote labor peace, including several committees with representatives from both labor and management to handle grievances, problems, and disputes. To begin with, there are few strikes due to jurisdictional disputes because LO unions are organized on an industry-wide rather than on a craft or trade basis. TCO unions are organized along both industry and craft lines, but generally in such a way that an employer confronts just one TCO union. Moreover, there are grievance procedures and provisions for mediation, should contract negotiations break down. Although collective bargaining is not subject to compulsory arbitration, legislation does enter at three points:

> It makes existing collective agreements enforceable and compels arbitration in case of disputes over their interpretation or application. [It also] makes the intervention of a government mediator obligatory if the parties cannot reach agreement in negotiations for new contracts. . . . Once entered into, a contract is binding all along the line, from the national federations to the individual employers and union members.[14]

The role of mediation is crucial and is probably made easier by the policy of equal pay for equal work, which allows a mediator to suggest settlements with less specific information about each separate case. In addition, contracts are automatically renewed if neither labor nor management gives notice, usually three months before expiration.

Until recently (1977), in case of dispute over the interpretation of an existing collective agreement, the employer's interpretation prevailed, this being part of his extensive rights to manage. The union could then appeal to the Labor Court (where it usually lost), but it could not legally strike over an interpretation. Today, the union's interpretation prevails until the matter has been settled by court decision, and the employer may not lock out his workers or take punitive action against them in the meantime. Nor can strikes or lockouts occur legally while negotiations are in progress. In the event of illegal strikes, "the individual worker is personally responsible for a breach of the obligation to keep the industrial peace, and he may be brought to the Labor Court and sentenced to pay damages to the employer. Such cases happen several times every year."[15] Moreover, industrial actions taken in sympathy with illegal strikes or lockouts are themselves illegal.

When contract talks fail, employees may not strike nor may firms lock employees out until one week after official notice has been given. This week is filled with last-ditch efforts to avoid conflict, and it is only then that government mediators will enter a dispute to lead the negotiations. In fact, a mediator can only suggest a solution—or else that the parties agree to binding arbitration—but such is the prestige of the Mediation Commission that public opinion puts pressure on both LO and SAF to accept the mediator's recommendations. Prior to the 1980 general strike, there had been no major conflict between LO and SAF since the 1944 Metalworkers' strike. Today's commitment to labor peace contrasts with the agitation and strife of earlier periods, notably the General Strike of 1909 and the conflicts of the Great Depression years.

Although there was no contemporary follow-up, the first step toward peaceful settlement of disputes came in 1906 when SAF agreed to allow unions to organize freely and bargain collectively, in return for the following provision, written into most collective agreements until 1977: "The employer is entitled to direct and to allot the work, to hire and to dismiss workers at will, and to employ workers, whether they are organized or not." This became Article 32 of the SAF Constitution, which meant that SAF would withhold approval of collective agreements not containing it. Basic union rights were thereby exchanged for company rights to manage that were among the most extensive in the world. In 1928, the Riksdag passed the Labor Court Act, which still prevails, and the Collective Agreements Act, over bitter opposition from the Social Democrats and LO. The Labor Court Act set up the Labor Court, and the effect of the Collective Agreements Act, along with the Labor Court's interpretation of it, was to impose on both labor and management a firm obligation to settle disagreements peacefully.

Then, the Great Depression brought further labor-management unrest. In 1931, striking workers, backed by Communist sympathizers, attacked strikebreakers in the small northern town of Adalen. Police and soldiers guarding the strikebreakers opened fire, killing four strikers and one bystander, a ten-year-old girl. It was the worst incident in Sweden's history of labor-management relations. In 1933–34, a bitter ten-month strike in the construction industry embarrassed the newly elected

Social Democratic government, in view of its public works program designed to stimulate economic activity. At this time, Sweden had one of the worst labor-relations records in the Western world, and public pressure for government control over LO and SAF was growing. Historically, these organizations had been mutually acrimonious, but more conciliatory leaders had recently come to power on both sides, and each wanted to avoid government interference. This led them to open talks at the resort town of Saltsjöbaden, about twenty-five miles from Stockholm, in the spring of 1936. It was the off-season for the resort.

Thus, negotiators from SAF and LO "had their meals together, spent their evenings together, and, as they got to know each other better, talked openly and amicably about many things. The employers learned . . . about the union movement's aims, structure, and activities. The workers learned . . . about economics, management, and business. And so there was born a . . . new attitude, . . . a willingness to listen [and] to understand. . . ."[16] While traditional class antagonisms scarcely melted away, they did mellow, and the new attitude is referred to as the "Spirit of Saltsjöbaden." It implies mutual respect and responsible, realistic bargaining positions, which have been a part of most negotiations since the Saltsjöbaden Conference.

The Spirit of Saltsjöbaden, although intangible, was the most important outcome of the Saltsjöbaden meetings, but a Basic Agreement was also signed. It reinforced and went beyond the Collective Agreements Act by imposing a peace obligation on employers and unions. As a rule, LO and SAF stipulate that the old agreement shall remain in force until the new agreement goes into effect. The Basic Agreement also set up the Labor Market Council as a means of resolving industrial disputes covered by the peace obligation before taking them to the Labor Court (whose decisions cannot be appealed). This council consists of three delegates from LO/PTK and three from SAF under an impartial chairman. It will arbitrate disputes if both sides agree, but it usually acts as a negotiating forum. Finally, the basic agreement forbade coercion, discrimination, retaliation, and actions against parties not directly involved in a conflict. It also defined procedures for dismissing or laying off workers.

15-5. Storm Clouds

Thanks to Saltsjöbaden, government legislation to interfere in collective bargaining or to regulate LO or SAF was not brought down. Until the mid-1970s, Sweden had few labor laws. Nevertheless, by 1970, LO's goals were shifting toward more specific job protection and more extensive employee participation in management. The emphasis on wage solidarity grew, just as the costs of this policy were surfacing. Finally, the energy crisis struck in 1974. These and other factors have strained Swedish labor relations, increased the cost of labor disputes (although this remains low by international standards), and added an element of uncertainty to the future direction of Swedish society.

To begin with, an outbreak of wildcat strikes occurred over 1969–70, mainly among higher paid workers, and notably among iron-ore miners in the north of Sweden, working in government-owned mines. There were a number of grievances, including a gradual speedup of work pace and a deterioration of the working environment over many years. But wage solidarity was also a factor, and thus the strike was directed partly against the union movement. Strikes and lockouts also took place in the public sector in 1966 and 1971, where the right to strike had only existed since 1966. Again, relatively well paid employees were protesting efforts to level incomes, and there was a renewed burst of wildcat strikes over 1974–75 amid record industrial profits. This period witnessed disaffection, frustration, and resentment among wage and salary earners that went beyond the open disruption. LO reacted to these events in two ways. First, it sought and won a reduction of traditional management rights, culminating in the 1976 Industrial Democracy Law. Second, over 1971–76, it stepped up its pay demands, which met decreased employer resistance. Let us look first at the latter phenomenon.

Most employer bargaining associations, aside from SAF, are small, but a major exception is SAV, the National Collective Bargaining Office, which bargains with public employees on behalf of the central government. SAV is supposed to follow the LO-SAF negotiations in its own wage offers, but in 1971, it broke ranks with SAF by agreeing to a pay raise (30 percent over three years) that was quite generous by standards of the time.[17] SAF then had to sign a similar agreement. Thus, the government rather than Sweden's key export industries determined the basic wage increase—a dangerous precedent given Sweden's dependence on world trade—which tended to establish the public rather than the export sector as pay leader, a position it has not yet clearly relinquished. Not only did SAV make a large offer, it made one favoring less well paid employees even more than LO usually did, causing an increase in the wage drift over 1971–73. Today, the pay structure is much more compressed in the public than in the private sector.

SAV again settled before LO-SAF in 1975 and again offered larger raises to its less well paid employees, in order to get a two-year pact, thereby avoiding negotiations in 1976, an election year. (By this time, unions were favoring shorter agreements because of growing uncertainty about future inflation.) Over 1975–76, the average wage-cost increase in Swedish industry soared to 40 percent, exceeding increases in other OECD nations whose products compete with Sweden's on world markets. This was just when it needed to expand exports to pay for the oil-price explosion. Instead, over 1974–76, average export prices of Swedish manufacturers rose by 29 percent, or three times the average increase of other OECD countries. By 1978, Sweden had lost more than 20 percent of its shares of OECD markets, and Swedish industrial output had fallen by over 10 percent in 1974. It did not surpass the 1974 level until 1984. Meanwhile, consumer goods from Japan and several developing nations achieved growing penetration of the Swedish market. (By 1981, for example, Japan had about 15 percent of the new-car market.) The current account of Sweden's balance of payments swung sharply negative in 1974, and external deficits persisted until 1984.

Aside from zealous pursuit of wage solidarity by LO and then by the Social Democratic government, a major cause of the balance-of-payments crisis was the sharp rise in oil prices after 1973. The energy crisis created greater problems in Sweden than in other market economies, not only because Sweden had the world's highest per capita oil imports—and a high energy content of its manufactured exports—but also because of the havoc which it played with the guidelines followed by each side in the central wage negotiations. As we have seen, LO is supposed to show restraint in its wage demands to help keep down the rate of inflation. In return, it is assured low unemployment, and the government also monitors price increases. But LO cannot relax its wage demands too much without losing blue-collar support. It must settle for wage increases that the export industries can afford, but which are also large enough to keep the allegiance of workers. In practice, this can be a fine line, which must be charted by observable indicators.

In principle, both LO and SAF accept the formula for maximum permissible wage increases, defined by what is known as the EFO model.[18] It divides the economy into a C (or competitive) sector, accounting for about 25 percent of total employment and 30 percent of GNP and a P (or protected) sector accounting for the rest. The C sector should be pay leader—that is, determine permissible average wage and salary increases for the entire economy. Suppose world market prices for Swedish imports are rising at about the same rate as world market prices of Swedish exports. Then, allowable wage increases will equal this expected rate of inflation—which is taken to be outside Sweden's control—plus the expected rate of labor productivity gain in the C sector. Such a wage increase is not consistent with stable prices at home, but will allow a rate of domestic inflation that does not harm Sweden's ability to export. For instance, if prices charged by Sweden's competitors are expected to rise by 5 percent per year over the life of an LO-SAF agreement, while C-sector productivity gains are expected to be 4 percent per year, the permissible annual rise in wages and salaries plus fringe benefits is about 9 percent. This must include all payroll fees (which finance social insurance) and the wage drift, as well as negotiated pay increases.

If wages and benefits do rise by 9 percent in the C sector, and if expectations are borne out, Sweden's export prices will rise by 5 percent, on average, just allowing it to keep its competitive edge on the world market. If labor productivity grows by only 1 percent per year in the P sector, however, prices there would rise by 8 percent. In fact, during 1960–71, average wage gains were just over the 9 percent annual increases that the EFO model would have allowed, because its guidelines were being followed, in effect. LO won wage increases that drove inefficient firms out of business and put profit squeezes on many efficient companies. If the latter were established, however, they usually had a margin for survival and growth. Moreover, the most efficient export firms—generally large and capital intensive—benefitted during the 1950s and 1960s from wage solidarity, because their workers are relatively well paid. Nevertheless, an ominous sign, especially after 1965, was growing investment abroad by these companies, and this expansion has continued into the latter 1980s.

Because of balance-of-payments considerations, allowable increases in wages and benefits in our above example would be less than 9 percent, if world prices of Swedish imports are rising more rapidly than world prices of its exports. Thus, no sooner did the EFO report appear, than the world on which it was based (Sweden in the 1950s and 1960s) was wrenched apart. First, SAV broke ranks with SAF and made the large offer to public-sector employees described above. In effect, the solidaristic wage policy got the better of the EFO guidelines, and not for the last time. But because price increases in nations whose exports were competing with Sweden's were also greater than foreseen, Swedish exports boomed at first, helping to achieve a record 6-billion crown surplus on current account in 1973. But then came the quadrupling of oil prices, which directly and indirectly caused the value of Swedish imports to jump by more than 70 percent between 1973 and 1975, as the balance-of-payments surplus turned into a long-term deficit. Yet, company profits soared at the same time—the worst possible result under the circumstances, because this served as a sign to union members that previous wage demands had been too low.

In fact, the opposite was true. The 40 percent wage explosion over 1975–76 far exceeded increases allowed by the EFO guidelines. At the same time, labor productivity was stagnating. Despite exchange controls, direct investment abroad by Swedish firms expanded rapidly after 1973, reaching 30 percent of industrial investment in Sweden by 1977 and nearly 65 percent in 1984. It has been running several times foreign direct investment in Sweden. By the late 1970s, the scope for real wage increases was smaller than at any time since World War II, and the unions were in a difficult position. In the past, union leaders have argued that rapid wage gains not only force inefficient companies out of business, but also compel surviving firms to raise investments and to take other measures to enhance their efficiency. But in the long run, the wage squeeze on profits reduces domestic investment yields, as well as voluntary savings, and may thereby reduce domestic capital formation, on which growth and future wages depend. Because of Sweden's commitment to full employment, wage increases which create excess supply of some types of labor also trigger increases in government spending, which are potentially inflationary.

During the 1970s and 1980s, real investment yields have been historically low in Sweden and lower than in several developed OECD nations. Industrial investment has also been low. By the latter 1970s, Sweden had a list of problem industries—shipbuilding, iron and steel, textiles, clothing, mining, even part of the forest-based sector. It is now clear that over 1960–75, some sectors (notably shipbuilding and steel) expanded too rapidly, despite a declining overall trend of investment, and some observers argue that the public sector was the biggest offender in this regard. Meanwhile, small- and medium-sized firms with growth potential, but needing breathing space to get started, were hard hit by the solidaristic wage policy, as well as by taxation plus the costly need to supply information and other services to government agencies.[19] The number of industrial enterprises in Sweden fell by more than 40 percent between 1967 and 1982, while the number of employees per firm rose by over 50 percent. Large, efficient export firms, notably in engineering, shifted investment abroad. A proposal to transfer control over most of Swedish industry to the labor unions—the Meidner Plan, discussed below—provided further incentives in this direction.

Following election in 1976 of the first non-Social Democratic government in 44 years, wage settlements became more moderate. Over 1976–77, Swedish labor costs reached their peak relative to those of other nations—a comparative gain of more than 16 percent vis-à-vis the already high level of 1970–71, when Swedish foreign payments were roughly in balance. Thanks to a 17 percent devaluation in 1977, and to moderate wage gains over 1977–80, Sweden's comparative labor costs were about the same in 1980 as in 1970. Yet, its export prices were higher relative to those of competitor nations, and its shares of markets in other OECD countries were lower, in addition to which its share of OPEC markets was (and remains) comparatively low. Despite relatively modest pay increases over 1981–86 and further devaluations of the crown in 1981 and 1982, Sweden has not recovered the export market shares it held in 1970. The balance of payments has improved, however, and increased growth of industrial investment and output is forecast over 1986–90.

15-6. The Tax Effect

In recent years, Sweden's high marginal tax rates on personal incomes have also affected labor market negotiations, by threatening to inflate pay demands. In 1985, an average industrial worker earned about 5.6 times as much as in 1900, in terms of real purchasing power. But his take-home pay in 1985 was only 45 percent of what he actually earned. About 25 percent was withheld for income taxes, and another 30 percent consisted of payroll fees used to finance social insurance. Individuals in high income brackets have long faced steeply progressive personal income taxes, and by the early 1970s, this problem was also confronting blue-collar workers in industry. Assar Lindbeck wrote in 1973 that, "We can see the difficulties arising for Swedish firms to employ internationally outstanding specialists; to give them a salary of $22,000 *after* tax, a firm has to pay $111,000 *before* tax. However, 'ingenuity' often solves the problem."[20]

In fact, wealthy Swedes have often escaped high marginal taxes on their personal incomes through the loophole of unlimited interest deductibility. Those who borrowed to pay for homes, cottages, land, autos, boats, and so forth were able to deduct all interest payments from their taxable incomes. By 1980, such deductions were as great as the total revenue from the personal income tax. Historically, the government has restricted the volume of credit available for consumer loans on official credit markets. Swedish banks, which were forced to ration funds among would-be borrowers, have sought to limit the risk in their loan portfolios. They favored relatively well-to-do borrowers with expensive, blue-chip assets to put up as collateral for loans. Blue-collar workers found their access to credit correspondingly limited.

In 1982, marginal taxes on most personal income varied between 30 percent and 85 percent. An average industrial worker faced a marginal tax of 56 percent, while one with an income 70 percent higher faced a marginal rate of 78 percent. As their incomes before tax rise, moreover, individuals became eligible for lower levels of means-tested benefits, notably housing allowances and public day-care assistance. A full-time single working parent, with two children in day care and an average wage in 1982, faced a marginal tax-plus loss-of-subsidy rate of 89 percent. He or she would have been able to keep just 11 crowns of a 100-crown raise. A Swedish investor who owned equity in a small company, was able to keep just 6.75 of every 100 crowns in profit earned on his shares.

The steeply progressive nature of the tax-transfer system, plus the fact that everyone is taxed separately on his own income, helps to explain why about 52 percent of the population is in the labor force—virtually the highest participation rate in the Western world—although the average work week is comparatively short. As of 1987, almost 90 percent of all men and just over 84 percent of all women aged 20 to 64 were in the work force, which includes nearly as many women as men, although 40–45 percent of the women work part-time. Recent years have also seen a growing use of "black" labor, which goes unreported and, thus, pays no taxes or social insurance fees, thereby costing the government 5–10 percent of potential revenues. Individual financial incentives to work longer hours, to move to better paying jobs, or to improve on-the-job performance have been low, and workers have heavily discounted wage increases, unless they went hand-in-hand with marginal tax cuts. Swedish unions have also sought nontaxable benefits, such as shorter working hours, goods and services paid in kind, a better working environment, and longer holidays. (Since 1977, all Swedish employees receive at least five weeks' paid vacation.) Prior to recent bargaining rounds, the government had offered tax cuts, lower interest rates, price freezes, and other benefits conditional on moderate pay demands by the unions. With the weakening and now the demise of centralized negotiations, this type of incomes policy (less austerity in return for lower pay demands) has played a growing role in restraining labor-cost increases.

Because of the disincentive effects of high marginal tax rates, most political parties have also sought tax reform to reduce these rates, largely by broadening the tax base. On April 24, 1981, after a "wonderful night" of bargaining, the Social Democrats and two nonsocialist parties (the Center party and the Liberals) agreed to a basic reform designed to solve the marginal tax problem. Following reelection of the Social Democrats in 1982, the reform was implemented in three stages over 1983–85. Marginal tax rates fell to 50 percent or less for about 90 percent of all income earners, and a complementary 1986 reform lowered the top marginal rate to about 75 percent on average. However, if we add indirect taxes and loss of income-dependent subsidies, the full marginal rate was still around 70 percent in 1985, and a new reform to lower this again has been announced for 1991. Additional changes, passed in 1983, altered corporate profits taxation and increased the incentive to invest in small- and medium-sized firms by turning shares in these companies into tax shelters. (For purposes of the wealth tax, such shares are assessed at just 30 percent of net asset value.) Finally, interest earned on small savings accounts in Sweden's new national savings system became tax exempt as of April 1, 1984. There are now over 3 million accounts in this system.

The unions have been anxious not to jeopardize the welfare state, of which their members are the main beneficiaries. Thus, they have insisted that revenue lost because of the marginal tax cuts be made up—via a 2 percent payroll tax, as well as by increases in taxes on energy, capital gains, alcohol, and tobacco, and by new taxes on transactions and property. In addition, no more than 50 percent of individual interest payments are now deductible from taxable income, and there will be less future adjustment of tax rates to compensate for inflation when price increases are relatively high. After following a rising trend for many years, the share of current government receipts in GNP has now stagnated at around 60 percent.

15-7. The Social Democratic "Platform"

A. The First Stages

Originally, the term "social democracy" was a synonym for democratic socialism and a revisionist offshoot of the legacy of Marx. Marx had foreseen a violent transition from capitalism to socialism, marked by a revolution in which the workers would seize the material means of production and establish a "dictatorship of the proletariat." Prior to this time, the bourgeoisie (class of owners and managers) would have dwindled, and the exploited class of laborers grown, through a succession of increasingly severe economic depressions that would drive small businessmen into bankruptcy and into the ranks of the proletariat. This evolution of modern capitalism was inevitable, in Marx's view. Finally, at the depth of the last great depression, the workers would become strong enough to seize the reins of power.

Events have not borne Marx out in two respects, however. First, the century since his death has seen the rise of the middle class in developed capitalist countries, rather than the burgeoning of a relatively impoverished proletariat. Second, the severity of recessions under capitalism reached a peak in 1932, with the Great Depression, and nothing comparable has occurred since. Yet, capitalism did not disappear, and the working class has become less oriented toward revolution. Disaffected intellectuals now control the leadership of revolutionary movements in the West and in Japan. Even before the Great Depression, Marxists were splitting into two camps that grew further and further apart. Those who remained revolutionary embraced Lenin's strategy of seizing power, which stressed leadership by a small, tightly knit revolutionary élite, making use of a disaffection by the masses where possible, but replacing democracy with democratic centralism. This allows discussion of issues and alternatives until a decision is taken—generally by the party élite—but then everyone must close ranks behind it. Balking or further dissension is not tolerated. Today, most Communist parties stress their Leninist origins, although not all stress seizing power by violent means.

The second group of Marxists became the democratic socialists, who believed in majority control of the instruments of power, as Marx had, but who also wanted to reach power peacefully via the electoral process and who came to accept the canons of Western democracy. (For this, they have been denounced by the Communists.) As widespread nationalization of the means of production became less popular, due to post-World War II prosperity, Social Democrats in most Western countries retreated from advocating it, except as a very long-range goal. Albin Johannsson, former head of the Swedish cooperative movement, once said that what matters is not who owns the means of production, but how they are used, and such sentiments were popular in Sweden during the 1950s and 1960s. Yet, in principle, Social Democrats are committed to eventual work-place democracy.

When we talk about a Social Democratic "strategy" for the evolution of Swedish economy and society, we are inferring from past actions and apparent present aims rather than reciting a master blueprint. Nonetheless, we can distinguish a three-stage evolution that brought the Swedish economy in general and the union movement in particular to the state of affairs prevailing around 1970, when the fourth stage began. The first stage was the struggle for universal suffrage, which accounts for much of the labor unrest of the late nineteenth and early twentieth centuries, in Sweden and in several other European countries. With the coming of the factory system of large-scale production, workers were crowded together, both during and outside of working hours, since they lived in factory towns or urban ghettoes adjacent to factory districts. This made them easier to organize for effective action. Sweden achieved universal suffrage in 1919. By then, it was clear the Social Democrats would eventually come to power, but they did not use this power to nationalize the means of production.

Instead, they sought first full employment and then industrial growth as the foundation of an affluent society. This was the second stage, and it was here that productivity, efficiency, and competition became watch words. Social Democratic governments used fiscal policy to maintain aggregate demand, and they pioneered, first in moderating cyclical fluctuations in income and employment, and then with an active labor market policy. Efforts to continually retrain workers and to relocate them in more productive jobs were also designed to keep down the rate of inflation associated with a high pressure economy and to support the policy of wage solidarity. During this time, neither the Social Democrats nor the unions seriously challenged management prerogatives—embodied in Article 32 of the SAF Constitution—that were among the most extensive in the world.[21] The Social Democratic view was that the pressures of a competitive market and the wage demands of strong unions would force companies to stay efficient or go under and that this was a good thing. Management retained control of hiring, investment, production, and marketing—and, to a decreasing extent, of layoffs and dismissals. Unions preferred to stay out of management, because this allowed them complete freedom to represent labor at the bargaining table.

The third stage was a series of measures to provide comprehensive social insurance and to redistribute the affluence created by a prosperous economy. This began when the Social Democrats first came to power in 1932, but the major emphasis dates from the 1950s. Here, the unions and Social Democratic governments collaborated through a "double pincer" strategy. If a major concession could not be won from SAF in negotiations, it was to be legislated. (In this context, much of public consumption, as well as large government subsidies for housing, agriculture, and employment creation or maintenance, can be viewed as complementary to wage solidarity.)

A major breakthrough in stage three was passage of the National Supplementary Pension Plan, which went into effect in 1960 after serving as the main issue of the 1958 elections (and passing in Parliament by just one vote). This plan created the quasi-public National Pension Insurance (ATP) Fund, originally to supplement the basic old-age pension. The latter is paid to every citizen from age 65, but is meager. It came to just over 2,720 Swedish crowns ($354 U.S.) per month in early 1986 for single persons and 3,980 crowns per month for married couples. A pensioner forced to live on this alone always receives a municipal housing allowance, which may cover the full cost of his or her lodging, and he is usually exempt from personal income tax.

The ATP pension better fits the welfare state image. A full ATP pension comes to 60 percent of an individual's average real earnings during his or her fifteen best-paid working years, although income in excess of a fairly high ceiling does not count in computing the pension. Together with the basic pension, it amounts to about two-thirds of best average real earnings, and both pensions are tied to the consumer price index, so that they rise with the cost of living. To receive a full ATP pension, it is necessary to have retired after mid-1981 and to have earned pensionable income for at least thirty years. (The pension is reduced by one-thirtieth for every year less than thirty.) By early 1987, about 1.6 million people were receiving full or partial supplementary pensions. ATP is entirely financed by a payroll tax on employers, which rose from 3 percent to 10.2 percent of wages and salaries over 1960–87, in addition to which the basic pension took 9.45 percent in 1987. In effect, the government has legislated wage increases and required employees to save these raises until retirement.

The birthdate requirement for receiving ATP benefits meant that, over at least the first 25 years of the Fund's existence (i.e., until 1985), payments into it exceeded outlays to pensioners in every year. By end-1985, the Fund had accumulated a balance of 254 billion crowns—in per capita terms by far the largest pension fund accumulation of any country in the world. Over 1980–82, the increase in the Fund's assets came to about 75 percent of net financial saving in Sweden, and this ratio was still as high as 36 percent in 1985. "Forced" saving, in the form of the payroll tax which finances ATP, has raised the savings share of national income, recalling our earlier observation that successful exercise of union bargaining power over the long run may require a way of increasing the percentage of labor's income that is saved (although payroll fees in Sweden also come partly out of profits). However, the positive effect of ATP on savings has declined, as more and more Swedes have become eligible for the full supplementary pension.[22] In the meantime, the Fund's managers have invested its assets, mainly by lending to low-risk borrowers. In 1985, the Fund held more than a fourth of all outstanding Swedish bonds, by value. It has tended to earn more than the average rate of return in Swedish industry.

Until 1974, ATP's managers were required to lend all proceeds available to them. Then, a new law allowed the Fund to buy equities, and it promptly purchased 585,000 shares of Volvo. The general reaction in business circles was one of alarm, since ATP had the means to buy control over most of Swedish industry, and Prime Minister Olaf Palme did not appear to be opposed to such back-door nationalization. However, these fears receded with election defeats of the Social Democrats in 1976 and 1979 and the expected peaking of the Fund's assets during the 1980s. Today, there is more concern, in Sweden as in other Western nations, about the ability of ATP to finance future pensions, as the average age of the population rises.

Nevertheless, the Fund has been obliged to invest most of its resources in housing and government bonds (39 percent and 34 percent, respectively, in 1985), reflecting Social Democratic priorities under stage three. Less than a fifth of its investment has gone back to industry, much less than the contribution to ATP from that sector. (Another 6 percent has been loaned for construction of power plants.) The EFO guidelines suggest that labor should bear most of the burden of pension payments and other payroll fees by accepting lower wages. Over 1950–79, however, only about half the total increase in payroll fees (from 6 percent to 40 percent of wages and salaries) was borne by labor. The rest fell on capital, in the form of reduced profits and other property incomes.[23] One result was a drop in the share of internally financed investment between 1960 and 1980 and a transfer of funds from the C sector to the P sector. In 1977, the share of wages, salaries, and payroll fees in gross domestic product peaked at 75 percent, after rising for many years. Since then, it has fallen to 68 percent, and incomes from property and entrepreneurial labor have correspondingly increased, although the share devoted to gross fixed investment remains low—around 18–19 percent vs. 23 percent in the 1960s and early 1970s. As a share of disposable income, net household saving has generally been less than 1 percent since 1982.

15-8. The Industrial Democracy Stage

A. New Legislation During the 1970s and Early 1980s

Ultimately, Social Democrats distinguish themselves by their advocacy of industrial democracy. In Sweden, this has been seen as a luxury good, to be achieved after the welfare state was created on the back of a prosperous economy. Prosperity has come from well-managed firms plus a remarkable record of innovation. According to psychological theories of motivation, individuals first try to satisfy their drives for material well-being and financial security. Once these lower order needs are fulfilled, they become harder and harder to motivate simply with higher earnings. Instead, they require greater social recognition or self-fulfillment, which advocates claim must be achieved through industrial democracy. In a welfare state financed by high marginal taxes on personal income, pay incentives are also weak, because changes in gross incomes are mostly offset by changes in individual tax obligations. Finally, the tendency for higher current wages to reduce investment and growth at least partly nullifies labor's bargaining power and makes it more likely that unions will develop alternative goals, notably those related to industrial democracy. This would give Swedish unions at least partial control over the means of production, in the name of employees. In return, labor would receive property income, which could be paid as profit shares or profit-linked bonuses. Hopefully, the propensity to save out of such income would be no lower than when it goes to traditional owners of capital, although this is not guaranteed.

During creation of the welfare state, extensive rights of traditional management, representing private owners of capital and featuring traditional patterns of authority and hierarchical relationships, were acceptable to Social Democrats. These would have to erode, however, with the start of the drive toward industrial democracy. This marks the fourth and most difficult stage in the above evolution. Even in favorable conditions, it demands a maturity and sophistication—what Marxians call a "level of consciousness"—on the part of workers that is not easily established. If workers' management is genuine, professional managers and foremen will become accountable and ultimately subordinate to elected employee representatives at all levels of the company. Work discipline must be maintained, but labor representatives will have to set and enforce directions for all phases of a firm's operations.

The fourth stage began in Sweden in the early 1970s. During the next few years, the Riksdag passed more new laws to govern labor relations than during the entire previous period of Social Democratic rule. In progressive companies, these codified existing practices and advanced them marginally. Elsewhere, they clashed with established procedure and set the stage for eventual confrontation. LO got passage of each law through its ties with the Social Democrats, after failing to negotiate a similar concession from SAF. Nevertheless, it is unclear how far union or Social Democratic leaders would have pushed the transfer of management rights to union representatives, if the leaders had not been pushed by discontent on the part of union members.

In Sweden as in other Western countries, the 1950s and 1960s were an era of comparatively large increases in labor productivity, as well as of rapid structural change. The average size of the firm grew, amid many mergers and failures and a fall in the number of successful new enterprises. Partly to allow higher wages to be paid, the work pace was speeded up. Jobs became more repetitive, monotonous, and in some cases, more dangerous. Stress in the working environment rose, and many jobs were eliminated.[24] Labor turnover grew, reaching almost a third per year for Volvo, usually considered a model employer. LO became less enamored of piece rates, and the Labor Market Board expanded its measures to retrain and relocate workers displaced by technological and structural change.

Although complaints about the working environment were multiplying, it was probably more pleasant in Sweden, on the whole, than elsewhere. Part of the problem was a declining tolerance by younger workers, whose lives had been relatively easy and who had not experienced unemployment for any substantial length of time. As well, the Swedish labor force could only expand after the mid-1960s by hiring women (whose participation rate rose from 35 percent to nearly 80 percent over 1965–85, to become the highest in the Western world), as well as immigrants, who now comprise about 5 percent of the labor force, and people with physical, social, and psychological handicaps. Of course, greater employment opportunities often helped to bring the latter into society and gave them a chance to develop more self-respect.

Nevertheless, much of the increase in the labor force had adjustment problems, just when technological change was making work more demanding and opening new areas of work hazard. Workers displaced by structural or technological change also found it harder and harder to readjust. The Labor Market Board found it more difficult to permanently place workers it had retrained. To cope with this situation, it raised its subsidies to business firms which agreed to set up or to expand semi-sheltered workshops, where handicapped people do useful work in normal employment situations, but shielded from normal competitive pressures. It also expanded its own programs for employing hard-to-place workers.

However, the government did not consider these measures adequate, and it therefore ended its policy of legislative nonintervention in the labor market. To begin with, the 1974 Act on Security of Employment stipulates that, as a basic rule, employment is to last indefinitely. Temporary employment contracts are allowed, but only under special circumstances (e.g., seasonal farm work). Both employer and employee must give at least one month's notice before terminating employment. As the employee grows older, he or she becomes entitled to a longer period of notice—up to six months—and receives full wages during this time. The employer must have "reasonable" grounds for dismissing workers, which may be contested in the Labor Court for substantial damages. (However, both falling product demand and technological change are normally considered reasonable grounds.) It is especially hard to lay off union officials or workers over age forty-five, and a laid-off employee has first refusal rights for up to one year.

According to the 1974 Promotion of Employment Act, the employer must also give the county employment board two to six months' notice before layoffs, depending on the numbers involved. This board may also force employers to provide more and better job opportunities for elderly and handicapped workers. An apparent cost of greater protection against dismissals was a rise in the rate of youth unemployment (of workers under 25), from under 3 percent in 1970 to 9.5 percent in early 1982, despite a succession of relief work projects for young people. With the growing cost of laying employees off, firms became less willing to hire new workers. Two-thirds of all people on relief work were under 25, and this age group was finding it especially hard to obtain permanent employment. Partly in consequence, the Riksdag passed a revised Act on Security of Employment in 1982, which made it legal to hire employees on a trial basis for up to six months, in the hope of encouraging job creation. Subsequent measures (to be outlined in chapter 16) eliminated most unemployment among teenagers and helped to push the rate of youth unemployment back down to 5.8 percent in 1985.

Legislation first passed in 1974 and strengthened by the 1978 Working Environment Act, seeks to adjust work to the physical and psychological needs of workers. Employees have the right to help design their work places—in practice through their local union representatives. Workers with adjustment problems get help from tripartite adjustment groups, consisting of representatives of the employer, the local union, and the county employment office, and financial support is available for investments to alter the work place. Finally, the Working Environment Act requires a safety steward to be appointed in all work places employing five persons or more. Management must inform these stewards in advance about any proposed change in the work environment, and the latter may rule such proposals unsafe on either physical or psychological grounds. The stewards also have the right to stop work they consider dangerous. In addition, each firm with at least fifty employees must have a joint labor-management safety committee.

Finally, the 1980 Law on Equality Between Men and Women explicitly forbids all forms of sex discrimination on the job. Women must receive equal pay with men for work of equal value, along with equal employment, training, experience, and promotion opportunities. This law established the office of Equality Ombudsman to enforce its provisions, and the first Equality Ombudsman was a woman, Mrs. Inga-Britt Törnell.

The above laws curtailed traditional management rights, albeit in a way that is fairly common in Western Europe. Other plans were also afoot, however, that relate more specifically to industrial democracy. We recall that 1969–70 saw an outbreak of wildcat strikes, over two hundred taking place in 1970. They came at the end of a decade when labor turnover, absenteeism, and suppressed labor discontent were rising, and when the commitment of many workers to the union movement was faltering. The main causes of the strikes are unclear. Many of the wildcat strikers were well paid, and some resented the wage solidarity program. But LO could not go back on this commitment without alienating other workers—and threatening the legitimacy of its own power over national unions—and the Social Democrats risked losing support to splinter groups on their left. Complaints about the working environment also lay behind the unrest, and the new left was winning support by challenging traditional concepts of property and authority. Both LO and the Social Democrats therefore moved to expand employee decision-making rights.

Indeed, SAF had perceived the same need and reacted more quickly (thereby increasing the pressure on LO) by fostering a series of "job enrichment" experiments in work reorganization. At Volvo plants, for example, an effort was made to divide automobile assembly into operations, each of which produces an identifiable part of the final product. The Volvo factory at Kalmar did away with the conventional assembly line.[25] Instead, each operation was assigned to a specialized work team of fifteen to twenty members. Every team has leeway to control the flow of work to its station and to determine its internal distribution of work. The number of supervisors is reduced, many jobs are more complex than in conventional assembly plants, and jobs are rotated among team members. The idea is to make work more challenging, less monotonous, and more humane, as well as to build up team spirit through identification of the worker with his or her team and its product.

Experiments also took place at Saab-Scania (Sweden's other major auto producer), at the state-owned Arvika tobacco factory, at Essem Simtar, at Almex (a maker of parking meters and ticket machines), and at other factories. These have relevance for wage solidarity, since job rotation allows comparative equalization of individual wages within a work team, even when the marginal productivities associated with different jobs are far apart. When piece rates or bonus payments are used, they are geared to the performance of the team, rather than to that of the individual. While experiments in humanizing the work place are described by advocates as qualified successes, output per worker is higher at leading Japanese firms than at Volvo. Volvo's labor productivity also compares unfavorably with Mercedes-Benz, which has undergone no large-scale reorganization to humanize the work place, but which is one of the few European car makers to expand its market share in the face of the Japanese "invasion."

In any event, LO and the Social Democrats seized the initiative on industrial democracy by launching a two-pronged assault on traditional management rights. Each prong was enacted into law after LO failed to negotiate it at the bargaining table. First, a 1972 law required most unionized, nonfinancial companies with over one hundred (later twenty-five) employees to seat two union representatives on their boards of directors. In most cases, one blue-collar representative was to come from LO and one white-collar representative from TCO. These delegates did not need to be employees of the firm on whose board they sat, although in virtually all cases they have been. The new law went into effect April 1, 1973 for a three-year trial period, after which it was made permanent. LO and TCO immediately set up courses in corporate decision-making techniques, personnel management, and basic company law for prospective labor representatives. This was a breakthrough, although progressive companies, including Volvo, had already invited employee representatives to join their boards—partly to improve feedback and worker morale and, thereby, to raise productivity and profits. In 1988, the number of union representatives was raised to three in most companies having 1,000 or more employees. In all cases, however, they remain a distinct minority of board members and do not pose a threat to traditional owners or managers.

However, the 1976 Industrial Democracy Law enables unions, mainly at the local level, to negotiate the entire range of managerial decision-making prerogatives within any unionized company. Unions may codetermine job assignments, arrangement of the work place, price setting, investment programming and finance, hiring and firing, marketing, and any other decision area with management. In practice, union representatives have tended to confine themselves to issues of direct interest to employees—namely, wages and benefits, layoffs, and working conditions. (In this respect, Sweden's experience parallels those of other nations that have tried industrial democracy.)

Nevertheless, the law intends that management will share authority and responsibility with union locals. It is up to management to initiate whatever negotiations are necessary to obtain union approval for changes in company operations. If there is a dispute, the union's view prevails until the Labor Court rules otherwise. This applies to working conditions, security of employment, and virtually every issue except wages, where management retains its traditional priority of interpretation. At union request, the company must negotiate any issue and is obliged to supply whatever information about company operations and plans the union may ask for, even if this is considered confidential and/or an expensive research effort is required. (Management pays research costs.) Moreover, the fact that a wage agreement has been signed does not bar a union from striking to obtain an acceptable collective agreement on participation in decision making. (However, when the latter is also concluded, the traditional peace obligation prevails.)

In this way, the positions of shop stewards and union board representatives have been strengthened. A major benefit of the Industrial Democracy Law to the union movement is its assignment of important functions to local union bodies, which had gradually atrophied as the centralized collective bargaining grew in coverage and importance. The law has brought fewer changes than we might expect, given its sweeping provisions, partly because the Swedish economy has run a string of potentially dangerous internal and external deficits. In addition, unions have needed time to learn how to exercise their increased powers and, perhaps, to further raise the "consciousness" of the workers. SAF did not sign a basic framework agreement with LO and PTK to implement the law until April, 1982, although it was the last employer association to do so. As a result of this agreement, large Swedish factories have been divided into small, quasi-independent work areas, and decision-making authority has been decentralized to lower level managers, foremen, and even to individual workers and work teams. (Once again, however, we should not overestimate the impact of this on day-to-day operations.)

B. The Meidner Plan

From the unions' point of view, the Industrial Democracy Law did not represent labor's main thrust toward industrial democracy during the 1970s. In 1976, LO adopted the Meidner Plan, a formula that would enable the unions to gain ownership of most of Swedish industry, in the name of company employees. The transfer would take place gradually over twenty years or more. Although it could be seen as a logical culmination of the drive to industrial democracy, it split the Social Democratic party, whose political opposition made it a major election issue. The Meidner proposals quickly became one of the country's most controversial socioeconomic questions.[26]

Their keynote is the creation of "employee funds" (löntagarfonder), which would be used to take over private companies. According to the original proposal, 20 percent of the pretax profits of every company with 500 employees or more— about 200 enterprise groups, producing some 85 percent of Swedish exports— would have to be deposited each year in union-controlled funds, of which there would be at least one for each industry. These deposits would be tax free. Other companies quoted on the Stockholm exchange would also have to participate in the program. Cooperatives, publicly owned enterprises, and other not-for-profit companies would be exempt, although they and smaller private firms could join the scheme voluntarily and would receive tax advantages for doing so. All nonparticipating firms would have to pay an extra 1 percent payroll tax, whose proceeds would be used to promote "employee democracy" within them.

The systems of reporting and monitoring profits would have to be improved, since the employee funds would give management an incentive to understate profits, as well as a disincentive to earn them. However, no monies would actually transfer to the funds being created, and all profits would remain within the firms that generated them. The employee funds would consist, not of cash, but rather of shares in the companies concerned, which their managers would be required to issue each year, priced at book value. The employee funds would have to hold their shares in trust; these stocks could not be bought or sold. Normal dividends would be paid on them and would go into a single central fund for the entire country. It would be used to train employee representatives or other union officials, to invest in research on the working environment, and/or to provide public benefits for union members. The central fund would be controlled by LO, perhaps jointly with TCO.

Individual employees would not be allowed access to the employee funds. Instead, as they accumulated shares, the funds would acquire more and more voting rights at annual company stockholder meetings. Eventually, the unions would be able to nominate a majority of the firm's board of directors—to help out, they would retain the representatives they had initially—on which occasion they would gain control over the enterprise. The most profitable firms would come under union control first. If this process caused the original owners to withdraw their capital from the company, the loss would be made good from the ATP Fund, which, we recall, is financed by a payroll tax.

Besides promoting union-based industrial democracy, Meidner designed his proposals to support wage solidarity and equalization of wealth.[27] As in other Western countries, the distribution of equity capital in Sweden is lopsided. According to a 1981 study, just over 1 percent of all households owned 75 percent of all shares owned by individuals, and 80 percent of households owned no shares. However, equities comprised just 5 percent of personal wealth. Moreover, these figures fail to take into account the impact of changes in the tax laws passed in 1978. The latter introduced tax concessions for individuals who bought into share investment funds (mutual funds for purchase of equities on the Stockholm exchange) by saving small amounts regularly through them. The result was a rise in the number of households owning equities, especially after 1980.

Proponents of the Meidner Plan have argued as well that the most profitable companies in Sweden have been made more profitable still by the union drive for wage solidarity, which has restrained pay demands. The unions have made this contribution reluctantly, as an alternative to higher average wage increases, which would have meant more bankruptcies among marginal firms and more layoffs. Other proponents have made a somewhat contradictory argument. They claim that the most profitable companies have contributed the most to the wage drift, and in this way, to thwarting the solidarity program. This result is not firmly established, although it is widely believed. Under Meidner's proposals, the most profitable firms would come soonest under the control of employee (or union) nominated directors and in this sense their excess profits would be "socialized." Once the transfer of power takes place, the profits of efficient firms are supposed to be used to benefit all of society, although exactly how is unclear.

When the Meidner Plan was introduced, the performance of the Swedish economy was deteriorating rapidly. A feature of this decline was a rapid fall in the rate of savings, as the public sector budget surplus dwindled and turned into a long-term deficit, and as the share of wages, salaries, and payroll fees in national income peaked at 75 percent in 1977. Thus, a joint LO-Social Democratic task force added a new goal and a new proposal to the Meidner Plan in 1978. It called for large new investment funds, to be managed by employee (union) and government representatives. These would be in addition to the employee funds described above and would mainly finance investment in export industries, whose need for restructuring and rationalization was greater than in many years. To create the investment funds, all firms—regardless of whether they were participating in the employee funds program—would have to pay a capital formation fee amounting to a percentage of payroll. In principle, the ultimate financing of this tax would come from employees, who would agree to smaller wage increases, although there would be no guarantee of this.

The revised Meidner Plan foresaw twenty-six investment funds—two at the national level and one to be administered by each county government. Of the national funds, one would be managed by a board on which employee (union) representatives had the majority of seats. The other would be administered by a majority of government officials, civic and business leaders, etc., although with some union representation. A similar tripartite board—government, traditional management, unions—would manage each county fund. Before long, the capital formation goal was pushing aside the three which had given Meidner his original inspiration.

Critics argue that the Meidner Plan would lead to a concentration of economic power—even to the extent of eroding the pluralistic nature of Swedish society—and also that it would reduce efficiency and lead to a state of affairs in which the unions represent management and hence come into conflict with their own members. It is not clear how wages would be determined, once the employee funds control a firm or industry. LO rejects the Yugoslav notion of firms managed by workers' councils, consisting of employee representatives (to whom professional directors are responsible), arguing that "solidarity should not be limited to one's own company."[28] That is, the workers in more profitable firms should not be allowed to vote themselves higher wages because they are more profitable.

This raises a key question. At what level would an enterprise be managed, once its employee fund has the votes to control it? Union spokesmen have pointed out that the employees at each company will be the ones who elect representatives on the boards of the employee funds. Meidner is well aware of his country's exposed position on the world market. "He stresses that his proposals would not change the basic structure of Swedish companies, but only give more power to workers, which would give them greater possibilities to influence decisions concerning their jobs and life-styles."[29] The twenty years or more required to transfer control over most of Swedish industry to the employee funds would permit a pool of union officials to emerge who are qualified to take over the reins of management. However, it would also be a period during which present owners are less and less willing to invest in their own firms—since they will look forward to capturing less and less of the return on such investment—and during which present management is less and less motivated to manage efficiently. (Socialist advocates of nationalizing industry have usually argued that such a step must be taken quickly.)

Nor would it be possible for the basic structure and mode of operation of the Swedish economy to remain unchanged after power had passed to the employee funds. To begin with, each firm affected by the program would come under control of its union, which is organized nationally. If the locals continue to be subordinate to the national union, one industry after another would be turned into a monopoly, insofar as most domestic competition is concerned. The problems that this would create might then lead to further centralization, eventually resulting in a Soviet-type economy. In such a system, management could easily be remote from the workers and less willing than traditional owners to bear entrepreneurial risk as well. It makes a difference whether industrial democracy is based on the enterprise or on a larger entity—normally, an industry or region—and wage solidarity would require union control to be based on the latter. Otherwise, employees of more profitable firms would find ways to pay themselves higher wages. (We also recall that the goal of wage solidarity on the union side played a major role in promoting centralized collective bargaining.)

According to Meidner's original proposal, industries were to be managed as cartels, with all employees in each industry electing a board of directors for that industry. This led to charges that the Swedish economy would eventually centralize along the lines of the Soviet model. In reply, an LO-Social Democratic task force modified the original proposal by adding the investment funds described above and by replacing management at the industry level with management by regional assemblies, one for each county. Every assembly would have 300 members elected by employees of participating firms in that county. Eventually, these assemblies would gain the power to name employee delegates on company boards of directors and, thus, to control enterprise management.[30] The regional assemblies would also appoint a congress that would, in turn, appoint employee representatives to the boards of the regional investment funds. Ultimately, much control would be exercised above the regional level, owing to the relatively centralized character of Swedish unions. In addition, the national union organizations would control two central funds—one of the national investment funds and a fund fed by dividends on company shares issued to the employee funds. If excess profits are "neutralized," to keep them from becoming part of wages, they would have to go into the second fund. The majority of other financial institutions would also come under union control or be nationalized.

Under the revised proposal, unions would still control the boards of major companies through the regional assemblies. Moreover, LO, together with the Social Democratic party and, perhaps, TCO, would be able to decide which firms have access to funds for expansion, research and development, and modernization. Supporters of the Meidner Plan have argued that the market economy would remain and be strengthened. Yet, many decisions would be taken above the enterprise level, and because of the strength of unions' national organizations, it is hard to imagine competition flourishing between firms, once union control is established. A crucial difference between a market and a Soviet-type economy is that firms do not compete for customers in the latter.

In this context, profits and losses play two key roles in an efficient market economy. First, they act as a spur to innovation—and, more generally, to risk-bearing—when the innovator(s) can capture part of the profits that result from putting a better product on the market or from using new technologies that cut costs.[31] Historically, the Swedish economy owes much of its success to innovation. This process is symmetrical. Low profits or losses punish poorly managed companies or those failing to introduce new technologies or products that people want. Second, excess profits or losses cause supply to expand or contract. Excess profits mean that buyers want more of a good, and the industry will expand as firms enter it or as already established enterprises increase their production capacity, in competition for these profits. Losses imply that buyers want less of the goods in question (or that the costs of some producers are excessive) and will motivate companies to leave the industry, to contract production, or to reduce their costs. The system will not work well, however, when excess profits are neutralized, because this removes much of the incentive to respond to shifts in demand, as well as to minimize costs, and to innovate. (Indeed, neutralization of profits would be a Swedish version of the soft budget constraint.) Innovation also requires that firms be forced to compete for customers.

Meidner designed his plan to break the concentration of private power in the business sector, which LO believes results primarily from internal financing of investment. But the possibility is more than remote that it would wind up centralizing economic decisions and reducing competition. This would also make Western-style democracy more difficult to sustain. Moreover, we may ask whether the right to vote for one or more of three hundred representatives to a regional management assembly—and an even more indirect right to elect managers of the investment funds—will satisfy worker desires for more influence over their conditions of work. Part of the Swedish economy would remain outside the employee-funds scheme, although control over taxes and credit by LO and the Social Democrats would eventually make this difficult. The knowledge that a firm must join the plan once a certain size is reached also gives it little incentive to exploit its market opportunities to grow. A small- or medium-sized enterprise would therefore hesitate to develop an innovation in Sweden.

The threat of centralization embodied in the Meidner Plan invites comparisons with the smaller East European command economies. All are well below Sweden's level of per capita income and output. All have achieved more rapid growth, but the possibilities for extensive growth were largely exhausted in Sweden by 1950. Eastern Europe has had trouble exporting manufactures to the West, which has been Sweden's *forte* and her ticket to prosperity. They also consume relatively large amounts of raw materials and energy per unit of national income. Finally, we have seen that pressures to decentralize have been growing in several of these countries.

In any event, the 1982 elections returned the Social Democrats to power, after six years in opposition, and they introduced a third version of the Meidner Plan, which passed the Riksdag to become law on January 1, 1984. The new version, known as the Edin Plan, emphasizes the need to raise saving and investment. It set up five regional "employee-investment" funds, each of which is managed by a nine-member board, including five union representatives. The government has appointed all nine members of each board—a point of controversy since Meidner had foreseen that employee delegates would be elected, as industrial democracy would seem to require. The funds may invest up to 400 million crowns per year, mainly by purchasing stock on the Stockholm exchange, but also by buying into small- and medium-sized companies which are not quoted. Their function is to "improve the supply of risk capital to benefit Swedish production and employment." Each fund is required to earn at least 3 percent plus the rate of inflation on its outlays and to pay this amount into the ATP Fund every year. A major difference from the Meidner Plan is that each fund must buy shares at market, rather than book value. Over 1980–85, the average market value of shares on the Stockholm exchange rose to more than nine times its previous level, and the boom has continued through 1988. This dilutes the purchasing power of the employee-investment funds.

Initially, the system will run until 1990. During this time, no fund will be allowed to buy more than 8 percent of the voting rights or total capital in any company, and all five funds together plus the ATP Fund must not control more than 49 percent. By 1990, the five funds combined are expected to own 5–10 percent of the aggregate value of all shares quoted on the Stockholm exchange. However, each fund is to be managed independently, and if a firm's union local so requests, any fund must transfer up to 55 percent of its voting rights to the local. The funds draw their capital from the ATP Fund, and these drawings are financed by a small payroll tax, as well as a 20 percent tax on "excess" profits. For small- and medium-sized companies, these will be profits in excess of 6 percent of payroll, which may give them an incentive to expand employment.

The Edin Plan is a compromise that has infuriated both left and right. The left considers it so ideologically watered down from the original Meidner proposal as to be incapable of promoting employee democracy. According to the head of the Communist party, "The discussion of power within companies should start again, from the beginning." The right wing described the proposal as a "declaration of war," in the words of SAF's managing director, since the employee funds are becoming major shareholders in leading firms.[32] By cooperating, they may acquire controlling interests in some enterprises by 1990, since as little as 5 percent of voting rights can be enough to control a company quoted on the stock exchange. Since the 1970s, however, there has been growing acceptance in Sweden, as in other Western nations, of the long-term link between profits, growth, and future employment. Thus, it now appears that the Edin Plan will be discontinued after 1990, with the funds retaining the shares they have accumulated at that time. In the meantime, they have been earning above-average returns on their investments. Whether they are accepting an above-average share of risk is less clear, and the mandating of a 3 percent floor on real yields suggests that, without this, economic criteria might be secondary in determining a fund's investment choices.

Only a small percentage of Swedes actively support the basic employee-funds concept, and many are strongly opposed. The nonsocialist parties consider the system of investment share funds mentioned earlier, which includes company-sponsored funds for their employees, to be an adequate way of popularizing stock ownership. Over 1980–83, these funds really caught on. More than 500,000 people save through them regularly, since capital gains and dividends worth up to 7,500 crowns per year are tax exempt, provided savings are locked up for five years or more. In addition, the tragic death of Olaf Palme on March 1, 1986 removed a powerful and passionate supporter of the employee-funds idea. The Social Democratic party then moved back toward the political center, seeking a better accommodation with traditional owners and managers. Present union leaders are also more tolerant of private capital than were their predecessors in the 1970s. During the 1988 election campaign, Prime Minister Ingvar Carlsson suggested that environmental improvement would become the new fourth stage of Social Democratic commitment. This was a time of rising worldwide concern about the environment, and in Sweden the Green party obtained seats in Parliament for the first time.

Yet it remains true that Social Democrats distinguish themselves by their advocacy of industrial democracy. It is too early to know whether they have made an historic retreat from this goal, and a stronger version of the 1976 Industrial Democracy Law might provide another vehicle for its realization. This issue represents one more chapter in Sweden's role as a social and economic laboratory, but one whose conclusion cannot yet be written.

Notes

1. See David Jenkins, *Sweden and the Price of Progress* (New York: Coward-McCann, 1968), pp. 166–67, and Marquis Childs, *Sweden: The Middle Way* (New Haven: Yale University Press, 1936).

2. See Nils Lundgren, "Poised for a Comeback," *Sweden Now*, No. 5, 1983, as well as Guy de Faramond, "The Fixers," *Sweden Now*, No. 6, 1986.

3. At end-1986, Dr. Lundgren wrote, "The growth rate is falling, nominal wage increases are nearly twice as high as in Germany or Japan, interest rates are 2.5 percent–3 percent higher than in the U.S. . . . On the other hand, the current account displays a handsome surplus . . . the manufacturing sector is in good shape, and current inflation is lowest since the 1960s." *PK Banken Outlook on the Swedish Economy*, December 1986, p. 1.

4. Andrew Shonfield, *Modern Capitalism: The Changing Balance of Public and Private Power* (London: Oxford University Press, 1965), p. 399. For a brief discussion of the Freedom of the Press Act, see "Constitutional Protection of Rights and Freedoms in Sweden," *Fact Sheets on Sweden*, No. 4c (Stockholm: The Swedish Institute, June 1986).

5. In contrast to competition policy in the United States, the Swedish government is more interested in the performance of an industry than in its structure. It pays more attention to whether prices are high or low and to other potential abuses of market power than to the simple possession of such power, although the Price and Cartel Office does follow trends in market concentration. A restriction on competition is deemed harmful if it unduly affects prices, restricts productivity, or impedes or prevents commerce, contrary to the public interest. According to an official (Jenkins, *Sweden and the Price of Progress*, p. 181): "We have monopolies in certain industries—containers and cement, for instance—but our investigations have not shown that these enterprises have unjustifiably high prices." Market structure is more concentrated in Sweden than in the United States, Canada, the United Kingdom, or West Germany, and three firms or less dominate the markets for a number of products. But this concentration results from the small size of the Swedish market—a fact of life that goes a long way toward explaining the Swedish government's approach. Import competition is also a major factor in the Swedish market, except in agriculture.

6. For example, SAF has established an Industry Council to Promote Competition, which will often take the lead in trying to dissuade businesses from engaging in monopolistic practices. A major reason is the threat of retaliation, either directly or through Parliament,

by associations representing labor and consumers. (Also, such activity would probably come to the attention of the Anti-trust or Consumer Ombudsman, if it persisted.) Similarly, LO tries to educate its members to understand (although not necessarily to sympathize with) management problems and points of view, as well as the "mechanics" of society. As a rule, LO is intolerant of featherbedding and often cooperates with management to increase efficiency, as a means of achieving eventual wage increases.

7. See OECD Department of Economics and Statistics, *National Accounts*, 1970–85, Vol. 1, supplement, "Purchasing Power Parities" (Paris: OECD, 1987), Table 13, p. 16, plus national statistical yearbooks. OECD membership comprises Western Europe, North America, Japan, Greece, Australia, New Zealand, Turkey, and Yugoslavia.

8. LO has 24 member unions, most of which are organized according to industry rather than craft. TCO has twenty member unions, organized along both industry and craft lines, while SACO/SR has twenty-six national professional associations and, thus, is organized according to occupation. TCO has less authority over its affiliates than LO, but SACO/SR is the most tightly knit of the three.

9. Higher wages and salaries will correspond to a higher wage-and-salary *share* of national income if and only if the elasticity of substitution between labor and capital is generally less than one, as is believed to be the case. The higher this elasticity, however, the greater the unemployment consequences of wage increases above competitive levels.

10. See Rune Aberg, "Economic Work Incentives and Labor Market Efficiency in Sweden," paper presented at the International Conference on Active Labour Market Policy, York University, Downsview, Ontario, Canada, December 1986, p. 7. However, this result may be due at least partly to the absence of a good measure of the marginal productivity of labor in different enterprises.

11. However, surveys have shown a large majority of blue-collar unionists in favor of wage solidarity, and the majority has been greater among the higher paid workers who have paid the price of this policy. See Karl-Olaf Andersson, "How Democratic is the Trade Union Movement?" *Current Sweden* No. 65, February 1975; and Leif Lewin, "Union Democracy," *Current Sweden*, No. 172, September 1977. See, as well, Kristina Ahlén, "Recent Trends in Swedish Collective Bargaining: Collapse of the Swedish Model," *Current Sweden*, No. 358, March 1988.

12. Quoted by Frederic Fleisher, *The New Sweden* (New York: David McKay, 1967), p. 73.

13. However, we note that, while 77 percent of all cases of illness were shorter than one week in 1985, these accounted for just 18 percent of all days lost through illness for which benefits were paid. See Birger Viklund, "Absenteeism in Sweden," *Current Sweden*, No. 264, February 1981 and The Swedish Ministry of Finance, *The Swedish Budget*, 1987/88 (Stockholm 1987), p. 146.

14. Martin Schnitzer, *The Economy of Sweden* (New York: Praeger, 1970).

15. Svante Nycander, "Industrial Relations and Workers' Participation," *Current Sweden*, No. 41, September 1974.

16. Quoted by Jenkins, *Sweden and the Price of Progress*, p. 137.

17. County and municipal government authorities also had to extend comparable packages to their employees. As the biggest percentage increases were offered by SAV to relatively less well paid workers and the lower levels of government have higher proportions of these, the cost of the settlement was much greater to them than to the central government. See Svante Nycander, "The Swedish Labor Market Organizations," Swedish Royal Ministry of Foreign Affairs Information Service, May 1972.

18. See Gösta Edgren, Karl-Olaf Faxen, and Clas-Eric Odhner, *Wage Formation and the Economy* (London: Allen & Unwin, 1973). This study, itself, reflects cooperation across the bargaining table, since Edgren, Faxen, and Odhner were, respectively, the chief economists for SAF, LO, and TCO. It should be noted, however, that the division of the

564   COMPARATIVE ECONOMIC SYSTEMS

economy into C and P sectors (reported below) was accepted long before this study appeared.

19. Sweden's export mix of goods and services is constantly changing, as is that of any developed nation, since new firms and products are constantly acquiring footholds on world markets, and old products are declining. In starting a new product line (or in getting started itself), a firm encounters high costs for several reasons, including lack of experience with the technology in question. In Sweden, such a firm would have to pay wages commensurate with those in factories turning out established product lines and would receive little protection from international competition. This is the opposite of what a Japanese company would encounter in similar circumstances, which may help to explain greater Japanese success in expanding export market shares over 1960–80.

20. Assar Lindbeck, *Swedish Economic Policy* (Berkeley: University of California Press, 1974), p. 207.

21. Article 32 never became law, but it acquired the force of law through rulings in its favor by the Labor Court. With intentional irony, the 1976 Industrial Democracy Law, described below, contained the following Article 32: "The contracting parties to collective agreements on wages and general conditions of employment should, if the employee side requests, also sign collective agreements on the right of employees to participate in decision making on matters concerning the direction and allotment of work, the inception and termination of employment agreements, or other management matters." This nullified Article 32 of the SAF constitution, and the Law itself replaced the Mediation Act of 1920, the Collective Contracts Act of 1928, and the Act on the Right of Association and Collective Bargaining of 1936.

22. See Ann-Charlotte Stahlberg, "Effects of the Swedish Supplementary Pension System on Personal and Aggregate Household Saving," *Scandinavian Journal of Economics*, No. 1, 1980. Sweden also allows early retirement with reduced pension or late retirement (after age sixty-five) with increased pension. Another plan permits individuals to gradually scale down the amount of work they do between the ages of sixty and seventy.

23. See Bertil Holmlund, "Payroll Taxes and Wage Inflation: The Swedish Experience," *Scandinavian Journal of Economics*, No. 1, 1983.

24. One author notes that "It would be oversimplified . . . to say that this development originated in the profit motive of private capitalism alone. The Social Democrats and LO both sanctioned and forced the pace of rationalization. . . . It was LO which, above all, wanted to increase the amount of piecework within industry during the 1950s. The [resulting] disadvantages were to be made up by increased earnings and progressively shorter work hours. . . . It was not until the 1970s that people began to become aware of the social disadvantages of this development. . . . Not even the idea that increased leisure would provide significant compensation seems to hold true. Commercialized and passive use of leisure appears to be most common among those who have an impoverished work situation." Se Bertil Gardell, "Production Techniques and Working Conditions," *Current Sweden*, No. 256, August 1980, pp. 3–4.

25. Replacement of the assembly line by a layout conforming to the operations team approach raised the cost of the plant by 10 percent. According to a Volvo official, the extra cost has been entirely offset by faster assembly times, fewer required supervisors, greater ease of altering production arrangements, and reduced rates of turnover and absenteeism. However, Kalmar also represented an early Swedish experiment with modern industrial robots, which made the "humanization" possible. See Berth Jonsson, "The Volvo Experience of New Job Design and New Production Technology," *Working Life in Sweden*, No. 19, October 1980, and Stefan Aguren, Reine Hansson, K. G. Karlsson, *The Volvo Kalmar Plant* (Stockholm: SAF-LO Rationalization Council, 1976). See, as well, Per Ahlstrom, "Codetermination at Work: The Almex Experience," *Working Life in Sweden*, No. 17, April 1980.

26. For discussion see Lennart Forsebäck, *Industrial Relations and Employment in Sweden* (Stockholm: The Swedish Institute, 1980), pp. 120–26; Per-Martin Meyerson,

Company Profits: Sources of Investment Finance: Wage Earners' Investment Funds in Sweden (Stockholm: Federation of Swedish Industries, September 1976); Dave Noble, "Rudolf Meidner and 'Worker Power'," *Current Sweden*, The Swedish Institute, No. 106, February 1976; Elisabet Hoglund, "A Proposal for Employee Funds—Another Step Toward Employee Power in Sweden," *Current Sweden*, No. 192, June 1978; Rudolf Meidner, "Employee Investment Funds and Capital Formation: A Topical Issue in Swedish Politics," *Working Life*, No. 6, The Swedish Information Service, June 1978; Staffan Sonning, "Election Year, '82: Employee Funds," *Current Sweden*, No. 286, May 1982; and Staffan Sonning, "The Employee Fund Issue Moves Toward a Decision," *Current Sweden*, No. 309, October 1983.

27. Meidner was charged by LO with finding a way to achieve three goals: increased control by employees over their companies, neutralization of excess profit to benefit the wage solidarity program, and a more equitable distribution of wealth. See Forsebäck, *Industrial Relations*, pp. 126–28; and Meyerson, *Company Profits*, pp. 6–11.

28. Forsebäck, *Industrial Relations*, p. 123.

29. Noble, "Rudolph Meidner and 'Worker Power'," p. 2.

30. Until the employee proportion of a company's shares reached 40 percent, voting rights at company annual general meetings would be divided equally between the employees of each firm and the relevant regional assembly.

31. The innovator is the individual responsible for marketing a product or for putting a new technique into practical operation. He or she is not necessarily the inventor. Schumpeter gives the strongest defense of innovation and entrepreneurship as the engines of progress. See J. A. Schumpeter, *Capitalism, Socialism and Democracy* (New York: Harper & Row, 1950), especially Part 2.

32. See Sonning, "The Employee Fund Issue Moves Toward a Decision," pp. 7–8.

Questions for Review, Discussion, Examination

*1. Why is Sweden's "active" labor market policy a key element in the package of economic and social policies on which its reputation as a "middle way" is based? Why is it a potential model for reformers in Eastern Europe and the USSR?

2. What attitude have Swedish labor unions taken toward firms threatened with closure because of declining product demand or foreign competition? How did this attitude change following the energy crisis and resulting growth slowdown?

3. Briefly explain what is meant by the "Swedish model."

4. From an efficiency standpoint, what is the main potential advantage of centralized collective bargaining over more decentralized variants? Why was the more centralized version chosen in Sweden?

*5. Why may an increase in union bargaining power prove to be self-defeating over the long run, at least in part? What else may have to happen, in order to remove this self-defeating property? Explain briefly.

How has the share of Swedish gross domestic product going as wages, salaries, and payroll fees evolved since 1960?

*6. What are the goals of the policy of "wage solidarity" of the Swedish union movement? How may wage solidarity have helped to promote Swedish exports over the post–World War II era (except during the 1970s)? Was wage solidarity pursued more successfully during the 1970s or 1980s? Explain briefly.

7. What is "wage drift"? How does it arise and how does it help to undo wage solidarity?

8. On what grounds does SAF oppose wage solidarity? Why might wage solidarity reinforce the effect of high marginal taxes on income in reducing labor mobility toward more productive jobs?

9. What did SAF receive in exchange for accepting the central wage negotiations? Discuss briefly. What role did government play in these negotiations?

*10. According to the EFO guidelines, how are maximum permissible increases in wages plus benefits supposed to be determined? How did the policy of wage solidarity plus soaring company profits get the better of the EFO guidelines to cause a wage-cost explosion over 1974–76? Explain briefly, noting the effect on exports and the Swedish balance of payments.

11. How has the Swedish tax system affected labor market negotiations? Explain briefly. What has been the nature of recent tax reform?

12. What kind of deduction has constituted a major tax loophole in Sweden? Has it now been closed? Discuss briefly.

13. Why does Sweden have such a high labor-force participation rate (especially among women), in combination with high rates of absenteeism and little use of overtime?

*14. How has the Social Democratic "Platform" evolved since the end of the nineteenth century in Sweden? (How have the party's immediate goals evolved since then and what stages in this evolution can we distinguish?)

15. Under what stage in the evolution referred to in question 14 do we find the rapid advance of social insurance? How did the national pension system change? How did this affect net household saving in Sweden? Why?

*16. What stage in the evolution referred to in question 14 distinguishes Social Democrats from other political parties? Why might we expect that pursuit of higher wages would eventually no longer be an adequate goal for a successful labor movement in a society with a relatively high living standard?

17. The period 1972–76 saw a marked increase in labor market legislation in Sweden. Why, apparently, did it help to cause an increase in youth unemployment?

18. What is the Working Environment Law?

19. What is the Industrial Democracy Law? How did it propose to alter previous management practices and prerogatives in Sweden? Does the traditional peace obligation in Swedish labor relations still prevail?

*20. What was the Meidner Plan? How was it an outgrowth of the policy of promoting wage solidarity, as well as the drive toward industrial democracy? Broadly speaking, how did the goals of the Meidner Plan evolve, from its inception to the Edin Plan that became law in 1984? Could we have predicted that such an evolution would take place? Explain briefly.

*21. What problems might economists find with the Meidner Plan, insofar as preservation of the present efficiency of Swedish industry is concerned? Explain how these problems are related to innovation and competition.

* = more difficult.

16

THE SWEDISH ECONOMY: POLICY AND THE WELFARE STATE

16-l. Sweden as a Mixed Economy

A. *Industrial Policy in Sweden*

The sheer weight of government spending gives the state leverage over all aspects of economic life in Sweden, and government agencies do interfere directly with production, pricing, employment, and investment decisions at the enterprise level. Without such interference, Sweden's record in reducing unemployment and pollution, in bringing handicapped people into working life, in humanizing the working environment, in recycling waste products, and more generally, in controlling the harmful effects of industrial development, would probably not be as good. Nevertheless, Sweden has a market economy that still relies on decisions of individual firms and households to allocate well over half the gross national product. It is also a mixed economy. Besides the active labor market policy, to be explored in section 16-6, we may divide the government's industrial policies into four broad categories:

(a) Assistance to sectors facing long-run decline, to permit an orderly run-down of capacity and to speed up redeployment of displaced workers. Between 1974 and 1983, Swedish industrial output showed a net decrease, which fell disproportionately on some basic sectors—notably, iron and steel, shipbuilding, and textiles, where employment was cut in half. Ironically, nonsocialist governments in power over 1976–82 nationalized more industrial assets, generally to keep down the number of bankruptcies and lost jobs, than the Social Democrats had done in the previous 44 years. However, by gradually shifting aid toward automating and computerizing production, upgrading products, and reducing the number of product lines, Sweden was able to save portions of most afflicted industries and make them cost competitive.

(b) Assistance to sectors with sound long-term growth prospects, to carry them over temporary difficulties, such as structural problems or a cyclical downturn in demand. In many sectors of the Swedish economy, the last twenty-five years have witnessed a dramatic fall in the number of production facilities and a dramatic rise in the capacity of each. By realizing scale economies in this fashion, the sectors in question have been able to remain viable and even to prosper.

(c) Assistance to sectors with good long-run growth prospects, but needing additional investment capital. During the 1980s, information technology has been the fastest-growing industry, and it has enjoyed government support for research and development, innovation, and expansion of plant capacity.

(d) Assistance to firms accepting undesirable locations, additional handicapped or elderly workers, or some other less profitable but more socially advantageous input mix. In this context, the 1985 Regional Policy Act aims at achieving "balanced demographic development in the various regions of the country and at making employment, services, and a good environment available to everyone in Sweden."[1] Government-owned firms are major employers in the north of Sweden, where mechanization of farming, forestry, and mining has raised the rate of unemployment to over 4 percent. These companies must balance considerations of profitability with those relating to employment and community welfare.

During the postwar era, the government has channelled low-cost loans into housing, and to a lesser extent, into power generation, export industries, and firms locating in the north of Sweden. Grants have also encouraged private companies to hire the handicapped, and in the 1970s, the state subsidized up to 75 percent of wage costs to prevent layoffs in industries and regions with employment problems. (We may also view these as subsidies for the wage solidarity program.) In addition, there is a uniquely Swedish form of accelerated depreciation—the investment reserves, discussed below—which has been used to combat business cycles and to stimulate expansion in depressed regions. Finally, just by maintaining the world's foremost welfare state, the Swedish government has stimulated the growth of industries (notably health care) whose products are used intensively by social insurance recipients.

In connection with (c), the state-owned Swedish Investment Bank lends for "large, long-term, risk-bearing investments in the business sector"—that is, mainly for projects that appear to be in the national interest, but which would not have enough access to finance without special help. Similarly, the National Board for Technical Development (STU) supplies venture capital for developing new products and production processes, including manufacture of prototypes and construction of pilot plants. The Board assumes much of the risk of projects that are approved, by requiring no security for these loans other than the projects themselves and by permitting repayment to depend on project profitability. Finally, the Swedish Industrial Fund was set up in 1979 to complement support from STU and from regional development funds, which had been established in each county. The Industrial Fund also lends to foster innovation, with conditional repayment depending on a project's success. In this way, it absorbs part of the risk involved, although, as in the case of STU, the borrower is expected to bear a substantial share of the total cost on his own.

To further stimulate investment and to make the increase in profits resulting from the October 1982 devaluation of the crown acceptable to unions (without encouraging excessive wage demands), the government set up Special Investment Funds.[2] Companies had to deposit 20 percent of their pretax profits into a special, non-interest-bearing account at the central bank, which could then be used for investment, with the consent of local union branches. In 1986, these Funds were replaced by Renewal Funds, into which firms must deposit 10 percent of pretax profit. These deposits are tax deductible, but again require local union approval, and must be used for investment, research and development, or educational and training programs for company employees. About 1 percent of GNP went into the Renewal Funds in 1985.

Prior to this, the nonsocialist parties in power over 1976–82 had raised grants and loans for regional development, research, and export promotion, and it was they who evolved a comprehensive program to improve conditions for small and medium-sized firms, which still account for half of private sector employment. Government support includes risk absorption—plus help with finance, marketing, research, technical production problems, and product development—and is mainly channelled through the regional development funds. In 1980, the government launched an enquiry which led to changes in the tax code, passed in 1983 and supported by all parties, including the Communists.[3] These reforms turned shares in small and medium-sized firms into tax shelters and created an over-the-counter market in which they are traded. Over 1977–85, the number of new enterprises soared to record levels. However, the labor legislation of the 1970s also provided part of the encouragement for this, as did the relatively high unemployment. Rather than hire new employees, with the commitments and costs that this now entails, large companies are contracting out more of their work, and new small firms are arising to fill this demand.[4]

Between 1974 and 1982, the Swedish government gave a large percentage of its aid to sectors whose long-run growth prospects were poor. Over 1982–83, central government subsidies to industry reached nearly 3 percent of GNP, and the main beneficiaries were shipyards, steel, mining, and forestry—which were also industries owned or taken over by the state.[5] Despite the government's weight and its formal long-range planning, it did not have a forward-looking industrial strategy in the mid-1970s, with growth sectors targeted for future promotion. This forced it to subsidize job preservation in declining industries and job creation in the public sector, in order to prevent a rapid increase in unemployment following the energy crisis. The option of creating jobs in sectors with good export growth potential did not exist because the way had not been prepared with the necessary investments, and the subsidies in question became a major reason for Sweden's poor growth and export performance during these years. Not only did state aid tie up resources in crisis sectors, but some of these continued to pay the highest wages in industry, although they would have shut down immediately, had assistance been withdrawn. In particular, subsidies continued to prop up shipbuilding after its value-added became negative; yet, most yards eventually had to close. (The government managed to ease the unemployment consequences, however, by getting Saab and Volvo to locate auto assembly plants near the sites of two major shut-down yards.)

A bright spot was that aid increasingly went for restructuring, rationalization, and cost reduction. By 1982, the government was committed to progressively reducing assistance under category (a) and expanding help to sectors with growth potential, notably in the high technology area. Key determinants of this shift were Sweden's deteriorating export performance and the growing relative size of the protected sector, as well as the rising public deficit. "The reorientation of industrial policy was confirmed in a bill presented to Parliament in March, 1984, which stressed the importance of . . . forward-looking measures. As a result, government support to industry was reduced from about 17 billion crowns in fiscal 1982/83 to 6.5 billion crowns in 1984/85. On the other hand, support aimed at promoting innovation and technological change, small and medium-sized enterprises, exports, and regional development was increased."[6] Sweden appears to have come through its worst postwar crisis in a humane fashion, sustaining one of the lowest unemployment rates in the Western world, although at high cost in terms of inflation, stagnation, and internal and external deficits. Moreover, the recovery is still vulnerable to large increases in labor or energy costs.

B. The Policy Roles of the Ministries and Boards[7]

Most economic policy making, planning, and forecasting devolves onto the various ministries with responsibilities for economic matters. Yet, with the exception of the Ministry of Foreign Affairs, Swedish ministries are small and nearly always have staffs of under one hundred. A unique feature of Swedish government is that ministries formulate policies, but do not carry them out. Laws limiting ministerial influence go back more than 300 years, with the result that Sweden has a separate set of agencies to implement policy. In the main, policy execution is entrusted to bureaus known as boards (also agencies or directorates). No minister, including the prime minister, may issue direct orders to the boards, which also supply crucial input for policy formation, because they constantly hold hearings and make recommendations about how laws should be changed or interpreted. The approximately one hundred boards have larger staffs than the ministries, although several are internally decentralized. The most prominent board in the sphere of economic policy is the Labor Market Board. With 10,000 employees it is also second largest, after the National Board of Health and Welfare.

Basic policy recommendations to guide the future development of society usually originate in the ministries. To be effective, they must pass the Riksdag to become laws or be approved by cabinet to become ordinances. Both boards and ministries are responsible to cabinet as a whole, and Figure 16.1 gives a simplified view of social goal formation and implementation in Sweden. Usually, ministerial recommendations will be approved—the relevant minister will have sought out many opinions, both formally and informally, beforehand—although modifications and compromises are common. Subsequently, the modified proposals become laws or ordinances to guide policy execution by the boards. Much information also passes informally among these bodies.

An advantage of the Swedish system is that it tends to separate goal formation from goal implementation and allows democratic approval procedures to play a role at every stage of policy formation. (In fact, the appeals procedures can play a role in amending policies even after implementation has begun.) A second advantage is that it frees the ministries from executive and administrative detail, allowing them to focus on major policy issues. Within the broad framework that they lay down, the boards determine much of the practical content of policy, as well as its evolution through time. Each board is headed by a director general, appointed by the cabinet. Traditionally, these are men of strong personality. As they operate under loose directives, it is sometimes said that Sweden is run by directors general, although recent years have witnessed efforts to dilute their power. Formerly, the boards were headed by directors general alone; now, the tendency is to head them by a directorate, which is chaired by the director general and composed at least partly of representatives of the special interest groups affected by the board's activities. These management bodies are supposed to deal with questions of principle—including interpretation of the board's policy guidelines from cabinet—while the director general runs the board on a day-to-day basis.

For example, we have seen that the Labor Market Board's directors include representatives of industry, labor, and farming. The directorate of the Board for Consumer Policies includes representatives of consumers, labor, and business, as does the Market Court. Its director general is also the Consumer Ombudsman (KO). Similarly, the directors of the National Industrial Board include two members of Parliament, one from LO, one from TCO, and one from each of the major industrial federations. The directors general of the Labor Market Board and the Board of Commerce also sit as directors on the Industrial Board. Overlapping membership is common when areas of responsibility overlap, and close cooperation prevails between the various boards and ministries dealing with a given problem area.

Moreover, while the boards must apply their own judgment in specific decisions, they are charged with obeying the spirit rather than the letter of directives. This is more than an abstract constraint, because any statute will have opinions and reports attached to it that give the views of members of Parliament, public servants, the board's directorate, other boards, technical experts, and the various special

Figure 16.1. **A Simplified View of Social Goal Information and Implementation in Sweden.**

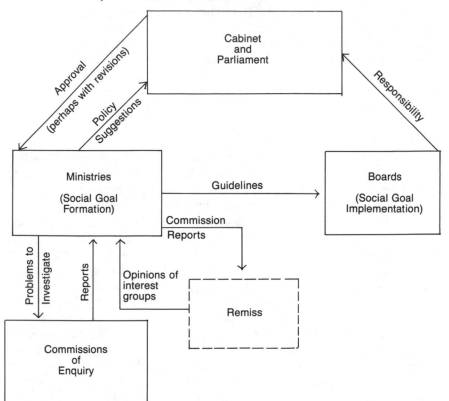

interests affected by the statute. These opinions reflect a statute's history from the time it first becomes a gleam in the eyes of its originators. In this connection,

> the Swedish Constitution does not allow questions to be asked in Parliament concerning individual administrative decisions taken by the [boards]. . . . Only questions of a general nature may be raised concerning the manner in which the subordinate [boards] apply legislation and regulations . . . as Ministers are unable to influence the decisions of [boards] in particular cases.[8]

A statute will often originate in the work of special committees called commissions of enquiry, which are formed by a ministry, by Parliament, or by the cabinet to investigate problems and propose reforms. Like the boards, such commissions do work performed by ministries in most countries. When the government contemplates policy changes, it usually appoints such a commission on an *ad hoc* basis, whose membership will depend on the nature of the problem to be investigated. Where potential economic reforms are concerned, commissions will normally include senior civil servants, members of Parliament, and representatives of such special interests as LO, SAF, KF (the Consumer Cooperative Union), and others who are likely to be affected if the reforms go through. The Swedish approach thus brings lawmakers and groups affected by proposed changes into contact with policy formation at the earliest stage. When major reforms are contemplated, the commissions will include representatives of all major parties in the Riksdag.

Once a commission of enquiry has finished its work, the assigning ministry will publish the resulting recommendations. The commission's report then circulates among special interest groups, local and regional levels of government, the boards that would have to implement the policies, and any other interested organizations. This is called the remiss procedure (Figure 16.1), which allows consultation of a wider range of views than could be represented on a commission of enquiry. Only after a proposal has been modified through remiss will it go to cabinet or Parliament. By then, the original version will have been revised many times and attracted diverse commentary and opinion. When a proposal is presented to Parliament, a standing committee of the Riksdag is likely to go over it again, and further modification is probable. By the time it passes Parliament or is approved by cabinet it has a history, which the boards charged with policy execution are supposed to know and to take into account.

C. Indicative Planning, Forecasting, and Budgeting

As a rule, economic planning in Sweden does not use obligatory production targets, and this sets it apart from practice in Soviet-type economies. Even state-owned companies stress their short-run autonomy, although they must get parliamentary approval for major expansions. During the late 1970s and early 1980s, they also depended heavily on subsidies for survival. The Finance Ministry's Economic Planning Secretariat does issue indicative long- and short-term plans covering different sectors of the economy and different components of GNP.

The functions of planning and budgeting merge in the Finance Ministry's annual presentation to the Riksdag of the budget and related documents. Any budget is a plan, at least in the sense of giving a detailed breakdown of how the government will spend its money. If we think of the budget as a one-year plan for the government sector, there is also a *long-term budget* or plan projecting the outlines of the budgets to come over the next four years. This is presented to Parliament each year with the regular budget and, in a sense, projects ahead the economic consequences of decisions already made by the cabinet and Riksdag. In particular, it gives cost estimates of government policies, along with expected revenues. The long-term budget is revised every year, in the light of recent developments, and a year is added on, so that it becomes a kind of "rolling budget." Unlike the budget proper, it need not be passed by the Riksdag.

The government also presents two other documents with the annual budget. The first is the *Budget Statement*, which acts as a guide to and interpretation of the budget. It gives the government's views on the state of the economy and the reasons for its current priorities, as well as a longer run perspective on the role of the public sector. It is discussed in Parliament, along with the budget, but not voted on. The second document is the *Economic Survey*. It forecasts the development of the Swedish economy over the next eighteen months and can be viewed as a broad economic plan for that period. In particular, it discusses government policies and goals, including any expected changes in taxes and subsidies, and indicates how these will affect the profitability of private investment. It also projects aggregate demand for goods and services and balances this against expected supply.

In drawing up the Economic Survey, the Ministry of Finance gets help from two outside agencies—the Council for Economic Planning and the Economic Research Council. The former brings in representatives of other ministries plus those of industry, labor, and various special interest groups. The Economic Research Council is a body of experts, including professional economists, representing interest groups, the Bank of Sweden, the Statistical Secretariat, private research organizations, and other government bureaus. In this way, a fairly wide representation is assured.

A final economic plan, *The Medium-Term Survey*, tries to project economic developments over the next five years and over the next twenty years in areas related to population growth and labor supply. The result is a forecast, in whose construction people with varied backgrounds will participate. The Survey also indicates current priorities and serves as a backdrop for political debates over economic policy. It is drawn up by the same bodies that work on the Economic Survey—each is done with the other in mind—but the Medium-Term Survey goes through the remiss procedure, and the resulting briefs and comments are published. However, neither survey is voted on by cabinet or Parliament. If the Medium-Term Survey's forecasts become obsolete quickly, it will be revised. For example, the 1980 Survey projected two possible paths for the Swedish economy in the years ahead, the worst of which was described as the "catastrophic alternative." It featured a continuing loss of world market shares by Swedish industry, growing external and internal deficits, low economic growth, and rising unemployment. Actual developments were even worse, and a revised survey appeared in 1982. Fortunately, exports and economic growth revived soon afterward.

16-2. Fiscal Policy

We usually divide government policies to influence the demand for goods and services into two categories. First, *monetary* policies affect the rate of expansion of the money supply, as well as the cost and availability of credit (including interest rates). Over most of the postwar era, the Swedish government has regulated loanable funds markets, using its leverage to depress interest rates and to steer funds toward priority sectors—notably, homebuilding and public investment. Low priority borrowers, including households, have had relatively low access to loans on official credit markets. This is why households were unable to borrow enough to compensate for forced saving via payroll taxes paid by employers on their behalf to finance social insurance. During the 1960s and 1970s, these taxes raised the rate of saving in Sweden, as noted earlier. During the 1980s, however, Swedish financial markets have undergone deregulation. As in Japan, this has resulted, in part, from a string of government budget deficits and a large cumulative public debt, which has reduced the state's leverage over interest rates and the direction of lending. In addition, the demand for new housing has declined.

Second, *fiscal* policies affect government spending, taxes, and transfer payments (subsidies) to households and firms. In this section, we focus on Sweden's "active" fiscal policy, which falls under the jurisdiction of the Finance Ministry and the Labor Market Board. In principle, monetary, fiscal, and labor-market policies support each other in Sweden. The Labor Market Board coordinates the fiscal policies of different levels of government, along with labor market policy, which is its primary concern. Guidelines for Swedish fiscal and labor market policies were spelled out during the late 1940s by the LO economist, Gösta Rehn, also the father of wage solidarity.[9] Rehn's work became part of LO's platform. He focused on active labor market policies, later adopted, to break down occupational and geographical barriers to labor mobility. These would be necessary, in part, because pursuit of wage solidarity would force marginal firms to close or to contract and lay off workers.

To prevent high unemployment, Rehn also advocated some assistance for marginal firms and to support production in depressed regions. However, he proposed keeping the aggregate demand for goods and services *below* its full employment level—specifically, at 96–97 percent of potential output—through restrictive fiscal policy. As a result, profits would be squeezed between restricted demand and union wage pressures on the cost side. Employers would be unable to pass along pay raises by putting up their prices, which was supposed to increase their resistance to inflationary wage hikes. Since excessive wage demands would also lead to unemployment, union leaders could more easily restrain pay demands without alienating their memberships. Moreover, with domestic demand restricted, Swedish firms would have added incentive to develop and expand their export markets. Other nations which rely heavily on exports—including West Germany, Sweden's main competitor on world markets—try to maintain a basically restrictive macroeconomic policy stance.

Where pockets of unemployment did appear, expansionary but highly selective policy measures should be used to eliminate them. In this way, Rehn hoped to combine full employment with price stability. (Of course, the selective policies referred to would raise aggregate demand, but if they were selective enough, most employers might still be unable to pass along inflationary wage increases.) It was important to Rehn that full employment not be guaranteed; an unreasonable union should have to live with the unemployment consequences of its unreasonable wage demands. Hopefully, unions would push their demands just far enough to squeeze profits, without adding to unemployment. In this sense, Rehn's model is a forerunner to the EFO guidelines.

The Swedish government has accepted Rehn's proposals for promotion of labor mobility and wage solidarity. But while Sweden had a restrictive fiscal policy stance in the early 1950s, it did not sustain this. Policy makers became more and more accommodating toward wage-cost increases, in the sense of tending to accept whatever raises were agreed to in the centralized bargaining and then doing what was necessary to keep unemployment low. Underlying fiscal policy became more expansionary, and government contributed to labor-cost increases by raising payroll fees and making generous pay offers to less well paid public employees. Eventually, the EFO guidelines replaced Rehn's, in setting a benchmark for allowable wage-cost increases, but even they were violated during the 1970s. After the energy crises, the government could only keep unemployment down by expanding the public sector, along with protected and subsidized employment.

With hindsight, we can say that failure to keep aggregate demand marginally below full employment was a major policy error. Since their return to power in 1982, the Social Democrats have tried to reestablish a restrictive policy stance, with resulting frictions between public and private sector unions and between unions and the finance minister. (Being "branches of the same tree," the unions and Social Democratic party are supposed to settle their differences privately and present a united front in public, but this has not always happened in recent years.) To better understand the problem, let us distinguish three broad components of fiscal policy:

(1) *Contracyclical Policy*. The government tries to counteract cyclical and seasonal changes in demand for goods and services, so as to dampen fluctuations in employment and output. If fiscal policy has this job, as in Sweden, public spending should rise and net taxes fall to combat recessions, while the reverse should take place to counteract booms.

(2) *Underlying Macroeconomic Policy Stance*. If neither recession nor boom threatens, should policy be expansionary, neutral, or restrictive? Alternatively, if the government follows contracyclical policy, what basic policy stance should this revolve around? Rehn's reply was that it should be restrictive, which would require the government to run a modest budget surplus. In the Swedish context, government expenditure, taxes, and social insurance fees are also high, relative to GNP, which is another part of the underlying policy stance.

(3) *Selective Policies*. These refer to the composition of public sector expenditure and revenues, and, thus, to social welfare, redistributive, and labor-market policies, as well as to aid for specific industries, regions, and activities. In Sweden, the latter would include generous support for humanizing the workplace and preserving the environment.

The policy drift referred to above relates to (2), which became more expansionary over 1953–82. In part, this may be due to shorter political time horizons. After 1970, the period between elections was cut from four to three years, and elections have been won or lost by razor-thin margins. In 1989, the Social Democrats appear stronger than they were in 1971, and this may allow the government breathing space to reestablish a basic budget surplus. In part, Sweden's failure to follow Rehn's guidelines may also have been a failure to prevent the selective increases in government spending which he advocated to remove unemployment from spilling over into the rest of the economy and causing a more general stimulus to aggregate demand. Whatever the cause, the ability of Swedish policy makers to avoid a renewal of drift in the underlying policy stance may be their major test over the rest of the twentieth century.

By contrast, readers may think of fiscal policy largely in terms of (1), and it is here that Sweden has been a pioneer. Every budget contains appropriations to be spent if and as measures to raise employment become necessary. The Labor Market Board maintains lists of public works projects that can get underway quickly, and local governments make up their own lists, which are continually updated. "Most government agencies . . . nowadays know that if they do not have their own ready projects when the next recession comes, other agencies will be allowed to fill the vacuum for increased public investment."[10] This activity can also be used to level seasonal employment fluctuations and to provide temporary employment to older or handicapped workers.

In addition, "the government has a stand-by program for placing orders with industry to compensate selectively for loss of [private] orders caused by a recession." Central government subsidies may also be extended to local authorities to help with their purchasing and public works programs, and "government orders have been used to defer local shutdowns of industrial plants from winter to spring or summer, when the chances of finding new jobs are more favorable."[11] By and large, Swedish authorities have used contracyclical policy tools with skill and imagination. When old tools proved inadequate, new ones have been introduced, such as the investment reserves, to be explored below. Nevertheless, as underlying policy became more expansionary, Sweden had to accept a higher cost of low unemployment, in terms of higher inflation and reduced growth.

All Western nations began a period of growth stagnation in 1974, during the first energy crisis. Most went into recession, which reached bottom in 1975. Sweden postponed this downturn with expansionary policy that was effective in maintaining full employment (indeed, in reducing unemployment below levels characteristic of 1971–73). Through wage subsidies, labor market support, increasing the period of notice for layoffs, a 20 percent subsidy for inventory buildup, and, to a lesser extent, the investment reserves, it was able to postpone the trough of its post-energy-crisis recession from 1975 to 1977. This was a "bridging strategy," which for a time successfully offset the deflationary impact of the first oil price explosion on the Swedish economy. Its aim was to build a bridge over the energy-crisis recession.

But short-term success was bought at a high price in terms of long-run growth, and Sweden's experience raises questions about the value of an active fiscal policy not backed by structural planning, which channels expansionary impulses into sectors with good long-term growth potential. The period of the bridging strategy (1974–76) was also one of wage explosion, which helped Swedish industry to lose shares of nearly every major export market. Several industries that received bridging subsidies became crisis sectors that were still benefiting from large doses of state aid in 1982. The bridging strategy also marks at least the temporary end of deliberate contracyclical policy in Sweden.

Because it tries to maintain fixed exchange rates, fiscal policy should be used to keep unemployment low, while monetary policy is used to maintain balance-of-payments equilibrium.[12] If imports persistently exceed exports, this requires Sweden to have real interest rates above those of other countries, in order to produce offsetting inflows of money capital, which take advantage of the higher return in Sweden. But the latter is unacceptable; the Swedish government wants to follow a low interest rate policy. To preserve at least a balance between imports and exports, Sweden must therefore set an exchange rate and then remain cost competitive at this rate. Failure to do so requires devaluations, as over 1976–82, which are incompatible with fixed exchange rates, except as an occasional aberration.

For this reason alone, underlying fiscal policy must be restrictive. In recent years, moreover, economists have reduced their evaluation of what contracyclical policy can do. Expansionary measures may raise wages and prices, for the most part, rather than output and employment. The division between a price effect and an output effect depends on the extent to which suppliers of goods and services, including labor, are able to foresee the government's policy stance. When expansionary policy is foreseen, suppliers expect the demand curves facing them to rise and become more aggressive in putting up prices. Expansionary policy would be most effective in raising output, according to this argument, when it is completely unexpected, and Sweden's commitment to full employment has made this unlikely, once a recession was in progress.

Even if perfectly foreseen, expansionary policy may work well when price ceilings preserve shortages of key goods. In Sweden, rent controls maintained an excess demand for housing until around 1970. The authorities could always stimulate apartment construction, with assured demand for what was built, just by expanding grants and low-cost loans for this purpose. But rent ceilings were also a major reason for the regulated credit market, which was probably unfavorable to growth. In the present era of deregulation and decontrol, traditional contracyclical policies will be less effective, not only because of the expectations problem, but also because high marginal tax-plus-loss-of-subsidy rates have eroded the incentive effects of policy changes. Finally, business cycles often have a structural dimension. They are associated with shifts in the composition of supply and demand, when advancing industries are unable to absorb inputs as fast as they are shed by declining sectors. This may result from immobility of resources or failure of industries with growth potential to obtain investment funds or to realize experience economies quickly enough to take maximum advantage of their opportunities. By making it easier for these industries to expand, selective policies may lighten recessions and raise long-term growth. Swedish experience during the 1970s shows that they may also have the opposite effect.

16-3. The Investment Reserves

For any kind of fiscal or monetary policy designed to combat the business cycle, the timing of impact is crucial. Ideally, the full thrust of expansionary policy will be felt just as the economy starts to turn down, and it should definitely take hold before a recession ends and the following expansion begins. Otherwise, the government will fuel inflationary pressures, and it may worsen a downturn in the same way, if it is still trying to control the preceding boom. In short, fiscal and monetary policies can easily intensify the business cycle instead of smoothing it out, even if we ignore the expectations problem.

Sometimes we describe this dilemma in terms of the lags with which policy measures operate. Basically, these are lags between perceiving a need for shifts in policy—e.g., because the economy is going from boom to recession—and the change in output that results from the policy changes taking hold. The lags in question may be long and will vary from one business-cycle turning point to another. Thus, the government may be unable to time the impact of policy revisions. Suppose it decides to increase spending. Decision making will, itself, take time, as will the drawing up of plans. Administrative orders will have to go through some bureaucratic red tape before projects are set in motion. Even then, the entire rise in spending will not occur right away, but will spread over a period of time during which projects achieve fruition. Built-in stabilizers, such as social welfare payments and progressive income taxes, work more quickly because they automatically begin to buoy the economy when incomes fall. No one has to perceive a need, and red tape is therefore bypassed.[13] The lag for discretionary spending can also be shortened by having a shelf of projects ready to go plus a transmission belt that by-passes bureaucratic channels.

In Sweden, the design and manipulation of tax rates has been used mainly to achieve long-run growth and distribution goals. Shorter-run stabilization has relied on changes in public spending, labor-market policies, and special devices, such as the investment reserves, a uniquely Swedish institution. We shall now explain the latter, using figures for 1987. Then, the main direct tax on corporations was a national profits tax of 52 percent.[14] Suppose a firm had 100,000 crowns of eligible profits, of which 52,000 crowns would potentially be taxed away. However, if it wished, the enterprise could set aside up to 50 percent of its taxable profit (50,000 crowns) in a special fund called an investment reserve, which is tax free. The catch is that 75 percent of the reserve (37,500 crowns) would have to be deposited in a blocked account at the Bank of Sweden that bears no interest.

The firm could do with the rest of its investment reserve (the remaining 12,500 crowns) as it pleased. But if it would draw on the portion deposited at the Bank of Sweden without permission, the entire investment reserve that is used would be taxed at the usual rate for profit plus 20 percent of the amount withdrawn.[15] This is rarely done. By contrast, when the Labor Market Board gives the go-ahead to spend the investment reserves, the gain is substantial. The cost of *all* investment made with the released funds can be deducted from taxable profits, and during the following year, the enterprise can deduct another 10 percent or 20 percent of this investment cost. However, when the blocked accounts at the Bank of Sweden are released, the enterprise must reproduce the original 25 percent of its investment reserve that it was allowed to keep. To extend the example above, let a company earn 100,000 crowns in pretax profits every year for five straight years. Each year, it sets aside 50,000 crowns as its investment reserve, depositing 37,500 crowns into its blocked Riksbank account and spending the other 12,500 as it wishes.[16] In the sixth year, suppose a recession threatens, which causes the Labor Market Board to unblock the investment accounts. Now, our firm has 187,500 crowns to invest ($5 \times 37,500$), but only if it produces another 62,500 crowns on its own, representing the 25 percent of its investment reserves it was allowed to keep. Whatever it withdraws, it must match on a one-for-three basis from other sources.

Depending on government preferences and perceptions, investment reserves may be released for any combination of construction, acquisition of new machinery and equipment, production for inventory, development of mines, or export promotion. When a release occurs, the funds must be spent within a given time period— ideally, coinciding with the recession trough. The basic goal is to keep the additional demand generated from spilling over into the next boom. Each 3 crowns unblocked from an investment fund account at the central bank will generate 4 crowns of additional spending. However, firms expecting a release of investment reserves may try to build up their idle money balances at a time when recession is already underway. Thus, timing becomes crucial, and the Labor Market Board— which keeps in close contact with employers about employment prospects at least three to four months in advance—must make reasonably accurate forecasts in order for the scheme to achieve good results. It is also up to the Labor Market Board to ensure that funds are actually spent during the period of release.

Swedish firms have responded to investment reserves with an enthusiasm that has been declining. Major releases of funds occurred during the recessions of 1958–59, 1962–63, 1967–68, and over most of 1975–84. (For practical purposes, the plan dates from 1955.) Generally, the reserves worked well through the mid-1970s. The impact of the release was usually a bit late, but not too late to do some good. Once the funds had been released in mid-1975, however, it became hard to end the release—which was extended again and again—because of the prolonged stagnation which followed. In recent years, the tool has become more an instrument of selective than of contracyclical policy, and this is recognized in the 1979 Investment Funds Law. Thus, the reserves were available virtually throughout the 1970s for construction, a depressed industry because of the decline of home building. Since 1963, it has been easier to get a release if part of the reserve is invested in a depressed area.

There have been several supplements to the investment reserves program. During the 1960–61 inflation, firms received a tax break for putting the entire investment reserve into their blocked Riksbank accounts. In this way, income was temporarily withdrawn from circulation, reducing aggregate demand. In 1974, when prices were rising rapidly in the wake of the energy crisis, and profits in Sweden were relatively high, firms were required to deposit 20 percent of their net profits with the Riksbank for subsequent investment in improving the work environment. A second special investment reserve, introduced late that year, absorbed another 15 percent of net profits. The Special Investment and Renewal Funds, described earlier, which were set up after the Social Democrats' return to power in 1982, are also a form of compulsory investment reserve.

From one point of view, the voluntary investment reserves are a form of super-accelerated depreciation. A firm can write off the entire cost of an investment from its taxable profits in one year and take a 10 percent or 20 percent bonus the following year. Thus, we may view the scheme as a component of Sweden's liberal depreciation laws, which are mainly designed to promote long-term growth rather than to combat recessions. In their present form, the investment reserves began in 1955, as part of a tightening of depreciation rules. Prior to then, most large firms could depreciate their fixed assets more or less as they chose. A company acquiring a factory worth 100 million crowns in 1953 could deduct the entire 100 million crowns from its taxable profits in 1953, provided the latter were high enough.

Of course, such a company could not deduct further depreciation charges on this investment. But as a rule, firms would rather have funds sooner than later. Accelerated depreciation is an interest-free loan of foregone taxes by the government to a firm taking advantage of such a plan and fits in with the general policy of keeping interest rates low. When a bad year comes along and pretax profits are poor, the company can defer most depreciation charges to more prosperous times. During recessions, the Swedish government sometimes sweetens depreciation allowances or gives special investment subsidies. On occasion, it has also surtaxed low-priority investment. Moreover, the basic 52 percent profits tax is mainly for firms that stop growing and therefore maintain low levels of investment. In this way, the corporate tax laws seek to motivate growth.

16-4. Rent and Price Control

Sweden has relied fairly heavily on price controls since World War II, although these were mainly selective between expiration of the comprehensive wartime law in 1956 and passage of a new law in 1973. The latter gives the government power to prohibit price increases and requires the Price Control Board to receive notice of increases one month in advance. Especially since 1977, both socialist and

582 COMPARATIVE ECONOMIC SYSTEMS

nonsocialist governments have made liberal use of controls on an on-again, off-again basis. As in other countries, there is little evidence that price ceilings have reduced inflation, except (possibly) over very short periods. In a few cases, this may be enough. For example, the general price freeze imposed by the Social Democrats on their return to power in 1982 may have provided breathing space to implement a combination of restrictive fiscal policy, devaluation, and selective subsidies which turned the Swedish economy around.

Beyond this, Assar Lindbeck has described Sweden as an economy with dual allocation.[17] While access to most goods depends on willingness and ability to pay the going price, the prices of other goods are kept permanently below their equilibrium levels, creating shortages. Allocation of the latter is partly by queuing, as well as by government priority, assessment of "need" or "merit," and so forth. Over most of the postwar era, loanable funds fell into this category, and many public services, along with education and health care, still do. For many years, rent control was a major example. From 1942 until the early 1970s, over half of all apartments in Sweden were subject to rent ceilings, which did not come off entirely until 1976. (Moreover, rent freezes were part of the brief general price freezes of 1980 and 1982.)

Historically, rent ceilings date from 1942 when rents were frozen as part of wartime emergency controls, and by 1945, a slight shortage had emerged. They remained frozen into the 1950s, as part of a general system of price restraints. In the meantime, the slight excess demand was becoming a major shortage, due both to rural-urban migration and to better enforcement of rent ceilings than of other price controls. Over the 1940s and 1950s, rents fell by about 20 percent relative to the consumer price index, and a critical housing shortage developed. During the latter 1950s, for example, a Stockholm family following the legal procedure put its name on an apartment list and waited up to ten years for a modest flat.[18] This was because rent ceilings kept monthly payments far below their equilibrium levels. At one time, over 15 percent of Stockholm's population had their names on an apartment waiting list. Families and individuals had to take whatever apartments became available—they could not choose one to suit their tastes—and Swedish apartments became highly standardized. By 1955, when the last of the other ceilings were being relaxed, rents could not be decontrolled for political reasons. The resulting increases would have been too great and too obvious. Instead, the government blamed the growing shortage on urbanization and on the large number of marriages during and just after the war. The authorities vowed to "build away" the shortage—that is, to end it by subsidizing the construction of new dwellings.

Until the early 1970s the state also manipulated the structure of the housing market, suppressing the demand for detached houses in favor of apartments, through greater subsidies for the latter and higher property taxes, more red tape, and even construction ceilings for the former. The entire structure of controls, including comprehensive rent ceilings, resulted in an excess demand for nearly every type of home. It was during this era that the expansion and contraction of homebuilding loans found major use as a contracyclical tool, since demand was assured for nearly all dwellings that were built.

Swedish experience with rent control is a textbook example of how supply and demand forces often reassert themselves in the face of controls. Figure 16.2 tries to summarize Swedish housing policy, which has been at odds with itself. Rent ceilings discouraged construction of rental housing, by lowering the return on such an investment. But the government offset this by subsidizing both the supply and the demand side of the housing market, shifting these curves outward from D'D' and S'S' to DD and SS, respectively. These subsidies took several forms, including direct grants to homebuyers or renters, the right of owner-occupiers to deduct mortgage interest payments from taxable income, and a plentiful supply of low-interest loans for construction and mortgages. As a rule, mortgage interest rates have been below those on other types of loans.

In Figure 16.2 with rent ceiling, R_C, plus subsidized demand and supply curves, DD and SS, the shortage equals 1.2 million apartments. Demand at the ceiling rent is 3.3 million flats, but only 2.1 million are available. This roughly describes the state of affairs in Swedish cities during 1950–70, if we add that, during most of this period, the shortage was growing. In 1955, the National Board of Building and Planning was forecasting that, if 65,000 apartments were constructed annually, the housing shortage would be ended by 1965. In fact, an annual average of 73,000 apartments were built during this period, and the excess demand, as measured by the lengths of waiting lists, grew in nearly every year.

Over 1950–70, Sweden probably completed more housing units per capita than any other country, although it also built a larger percentage of apartments than any other Western developed nation except Switzerland.[19] The average number of people per room of living space fell from 1.35 in 1945 to 0.78 in 1973. (It is now under 0.6 people per room.) Such amenities as running water, indoor toilets, central heating, and baths and showers became much more common than they had been. Today, over 90 percent of all dwellings have these conveniences. Between 1946 and 1975, about 2.22 million new dwellings were built and 845,000 were demolished or converted to other uses, for a net gain of 1.375 million, or more than one new home for every 6 residents. Nearly half the homes in Sweden were built during this period. Rents fell to absorb just 14 percent of gross family incomes in 1973, vs. 25 percent to 40 percent in the 1930s. (However, the tax share of income was much lower in the earlier period.)

Unfortunately, these gains were not without cost. The rate of demolition of older units was abnormally high because rent controls reduced the incentive to proper repair and maintenance and because it was often profitable to pull down apartment houses and to replace them with warehouses or office buildings, which were not controlled. When rent ceilings were abolished for apartment buildings completed after January 1, 1969, it sometimes became profitable to tear down old apartment buildings, whose rents were controlled, and replace them with new buildings that were decontrolled. The ratio of dwellings removed from the housing stock to new

584

Figure 16.2. **A Shortage of Housing Caused by Rent Control.**

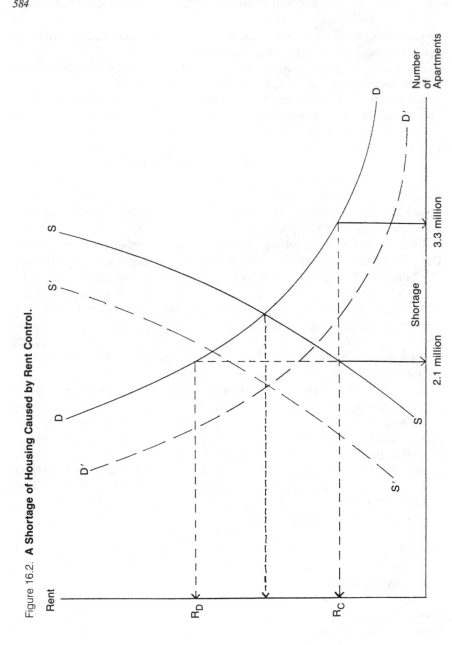

homes built rose from 20 percent over 1941–45 to 52 percent over 1961–65. In 1965, a commission was appointed to investigate the "mystery of the disappearing dwellings."[20] Subsequently, as rent ceilings were lifted in stages, this ratio fell back until it is now below one-third.

With the shortage of apartments, many families were willing to pay more than the ceiling rent to obtain a flat. In Figure 16.2, the demand price for the 2.1 million apartments available is R_D, which is above R_C and also above the rent that would prevail in market equilibrium where demand equals supply. If an apartment were *not* subject to rent control, it would rent for R_D (or what buyers are willing to pay), and if it could be sold without any price ceiling, it would sell for the capitalized value of R_D. Since families were willing to pay more than the ceiling rent, they often did end up paying more, especially in Stockholm, where the excess demand for housing was greatest. A black market for apartments developed in which individuals with access to flats, whether because of political connections or because their names were at the front of the queue, sublet to others whose housing needs were more urgent. The rent ceilings applied to the sublet, but ways around this were found, such as selling the keys to the apartment.

In other cases, outright bribes were paid. Writing in 1968, Assar Lindbeck observed that "according to . . . sketchy empirical evidence, only 20 percent to 25 percent of those who have moved into apartments in recent years have obtained them via the official queues . . . the usual way to get an apartment in Sweden seems to be via relatives, friends, and employers . . . the black market also seems to play an important part."[21] Worse, pregnant mothers without sufficient housing space got abortions, couples broke their engagements or moved in with relatives because they could not get apartments of their own, and parents short of space turned over their children for adoption.[22] Many people who were lucky enough to have apartments before the shortage became severe, or to have spots near the front of the queue, had a lower valuation of housing—and a less urgent need of it by any reasonable standard—than many at the back. Some individuals even put their names on waiting lists in order to sell their places on the black market at a profit. At the same time, suppliers tried to regain part of the income diverted from them by rent ceilings—e.g., by collecting disguised rent payments, by allowing the quality of apartments to deteriorate, and by shifting supply into uncontrolled uses.

Thus, a lesson from Sweden's experience is that rent ceilings cause waste and that they hurt many prospective tenants, although they also help others. The Swedish government began relaxing rent controls on a step-by-step basis in 1958, especially for areas where excess demand was not too great and for buildings owned by municipalities and consumer cooperatives. The latter were, in fact, a large and growing share of the total housing stock, and private contractors accounted for only about half of all new construction vs. 90 percent before World War II. Since cooperative apartments (similar to condominiums in North America) were effectively owner purchased and occupied, the market value of such a unit rose to the capitalized value of R_D, which made them good investments, as long as rent control was in force. After 1958, rents were allowed to rise enough to cover increases in interest and maintenance costs, although until 1969, ceilings remained tighter on privately owned dwellings than on others. In 1960, the index of rents caught up with the overall consumer price index, but the housing shortage remained through the 1960s, and threatened to cause defeat of the Social Democratic party in the 1968 elections. This led to a final lifting of rent ceilings on all homes completed after January 1, 1969. Rents on older homes were decontrolled by 1976.

As rent ceilings were lifted, a surprising thing happened. The number of housing starts reached an all-time high in 1968—just before decontrol—and the number of completions peaked over 1969–70. It has remained below 60,000 per year since, with most of the decline taking place in construction of apartments. Yet, the great housing shortage, that could not be built away in twenty years, disappeared as a general phenomenon. By the early 1970s, a few areas had 20 percent apartment vacancy rates, something previously unheard of, and many owners of cooperative dwellings watched the market values of their homes depreciate (as R_D fell toward $\overline{R}$ in Figure 16.2), even as rents in privately owned apartment buildings were rising (also toward $\overline{R}$). It is hard to explain the elimination of the housing shortage, except as a reduction in quantity demanded due to higher rents and to the disappearance of opportunities for resale at a profit on the black market. Buyers who put low values on homes for their own use were finally excluded, and the government had underestimated the importance of this segment of demand. Moreover, when consumer preferences reasserted themselves, single and two-family houses rose from a low of 25 percent of all dwellings started during the 1950s to about 30 percent over the 1960s and to more than 65 percent since 1975.

Today, rents are decontrolled, although not completely free. Primarily, they are determined in collective bargaining between the Swedish Tenants' Association and the Swedish Landlords' Association. The largest member of the latter is the Local Authorities' Association, representing municipal governments, which owns about 20 percent of the total housing stock, including over 40 percent of all rented dwellings. There are also rent review boards, to which tenants can appeal, and which will generally be guided by rents in municipally owned dwellings. In the main, rent ceilings have been replaced by means tested rent subsidies, which are paid to nearly all pensioners and to half of all families with children, although to few others. These subsidies depend on income, size of family, and amount of rent charged, so that there is some disincentive to accept low quality housing. For retired people with only the basic pension, housing is usually free. For others, the subsidy can come to over half the rent, although 30–40 percent is more usual.

16-5. Health Care

Sweden has had national health insurance since 1955, financed largely by payroll fees and to a lesser extent from general budget revenues. Thus, medical care is underpriced or free, and a person in normal income brackets unable to work due to illness is entitled to sick pay totalling 90 percent of regular earnings. The prevailing view is that inexpensive medical treatment should be denied to no one in need, and that nearly all costs of catastrophic illness should be borne by society. According to a Swedish source: ''The health insurance system is mainly an instrument for creating greater socioeconomic equality. It enables people with small resources and/or extensive medical care needs to take advantage of health care services on the same basis as others.''[23]

Generally speaking, Sweden has one of the world's best health care systems. However, low prices for medical care have led to an excess demand for all aspects of it—despite the heavily subsidized supply—including shortages of doctors and trained personnel. Waits of several weeks to several months are normal for routine doctor appointments. While emergency care is reasonably fast—and often abused because of this—Swedes have had to wait over a year, on occasion, for elective surgery, including routine operations. In some cases, it has been possible to speed up treatment by paying higher, black-market prices. Hospital space has also been used by people who could have been treated as outpatients, but who would then have had to pay more, because laboratory tests are only free to those admitted to hospital. Doctors rarely get to see the same patient more than once, which reduces their incentive, since they cannot follow a case and see the effects of their treatment. In addition, Sweden has a shortage of facilities to care for the aged, which are a rising percentage of her population, and treatment of mental disorders is on a low level. However, because doctors' earnings are largely independent of the amount of medical care they prescribe, they rarely prescribe expensive care that is not needed. They also have considerable freedom and funding for research. Swedish doctors are responsible for many of the major medical advances of this century.

Health care is permanently part of the queuing sector of the Swedish economy, with the county councils picking up most of the cost.[24] (Just 4 percent of health care costs are financed from patients' fees.) About 95 percent of all doctors and half of all dentists work for the government, while the remainder are in private practice. In 1986, the basic charge for an outpatient visit was 55 crowns ($7.15 U.S.). Outpatients never paid more than 55 crowns for drugs prescribed at any one visit, and life-saving drugs are provided free. Inpatient care is even more heavily subsidized. By contrast, individuals pay 50–60 percent of dental care costs, although this is free for children under 16. The goal of price policy is to keep medical fees reasonable, but still high enough to exclude much of the demand by people who don't really need the treatment. (Ideally, the fee for each type of care would lie just above the most elastic segment of the demand curve.) Nevertheless, the trebling of county income taxes over the past twenty-five years or so has gone mainly to finance health care, which now absorbs about 10 percent of GNP vs. 2.5 percent in 1950. The health care field employs almost 10 percent of the Swedish labor force, although many work on a part-time basis. As in other countries, costs of these services have soared, and Sweden is close to world leadership in terms of per capita expenditure on them.

16-6. Labor Market Policy

A. *The Basis for Labor Market Planning*

In principle, Swedish labor market planning aims to make labor markets work like the competitive markets in economics textbooks. Workers should be paid according to the values of their marginal products, and two individuals doing work of comparable quality with similar skill requirements and disutility costs (in terms of boredom, exertion, danger, dirtiness, and so forth) should receive about the same real wage. Where this rule is modified, it should be in favor of greater equality. The Swedish authorities have also tried to reduce income inequality by expanding the supply of skilled and professional workers, and labor market programs to increase mobility across geographical and skill boundaries are an outgrowth of the wage solidarity policy. Retraining first became a major concern of the Labor Market Board during the 1960s, when the number of company closings accelerated to about three times its former level, partly due to wage pressures. The 1970s and 1980s have seen a rapid expansion of labor market programs, which in 1985 covered about 3.7 percent of the labor force.

The Labor Market Board has also made a special effort to bring married women, the handicapped, and older workers into productive employment. Its courses have played a major role in facilitating a dramatic expansion of labor force participation by women over the past twenty years. The Swedish government will train or retrain anyone who is unemployed or in danger of losing his job and unable to find suitable work easily, provided the individual demonstrates the necessary aptitude. It will also train any competent person for short-handed jobs, regardless of whether he or she is in danger of becoming unemployed.[25] Training is free, not only in the sense that the trainee pays no fees (virtually all education in Sweden is free in this sense), but also in that all living costs, including child support, are borne by the state. In addition, the trainee receives a stipend, which, on average, will be 60–65 percent of the average, pretax industrial wage.

As noted above, labor market measures were conceived as support for wage solidarity, and Figure 16.3 shows how retraining can help to equalize earnings. Ideally, these programs expand the supply of skilled labor from S_sS_s to $S'_sS'_s$ in Figure 16.3(a), thereby lowering the average skilled wage from W_s to W'_s. The newly-trained workers come from the ranks of unskilled, whose supply therefore shrinks from S_uS_u to $S'_uS'_u$ in Figure 16.3(b), causing the average wage in this market to rise from W_u to W'_u. The Labor Market Board will also retrain individuals whose skills have become obsolete. Over a typical year, 2–3 percent of the labor force will acquire new skills or upgrade old ones in courses supervised by the Labor Market Board and the Board of Education. Since up to 25 percent of LO's members will change jobs over a period of three to four years, the unions want assurances that most will go on to better paying work fairly quickly. As this became less likely in the 1970s, Swedish unions became more protective of specific jobs for specific

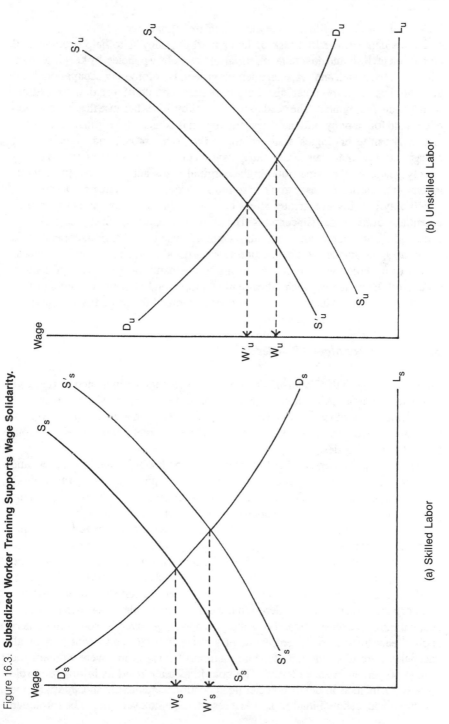

Figure 16.3. **Subsidized Worker Training Supports Wage Solidarity.**

(a) Skilled Labor

(b) Unskilled Labor

individuals and less willing to see marginal firms shut down.

In this context, the first task of labor market policy is to help promote full employment. It should dovetail with fiscal and monetary policies, by keeping down structural, frictional, and seasonal unemployment. By promoting occupational and geographical mobility, it can also help to reduce the rate of inflation compatible with low unemployment. The need for active policy arises because the composition of demand for labor by skill, industry, and region is constantly shifting, in response to changes in technologies, tastes, competition from abroad, and availability of energy and raw materials. Such shifts have been rapid in Sweden over the past twenty years. At the same time, high marginal taxes and pressures to equalize incomes reduce incentives to move or retrain, in order to take more productive jobs, which may also involve greater stress or responsibility. Labor market measures potentially offset these disincentives. The more successful they are in matching the composition of labor supply with labor demand by skill and region, at negotiated wage rates, the smaller will be the pressure on fiscal policy to remove the excess supply of unskilled workers by expanding the demand for them. Thus, the more successful the match between labor-market supply and demand, the smaller will be the wage drift—which results from excess demand for skilled labor—and the weaker inflationary pressures will be.

B. Kinds of Labor Market Policies

The explosive growth of labor-market measures in Sweden is indicated by the large numbers of people taking advantage of them, as well as by the size of appropriations, which have run altogether 3.5–4.0 percent of GNP in recent years—over ten times their share in the early 1960s. The main labor market programs fall into four overlapping categories:

(a) Measures to increase the flow of information about jobs to job seekers and about job seekers to employers. This is a major prerequisite of a well-functioning labor market. (The textbook market model presupposes perfect knowledge on the part of both employers and workers.) The Labor Market Board controls all employment agencies in Sweden, which keep updated, computerized lists of job vacancies plus records of the characteristics and qualifications of those looking for work. Employers must give the Labor Market Board advance notice of layoffs, and they must list all job vacancies with the public employment service. The board itself collects a variety of information via regular sample surveys. At any employment office, the staff can now determine where in the whole of Sweden a specific occupation is in excess demand or supply. On average, over 300,000 job seekers applied each month to the employment service in 1986, and about half of all vacancies were filled through it. More than half the applicants were women, and around 40 percent were under 25. The board has interpreted its information role broadly to include in-depth counseling, vocational guidance, and aptitude and psychological testing. Finally "as a last resort, the employer can . . . be forbidden to hire workers not approved by the employment office.''[26]

(b) Measures to promote occupational and geographical mobility. This notably includes a large vocational training program, with courses in 50 cities and towns, covering about 250 trades and divided into two main types—retraining courses ''to learn the basic knowledge needed for a trade'' and advanced courses ''to build up personal skills in an existing occupation.''[27] Follow-up studies showed that 66 percent of those completing their training in the second quarter of 1985 found jobs on the open market within 6 months, a success ratio which is lower than in the early 1970s and 1960s.[28] In addition, four kinds of in-house (company) vocational training qualify for state subsidies: (i) training for skilled jobs where there are too few qualified people; (ii) training for employees whose jobs are being transformed or eliminated by technological change; (iii) training for workers who would otherwise run an ''imminent risk'' of being laid off; (iv) training of women for traditionally male occupations or vice versa.[29] Labor market training was expected to absorb more than 20 percent of the central government's budget for labor market programs over 1987–88.

Once an applicant has been (re)trained, the Labor Market Board will give the individual a free round trip, where necessary, for a job interview. When he or she obtains employment, all moving expenses are paid, and there is a starting allowance to tide the worker over until the first paycheck. If housing difficulties cause a delay in moving his family to a new town, the worker receives compensation for the expense of maintaining two homes. The board even buys the old house, if it cannot be sold except at a heavy loss (as might be the case if the worker is moving away from a location in the north of Sweden). Over 30,000 people, or more than 20 percent of all movers to new jobs, qualified for the board's removal grants in 1985. Cost-benefit research has indicated that the gain to society from individuals moving to more productive work usually exceeds the cost of removal subsidies.

(c) The Labor Market Board makes a special effort to help disadvantaged workers. These include people with physical, mental, or social handicaps, as well as those coming onto the job market for the first time, people returning to the market after a long absence (such as housewives), and elderly workers. During the 1970s, it became harder for the board to find jobs for the growing numbers of older workers being laid off due to mechanization and automation. For this reason, their welfare benefits have been expanded, and employers can be forced to accept them. The board also goes to greater lengths than usual to assess the work capacities of disadvantaged workers, including ''a medical, psychological, and social analysis, as well as a test of mechanical ability, manual dexterity, and the like,'' and then to retrain them.[30] The latter program includes ''work training . . . in which the handicapped build up their physical and mental working capacities in occupational forms under medical control.''[31]

Once a disadvantaged worker is hired, there are grants to equip his workplace with special facilities and tools that are required and to help pay for the services of a work assistant, if one is needed to enable him to do his job properly. If a worker remains disadvantaged, despite rehabilitation measures, the Labor Market Board, in consultation with the union local, can arrange *semisheltered* or wage-subsidized employment at approved work places in local firms. Normally, these should be permanent jobs, and the government will reimburse up to 50 percent of full labor costs during the first two years plus 25 percent thereafter. If occupational disabilities are severe, wage subsidies may rise to 90 percent of labor costs during the first year and 50 percent during the following three years, with possible extensions. The placing of adjustment groups at all workplaces with over fifty employees, whose task is to physically and psychologically adapt the workplace to the individual worker, has given semisheltered employment a boost. Finally, grants are available to help older or handicapped persons who want to go into business for themselves. As of mid-1986, some 41,000 people were employed with a wage subsidy.

In more severe cases, handicapped persons cannot find work on the open market, even after training and rehabilitation and with wage subsidies. Thus, for disadvantaged blue-collar workers, there are *sheltered* workshops, operated by local governments with central government financial support, mainly in metalworking, woodworking, plastics, and papermaking. "Work at home can [also] be offered to persons who cannot get about or who have mental handicaps that prevent them from travelling to work."[32] There are also *special relief work* projects for disadvantaged workers, which were originally designed to counteract seasonal and cyclical employment fluctuations, although they now serve a broader purpose. Finally, for handicapped white-collar workers, there is *archive* work, mainly in the records offices of government agencies. In 1980, archive, special relief, and sheltered work were grouped into a special production and sales enterprise called Swedish Communal Industries, with 320 workshops and 27,500 employees in mid-1986. All three categories are referred to as *sheltered employment.* Since 1985, the central government has reimbursed public employers (mainly municipalities) up to 75 percent of the wage costs of people on special relief work projects. In 1987–88, measures for the disabled were expected to take one-third of the central government's budget for labor market programs. However, it would be more expensive to put these people on welfare, even ignoring the cost of keeping them apart from work and society.

(d) Programs under (a) above are efforts to achieve a better information link between supply and demand. Those under (b) are supply-side or human-resource development programs, while those under (c) are demand-side or job-development programs. Finally, some involuntary unemployment is inevitable, even when labor market programs work well. In Sweden, unemployment benefits are paid as a last resort and represent just 30 percent of the budget for labor-market policy. They are intended for people who are unemployed and not training, who are willing and able to work, and who are registered with the public employment service. As a rule, a jobless person must have worked for five of the last twelve months to qualify for support, but an individual is also eligible if he or she has not found work for three months after completing a job-specific training course.

The highest rates of unemployment compensation are paid to members of unemployment benefit societies, which are linked to labor unions, although they are formally independent. Just 5 percent of their benefits come from membership fees. The rest are paid by the state—65 percent coming from payroll fees and 35 percent from general revenues. There are now 43 unemployment benefit societies with nearly 3.5 million members. They pay compensation averaging around 80 percent of regular pay for up to 300 consecutive days, which becomes 450 days for members 55 or older. If a member over 60 cannot find work during this time, he or she becomes eligible for an early retirement pension. Those who do not belong to a benefit society may obtain much lower cash assistance for up to 150 days (300 days, if they are over 55) from a program financed one-third by central government revenues and two-thirds by a payroll tax. To reduce the incentive to remain unemployed, unemployment compensation is taxed like earned income. Moreover, the person collecting benefits must accept "suitable" work when this is offered, and "work outside the claimant's trade may be deemed suitable."[33]

C. Recent Labor Market Problems

As in other Western countries, the average duration of unemployment in Sweden has been longer during the 1980s than at any time since World War II—especially for young workers and for those nearing retirement age. Partly because of the constraints on laying employees off and the protection for older workers embodied in labor legislation of the 1970s, the jobless rate among young people (under 25) rose from 5.1 percent to 8 percent of the youth labor force over 1980–83, although the 1983 rate was still one of the lowest in the OECD. In 1983, the under-25s constituted over 35 percent of all unemployed, and among 18- and 19-year-olds, unemployment was running 12–13 percent. Young people have been taking longer to find permanent jobs, and joblessness among workers over 55 is up as well. After six months in unemployment, the ability to find new work falls drastically with age. As in other countries, moreover, employers have used the unemployment insurance system as a step toward early retirement, with tacit union support. "Employees older than 58 have been dismissed, regardless of what priority they may enjoy [in job retention] and have then received unemployment benefits for 450 days [after which] it has been assumed they would be eligible for disability pensions."[34]

Mainly to combat youth unemployment, the government introduced a recruitment subsidy in the fall of 1983, amounting to half of wages over a period of six months, and reserved for jobless young people or long-term unemployed. The Young Persons' Law, which took effect on January 1, 1984, guarantees that no one under 20 will remain completely unemployed. It requires local governments to hire all 18- and 19-year-olds and all handicapped workers between 18 and 25, for whom no other job (or suitable training) can be found. It entitles eligible young people to an average of four hours' work per day, five days per week, at going rates of pay, in what are called "youth teams," financed by the central government. Their purpose is to help team members do all that is necessary to make the transition from school to working life, down to conducting a successful job interview. (Since mid-1985, job-seeking is a compulsory part of youth-team programs.) Youth teams complement a program of "youth jobs" for school leavers aged 16 and 17, and there is, in addition, a system of "induction places" or wage subsidized employment for young people in the private sector. At end-1986, there were about 18,000 places in youth teams, a similar number of youth jobs, and 5,000 induction places. A follow-up study found that 42 percent of those leaving youth teams in 1985–86 (after an average six months of team membership) had taken regular employment, while another 40 percent had entered vocational training.[35]

Yet, the system of youth teams and induction places does not appear to have reduced unemployment among workers aged 20 to 24, which fell only slightly during the 1983–85 expansion. More generally, the number of people covered by labor market measures grew from under 28,000 in 1963 to more than 160,000 in recent years. In many cases, these individuals go on to better paying jobs or are brought into work and society, when they would otherwise be excluded by disability. But some people now view labor market programs as alternatives to normal jobs. According to a recent survey, many young people prefer vocational training or relief work to permanent employment in industry. Within vocational education, it has been hard to recruit enough trainees for traditional blue-collar jobs.[36]

Government support for labor-market measures has been generous. Without them, open unemployment would be higher, and many individuals would face a bleaker future. More people now take advantage of these programs more often and/or for longer periods. The problem is that despite large expenditures on them in recent years, shortages of skilled workers have been growing in the private sector, along with the wage drift, which averaged 80 percent of negotiated wage increases over 1984–86. Most Swedes do not want to drastically curtail labor market programs, which remain one of the model aspects of the Swedish economy. Perhaps the best policy prescription is therefore Gösta Rehn's original recommendation that underlying fiscal policy should remain restrictive. This will put more pressure on labor market measures to serve as an efficient bridge to productive employment within a "harder" (less elastic) budget constraint than in the past.

16-7. Consumer Cooperatives

> The Social Democratic party, the LO, and the cooperative movement are 3 branches off the same trunk. The Social Democratic party gave the working classes a voice, the trade unions strengthened their position on the labor market, and the co-ops tried to give them the necessities of life at a low price.
>
> —Nils Thedin (former Information Officer of KF)

A. The Role of Sweden's Consumer Cooperatives[37]

A consumer cooperative is a firm controlled by the consumers of its products, whose elected representatives make or at least ratify its basic production, pricing, financial, and investment decisions. Except in the smallest enterprises, efficient production is only possible when direct management is in the hands of experts, which consumer representatives must therefore supervise. Consumer cooperatives are manifestations of "consumer democracy," just as worker-managed firms are manifestations of "industrial democracy." To date, Sweden is more the land of the former than of the latter, although the two are compatible, in the sense that worker and consumer delegates may share control of a company's board of directors.

Swedish consumer co-ops handle 16.5 percent of all retail sales, including 20 percent of the everyday or convenience goods trade and 11 percent of the specialty trade. Folksam, the cooperative insurance group, writes more policies than any other company, and the government has assigned all sick pay insurance to Folksam. The OK Union, a consumer oil cooperative, has 15 percent of the retail market for petroleum products; it introduced the self-service gas station to Sweden. Cooperative housing societies have built nearly 600,000 homes, out of a total stock of about 3.7 million—including more than 25 percent of all apartments.[38] Finally, the cooperative sector accounts for 5 percent of total employment, including 7.5 percent of industrial employment, and 5 percent of industrial output. About 3 million Swedes belong to one or more consumer cooperatives, and nearly one million (including farmers) belong to one or more producer cooperatives.

If price competition is weak, a consumer cooperative will charge a lower price than a profit-maximizing firm, when both face the same demand and cost conditions. Because of this, co-ops have played an important role in the protected sector of the Swedish economy, where the small size of the market makes workable competition difficult to achieve. The Price and Cartel Office and the Anti-Trust Ombudsman must therefore rely on monitoring to keep prices low. Where possible, they use as reference a firm that does not profit maximize, but rather prices to approximately cover its costs. Generally, these are consumer cooperatives or public enterprises. This is an effort to substitute user democracy for competition, and Swedish co-ops receive tax breaks for practicing internal democracy.

A consumer cooperative will set its prices lower and its output higher than a profit maximizer because co-op members benefit, not only from sharing in its profits, but also from consuming or using the products it sells. A co-op acting in the best interests of its members will never exercise market power over them because the members would, in effect, be exploiting themselves. In Figure 16.4, a profit-maximizing firm would set price, P_π, and supply quantity, Q_π, where marginal revenue equals marginal cost. This is the classic textbook solution. But a consumer co-op would set the lower price, P_c, and higher quantity, Q_c, where the demand and marginal cost curves cross. Here, the cooperative supplies twice as much as the profit maximizer.[39] Thus, the entry of a co-op into a market dominated by one or two sellers will bring down prices, provided it can cost compete with privately owned companies. The Swedish cooperative movement has a history of breaking up concentrations of selling power in this way, but it has also been pushed

Figure 16.4. **Price-setting by a Consumer Cooperative.**

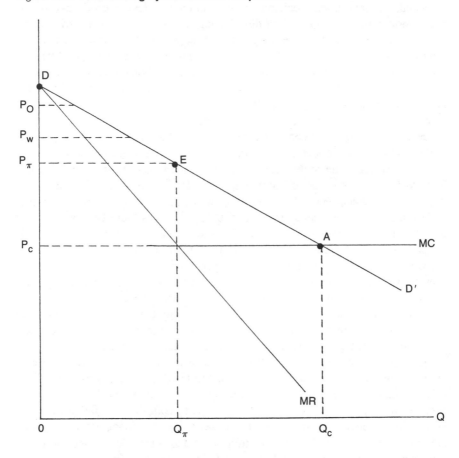

out of other markets by more efficient private firms.

Consumer co-ops acting in the interests of their members will try to maximize the sum of profit plus consumer surplus on the goods they sell. Consumer surplus is the maximum amount customers would be willing to pay for a good minus what they do pay. Thus, it is a measure of the welfare they derive from consumption. In Figure 16.4, a few consumers are willing to pay the high price, P_0. When the actual price is P_π, they receive a surplus of $(P_0 - P_\pi)$ times the quantity they buy. Others are willing to pay P_w and receive a surplus of $(P_w - P_\pi)$ times quantity bought. When the prevailing price is P_π, total consumer surplus received is the area of triangle $P_\pi ED$ under the demand curve and above P_π. When price is P_c, consumer surplus is the area of the larger triangle, $P_c AD$.

Suppose a consumer cooperative expands its sales by one unit at any given price. The addition to profit is the price it charges minus the marginal cost of supplying the good. The addition to consumer surplus is the maximum price that someone is willing to pay—read off the demand curve in Figure 16.4—less the price actually charged. The consumer surplus plus the profit on an additional sale is therefore the maximum price that someone is willing to pay minus the marginal cost of supplying the good. The total profit plus consumer surplus over *all* sales will reach its maximum about where the profit plus consumer surplus on an additional sale is zero. This will be where the demand and marginal cost curves cross and where the price charged, P_c, equals marginal cost. Not only is the higher quantity and lower price (Q_c and P_c vs. Q_π and P_π) a break for consumers, it is also the efficient pricing policy, provided the co-op is supplying Q_c at lowest possible cost. Unfortunately, a co-op has no way to concretely measure its major managerial success indicator (consumer surplus) and may therefore have trouble motivating management to maximize this index.

B. Development of the Swedish Cooperative Movement

The first known Swedish consumer cooperative was organized in 1850, and the oldest cooperative society still in existence, at Trollhatten, dates from 1867. Originally, these were organizations of poor craftsmen and farmers who banded together to satisfy their need for essential commodities of satisfactory quality at reasonable prices. "Artisans and farmers, confronted with competition from the mass-produced goods of industry and grains produced [in North America], resorted largely to self-help by founding credit societies and credit unions based on mutual guarantee."[40] The early cooperatives faced many difficulties, were weak financially, and a number of them failed. As late as 1910, all co-ops together had scarcely 100,000 members and fewer than 700 shops, each of which was small. Less than 3 percent of the population belonged to them vs. 23 percent today. From the outset, the Swedish co-ops have accepted the following principles first drawn up by the Rochdale Society of Equitable Pioneers in England in 1844:

(a) Voluntary Membership Open to All.
(b) Democratic Management by Elected Consumer Representatives According to the Principle of One Member, One Vote.
(c) Dividends to be Paid to Consumer-Members from Profits Earned by the Cooperative in Proportion to the Values of Their Purchases.
(d) Limited Interest to be Paid on Shares in the Cooperative that Members Must Purchase Upon Joining.
(e) Political and Religious Neutrality.
(f) Funds to be Allotted for Consumer Education and Informational Activities and to Otherwise Promote the Economic Interests of Members.

In order to qualify for special tax privileges, the cooperatives must accept (a) through (d) and the last part of (f). When an individual joins a retail cooperative society, he or she must buy a membership share for 200 crowns.[41] Once the share is fully paid, it will yield a small interest return, but it is only necessary to pay 10 crowns upon joining. A member can pay the rest by buying at co-op stores and not collecting part of the dividends normally paid on purchases. Each retail co-op usually pays a small dividend from its profits (officially called surplus) to each member.

The Swedish cooperative movement passed a milestone in 1899 when 40 local societies formed the Cooperative Union and Wholesale Society (KF) to act as their buyer, supplier, and banker. They were integrating backward to gain countervailing power against manufacturers, and eventually they succeeded. KF is today the center and heart of the consumer cooperatives. Until recently, it was the largest firm in the Nordic countries. Its 1985 sales were 30.3 billion crowns, of which over 55 percent went to the retail (Konsum) societies, and nearly 15 percent was exported. In 1902, KF joined the International Cooperative Movement, and in 1908, it started a fire insurance business, since many of its members were poor and unable to obtain private insurance. In 1914, together with LO, it started a cooperative life insurance society, and the two insurance societies eventually merged, in 1946, to form Folksam. Today, at least half of all Swedes carry some insurance with Folksam, which administers over 16 million individual and group policies of all kinds. It is controlled by KF, LO, and TCO.[42]

In 1909, KF acquired its first factory, a margarine-producing plant with which it would win its first major economic victory. Following World War I, Swedish margarine wholesalers merged to form a monopoly and temporarily kept prices high. KF refused to go along. Instead it used its production facilities to break the monopoly and force down the price by 60 percent. Soon after, KF broke the flour milling monopoly and subsequently won similar battles in electric bulbs, cash registers, china, fertilizers, detergents, and building supplies.[43] At present, KF controls 12–13 percent of the Swedish food processing industry and also maintains its own food laboratories and test kitchen. It is potentially able to take up production of almost any light industrial good, and this makes it a check on the exercise of monopoly power. As early as 1906, the co-op movement introduced the eight-hour day to Sweden. In 1941, the Stockholm Retail Society introduced self-service shops, and the movement also brought in the chain-store system, which has driven many small retail shops out of business.

Until around 1915, over 75 percent of Swedish cooperators were from the working class, and strong sentimental ties bound KF with LO and the Social Democrats. KF and LO have collaborated in a number of areas. In 1912, they jointly launched the Workers' Educational Association, and in 1937, they helped establish Reso, Sweden's second largest travel agency. (In 1977, Reso became a subsidiary of KF.) A joint LO-KF committee monitors consumer prices, and the two jointly promote consumer protection. They also operate consumer education and information services designed to promote rational buying. KF trains its own personnel in principles of home economics and household budget management, and it has elaborate facilities for product testing. Finally, LO and KF have collaborated on projects in developing countries.

Nevertheless, KF has stayed politically neutral and has not actively supported

LO's drive toward industrial democracy. Neither does it try to outbid SAF in wage negotiations. KF began to move a bit away from LO in 1915 when consumer cooperatives, whose popularity was growing rapidly, started accepting many new members who were neither unionists nor Social Democrats. By 1920, the retail co-op societies had 250,000 members, 2.5 times the number ten years earlier. On the eve of the Great Depression, there were around 450,000, and the Depression itself collapsed the resistance of middle-class families to joining. During World War II, membership rose to over 900,000 and passed the million mark in 1949. As of 1990, about two million Swedes belong to their local retail cooperative societies, approximately half of them women. Since just one member of a family will usually join, more than half of all Swedish families belong to the movement.

Nevertheless, to realize economies of scale in production and marketing, the Swedish co-ops have closed over 4,750 retail stores since 1965, most of them small, that could not cover their costs. The number of co-op outlets fell from 6,650 in 1965 to about 1,900 in 1985. This mirrors the general trend in Swedish retailing toward fewer and larger stores. Over half of all Swedish discount stores now bear the cooperative OBS! trade mark, and more than half of all co-op retail sales go through the larger stores. The co-op movement has been sacrificing service in the towns and villages that are its traditional bastions of support, in the hope of improving its prices and service in urban areas big enough to sustain the larger stores, whose unit costs are lower. Cooperative outlets in small towns have either gone out of business, or no longer offer clothing and durables, concentrating instead on food, detergent, light bulbs, and other everyday items. This "rationalization" comes at the expense of potential customers living outside urban areas and lacking easy access to affordable transportation.

The co-ops have also become more like businesses and less like societies in terms of their internal organization, although the one-member-one vote principle still formally prevails. To an extent, the movement is decentralized at the retail level, and the retail (Konsum) societies have some control over KF. (Internally, however, KF is fairly centralized.) Yet, the trend over the years has been toward fewer Konsum societies—as the smaller societies have merged—and therefore toward increasingly indirect democracy, even at the retail level. This has tied in closely with the replacement of many small stores by fewer large ones. As late as 1960, there were nearly 600 Konsum societies, with an average membership under 2,000. In 1985, there were just 142, averaging about 14,000 members each. The 15 largest societies account for over 70 percent of all retail sales, while the smallest 100 account for less than 3 percent. The number of retail societies is likely to fall even further, and meetings open to all members already draw less than 10 percent attendance, on average, this being higher in the smaller societies.

C. The Housing Cooperatives

Most Swedish housing cooperatives belong to HSB, the National Association of

Tenants' Savings and Building Societies, founded in 1923, or to Svenska Riks-bggen (SR), the Cooperative Housing Organization of the Swedish Labor Unions, started in 1940. Each of these is headed by a national organization, to which local societies belong and which serves the local societies in all matters of a technical, financial, legal, or administrative character. Individuals join the local societies and begin saving—usually toward an apartment in a tenant-owned block of flats, although one- and two-family houses are also available. Both HSB and SR have savings plans, under which members can make regular deposits. The local societies finance and plan the construction and later assist in managing the housing unit. For the most part, however, each co-op unit manages its own property through a committee elected by tenant-owners. HSB and SR also assist in managing munic-ipal apartment dwellings, which are run on a democratic basis.

HSB grew out of a protest movement against high rents during and after World War I, and it has played a pioneering role in improving the quality and amenities of Swedish apartments, including provision of playgrounds and day nurseries. It has about 460,000 members, of whom 295,000 have obtained HSB dwellings, and 165,000 are still saving toward this goal. In 1985, HSB comprised some 3,400 local housing societies. In addition, it has its own factories for making woodwork and furniture, and it designs apartments for municipal authorities, as well as its own members. Svenska Riksbyggen was started by construction unions to maintain employment after the outbreak of World War II had reduced building activity. In 1985, it comprised 1,250 local societies and managed 201,000 dwellings. SR is owned by KF, LO, and the Swedish Building Workers' Union, as well as its own local housing associations. It generally builds apartments and town houses for blue-collar union members, and because of the strong union influence on its board of directors, it qualifies as a joint producer-consumer cooperative.[44] A union-owned construction company builds 80 percent of SR's apartments.

Neither HSB nor SR owes its existence to rent control, but both prospered under it, partly because they were favored by government policy and partly because rent control raised the demand price of housing and, thus, the sales value of owner-occupied apartments and town houses. (Moreover, Swedish rent ceilings were tied to the cost of construction, finance, and maintenance, which suited co-op pricing policy.) With the end of rent control and shift in homebuilding toward one- and two-family houses, the co-ops have had to follow suit to a degree. Thus, in 1971, they completed 15,570 dwellings, of which just 254 were one- and two-family houses. But in 1987, 4,334 out of 9,864 co-op dwellings were in the latter category. In that year, the co-ops had 32 percent of the housing market. Of their share, HSB accounts for about 60 percent and SR for 30 percent.

16-8. Sweden as a Welfare State

> Swedish bureaucracy is an export item with considerable potential—but can it be
> made profitable? There seems to be some doubt about this. . . . The minister of
> Local Government Affairs, Karl Boo [has said] that the public sector . . . could

well become a major exporter of services. Many shared this view, including the state consultancy company, Statskonsult, which for three years has been attempting to sell Swedish bureaucracy abroad. The result so far has been a loss of 6 million crowns.

—*Sweden Now* (No. 5, 1980, p. 12)

A. The Welfare State and Its Cost

Social Democrats have assigned a high priority to building a welfare state, and today there is wide political and social consensus in favor of it, despite its high tax cost. Protection from financial distress is womb to tomb. No one has yet cured death; unpleasant accidents continue to happen; the sweet bird of youth still flies away, and unemployment remains a problem. But there is little financial anxiety or insecurity over the misfortunes of life in a country that, as late as 1920, had scant social welfare legislation.[45] Financial protection frees Swedes to develop their potential, and two basic principles govern social policy. First, social welfare benefits should be available to all citizens as a right, not as charity. Second, welfare benefits should form a protective net that keeps every citizen from falling into poverty.

Swedish experience suggests that it is possible to combine comparative efficiency with redistribution and comprehensive social insurance. Nevertheless, the high taxes needed to finance the welfare state loosen the link between performance and reward, making it necessary to rely more heavily on intrinsic incentives. (Individuals must be motivated to do useful work by factors intrinsic to the job, its surroundings, or the product being produced.) This is a fine ideal, but intrinsic incentives have proved to be insufficient by themselves. Even after the 1983–85 tax reforms, a typical full-time worker faces a marginal tax-plus-loss-of-subsidy rate on the order of 70 percent. Besides income taxes, there are also property taxes, including a progressive tax of 1.5 percent to 3 percent, levied on family wealth in excess of 400,000 crowns (excluding housing and household belongings), as well as housing and real estate taxes, personal gift and inheritance taxes, stiff excise taxes, and fairly high taxes on capital gains. Although joint taxation of married couples was abolished in 1971 for income from work, this has not been done for property income.

Thus, income plus property taxes could, in principle, take more than 100 percent of a well-to-do Swede's income in a given year, and this has happened. In 1976, Astrid Lindgren, a well-known writer of children's books, wrote a fairy-tale satire of her inability to pay taxes amounting to 102 percent of her income. Subsequently, a 1980 law set a tax rate ceiling of 85 percent, which was lowered to 80 percent by the 1983–85 reforms. In fact, until these reforms, most well-to-do Swedes avoided the highest marginal rates by borrowing money to finance acquisition of durables and property, since interest payments were fully deductible from taxable income.

Nonetheless, high marginal tax rates have helped to offset efforts to promote occupational and geographical mobility of labor. They have also made it hard for small, unincorporated businesses to survive, while large corporations and associations were getting off lightly—through accelerated depreciation, investment reserves, and other tax breaks. The need to keep the tax burden manageable has caused many mergers since the mid-1960s. Following the current tax reforms, marginal rates on income from work are lower, but still virtually highest in the world for most income categories. The offsetting payroll taxes have made labor more expensive, and new limits on interest deductibility have raised effective marginal tax rates for many well-to-do Swedes. Tax rates are likely to continue to be too high to allow national income to be maximized—considering their negative incentive effects and their tendency to raise the cost of labor relative to other productive inputs—and may even continue to be too high to maximize total tax revenue, when evasion is taken into account as well.[46]

In all, taxes plus obligatory social insurance contributions came to over 60 percent of GNP in 1985. For most of the post-World War II era, the Swedish ratio has been highest in the world, and while it is no longer rising, neither is it showing any significant tendency to fall. Transfers to households, in the form of rent subsidies, unemployment compensation, old-age pensions, training grants, child and study allowances, health benefits, and so forth came to about 32 percent of GNP in 1984, while public consumption was 25 percent, again higher than anywhere else in the world. Thus, "The Swedish system [also] limits the individual's freedom of choice in consumption. A person is 'forced' to finance public consumption with tax money, regardless of whether he or she has any reason, opportunity, or desire to make use of it."[47]

B. Provisions of the Welfare State

The high taxes finance security that begins in the womb. Maternity clinics conduct free pregnancy tests, provide pregnant women with free prenatal care plus free information about child care, and conduct a free calisthenics program. At the other end, pensioners receive good incomes plus social and home help, including care in the home. There are also special pensioners' dwellings and homes for old people needing permanent care, plus funeral allowances, subject to a means test. Thus, security follows the individual into his tomb. Nor are any steps left out in between. Sweden has the world's lowest infant mortality rate (about six infant deaths per thousand live births in 1985, vs. eleven in the U.S. and U.K., seven in Japan, and twenty-two in the Soviet Union) and one of the longest life expectancies.[48] It has around twice as many hospital beds per thousand residents as the U.S., but there are also shortages of many types of medical service. Sweden has spent no more per person on health care, but through a more equal distribution of benefits has been able to achieve a higher standard of care than the United States, albeit one fraught with inconvenience.

Often, this is especially true for the elderly, who require four times the care of individuals in prime working age. About 17 percent of Sweden's population is over

65, and this share will rise to 20 percent by 2025.[49] Some old or seriously ill patients requiring extended care are being turned down by hospitals short of staff or beds. Help in the home is also given to aged and handicapped people by home nurses, home helps, and home samaritans, and a variety of technical aids, special municipal transport services, etc., are available to help the elderly look after themselves and get around. Fees for such services are low and/or vary according to income. About 90 percent of people aged 65 or over live in ordinary dwellings. Despite shortages of help, service, and places in homes for the elderly, old-age care in Sweden is probably on a higher standard than in nearly any other country. A variety of programs and activities—including courses to teach people how to prepare for retirement—also seeks to enhance the life experience for pensioners. We may briefly outline Swedish social benefits as follows:[50]

Care During and Before Maternity. As noted, there are maternity clinics to conduct pregnancy tests and to provide prenatal care, postnatal checkups, and family planning:

> While still at the hospital maternity ward, the mother receives information on baby care and is told where the baby can get regular appointments with doctors and nurses during the first few years, [including] preventive measures such a physical examinations, vaccinations, and general counselling. The services, which are free of charge, also include house calls.[51]

There is a maternity allowance at birth, even if it is a stillbirth, and live births are registered so that the child may continue its womb-to-tomb protection. Child allowances come in regularly until the 16th birthday. The child also receives free prophylactic medicine, such as vitamins and iron.

Whole-Day Care of Children. This can begin as early as six months of age in day-care centers, for which a fee is usually paid, adjusted to parents' income. Since facilities are in short supply, there is a means test for admission, and mothers must have jobs. Even then, there is no guarantee that a place will be available. Following day care is kindergarten, from ages four to seven, which lasts three hours per day and is subject to the same qualifications as day care. Leisure-time centers also exist for children of school age outside regular school hours, and there is supplemental day care in private homes for children of school age or younger. Given the shortage of day-care facilities, a government decision not to allow private day nurseries operated "for profit" to qualify for state support has been controversial.

Free Education, Study Allowances, and Living Grants While Studying. Education is completely free in Sweden, including travel, meals, books, etc., and following the completion of compulsory schooling at age sixteen, the student who continues receives a "study allowance" through age twenty. We have already indicated the government's considerable support for vocational training. In addition, "Higher education in Sweden is free of charge. The students are, however, required to be members of the Student Union and to pay a small term fee. All students who need help to finance their studies receive [state] assistance . . . in the form of a nonrepayable grant plus a larger loan. For graduate students, there is also a limited number of special fellowships.''[52]

Home Furnishing Loans for the Newly Married; Loans for Buying and Renting Homes; Housing Loans for Rebuilding; Mortgage Real-Estate Loans; Improvement Loans; State Rental Allowances to Families with Children, and the like. Here there is a means test. The housing must be neither too luxurious nor too crowded or cramped, and various other stipulations are laid down.

Old Age Pensions; Social and Home Help. The state is generous here, as we have seen, but there are shortages of personnel and facilities to care for the aged.

Medical Care. This is nearly free, subject to stipulations outlined earlier, although dental care is fully covered only for children under sixteen. Adults must pay up to 40 percent of these costs, which can be substantial. A full sickness allowance, equal to 90 percent of earned income for most people, is payable for as long as an illness reduces working capacity by half or more. There is also free medical treatment for industrial injuries, as well as an extended care allowance over and above the sickness allowance, for anyone unable to look after himself over a long period. Not only is there free outpatient examination and treatment of venereal disease, but anyone suspecting that he or she has such a disease must promptly consult a doctor. Special facilities exist for treating alcoholism and drug addiction; the latter are expanding.

Disability Aid. The goal is to enable those with disabilities to live like other people. Extensive means to this end include the various allowances and facilities for vocational training and rehabilitation discussed earlier. There are also life annuities for industrial injuries and pension benefits for widows and children, along with various other types of disablement compensation, including early retirement pensions and allowances for housing. A special transport service enables disabled people to visit stores, doctors, friends, relatives, to get to work, and so forth, for about the usual price of public transportation. In some cases, means-tested grants are available to finance trips from one municipality to another, via the national transport service. Moreover, nearly any type of invalid aid is available free, provided it has been prescribed. A handicapped person needing a car can obtain grants toward buying one and adapting it to his handicap, again subject to a means test.

Employment Service. Sweden has the world's most comprehensive employment service, as we have seen. We would add that it is easier in Sweden than in North America to combine work with welfare payments. The working poor can go on working and still draw additional assistance—such as rent allowances and child support—which brings their living standards up to a socially acceptable level.

Child Support Allowances. These are also available for children of divorced parents and children born out of wedlock. (In 1983, about 44 percent of all children born in Sweden had unmarried parents.)

Free Legal Aid. This is subject to a means test.

Finally, when all above benefits are exhausted, ''there remains extra blanket assistance, which is unlimited in form and amount, and which is at the discretion of local welfare offices. It may take the form of an immediate cash grant to avert pressing need or an advance against other benefits. . . .''[53] More than a half million Swedes—one in every sixteen—were accepting emergency social assistance, as of late 1985. Some listed high taxes as a cause of their need for this aid.

C. The State and the Individual

By North American standards and even by those of Western Europe, Sweden is a conformist society, where individual expression is muted. Respect for rules is deeply ingrained, and there are many boundaries which are learned instinctively, along with a fear of stepping over these and of the reproach and social ostracism that is likely to follow. It is also a group- and achievement-oriented society, the latter helping to offset the blunting of income-related incentives by the welfare state. During the 1950s and 1960s, sexual freedom was greater in Sweden than in most other developed countries. It has been alleged that the government deliberately promoted this to relieve frustrations built up because of the lack of freedom in other areas.[54]

In addition, not only does Sweden have an elaborate appeals procedure, but free use of courtroom facilities, although subject to a means test, is carried to extremes. One can sue to recover small losses with the same lack of financial anxiety that we have associated with old age, unemployment, catastrophic illness, or accidents. Yet, there are gaps both in the appeals procedure and in the law as far as protection of the individual is concerned. For example, child welfare authorities may force their way into any home, investigate conditions there, and remove children, if they believe this necessary. An appeal to an ombudsman is not likely to bring redress, although the authorities would probably be admonished if excessive force was used. Similarly, the Temperance Board may commit any person to an institution for alcoholism. On balance, Swedish law is designed more as an instrument of social policy than as protection for the individual.

Beyond this, a prominent observer has described the organized character of Swedish society as follows:

> Let us take . . . an ordinary worker; he probably lives in a building owned by a housing cooperative, or if not, he will be a member of a tenants' association; he buys his provisions at a cooperative store; his working conditions are fixed by an agreement between his employer and his union; if he wants to study, there is a workers' cultural association which organizes courses or study circles where he can go and hear lectures; if he likes sports, there is a sports association to organize everything for him; and when he wants to go on vacation, he has only to go to the travel association [Reso] of the workers' movements . . . the only thing . . . not organized for him is his sleep.[55]

In a modern nation state, workable democracy requires continuing interaction between government and special interest groups (called "associations" in Sweden) to help form social priorities. However, the Swedish government also tends to exclude other points of view in social goal formation. For example, when commissions of enquiry or government agencies hold hearings, they rarely invite *all* interested parties to appear or to comment (in the remiss procedure). Nor are the hearings open to the public or the press. The government hardly ever consults individuals, unless they represent special interest groups or government agencies, or qualify as expert witnesses. Instead, representatives of the major associations that will be affected by the proposed laws or regulations are invited to appear or to comment in a carefully controlled environment, conducive to negotiating workable compromise agreements.

The Swedish associations are internally democratic, for the most part, in the sense that their officers hold power because they have been chosen by the membership in free elections. Nevertheless, the associations with roots in popular movements—including the unions and cooperatives—have grown more centralized over time and more distant from individual members. The large role assigned to collective decision making implies a greater importance for association, as opposed to individual preferences. In this sense, individuals have been squeezed out of the complex equilibrium between power blocs that characterizes modern Sweden. The squeeze is made more acute by the welfare state, with its bureaucratic superstructure, which requires a retreat from the right of each individual to choose for himself, not only because of the taxes necessary to finance it, but also because of the need to apply and enforce its rules. As one Swedish newspaper editor put it:

> The charge that the growth of the public sector reduces each person to a number is not demagoguery. The impersonal relationship between institutions and individuals is built into the system. We all insist that public agencies treat us fairly, that they apply the relevant rules and regulations to the letter and apply them uniformly to everyone. If they do not, we call it corruption. But this impartiality is at the same time experienced as an outrage to our self-esteem, since it means that all human qualities—indeed, everything that makes us unique individuals— are regarded as irrelevant. So we approach civil servants with a double message: Be fair, but realize that my case is different from everyone else's. . . . The only way civil servants can protect themselves is to elevate their work routines to law.[56]

The vast welfare program is part of the underlying social contract that holds Swedish society together. It is in the collective interest of most people to support it, partly because it makes society more cohesive and reduces the level of crime and partly because of the freedom from financial anxiety which it brings. (Anyone may suddenly have to rely on it.) But individual incentives to abuse the welfare system require government enforcement of standards for receiving aid, as well as controls to ensure that it is spent for the purposes for which it is given. The same is true of any other form of subsidy. In this context, lower-level bureaucrats will have an incentive to be overzealous in applying the law—the source of many complaints about the Swedish bureaucracy—especially since the government has shown that it wishes to err on the side of protecting society's rights, as opposed to those of the individual.

Yet, despite the tradition of conformity and the group orientation of Swedish society, there is always a risk that collectivization of decision making will be pushed too far. In particular, most decisions relating to the production of wealth, as opposed to its (re)distribution, have not really been collectivized. They are still made by individuals or small groups (usually managers, bankers, or other business people), motivated to some degree by the prospect of financial rewards. Earlier, we said that Sweden has a remarkable record of innovation and entrepreneurship and that its companies are generally well managed. It will need to rely more heavily on those qualities over the next twenty-five years or so. "The dominant trend in Swedish industry in the 1980s is a shift from traditional dependence on iron, steel, and forest products to [goods embodying] advanced technology...."[57] Sweden will scarcely become an individualistic society, and its social insurance safety net will remain in place. But although the government will have to give better guidance to industry in the form of a forward-looking structural policy, it will also have to refrain from pushing the collectivization of management decisions and rewards too far, in order to preserve a climate in which innovation and entrepreneurship will flourish.

Notes

1. "Swedish Regional Policy," Fact Sheet on Sweden No. 72e (Stockholm: The Swedish Institute, June 1986), p. 2.

2. OECD, *Economic Survey of Sweden, 1985–86* (Paris: OECD, May 1985), p. 48. The 1974–76 wage explosion, from which it took Sweden at least ten years to recover, was triggered by excessive company profits over 1973–74.

3. The Social Democratic government passed these reforms in 1983. They were supported by all parties, including the Communists. See Roger Smith, "Doors Open for Venture Capital," *Sweden Now*, No. 6, 1983.

4. About half of small industrial enterprises subcontract for larger manufacturers.

5. OECD, *Economic Survey of Sweden, 1985–86*, pp. 45–47.

6. Ibid., p. 46. Moreover, "In some cases, the burden on labour market policy will increase as a result of the new industrial policy. The Government finds these measures less costly in the long run and more conducive to the restructuring and reshaping of industry, which has to be a continuous process (pp. 46–47)."

7. The following discussion borrows from Pierre Vinde, *Swedish Government Administration* (Stockholm: the Swedish Institute, 1971).

8. The Swedish Ministry of Economic Affairs and the Ministry of the Budget, *The Swedish Budget 1977/78* (Stockholm, 1977), p. 61.

9. This article appears (in translation) in R. Turvey, ed., *Wages Policy Under Full Employment* (Edinburgh: Hodge, 1952), ch. 3.

10. Assar Lindbeck, *Swedish Economic Policy* (Berkeley: University of California Press, 1974), p. 103.

11. The Swedish Institute, "Active Manpower Policy in Sweden," *Fact Sheets on Sweden*, No. 6d (Stockholm: The Swedish Institute, April 1972), p. 3.

12. See R. A. Mundell, "Capital Mobility and Stabilization Policy Under Fixed and Flexible Exchange Rates," *Canadian Journal of Economics and Political Science*, November 1963.

13. For further discussion, see A. Ando and E. Cary Brown, "Lags in Fiscal Policy: A Summary," in W. L. Smith and R. L. Teigen, eds., *Money, National Income, and Stabilization Policy* (Homewood, Ill.: Irwin, 1965).

14. Tax rates and ratios associated with the investment reserves have varied over time. Corporations must also pay an "excess profits" or "profit-sharing " tax, as reported above. The profit-sharing tax is deductible as a business expense, in calculating the national profits tax.

15. However, a firm may freely invest 30 percent of any allocation to its investment reserve account five years or more after the allocation has been made. When it does this without a government release, it loses the extra deduction from taxable profits in the following year.

16. It may not pay these out as dividends, however.

17. Lindbeck, *Swedish Economic Policy*, pp. 179–82.

18. The average waiting period for dwellings in Stockholm rose from 9 months in 1950 to 40 months in 1958, after which the series was discontinued. See Sven Rydenfelt, "The Rise and Fall of Swedish Rent Control," in M. A. Walker, ed., *Rent Control: A Popular Paradox* (Vancouver: The Fraser Institute, 1975), ch. 7.

19. For example, Sweden completed 8 homes per thousand inhabitants in 1955, 9 in 1960, 13 in 1965, and 14 in 1970. For the U.S., the corresponding figures are 8, 7, 8, 7; for France, they are 5, 7, 12, 9; for West Germany, they are 6, 6, 7, 6, and for Japan, 4, 5, 9, 14. Until recently, more than 70 percent of the homes being built in Sweden were apartments.

20. Rydenfelt, "The Rise and Fall of Swedish Rent Control," p. 175, which is an important source for this paragraph and the ones to follow.

21. Assar Lindbeck, "Theories and Problems in Swedish Economic Policy in the Post-War Period," *American Economic Review*, June 1968, pp. 67–68.

22. Frederic Fleisher, *The New Sweden* (New York: David McKay, 1967), p. 217.

23. "The Health Care System in Sweden," *Fact Sheets on Sweden*, No. 76n (Stockholm: The Swedish Institute, April 1986), p. 2.

24. Part of this is reimbursed by the national health care system. The central government also supervises health care, to ensure that efficiency and high quality standards are maintained throughout Sweden, along with equal access to health care and to legal protection regarding health and safety matters.

25. In addition, according to a 1975 law, Swedish employees have a general right to leave work for adult education. No restrictions exist on the type or duration of studies pursued.

26. "Active Manpower Policy in Sweden," p. 4. See, as well, Allan Larsson, "Flexibility in Production, Security for Individuals—some aspects on Sweden's active labor market policy," *Working Life in Sweden*, No. 35, May 1988. Mr. Larsson is Director-General of the Labor Market Board over 1988–89.

27. The National Labor Market Board, *The Public Employment Service in Sweden* (Stockholm: The Swedish Institute, 1973), p. 11.

28. Swedish Labour Market Administration, *The Swedish Labour Market, 1985–86* (Stockholm: The Swedish Institute, 1986), p. 15. See previous annual reports of the Labor Market Board for earlier figures.

29. "Swedish Labour Market Policy," *Fact Sheets on Sweden*, No. 6m (Stockholm: The Swedish Institute, April 1986), p. 4.

30. The National Labor Market Board, *The Public Employment Service in Sweden* (Stockholm: The Swedish Institute, 1973), p. 19.

31. Ibid., p. 20.

32. The National Labor Market Board, *Labor Market Policy* (Stockholm: The Swedish Institute, 1974), p. 32.

33. A. J. Gilderson, Eva Marshall, *Social Benefits in Sweden* (Stockholm: The Swedish Institute, 1972), p. 53.

34. Bo Jangenäs, *The Swedish Approach to Labor Market Policy* (Stockholm: The Swedish Institute, 1985), p. 56. See, as well, Jan Johanneson, "On Costs and Experiences of Sweden's Labour Market Policies and Programmes," paper presented at the International Conference on Active Labour Market Policy, York University, Downsview, Ontario, Canada, December 1986, p. 8.

35. *The Swedish Labour Market, 1985–86*, p. 16.

36. OECD, *Economic Survey of Sweden, 1981* (Paris: OECD, 1981), p. 41n. Regarding labor-force mobility and related issues, see *Economic Survey of Sweden, 1985–86*, Part 3.

37. See "The Cooperative Movement in Sweden," *Fact Sheets on Sweden*, No. 43m (Stockholm: The Swedish Institute, December 1986). Earlier editions of this fact sheet appear under slightly different titles.

38. In 1987, the housing co-ops built about 32 percent of all new homes, a percentage which has been rising and was about the same in that year as the previous peak in 1959, at the height of rent control (when the number of housing units completed was more than twice as high as in 1987). Fifty-six percent of co-op dwellings completed in 1987 were apartments.

39. This assumes a linear demand, horizontal marginal costs, and "open membership," in the sense given below.

40. "Cooperative Activity in Sweden," *Fact Sheets on Sweden*, No. 43c (Stockholm: The Swedish Institute, September, 1971), p. 1. See, as well, "The Cooperative Movement in Sweden."

41. The personal liability of each member in his or her retail society is also limited to 200 crowns.

42. Folksam has a fifteen-member board of directors, including six from KF, four from LO, two from TCO, and two elected by the employees through their unions. These fourteen nominate a fifteenth member, also the managing director.

43. Another case history is cited by J. W. Ames in *Cooperative Sweden Today* (Manchester: The Cooperative Union, 1956), p. 196:

> Toward the end of 1955, the private rubber companies announced their intention of raising the price of tyres and tubes, etc., from between 4 percent to 10 percent. The Movement's factory at Gislaved, however, stated that there existed no reason for the increase and therefore did not intend to adjust its prices. On January 8, 1956, the Price Control Board placed a [ceiling] on the price of these rubber products one day after it had received notice from Gislaved that the factory intended to retain its old prices. The next announcement by the factory finally killed completely the private companies' case for increased prices. This stated that from March 5, the prices of tyres, etc., would be reduced . . . 5 percent to 10 percent.

44. However, membership in local SR societies is open, not only to LO's members, but also to members of other "popular" movements, including the Konsum societies.

45. A 1986 opinion poll of Swedish households identified world pollution, world starvation, and war, in that order, as major worries. Concern over personal finances or unemployment was relatively minor.

46. See E. L. Feige and R. T. McGee, "Sweden's Laffer Curve: Taxation and the Unobserved Economy," *Scandinavian Journal of Economics*, No. 4, 1983.

47. *Sweden in Brief* (Stockholm: The Swedish Institute, 1982), p. 50.

48. However, there is about one abortion for every three live births.

49. See "Old Age Care in Sweden," *Fact Sheets on Sweden*, No. 8h (Stockholm: the Swedish Institute, February 1986).

50. For a fuller discussion, see *Social Benefits in Sweden*; Åke Fors, *Social Policy and How It Works* (Stockholm: The Swedish Institute, 1972); and Mats Forsberg, *The Evolution*

of Social Welfare Policy in Sweden (Stockholm: The Swedish Institute, 1984).

51. "The Organization of Medical Care in Sweden," *Fact Sheets on Sweden*, No. 76h (Stockholm: The Swedish Institute, June 1977), p. 2.

52. *Sweden in Brief*, p. 59.

53. R. Huntford, *The New Totalitarians* (New York: Stein and Day, 1972), p. 185.

54. Ibid., ch. 15. Chs. 4 and 10 of Huntford are sources for the following paragraph.

55. Quoted by Jenkins (from Gunnar Heckscher) in *Sweden and the Price of Progress* (New York: Goward-McCann, 1968), p. 75.

56. Arne Ruth, "The End of the Swedish Model?" *Social Change in Sweden*, No. 16, April 1980, p. 4.

57. Scandinaviska Enskilda Banken, *Some Data About Sweden, 1985–86* (Orebro, 1985), p. 3.

Questions for Review, Discussion, Examination

1. Over the period 1974–82, the Swedish government appears to have given too much assistance to sectors whose long-run growth prospects were poor and not enough to industries with good export growth potential. Besides the high priority attached to full employment, what accounts for this concentration of resources in declining sectors?

2. Why are Swedish ministries much smaller than their counterparts in other Western countries? What is the policy role of the Boards? Why has it been said that Sweden is "run" by directors general? What constrains the decision-making latitude of directors general in modern Sweden?

3. Guidelines for Swedish fiscal and labor market policies were spelled out after World War II by the LO economist, Gösta Rehn. Which of his proposals was not consistently followed, especially after 1970? What may have been a reason for this? What were the consequences?

4. How did rent controls over 1942–76 help to make contracyclical fiscal policy more successful in Sweden than in other Western market economies?

5. What are the Swedish investment reserves? Why is timing of the release of the reserves crucial to successful stabilization policy? How has the use of the reserves evolved over time?

*6. In 1965, the Swedish government appointed a commission to investigate the "mystery of the disappearing dwellings." This was after more than two decades of rent control, during which time the ratio of demolished dwellings to dwellings newly constructed rose from under 20 percent to over 50 percent, despite the fact that over 2.3 times as many dwellings were completed during 1961–65 as during 1941–45.

Why did this problem of destruction of dwellings arise? Is it what we would have expected, based on the analysis in part E-1 of section 1-1? What were some of the other costs of rent control?

7. Why did a spot near the front of a housing queue have a value during Swedish rent control, even for someone with no desire to rent?

*8. Why did rent control increase the value of cooperative apartments in Sweden? Why did removal of rent ceilings reduce the value of cooperative apartments, even as apartment rents were rising? What has replaced rent ceilings?

9. Why do you suppose Sweden's national health insurance system has led to an excess demand for many types of nonemergency health care? Why might an ideal fee for such a service lie just above the most elastic segment of the demand curve? Who are the beneficiaries of redistribution via this system?

10. How does Swedish labor market policy seek, in particular, to support Sweden's commitment to full employment, in a context where Swedish industry must maintain flexibility and cost effectiveness, in order to compete successfully on the world market?

*11. How have government labor market programs helped to support wage solidarity in Sweden? How do wage solidarity plus redistribution via personal income taxation and transfer payments to households help to make labor-market programs more necessary?

*12. Given the drive for wage solidarity, how does a failure of labor-market measures to achieve clearing of labor markets at negotiated wage rates increase the pressure for expansionary fiscal policy? Why does wage drift increase as policy becomes more expansionary? (*Hint*: Suppose there is an excess supply of unskilled labor at negotiated wage rates, in combination with an excess demand for skilled labor.)

13. In what way is Swedish labor market policy effectively a part of social policy? How does it help to keep down welfare payments?

14. Why may Swedish labor laws passed during the 1970s be increasing unemployment among older workers?

*15. Sweden has the world's strongest consumer cooperative movement, relative to the size of its economy, which also plays a role in consumer education and in restraining price increases.

Why would a consumer cooperative facing the same demand and costs as a private monopoly set a lower price? Then why have consumer cooperatives been forced out of some industries by private competitors, even though the cooperative movement has had success in breaking up concentrations of market power in other industries?

16. What two basic principles govern Swedish social policy? What is the main goal of disability aid?

*17. Briefly explain how tax rates could be too high to allow national income to be maximized, citing some examples of efficiency problems that might be created by high marginal tax-plus-loss-of-subsidy rates.

Do you think that such high rates could be effectively maintained in a much more individualistic society? Why or why not?

* = more difficult.

Suggested Further Readings

Note: The Swedish Institute publishes a large volume of material in English about all apsects of Sweden and Swedish life, including the economy. Particularly worth noting are the series, *Fact Sheets on Sweden* and *Current Sweden*. These are available from any Swedish embassy or consulate, as is the magazine, *Some Data About Sweden*, published every other year by the *Skandinaviska Enskilda Banken*, Sweden's largest bank. In addition, the annual *Economic Survey of Sweden*, published by the OECD, is valuable, as is the magazine, *Sweden Now*, published in Stockholm by the Swedish Engineers' Press, Ltd.

Agurén, Stefan, Reine Hansson, and K. G. Karlsson. *The Volvo Kalmar Plant*. Stockholm: SAF-LO Rationalization Council, 1976.
Ahlén, Kristina. "Recent Trends in Swedish Collective Bargaining: Collapse of the Swedish Model." *Current Sweden* 358 (March 1988).
Ahlström, Per. "Co-Determination at Work: The Almex Experience." *Working Life in Sweden* 17 (April 1980).
Alfredsson, Hans O. "Liberty and Freedom of Choice in the Swedish Election Debate." *Current Sweden* 334 (May 1985).
Ames, J. W. *Without Boundaries. Co-operative Sweden Today and Tomorrow*. Manchester, Eng.: The Co-operative Union, 1971.
Andersson, Ingvar, and Jörgen Weibull. *Swedish History in Brief*. Stockholm: The Swedish Institute, 1985.
Aniansson, Britt, and Bertil Hägerhäll. "The Major Environment Issues Facing Sweden in the 1980s—A Decade of Opportunity and Potential Conflict." *Current Sweden* 302 (May 1983).
Berke, Lena. "Economic Crime in Sweden." *Current Sweden* 322 (August 1984).
Brandelius, Pia. "Election Year '85: The General Political Scene: Retrospect and Current Tendencies." *Current Sweden* 332 (May 1985).
Brownstone, David, Peter Englund, and Mats Persson. "Effects of the Swedish 1983–85 Tax Reform on the Demand for Owner-Occupied Housing: A Microsimulation Approach." *Scandinavian Journal of Economics* 87, 4 (1985): 625–646.
Burton, Jeffrey. "The Swedish Steel Merger: Government and Worker Participation." *Working Life in Sweden* 21 (December 1980).
Childs, Marquis. *Sweden: The Middle Way*. New Haven: Yale University Press, 1947.
———. *Sweden: The Middle Way on Trial*. New Haven: Yale University Press, 1980.
Daun, Åke. "Setbacks and Advances in the Swedish Housing Market." *Current Sweden* 331 (May 1985).
Davidsson, Anders. "Swedish Industrial Policy at the Beginning of the Eighties." *Current Sweden* 262 (December 1980).
Edgren, Gösta, Karl-Olaf Faxen, and Clas-Erik Odhner. *Wage Formation and the Economy*. London: Allen & Unwin, 1973.
Eiger, Norman. "Labor Education and Democracy in the Workplace." *Working Life in Sweden* 22 (April 1981).
———. "The Education of Employee Representatives on Company Boards in Sweden." *Working Life in Sweden* 27 (May 1983).
Erikson, Robert. "Welfare Trends in Sweden Today." *Current Sweden* 330 (March 1985).
Fahlström, Jan Magnus. "Current Economic Trends in Sweden." *Current Sweden* 299 (January 1983).
Feige, E. L., and R. T. McGee. "Sweden's Laffer Curve: Taxation and the Unobserved Economy." *Scandinavian Journal of Economics* 85, 4 (1983): 499–519.
Fleisher, Frederic. *The New Sweden*. New York: David McKay, 1967.
Forsebäck, Lennart. *Industrial Relations and Full Employment*. Stockholm: The Swedish Institute, 1980.

Forsberg, Mats. *The Evolution of Social Welfare Policy in Sweden.* Stockholm: The Swedish Institute, 1984.
Gardell, Bertil. "Production Techniques and Working Conditions." *Current Sweden* 256 (August 1980).
Gilderson, A. J., and Eva Marshall. *Social Benefits in Sweden.* Stockholm: The Swedish Institute, 1972.
Gustafsson, Agne. *Local Government in Sweden.* Stockholm: The Swedish Institute, 1983.
——. "Decentralization in Sweden." *Current Sweden* 316 (April 1984).
Gustafsson, Björn. "Macroeconomic Performance, Old-Age Security and the Rate of Social Assistance Recipients in Sweden." *European Economic Review* 26 (1984): 319–338.
Haag, Martin. "Election Year '85: The Swedish Economy in the Right Direction?" *Current Sweden* 333 (May 1985).
Hadenius, Stig. *Swedish Politics During the 20th Century.* Stockholm: The Swedish Institute, 1985.
Hansson, Ingemar. "Inflation and Price Controls in Sweden." *Scandinavian Journal of Economics* 85, 3 (1983): 415–423.
Hansson, Ingemar, Lars Jonung, Johan Myhrman, and Hans Söderström. *Sweden: the Road to Stability.* Stockholm: Swedish Business and Social Research Institute, 1985.
Heckscher, Eli. *An Economic History of Sweden.* Cambridge: Harvard University Press, 1954.
Heckscher, Gunnar. "What is the Purpose of Welfare?" *Social Change in Sweden* 25 (May 1982).
Herrstroem, Staffan. "Swedish Family Policy." *Current Sweden* 348 (September 1984).
Höglund, Elisabeth. "Election Year, '82: End of Party Truce on Swedish Labor Market Policy." *Current Sweden* 288 (June 1982a).
——. "Election Year, '82: Cut in Health Insurance Benefits—A Controversial Austerity Measure." *Current Sweden* 289 (July 1982b).
Holmlund, Bertil. "Payroll Taxes and Wage Inflation: The Swedish Experience." *Scandinavian Journal of Economics* 85, 1 (1983): 1–15.
Huntford, Roland. *The New Totalitarians.* New York: Stein and Day, 1972.
Jangenäs, Bo. *The Swedish Approach to Labor Market Policy.* Stockholm: The Swedish Institute, 1985.
Jenkins, David. *Sweden and the Price of Progress.* New York: Coward-McCann, 1968.
Jonsson, Björn. "Sweden's Economic Development in the 1980's." *Current Sweden* 317 (May 1984).
Kjellander, Claes-Göran. "Election Year, '82: New Tax System Splits the Bloc Structure of Swedish Politics?" *Current Sweden* 287 (May 1982a).
——. "National Political Issues for the 1984–85 Session of the Riksdag." *Current Sweden* 295 (October 1982b).
Leijonhufvud, Sigfrid. "Election Year '82: New Departures from the Middle Road." *Current Sweden* 295 (October 1982).
Lindbeck, Assar. "Theories and Problems in Swedish Economic Policy in the Post-War Period." *American Economic Review* 58 (June 1968). Supplement.
——. *Swedish Economic Policy.* Berkeley: University of California Press, 1974.
Logue, John. "On the Road Toward Worker-Run Companies: The Employee Participation Act in Practice." *Working Life in Sweden* 9 (February 1979).
——. "American and Swedish Attitudes Toward New Technology on the Job." *Working Life in Sweden* 31 (May 1986).
MacLeod, Dan. "Why Sweden Has Better Working Conditions than the U.S." *Working Life in Sweden* 28 (April 1984).
Magnusson, Birgitta. "What is Being Done in Sweden for Unemployed 16- and 17-Year-Olds." *Current Sweden* 275 (September 1981).

Meidner, Rudolf. *Employee Investment Funds.* London: Allen & Unwin, 1978a.

———. "Employee Investment Funds and Capital Formation: A Topical Issue in Swedish Politics." *Working Life in Sweden* 6 (June 1978b).

Meyerson, Per-Martin. *Company Profits: Sources of Investment Finance: Wage Earners' Investment Funds in Sweden.* Stockholm: Federation of Swedish Industries, 1976.

———. "Capital Accumulation and Ownership Structure in Swedish Industry—The Employee Fund Debate in Perspective." *Working Life in Sweden* 10 (March 1979).

Öhman, Berndt. "A Note on the 'Solidarity Wage Policy' of the Swedish Labor Movement." *Swedish Journal of Economics* 71 (September 1969): 198–205.

Olsen, Gregg M., ed. *Industrial Change and Labour Adjustment in Sweden and Canada.* Toronto: Garamond Press, 1987.

Ruth, Arne. "The End of the Swedish Model?" *Social Change in Sweden* 16 (April 1980).

Ryden, B., and W. Bergström, eds. *Sweden: Choices for Economic and Social Policy in the 1980s.* London: Allen & Unwin, 1982.

Rydenfelt, Sven. "Sweden: The Rise and Fall of Swedish Rent Control." In M. A. Walker, ed. *Rent Control: A Popular Paradox.* Vancouver: The Fraser Institute, 1975, pp. 163–187.

Schnitzer, Martin. *The Economy of Sweden: A Study of the Modern Welfare State.* New York: Praeger, 1970.

Sonning, Staffan. "Election Year '82: Employee Funds." *Current Sweden* 286 (May 1982).

———. "The Employee Fund Issue Moves Toward a Decision?" *Current Sweden* 309 (October 1983).

Stahl, Ingemar. "From Job Mobility to Job Preservation: The Development of Swedish Manpower Policies, 1973–1978." Paper presented to Conference on Recent European Manpower Policies, Glen Cove, New York (July 1978a).

———. "Unemployment Insurance: The Swedish Experience." In Grubel, H. G., and M. A. Walker, eds. *Unemployment Insurance.* Vancouver: The Fraser Institute 1978b, pp. 120–142.

Stahlberg, Ann-Charlotte. "Effects of the Swedish Supplementary Pension System on Personal and Aggregate Household Saving." *Scandinavian Journal of Economics* 82, 1 (1980): 25–44.

Strandberg, Hans. "Election Year '88: Time for an Environmental Election?" *Current Sweden* 362 (May 1988).

The Swedish Institute, *Sweden in Brief.* Stockholm, 1985.

The Swedish Institute of Public Opinion Research (SIFO). "Swedish Collective Bargaining in Transition." *Current Sweden* 337 (August 1985).

The Swedish Ministry of Finance. *The Swedish Budget, 1987/88.* Stockholm, 1987.

The Swedish Ministry of Industry. *Swedish Industry and Industrial Policy, 1985.* Stockholm, 1985.

The Swedish National Commission for Industrial Policy. *Roads to Increasing Prosperity.* Stockholm: The Swedish Institute, 1979.

Thalin, Lillemor. "Current Economic Trends in Sweden." *Current Sweden* 320 (June 1984).

Törnell, Inga-Britt. "The Swedish Equal Opportunities Ombudsman at Work." *Current Sweden* 290 (August 1982).

Turvey, Ralph, ed. *Wages Policy Under Full Employment.* London: Hodge, 1952.

Vahlne, Jan-Erik. "International Enterprise in Swedish Industry." *Current Sweden* 343 (December 1985).

Vinde, Pierre. *Swedish Government Administration.* Stockholm: The Swedish Institute, 1971.

17

THE WEST GERMAN ECONOMY

The defeat, division, and chaos which Germany suffered in the 1940s did not wipe out the legacy of the past; it only lifted temporarily the pressure of history. When the Germans began to reconstruct their economy, they built upon the familiar structural foundation and plan, much of it invisible to the naked eye, as if guided by an archaeologist who could pick his way blindfolded about some favourite ruin.

—Andrew Shonfield, *Modern Capitalism*

17-1. Introduction

A. Background

West Germany's economic performance between the June, 1948 currency reform and the 1973–74 energy crisis has been called an economic miracle. In 1948, Germany was a wasteland, still devastated by war, and lacking both an indigenous government and an acceptable currency. During the 1950s, its real income per capita rose by twice as much as the net increase over the previous 150 years. By 1973, it was one of the world's most prosperous nations, and by 1981, the average West German household owned assets of nearly 250,000 deutsche marks, not counting its pension rights and income from work. Yet, its performance is scarcely more remarkable than those of Japan, Italy, the USSR, or several East European nations over the same period. Growth was at roughly the same pace in East and West Germany, on average, over 1955–85. In 1985, West Germany had a per capita GNP with the purchasing power of $12,250 U.S., which placed it eighth in the world (behind the United States, Canada, Norway, Switzerland, Luxembourg, Sweden, and Denmark), ignoring the oil-rich Middle Eastern States. This was about 73 percent of the U.S. level ($16,750). East Germany, the wealthiest socialist state, had an estimated per capita GNP of about $10,700.

Much interest in the Federal Republic (West Germany) stems from its reputation as one of the least planned of the above economies—an observation that is correct, but overdrawn. West Germany has consciously adopted a "social market" philosophy, stressing primacy of the market mechanism and freedom of contract, but equally a major role for social welfare. The market is supposed to coordinate the bulk of economic activity, but the state also provides one of the world's most comprehensive and generous safety nets. In addition, Germany is the home of classic finance capitalism—the "structural foundation" alluded to by Dr. Shonfield—and West German labor unions obtained important concessions in the realm of industrial democracy as early as 1951–52.

The heart of an ideal social market economy is what Walter Eucken, the founder of the modern neoliberal school, called the "competitive order." As a liberal in the classical sense of wanting diffusion of power, Eucken believed that a market economy with workable competition would be both the most efficient and the most humane economic order, because it would maximize individual freedom of choice. He contrasted the competitive order both with a command economy and with an economy dominated by monopolistic elements and political pressure groups. Indeed, he saw a state-managed economy as a system monopolized and dominated by its bureaucratic élite, which would run it against the best interests of the masses of its citizens. The neoliberals believed it essential to guard against all forms of concentration of economic power.

> . . . most neo-liberals would support the competitive order largely because it starts from the assumption that men work and do business in their own interest, and that this is a surer foundation on which to build an economic order than that of absolute ethical rules [such as those of the Catholic Church or of the Communist party]. They would also endorse the competitive order for the reason that it protects the individual from the arbitrary domination of others. . . . [Ideally], the only force to which the individual is constantly subject is the impersonal "objective" one of competition itself.[1]

Nevertheless, the neoliberals stressed government's role as a guarantor of competition, a combatter of business cycles, a defender of the value of money, a provider of social-welfare benefits, and a supplier of public goods. They recognized that public authorities would have to play a major role in combatting pollution, and they have generally favored a high level of government spending on education, public works, and culture. Otherwise, they agree with nineteenth-century English advocates of laissez faire on the importance of free trade and the primacy of the market.

The area now occupied by West Germany covers just over half of prewar

Germany, which also included the GDR, a large chunk of modern Poland, and a small piece of the USSR (then part of East Prussia). One consequence of territorial shrinkage is that 98 percent of West Germany's population consists of ethnic Germans. However, postwar prosperity has also created a demand for labor beyond the capacity of West German citizens to supply. After the flow of refugees from East Germany was shut off in 1961, large numbers of foreign workers flooded into West Germany, mainly from Italy, Turkey, Yugoslavia, and Greece. By and large, they have taken the least desirable jobs, and large numbers remain to this day, even though the energy crisis has turned the shortage of workers into an acute shortage of jobs.

West Germany has a population density roughly equal to that of India (1,645 people per square kilometer or 635 per square mile). Its territory is about the size of Wyoming, or a bit smaller than Labrador, but it is inhabited by over 61.1 million people (as of 1986) including nearly 4.5 million foreigners. There has been little population growth since 1972, however, thanks to one of the world's lowest birthrates, which the government is trying to raise by means of increased family allowances. Over 90 percent of West Germany's people live in cities and towns with over 2,000 residents, and because of World War II, 52 percent are females.

Historically, Berlin was the capital of Germany until the end of World War II. When the Allies divided Germany, Berlin was nearly 110 miles inside the eastern zone and was, itself, divided between east and west, with East Berlin eventually becoming the capital of the GDR. West Berlin is not officially part of West Germany, although close ties have developed between the two.[2] The Federal Republic had to find a new capital, and Bonn was chosen, partly because it was a pleasant university city, relatively undamaged during the war (owing to its lack of importance). No city has been able to replace Berlin as the heart of Germany, although Munich, Hamburg, Dusseldorf, Cologne, Hanover, and Stuttgart have become important regional centers, and Frankfurt is a major financial center.

B. Evolution of the West German Economy

We can identify three benchmarks in the evolution of the postwar West German economy. Until the currency reform of 1948, an excess supply of money (too much money chasing too few goods)—a legacy of the Nazi era combined with poor management by Allied occupation authorities—caused economic activity to stagnate. More than half of all exchange took place via barter or black markets, on which average prices were around fifty times official ceilings. A successful change of currencies in June 1948 finally started the three Western zones of occupied Germany on a path of sustained growth. Industrial production rose by 50 percent in the second half of 1948 and by 25 percent in 1949. Except for a brief pause in 1966–67, economic growth continued for nearly twenty-five years, until the first energy crisis in 1973–74. However, the currency reform also sealed the division of Germany into east and west zones by World War II victors with deep ideological differences. Thus, June 1948 is the first benchmark in the evolution of West Germany's economy, and the 1966–67 "recession"—although scarcely deserving of the name—is the second.

The period 1948–66 was, basically, one long expansion. Unemployment was reduced to 2.5 percent by 1959, despite an influx of 3.6 million more refugees between 1950 and the building of the Berlin Wall in August 1961. The jobless rate remained below 2.5 percent until 1974. However, in the first half of 1967, real GNP fell (by 2.3 percent) for the first time since 1948. This ended domination of the federal government by the Christian Democratic party, which had been in power since the founding of the Federal Republic in 1949. A "grand coalition" of Christian and Social Democrats ruled over 1966–69, and in 1969, the country shifted further leftward, as the Social Democrats came to power. Although supporting the basic social market philosophy, they have been less devoted to free-market ideology, more willing to expand the state's economic role, more oriented toward labor and industrial democracy, and more interested in expanding economic and political ties with the USSR and Eastern Europe (Willy Brandt's "Ostpolitik"). Under Brandt and then Helmut Schmidt (from 1974), they ruled until the fall of 1982, when the Christian Democrats returned to power. By the latter year, public sector outlays were over 49 percent of GNP.

To many observers at the time, the 1966–67 recession demonstrated the inadequacy of existing policy tools to combat the business cycle. This ensured passage of the 1967 Stability and Growth Law, which expanded the government's toolkit and signaled the start of a belated but brief fling with Keynesian economics. In retrospect, this exercise in raising aggregate demand-generated wage increases plus expectations of more to come that could not be sustained—especially once the energy crisis was underway. It also heightened employer interest in labor-saving technology, which now accounts for more than half of all enterprise investment. For the most part, the experiment with "der Keynes" was abandoned after the 1973–74 energy crisis, which is our final benchmark.

Because it depends heavily on imported oil, the energy crisis hit West Germany hard, causing her first year-to-year decrease in GNP and raising unemployment to over 3.5 percent for the first time in twenty years. No sooner did the economy pull out of this recession than the second energy crisis struck, in 1978–79. By 1981, the Federal Republic was paying nearly ten times as much for each barrel of imported oil as ten years earlier. The first energy crisis ended the economic miracle, and the second signaled the start of a period of relative stagnation. By late 1985, oil prices were falling, and exports had recovered to reach record levels. But growth was still slow, and unemployment was at its highest level since the Great Depression. In the Ruhr, center of the iron, coal, and steel industries, over 14 percent of the labor force was jobless. Bankruptcies also reached record highs (more than twice as many in 1984 as in 1980), and just 7.5 percent of GNP was going into productive investment vs. 12 percent in the early 1960s.

At the same time, the social welfare system was unable to finance itself on a pay-as-you-go basis, although social insurance fees came to more than 35 percent of gross wages and salaries in 1986. The energy crisis revealed structural flaws in the economy, and it is unclear whether the traditional bank-led entrepreneurial drive—which propelled Germany to world technological leadership in the early twentieth century—will be equal to the task of renewal this time around. To keep down unemployment, government subsidies have propped up declining industries and delayed structural change. Meanwhile, the Federal Republic lost market shares in exports embodying advanced technology to both Japan and the United States over 1972–84. With the high unemployment and uncertain future, the old consensus about the broad direction of economic policy appears to have vanished.

C. Subsidies and structure

Despite the long-standing commitment to social market philosophy, several sectors of the West German economy have enjoyed long-standing protection via subsidies from the rigors of the free market—most notably, farming, coal mining, housing, and transportation. In recent years, the list has grown to include shipbuilding, steel, textiles, and electronics. In the form of financial aid and tax relief, subsidies ran 6–7 percent of GNP over 1973–87. Despite campaign promises, the Christian Democrats, who came to power in 1982, have been unable to cut the subsidy share of the budget, because of the threatened loss of jobs. On balance, this aid impeded structural change by keeping resources in declining industries, which were its main recipients. Ironically, its net effect was to reduce economic growth and, thereby, to raise the rate of unemployment, despite an avowed aim of doing the opposite.[3]

As in other Western countries, agriculture is one of the most protected sectors. In 1985, total explicit plus implicit farm subsidies (including the cost to consumers of retail food prices above world market levels) were twice as high as value added in farming. Yet, the income gap between urban and rural areas, in favor of the former, was wider than at any time since the founding of the Federal Republic. The scissors index of prices paid to farmers divided by prices farmers pay for equipment and supplies fell by more than 20 percent over 1976–85. Despite several "Green Plans" designed to rationalize farming, to consolidate farms, and to reduce their number, only half of all farms consist of 25 acres or more. The wealthiest 10 percent of West German farmers earn more than 30 percent of total farm income, while the bottom 40 percent earn just 16 percent. Although not close to being cost effective in the absence of subsidies, most of the latter continue to farm, because of the subsidies and because alternatives are limited in a period of high unemployment. Yet, by 1985, there were fewer than 45 percent as many farms as in 1950, and many families were farming part-time. Just 60 percent of the income of agricultural households actually came from farming. (As a rule, women do most of the farm work, while their husbands hold other jobs.) The federal government also subsidizes the movement of industry into rural areas where the farm labor force is too large, and it now bears 80 percent of the cost of farmers' pensions plus nearly 40 percent of the cost of their health insurance.

However, the costliest assistance comes in the form of price supports for farm produce, which are mainly channelled through the European Economic Community (EEC). Guaranteed EEC prices are nearly always above world market levels, which raises the cost of food and housing to German consumers.[4] (Farm price supports raise the value of land used in agriculture, thereby restricting the supply for residential and commercial use, which helps to keep real estate prices high.) The EEC spends 65–70 percent of its budget to subsidize high farm prices. Partly because of this, West Germany is 75 percent self-sufficient in food, and an average farmer produced enough, by value, to feed 37 people in 1980 vs. 10 in the Soviet Union, 18 in East Germany, 36 in France, and 70 in the United States. Nevertheless, the Federal Republic is also the world's biggest food importer, most of which comes from other EEC nations at the high support prices. This has been a source of some dissatisfaction.

West Germany's comparative advantage lies in industry, and it is one of the world's most industrialized nations, as well as the world's leading exporter of manufactured goods. (With just over one percent of the world's population, it accounts for more than 20 percent of the world's manufactured exports.) During the 1950s, it developed new markets for its capital goods, which became famous for quality and after-sale service, and the demand for which proved to be income elastic. Thus, in a period of rising world incomes, the demand for West German exports grew even more rapidly and propelled a dramatic expansion of income and output at home. This was a formula that Japan would also use, but the Federal Republic still exports a much larger volume and variety of goods, even though just four industrial groups—machinery, motor vehicles, chemicals, and precision instruments—account for over half of German sales abroad. The Federal Republic exports 40–45 percent of its industrial output and 26–27 percent of its GNP. More than 20 percent of all jobs are closely related to exports. (One worker in nine produces directly for export; one in eleven produces the necessary inputs.)

In 1986, industry accounted for about 38 percent of West Germany's gross domestic product and construction for 5 percent vs. 1.7 percent for agriculture, forestry, and fishing. As in other developed countries, the share of industry has been falling as has that of commerce, transport, and communications (just under 15 percent). That of services (more than 40 percent) has been rising, although about half the increase since 1970 has been due to rising relative prices. Until the late 1950s, the Federal Republic had a fairly good natural resource endowment that formed the basis for its industries. The coal reserves of the Ruhr Basin are still the largest in Europe, but they are mostly 1,200 meters deep and more, and coal mining would not survive without price floors above world market levels, supported by subsidies and import quotas. West Germany also mines 20 percent of the world's potash. However, West German iron ore reserves are now mostly exhausted, forcing it to import most of its needs, along with over 95 percent of its oil, two-thirds of its natural gas, and half its total energy use. It is self-sufficient only in coal, which supplies about 30 percent of her total energy use, thanks to the import barriers and the highest subsidies of any sector on a per-worker basis. Twenty-one of the twenty-six main mineral raw materials used by industry must now be entirely imported.

Thus, the Federal Republic has joined the ranks of industrial powers that essentially add value to imported raw materials—although it does this more successfully than most, despite labor costs that are close to being highest in the world. West Germany also runs an export surplus with OPEC, thanks to an eight-fold expansion of export value to this region over 1972–82 and to domestic energy saving. Total energy consumption was less in 1984 than in 1973, although real GNP had grown by 28 percent, and the share of oil had fallen from 55 percent to 42 percent. Nevertheless, the economy suffers from structural defects, as well as high labor costs and low investment yields. Investment is still running below levels needed to achieve full employment by the early 1990s, and most fixed investment is directed toward economizing on labor. At least the medium-term outlook is for lower growth and higher unemployment than before the energy crisis, although the passing of the baby boom generation into the labor market by 1990 will ease the pressure on job creation.

D. West Germany's Political System

Finally, West Germany is a parliamentary democracy with a federal form of government, whose taxing and law-making authority are divided among three main levels—the local governments, the provinces (or *länder*), and the federal government in Bonn. There are now ten *länder* (eleven if we include West Berlin) and several thousand units of local government. A feature of West German federalism is an interlocking of federal and provincial (or land) levels through federal organs with a balanced regional representation, whose members adhere to instructions from their respective *länder*. There is also a German tradition of allowing the provinces to implement most laws, and these land powers are often delegated further to local governments. Federal implementation is largely confined to foreign affairs, defense, and labor-market policies (including the local employment offices). Otherwise, "the federal ministries are mainly concerned with the preparation of laws, and the corresponding land ministries with their administration."[5] For example, the *länder* physically collect most taxes, and this obliges the federation to negotiate tax-sharing agreements with them; the federation also uses tax sharing to redistribute revenues from more to less prosperous *länder*. Over time, the federal authorities have gained economic strength vis-à-vis the *länder*, while the local authorities have grown weaker. The latter have had to finance growing social welfare burdens and are in an almost permanent state of financial crisis. They depend heavily on land subsidies in exchange for which they are able to exercise less and less autonomy. Partly because of their own administrative and welfare burdens, the *länder* have also had discretionary control over smaller and smaller percentages of their budgets.

At the federal level, the West German government is presided over by a Chancellor or Prime Minister, normally the head of the political party or coalition with a majority in the lower house (or Bundestag) of Parliament. Three political parties have played major roles in government. The Christian Democrats (CDU) and their Bavarian sister party, the Christian Social Union (CSU) ruled the country from 1949 to 1966—until 1963 under Konrad Adenauer and over 1963–66 under Ludwig Erhard. We may consider these men as, respectively, the political and economic architects of the Federal Republic, although Erhard, who had been Adenauer's economics minister, was ineffective as Chancellor. The CDU/CSU occupies the right wing of the political spectrum, with the Social Democrats (SPD) on the left and the Free Democrats (FPD) in the center.

The Free Democrats are by far the smallest of the three main parties. Yet, with 6 percent to 13 percent of the vote, the FPD has held the balance of power at the federal level, except over 1953–61 and 1966–69. In every other election, it has been able to determine whether the CDU/CSU or SPD would rule. When the FPD moved to the left in 1969, switching coalition partners, the SPD came to power for the first time, despite the fact that CDU/CSU polled more votes (as it has in every election, save 1972). Similarly, when the FPD switched back to the Christian Democrats in 1982, the popular SPD Chancellor, Helmut Schmidt, lost his post to Helmut Kohl of the CDU, who has since been reelected twice and remained Chancellor, as of 1989. Because it holds the balance of power, FPD has exercised influence beyond numbers and has usually held at least one major cabinet post. As a rule, the Free Democrats take a relatively conservative stand on economic issues, in combination with a left-of-center position on social questions. They place a high value on restoring German unity and were enthusiastic supporters of the SPD's Ostpolitik for that reason. They also uphold a long-standing liberal tradition in German politics.

The SPD traces its origins to 1875, when the working-class movement founded by Ferdinand Lassalle merged with the Marxists to form the Socialist Workers' party. Thus, the SPD has quasi-Marxist origins and was revolutionary in its rhetoric—although reformist and pragmatic in its actions—until it adopted the Godesberg Platform in 1959. This reversed its commitment to abolition of private property and command planning, substituting the slogan, "Competition as much as possible; planning as much as necessary."[6] In 1963, the union movement adopted the Düsseldorf Program, in which it postponed its previous demands for a new economic and social order. Instead, it pledged support for the existing social market economy and promised to moderate wage demands, in return for government policies to promote full employment, growth, and a more equitable distribution of wealth.

The SPD's extreme left wing never accepted the Godesberg platform, and many unionists have been uneasy with the Düsseldorf Program, especially in the 1980s, when unemployment has soared to over 8.5 percent of the labor force. Nevertheless, the implied shift toward the center of the political spectrum raised the SPD's potential vote by 10–15 percent of the electorate and made it a serious contender for power at the federal level. This it achieved, first over 1966–69, in coalition with the CDU/CSU, and then over 1969–82, as the dominant partner in a coalition with the Free Democrats. However, in the 1983 and 1987 elections, part of its youthful left wing deserted it to vote for the Green party—a loose coalition of environmentalists, pacifists, and leftists—which therefore gained representation in the Bundestag for the first time.

17-2. Financial and Industrial Structure of the Economy

In this chapter, we focus on three basic ingredients of the West German economy. These are finance capitalism, or the close association between banks and firms; the government's policy role, and codetermination (*mitbestimmung*), the West German version of industrial democracy. We begin with finance capitalism.

A. Historical Background

In several respects, the modern West German economy is a continuation of the system that emerged in the second half of the nineteenth century. Perhaps the most important date dividing modern from medieval Germany would be January 1, 1834 when Germany became a customs union. Prior to then, Germans were never really united, either politically or economically. "In the centuries when England and France were laying the foundations on which the structures of their unified states were to be built, the German people were split into hundreds of principalities that fought and conquered one another. . . ."[7] As late as the early nineteenth century, Germany was divided into 38 largely independent states, of which Prussia was strongest, but most of which were fiefdoms of nobles of middling importance, who suppressed economic development by levying tolls on commerce passing through their realms. The customs union put an end to this and set the stage for industrial development, which began in earnest during the 1850s.

The German states were not politically united until 1871, when articles of confederation were signed at Versailles, at the climax of the Franco-Prussian War. During the signing at Prussian military headquarters, guns of the Prussian artillery besieging Paris were clearly audible to the other German leaders. The Prussian Emperor (*Kaiser*) became the Emperor of the second German Reich, which was dominated by Prussia. It lasted until late 1918, when military defeat in World War I ended the monarchy. Then followed the Weimar Republic (1919–33), Germany's first experiment with democracy. It ended with Hitler's ascent to power amid record unemployment following the Great Depression. The Third Reich itself collapsed in 1945, owing to crushing defeat in World War II. Following Allied military occupation, the present West and East German governments were founded in 1949.

Nineteenth-century Germany was also the home of classic finance capitalism, centered on the banking system. As in Japan and several other European countries, industrialization in Germany owed much to technological progress in agriculture, which raised farm incomes and savings, while creating a pool of surplus labor. A way was therefore needed of combining the savings of thousands of relatively small savers, mainly risk averse rural landowners, and of channelling these to investment projects in industry. Here, both risks and prospective returns were high, and the borrower would frequently lack security for a loan, other than the project itself. As in Japan and Sweden, this led to managerial and ownership ties between banks and firms, and it was also the origin of the universal bank, with a heavy long-term loan commitment, and of bank absorption of a significant share of client risk. The big banks concentrated on large-scale industry and became the centers of industrial empires. Credit cooperatives arose to finance small-scale industry, farming, and commerce.

German banks not only financed the investment and working capital needs of client firms, but also supplied them with technical and entrepreneurial expertise. These two functions were (and remain) closely related, and banks prided themselves on being able to judge clients' loan requests on scientific or engineering, as well as on financial grounds. In his *Industry and Trade*, Alfred Marshall wrote,

> [In Germany, an inventor] would take his proposal to one of the great banks with an industrial department; and the proposal would immediately be put before experts, scientific and technical, well known to the bank and thoroughly trusted, who (on the assumption that the proposal was really good), would report well on it and would be believed.

In Marshall's view,

> the German banks have surpassed even those of America in the promptitude and energy with which they face the risks of turning a large flow of capital into an enterprise . . . to which the future belongs.

Moreover,

> The German great banks are, as a rule, remarkably well-managed. But . . . some good judges think they are inclined to venture beyond their strength; especially by carrying to excess the locking up of their capital in [long-term] loans, which cannot be called in under grave emergency. It is, however, claimed that their intimate association with large industrial movements keeps them alert: that they earn a higher rate of interest on their advances and can pay higher interest rates to their depositors [in consequence].[8]

At first, banks made largely short-term loans, but these were gradually lengthened until banks were practically partners of the firms they were financing. Not a few of these partnerships survive to this day. Because of Germany's underdeveloped financial markets—and of the frequent need to combine the savings of individual savers to get enough funds for a single investment—banks had to satisfy most of the financial needs of industry, a role that the West German banking system still plays. A feature of finance capitalism is that a particular company will do much of its business with a single bank, which is therefore well placed to evaluate its financial condition. Moreover, banks exercise substantial ownership rights over much of German industry. By law, major decisions made by the board of directors or by the management of a large private company can be vetoed by any group of shareholders controlling the votes of just over 25 percent of the firm's stock. Such decisions require 75 percent approval.[9] This enhances the importance of large vis-à-vis small shareholders and makes it possible for large institutional investors to gain veto power in important firms.

Banks are especially favored because of their historical role as Germany's only stockbrokers—a role that has persisted in modern West Germany. When a bank buys shares for its clients, it can often induce them to deposit with it the voting rights attached to the stock. Through a practice called *stimmenleihe* (loaning votes), banks can further enhance their voting strength in specific companies by trading these proxy rights among themselves. Unless an owner controls a major proportion of a company's shares, such an arrangement can benefit both the bank and its clients. No small client can hope to accumulate 25 percent of the shares of a publicly listed company, and, thus, is nearly powerless to influence the behavior of management by himself. A bank can do this, however, by buying shares on its own and by accumulating proxy voting rights. If both a bank and its clients want a firm whose shares they own to maximize share value (long-run profit)—or if both agree on another company goal—the clients will gain by depositing their voting rights, whenever these raise the bank's influence over enterprise management.

Thus, banks place their representatives on the supervisory boards of directors of many firms whose stock voting rights they hold—whether through proxy or direct ownership—and it is fairly common for a banker to chair such a board.[10] The Deutsche Bank alone now seats directors on the boards of about four hundred different corporations. In 1905, the eight large credit (or joint-stock) banks were able to name the directors of 819 firms, producing the bulk of industrial output. A British historian wrote of the Imperial era (1871–1918) that "The joint-stock bank was not merely a credit organization, but a politico-economic agency for converting Germany into an industrial state."[11] Today, the power of West German banks is less and is more constrained by regulation, but it is still considerable.

In some respects, the Imperial economy was not very competitive. It was then that the great German cartels were formed—in iron, steel, electrical equipment, coal, chemicals, potash, paper, copper, textiles, ammunition, and so on. "By 1900, there was hardly a trade which had not its Kartell . . . upwards of 350 had come into existence, [although only] about 275 remained active."[12] It was the banks who were most active in promoting and policing cartel agreements. Clapham writes that "among the Germans [cartel] agreements were more ingeniously elaborate, far more general, and more frankly accepted as part of a rational organization of society than among any other people. Many international agreements in the years, 1890–1910, were designed and promoted by Germans.''[13] Moreover, ''while cartels and trusts had to fight a tough battle against public opinion in America and Britain, no influential section of opinion challenged Germany's need for them.''[14] Firms that refused to join a cartel were to be pursued ''like beasts'' and shown no mercy. Banks have always promoted mergers, takeovers, and cartels, although they have also rescued many companies in financial distress and reorganized them or found merger partners (or buyers) when the alternative would have been failure.

Moreover, while German banks have helped to suppress price competition, they have fostered dynamic competition. Historically, they have been the prime movers in promoting innovation and in introducing and spreading information about new products and production processes. They continue to play this role in West Germany today. Interlocking boards of directors help to disseminate such information, and banks frequently organize exchanges between firms on technical matters. As a rule, they know every phase of their clients' operations. The effect of innovation is frequently to enable one enterprise or cartel to invade the market of another, and this was especially true during the Imperial era. For instance, ''the introduction of reinforced concrete came at [a] time of increasing building activity: the cement trust took advantage of it . . . and practically captured the entire building construction and bridge-work markets by substituting concrete at a much lower [price] than steel girders could be purchased for from the [steel cartel].''[15] Subsequently, the steel cartel was forced to cut prices.

Similarly,

> while in France and Britain chemical manufacturers were increasingly hampered by obsolescent plant, . . . Germany was free to develop new methods, like the Solvay process. German sulphuric acid producers were free to attack the markets for dyestuffs and agricultural fertilizers. In every branch of production there were stupendous increases between 1870 and 1900—output of sulphuric acid and alkalis was multiplied eight times, that of dyestuffs about four times.[16]

Finally, by the early twentieth century,

> the telephone had for many purposes superseded the telegraph. In telephone work, Germany led the way for all Europe, including Great Britain . . . [by the second decade of the twentieth century,] there were sent daily more than three times as many telephone messages in Germany alone as telegraphic messages in all the world.[17]

German enterprises and cartels remained willing and able to introduce new technologies even when these would cause chaos, force other firms into bankruptcy, and result in early obsolescence of some of their own capital. The banking system was designed as a vehicle for importing new techniques, products, and ideas, and banks showed skill and enthusiasm in carrying out this task. Not only did Germany import technology at a rapid rate and adapt it to its own conditions, it soon became the world leader in developing new techniques and products.

> When Germany appeared on the world economic scene, the second phase of industrialization was beginning. In the first, the key industries had been textiles, coal-mining, iron-founding, railways, and ship-building, and most of the vital inventions had been British. . . . But in the second phase, where the key industries were steel, electricity, chemicals, optical goods, and the internal combustion engine, many of the inventions were German, as the names Daimler, Benz, Diesel, Zeiss, and Siemens testify, while two of the relatively few British innovations, the Gilchrist-Thomas process for steel-making and Perkins' discovery of aniline dyes, were mainly developed in Germany.[18]

Rapid diffusion of new technology continues to be a major reason for West German export success, and the close association between banks and firms has also been an avenue for spreading entrepreneurial talent over a larger number of enterprises. In addition, German governments have relied on banks to help them implement priorities over the past 130 years or so. When public authorities award low-cost loans or other subsidies, they usually ask the banks to help them choose recipient firms, in effect, by making recommendations based on credit-worthiness and merit.

B. The West German Financial System

At the apex of the current West German financial system we find the central bank, the *Deutsche Bundesbank*, which enjoys greater independence from the government and from domestic political pressures than any other central bank in the world. The Bundesbank has 230 branches scattered through the country, and many of its functions are decentralized into the hands of the 11 land central banks, which are effectively its divisions. As of end-1985, there were 245 credit or commercial banks, with about 6,000 branches. Most banks of all types are small, regional, and unincorporated, but the commercial banking system is dominated by the Big Three—the Deutsche Bank, the Dresdner Bank, and the Commerzbank—which together account for 38 percent of all commercial bank assets. By far the largest of these is the Deutsche Bank, with 1,200 branches and more assets than the other two combined, which is one of the largest non-Japanese banks in the world. It finances about a third of the foreign trade of West German industry.

A feature of all West German banks is the wide variety of services that they offer. In the words of a German banker, they are "financial department stores" or universal banks, that combine commercial and investment banking with all other kinds of financial services. Competition between German banks has been intense. Over 1957–85, the number of all kinds of banks dropped from 13,359 to 4,739, while the number of branches more than tripled, from just under 13,000 to nearly 40,000. The number of commercial banks fell from 364 to 245, while the number of branches was rising to about 5,950 from just over 1,900. Because of fierce competition at home, as well as constraints on domestic lending, the Big Three have also become heavily involved in international operations.[19] These account, e.g., for over a third of the Deutsche Bank's business.

For all West German producing enterprises combined, the percentage of capital assets ultimately financed from own funds was under forty in 1985, a share that has been falling for nearly twenty years. Over 60 percent were financed by borrowing, mainly in the form of bank loans.[20] New lending covered about 18 percent of gross or 68 percent of net investment by producing enterprises, and over 80 percent of such loans, by value, were contractually long term, maturing in four years or more. By comparison, sales of new stocks and bonds were minor, and this has been the rule in Germany for more than one hundred years. As banks are the country's only legal stockbrokers, they also handle nearly all sales of securities, and corporations applying for a stock exchange listing must have the support of a bank. The bond market is several times as large as the stock market. At end-1983, just 11 percent of outstanding securities were equities vs. nearly half in the United States and almost 60 percent in the United Kingdom. Only nineteen hundred of two million business firms were public limited liability companies, and as of end-1985, only 450 of these were listed on a stock exchange (a net decrease from twenty years earlier). Only about thirty were actively traded. As we have seen, banks often own shares of the companies to which they lend and are able to name directors of these firms. Borrowers return the favor by seating their own representatives on the boards of banks, although the direction of influence is from banks to firms. (Such arrangements do not violate West Germany's antimonopoly laws.)

In periods of tight money and relatively high interest rates, banks have often found their profit margins squeezed. They are locked into long-term loans made when rates were lower and are therefore unable to raise their average lending rates rapidly enough to keep pace with the rates at which they must borrow. (As a rule, they borrow from the central bank at favorable rates, but subject to quotas, and on the short-term money market where interest rates are volatile.) In periods of easy money and low interest rates, the above scenario is reversed. Thus, banks honor their long-term relationships with client firms by partially shielding the latter from risk in the form of fluctuations in borrowing cost, although the percentage of long-term lending at floating interest rates has been rising.

Banks are less likely to shield client firms from fluctuations in cash flow over the business cycle. When business conditions worsen, West German firms are already operating with high debt-to-equity ratios. It is difficult or impossible for them to offset the drop in cash flow with increased borrowing, because their managers may not want a greater debt burden and because banks are reluctant to allow borrowers to raise their debt-to-equity ratios even further. This reluctance stems not only from caution on the part of bank management, but also from government requirements for banks to maintain "adequate" capital and liquidity (which is governed by detailed regulations) and to accept only "prudent" risks. As a result, German firms react to a worsening of earnings by cutting investment and employment. When earnings improve, they do the reverse. Net investment by producing enterprises in the Federal Republic is more sensitive to changes in underlying business conditions than is the case in most Western countries.

As a third category of bank, we have about 600 savings banks, with more than 17,000 branches, plus over 3,660 industrial and farm credit cooperatives with 15,900 branches. These figures include the twelve central clearinghouses for the savings banks and the nine cooperative clearinghouses. The Westdeutsche Landesbank, the savings bank clearinghouse for the Ruhr area, is West Germany's third largest bank. These clearinghouses hold the reserves and guarantee the largest loans of the banks they serve. They also lend on their own. (For example, the cooperative clearinghouses lend mainly to small businesses, farmers, cooperatives, and professional people.) All banks in this category have a regional orientation.

A fourth category covers 16 special credit institutions, including the state-owned Reconstruction Loan Corporation (RLC), now the country's tenth largest bank. Originally, RLC was set up in the late 1940s to channel Marshall Plan aid to German industry. West Germany received $1.3 billion (7 billion DM) through the Marshall Plan, of which it ultimately had to repay $1 billion. However, the federal government repaid this from tax revenues and used the aid to set up a revolving fund, now known as the European Recovery Program (ERP) special fund, which has become a permanent source of investment finance. RLC was founded under the Economics Ministry to manage this fund.[21] At first, ERP resources were channelled to bottleneck sectors—mainly coal, iron, steel, energy, and transportation—where a shortage of capacity owing to war destruction and postwar dismantling threatened to prevent expansion in the rest of the economy. Some monies also went to export industries which, at the time, were facing serious difficulties. Subsequently, ERP funds were lent mainly to small- and medium-sized firms, whose access to normal borrowing channels was restricted, and for regional development or to companies willing to locate in West Berlin or close to the East German border. ERP now provides loans and investment guarantees for both of these purposes, and it also finances energy saving, protection of the environment, better adaptation of production capacity (e.g., to changes in demand), industrial restructuring, and improvements in working conditions.

Today, more domestic ERP credits go to promote small and medium-sized enterprises than for any other single purpose. By the end of 1985, the ERP Special Fund had made loans totalling over 68 billion DM, or nearly ten times the original Marshall Plan endowment. The Fund has grown through the years, as loans from it were repaid, and it is now larger than ever in nominal terms. (By law, its assets may not fall in value.) Recently, it has become a source of aid for developing countries. The domestic funds lent by ERP—now running just over 4 billion DM per year—came to around 2 percent of total gross investment or to a bit more than 7 percent of total net investment of producing enterprises in 1985. However, the Fund's potential leverage is raised by the fact that it usually lends to cover just part of a project's cost. The borrower must supply the rest from other sources.

Other special public credit institutions include the industrial credit banks, the Equalization of Burdens Bank, and the Berlin Industrial Bank. The first of these specialize in short- and medium-term loans to medium-sized firms. The second is partly financed by the Equalization of Burdens Fund, set up to aid victims of World War II. It now specializes in loans to less developed regions. Finally the Berlin bank specializes in financing industrial development in that city, which is heavily subsidized by the federal government. (Berlin aid has also accounted for more than 16 billion DM worth of ERP credits.)

At end-1985, savings banks, together with their central clearinghouses, had about 37 percent of the assets of all German banks vs. 22 percent for commercial banks (including 8.5 percent for the Big Three), and about 41 percent for credit cooperatives, mortgage banks, and all other banks combined. Over time, savings, commercial, and cooperative banks have become more alike and more in keeping with the financial department store image, although commercial banks are comparatively short-term in both assets and liabilities with respect to other kinds of German banks. On average, there is about one (commercial or noncommercial) bank office for every 1,400 residents vs., e.g., one office for every 6,000 residents in the U.S., and 95 percent of all German employees own bank accounts into which their earnings are regularly paid.

As a rule, close association with a major bank raises a company's return on investment, and this result is plausibly due to increased efficiency, as well (in some instances) as to greater concentration of market and political power.[22] According to a 1980 report of the Federal Monopolies Commission, banks held 145 seats on the supervisory boards of the 100 largest corporations (about 10 percent of the total number of seats). About 65 percent of the bank seats belonged to the Big Three. Banks had at least one seat on each of sixty-one supervisory boards, twenty of which were chaired by a bank representative. Bank directors are valued as sources of expertise, experience, and information, not least because of their wide contacts in Germany and throughout the world. Yet, some observers question whether the old bank entrepreneurial drive still prevails. In part, this is because banks are constrained by reserve ratios and the requirements to maintain "adequate" capital and liquidity and to accept only "prudent" risks, as noted earlier. These stem from the 1931 Banking Crisis, which is believed to have aided Hitler's rise to power, as well as postwar bank failures, notably of Herstatt Bankhaus in 1974. They push bank lending toward the low end of the risk spectrum, with potentially serious consequences for the financing of entrepreneurship.

C. Industrial Structure

Another feature of the German economy has always been a large sector of small- and medium-sized firms, which we define to be enterprises with less than 25 million DM (or $11.5 million U.S.) in annual sales, as of 1986. These account for around 60 percent of total employment, 35–40 percent of total sales and investment, and more than 80 percent of all apprenticeships. To a degree, West Germany has a dualistic economy, with relatively capital intensive large firms and relatively labor intensive small- and medium-sized enterprises. Within the latter, investment and employment are more subject to business-cycle fluctuations, partly because they have higher debt-to-equity ratios, pay higher borrowing costs, and are often more subject to business risks. Yet, this sector is essential to maintaining competition and entrepreneurship. From time to time, concerns are expressed about its prosperity or even survival, and there is a program of government assistance to it (the "Middle Estate" Policy). Nevertheless, large firms have an advantage in applying for subsidies, because of better connections and because the overhead cost of application and documentation can be spread over a larger output. Studies show that unpaid administrative services supplied to government agencies can easily absorb 5 percent or more of the sales revenues of smaller enterprises. The present régime is trying to reduce this burden, by abolishing or simplifying legal and administrative procedures and requirements.

Despite the proliferation of small- and medium-sized firms, ownership of private capital is concentrated in West Germany, with 20 percent of all households owning more than 85 percent of all productive assets.[23] Efforts to promote "people's capitalism" by subsidizing small shareholders have had a small effect. In addition, West German industry is concentrated in terms of output and employment. In 1986, the three largest firms in an industry accounted, on average, for 39 percent of domestic industry-wide production. Enterprises with over 1,000 employees constituted about 1 percent of industrial firms, but accounted for over 40 percent of industrial employment.

Between 1966 and 1986, the number of manufacturing enterprises was cut in half, and the annual number of mergers soared from forty-three in 1966 to an average of 608 over 1980–85. About two-thirds of recent mergers have been horizontal (between firms producing substitute products), but most have also involved small- and medium-sized enterprises. Many were competition-increasing, on balance, by creating units better able to stand up to rivals. Labor unions have often supported mergers on grounds that large firms offer greater security of employment. However, labor and capital productivity data fail to reveal any efficiency advantage for the hundred largest industrial enterprises as a group vs. industry as a whole. This is not to deny economies of increasing firm size up to a point, but some of these are political. Subsidies to avoid bankruptcy are easier for large enterprises to obtain. A case in point is the near collapse of AEG Telefunken, the country's second largest electrical and electronics firm and fifteenth largest corporation, in 1982. Its bankruptcy would have pulled down hundreds of small suppliers with it and threatened over 130,000 jobs, at a time of record unemployment. Thus, the federal and land governments had no choice but to subsidize a partial rescue. Recent efforts to help declining industries have involved mergers designed to stave off bankruptcies—as well as subsidies and cartels, which restrict output (and use import barriers) to keep up prices.

There are also government restrictions which fragment the national market and protect high-cost producers. For example, to transport goods by rail to a location more than fifty kilometers from the place of production, an enterprise needs a license issued by the Transport Ministry. The number of licences has expanded over the past thirty years, but is still limited, and complementary regulations raise the cost of substitute transport by truck. The free-market price of a licence is far above the nominal cost to a firm whose application is approved. This keeps prices of many goods above competitive levels. In addition, there are a number of officially authorized cartels (237 as of end-1985) and many informal restrictive agreements between enterprises. However, the latter are illegal and punished by stiff fines when caught.

On balance, West German industry is oligopolistic rather than monopolistic, and reasonably competitive in most sectors. The government also has a large ownership stake. The state sector includes large segments of coal mining, petroleum, natural gas, transport, iron ore, aluminum, shipbuilding, and other industries. One employee in ten works for a publicly controlled enterprise. In early 1984, the federal government owned 171 firms which, in turn, held at least blocking minorities (25 percent ownership or greater) in 386 others, and the government sector as a whole had an ownership share in nearly 900 companies. Large firms and conglomerates (including some that are publicly owned) are often fierce rivals, and many are large exporters. West Germany belongs to the EEC, which increases the size of the market served by its industrial firms, as well as their import competition at home. Falling trade barriers within the Common Market are at least partly responsible for the explosion of mergers and takeovers since 1973, as firms have sought to strengthen their competitive positions. By the end of 1992, all barriers to the movement of goods and labor within the EEC are supposed to disappear. But the European Community also enforces its own cartels, especially in agriculture and steel, which suffer from overcapacity. In 1983, a West German steelmaker (Kloeckner), one of Europe's most modern, almost went bankrupt, owing to fines levied against it for exceeding EEC output quotas. (To have remained within them would have cost the company even more, owing to the resulting low level of capacity utilization.)

17-3. The Government's Policy Role

A. Overall Fiscal and Monetary Policy

Despite its considerable weight, the West German government has been unable to use fiscal policy systematically to achieve any macroeconomic goal. One reason is that taxing and spending authority are divided between the three main levels of government. The local and land levels have usually spent more when their revenues were relatively high—i.e., when business conditions were relatively good—as well as just before elections, and they carry out 75 percent of all public investment. Thus, fiscal policy has been of little use in dampening business-cycle fluctuations, and we recall that private investment is also sensitive to business conditions. Fortunately, the period, 1949–73, between the founding of the Federal Republic and the energy crisis, saw just one recession of consequence, in 1966–67. The government's apparent inability to end this downturn quickly strengthened the influence of those who wanted to "rationalize" economic policy by giving the state more contracyclical muscle.

This led to the 1967 Stability and Growth Law, designed to give federal authorities more leverage over the revenues and spending of lower government levels, along with power to raise or lower taxes and depreciation allowances more quickly, so as to offset variations in spending by the private sector. The tax reform of 1969 subsequently expanded the income tax shares of the federal government and of the localities, at the expense of the laender, and gave the localities a more stable tax base, although in practice they continue to rely on land subsidies. However, the federal government is still ineffective in combatting the business cycle. While it now has more potential leverage over lower government levels, it can only exercise this leverage (according to the Stability and Growth Law) with the approval of land governments, who are jealous of their autonomy. Moreover, the effectiveness of fiscal policy has been reduced by the shift from fixed to semiflexible exchange rates in 1973.[24] This happened just before the first energy crisis, which raised the need for effective measures against recessions. Under flexible exchange rates, it is monetary policy that must take the lead in combatting cyclical fluctuations in output and employment. However, the Deutsche Bundesbank has only a vague obligation to support federal government policy—and only as long as this does not interfere with the bank's constitutional task of defending the value of the deutsche mark. The Bundesbank need not obey any specific instructions from the government, with the single exception that the latter may delay the bank's execution of policy for up to two weeks. If this is not time enough for compromise, the central bank becomes free to do as it wishes.[25]

Central bank independence results, in part, from Germany's experience with two inflations, one open and one repressed, after the two world wars, which we shall describe in chapter 18. These wiped out large amounts of individual savings twice within twenty-five years, and created a traumatic fear among Germans of inflation and, to a lesser extent, of government budget deficits. They explain the constitutional requirement that public borrowing not exceed public investment— unless this is the only way to avert "economic disequilibrium" (i.e., the only way to reduce cyclical unemployment)—and its emphasis on defending the value of the currency, institutionalized in an independent central bank protected from political pressures. Since the first energy crisis in 1973–74, budget deficits have been the norm, but the money supply has remained under control, and West German inflation continues to be low. Over 1974–86, the average annual increase in the GNP deflator was just over 3.5 percent, lowest of any market economy in the world.

When restrictive policy at home has made it hard for German companies to expand domestic sales, they have had the initiative to develop or expand foreign markets for their products, often with active government assistance. This has cushioned the impact of restrictive measures on unemployment. Indeed, the government's policy stance has been basically restrictive—both to combat inflation and to force German companies to seek export markets—a strategy on which the Bundesbank and the federal government could agree until the energy crisis. When credit has been tight, it has been relatively easy to borrow for purposes linked to export expansion. Moreover, while it has escaped most of the notoriety inflicted on Japan, the Federal Republic has also made some dubious use of product standards and other nontariff barriers to restrict imports.

Following the first energy crisis, fiscal policy under the Social Democrats became more expansionary, while monetary policy remained tight. With flexible exchange rates, this combination pushed up interest rates and the value of the deutsche mark (DM) in terms of other currencies, just when energy prices were exploding. The rising value of the DM against the U.S. dollar over 1972–80 mitigated the increase of energy costs—although it made German exports more expensive—but energy imports still jumped from 8 percent of total exports in 1972 to 23 percent in 1981. The appreciation of the DM also boosted German investment abroad. From next to nothing in 1960, cumulative foreign direct investment by German firms shot up to 120 billion DM by mid-1986, or 36 billion DM more than foreign direct investment in Germany.

The combination of energy crisis, wage-cost explosion, and rise in the deutsche mark's value finally pushed the current account of West Germany's balance of payments into deficit over 1979–81, following a long period of surplus. After 1980, fiscal and monetary policies were more in harmony, and the DM began to fall against the U.S. dollar, although it continued to rise against the currencies of most of the Federal Republic's trading partners. Yet, the balance of payments recovered dramatically, achieving surpluses after 1981 and record surpluses in 1985 and 1986, by which time the price of oil was down more than 50 percent from its 1981 peak. In 1986, West Germany passed the United States (with four times its population) and increased its lead over Japan (with about twice its population) to become the world's leading nation in total value of exports. "The particular strength of German business lay in the quality of its products, the after-sales service, prompt deliveries, the willingness to comply with customers' individual requests, and an increasing range of goods on offer," wrote the Deutsche Bundesbank in its 1985 *Annual Report* (p. 24). But the record performance in trade also coincided with record (and growing) unemployment.

B. The Central Bank's Monetary Policy Role

For regulatory purposes, the Bundesbank classifies every institution that carries out any financial function as a bank. Except for insurance companies and social insurance funds, virtually no financial institution escapes being so classified. As of

1986, about 4,700 different lenders were subject, either directly or via their central clearinghouses, to Bundesbank regulation. However, interest rates were decontrolled in 1967, and because of past experience with inflation, Germans do not suffer from money illusion. This has limited central bank influence over real interest rates (or nominal rates adjusted for inflation).[26] For example, if the Bundesbank increases the growth of money and credit, relative to the growth of real output, expected inflation will usually rise, and lenders will demand higher interest in consequence. Real interest rates (equal to nominal rates minus expected inflation) will stay about the same.

Thus, monetary policy seeks mainly to influence the volume of money and credit, rather than interest rates, and operates by varying bank liquidity. Banks may only maintain or expand their volume of lending if they are able to do so and continue to meet official liquidity requirements. Moreover, their willingness and ability to lend is an important determinant of investment and employment. Chief instruments of the central bank's monetary policy have been minimum reserve requirements, rediscount quotas, and "open market" operations, or buying and selling of short-term government bonds. The latter have become the most popular in recent years, as the market for government securities has become broader and deeper, but they still often consist of trading between the Bundesbank and financial institutions and operate by varying bank liquidity. Manipulation of minimum reserve ratios, the main tool of monetary policy until the 1980s, and of rediscount quotas (effective ceilings on borrowing by financial institutions from the central bank) also affect the liquidity of lenders.

For example, by lowering a bank's rediscount quota, the Bundesbank can force it to borrow less at the relatively low discount or bank rate. To borrow more, it would have to pay a higher rate, called the "lombard" rate, if it borrows from the central bank, or go to the short-term money market where rates are usually determined by (and are close to) the lombard rate. The money market is mainly an interbank market. Here smaller, regional banks, which deal mostly with households and smaller firms, lend (as a rule) to larger banks with close ties to large companies. Especially when money is tight, large banks are likely to be short of funds. By lowering all rediscount quotas (or raising required reserve ratios), the Bundesbank can reduce financial institutions' access to low-cost liquidity, which causes them to contract their loans, as well as to lower the average maturity of new lending. The raising of rediscount quotas has the opposite effect on the cost and availability of credit.

Each financial institution must keep its reserves in the form of noninterest-bearing accounts at the Bundesbank. Until the 1980s, the uniqueness of German monetary policy lay partly in the frequency with which reserve ratios and the rediscount rate were changed—about twice a year, on average, for each—as well as in the frequent borrowing by banks from the central bank. The latter continues, but reserve ratios were changed only twice in the five years after October 1, 1982 and will, in future, change far less often than in the past. Instead, the Bundesbank now relies mainly on open market operations, in common with other Western central banks. This is a more flexible tool, which permits better fine-tuning of policy (a larger number of smaller and better timed changes) to achieve a closer control over bank liquidity at any point in time plus a steadier growth of the money supply over time. Either an increase in reserve ratios or a sale of government securities could offset (sterilize) a potentially inflationary inflow of funds due to a balance-of-payments surplus. But constantly changing reserve ratios, designed to adjust to a continuously variable rate of inflow, would be costly and disruptive to the point of causing chaos, whereas a constantly changing open market position places no such stress on the system.

As noted, the Bundesbank seeks to control the volume of money and credit, in line with its constitutional mandate to promote price stability. Under quasi-flexible exchange rates, the central bank also has primary responsibility for keeping business cycles under control and, thus, for insulating the domestic economy as far as possible from shocks capable of causing changes in (and especially deterioration of) underlying business conditions. In particular, its own monetary policy should not produce erratic variations in the availability of money and credit. Thus, it has tried to orient policy around targeted annual increases in the money supply, using first a narrow measure of money—the monetary base, M_0, or currency in circulation plus required reserves on domestic deposits, adjusted for changes in reserve ratios—and since 1988, the broader money supply measure, M_3. Each December, the Bundesbank announces next year's target growth rate as a range—for example, 3–6 percent in 1988. One prominent view holds that the central bank should achieve a steady growth rate of M_3 or even of broader measures of money, as its major means of reducing cyclical fluctuations in output and employment. This follows the prescription of the monetarists, although such an approach is also rooted in German neoliberal philosophy, which is the foundation of the social market economy.

Monetarists argue for a steady growth of the money supply because they believe that, over the short run, the public's demand for money is approximately constant in relation to income. If so, a rise in the stock of money for any given level of GNP, will cause some households and firms to wind up holding more money than they want to. Thus, they will spend it, raising their demand for goods and services in the process. Sooner or later, this will lead to some combination of output and price increases. The reverse happens when the supply of money is reduced. By maintaining a constant growth rate of money, therefore, to which expectations of future prices and wages become oriented, a government would eventually be able to stabilize the growth of demand and minimize business-cycle fluctuations, given the right external environment (basically, flexible exchange rates and low trade barriers). Despite its power, however, the Bundesbank has yet to realize a steady growth rate, either of broad or of narrow money-supply measures. Indeed, it departs from the monetarist view in wanting room to vary the rate of money supply expansion when it deems this necessary to counteract unexpected short-term changes in economic activity, prices, or exchange rates.

C. Recent Unemployment

By comparison with Sweden, West Germany has experienced lower inflation but higher unemployment since the 1973–74 energy crisis. This reflects, in part, Sweden's overriding commitment to full employment plus West Germany's built-in commitment to low inflation. Nevertheless, we should not blame the Deutsche Bundesbank for most of the high unemployment of recent years, which has become increasingly a long-term, structural problem, rather than a macroeconomic, cyclical problem. Over 1973–85, the total number of jobs in West Germany fell by 1.8 million. This is partly due to real wage and benefit costs which are too high to clear many labor markets and which do not fall in response to excess labor supply. In Germany as in several other Western countries, real wages tend to remain rigid in the face of unforeseen shifts in labor demand, which therefore mainly affect employment. This behavior is consistent with the insider-outsider dichotomy discussed at the end of chapter 3. No one foresaw the magnitude of the economic miracle, which reduced the rate of unemployment from 10.4 percent in 1950 to less than 1 percent in 1962, after construction of the Berlin Wall cut the flow of workers to the West. It only rose permanently above the circa 1 percent range again after the first energy crisis in 1973–74. However, the second energy crisis (1979–80) soon put it into the 7–8 percent range, where it remained, as of 1988. Neither crisis (each of which was plausibly unforeseen) halted the growth of real wages.[27]

The structure of wages and salaries between occupations has also tended to be rigid. Firms have become less willing to hire workers because of the rising cost of laying them off, and discharged workers are often immobile between occupations and regions—partly because of generous social insurance and high marginal tax rates, as well as subsidies—so that some jobs go begging, even with over two million unemployed. Subsidies to declining sectors (including coal, iron and steel, shipbuilding, chemicals, and textiles) have maintained their ability to keep operating and, often, to pay relatively high wages, thereby suppressing the movement of resources to sectors with growth potential. Few employees laid off in declining sectors have found jobs in advancing industries, even though geographical mobility is often not required. Some growth industries, including much of the service sector, must pay wages well below those in older, smokestack industries, if firms are to remain competitive. As a result, discharged workers often collect unemployment benefits—paid at 63–68 percent of last after-tax wages for six to thirty-two months (depending on age and duration of previous employment) and then at 56–58 percent of last earnings—after which they may become eligible for early retirement (as early as age fifty-eight). Pensions are "dynamic"—i.e., indexed to the growth of average wages, as part of womb-to-tomb social insurance protection—and also depend on an individual's past earnings.

The Federal Republic has a cornucopia of product- and region-specific subsidies, some which are helping to promote growth in promising new industries. In 1987, for example, products developed within the past five years accounted for about 40 percent of sales turnover in the depressed Ruhr district. Yet West Germany has been losing international competitiveness in high-technology products. As in other Western countries, industries of the past, with political clout, absorb funds that could be spent to achieve scale and experience economies in industries of the future. Industries in which Germany now enjoys a comparative advantage (e.g., machine tools) are sometimes undercapitalized, and there has been a shortage of venture capital, especially for companies trying to get started. The combination of high unemployment, a decreasing number of jobs, and too much labor and capital tied up in declining or inefficient sectors (or, more generally, inelastic supply responses to structural shifts in demand) is what a good industrial policy should avoid. Such a policy is harder to negotiate and to implement, however, in a federal system where the land governments administer over half of all subsidies.

Lobbying pressures to protect declining sectors and their laid-off workers tend to be greater, the more attractive are earnings there relative to earnings-employment opportunities elsewhere. Such pressures are therefore bound to be strong when high-wage industries are declining. But it is also true that growth sectors were not identified early enough, nor were sufficient measures taken to move labor and capital into them. Job opportunities have therefore been fewer and less attractive than they might have been, and many unfilled vacancies have called for skills which are in short supply. Recent policy responses to unemployment recall Swedish labor market measures (described above in section 16-6). They include greater funding to promote geographical and occupational mobility, as well as vocational education, which has been expanding. Legal changes have made it easier to hire part-time and temporary labor and to institute work sharing. Wage subsidies are also available to employ long-term jobless, mainly in the public sector. Subsidies to some crisis industries, notably steel and shipbuilding, have been drastically cut, and the steel industry has undergone restructuring designed to make it competitive without further aid. West Germany retained the combination of relatively high unemployment, high-capacity utilization, and sluggish business investment through 1987, although a new surge of investment and optimism had occurred over 1988–89.

D. Promotion of Homebuilding

On a more positive note, West Germany has public works that are second to none. It has the best road and one of the best rail networks in Europe, and it is a leader in pollution control, with the EEC's best toxic waste treatment and disposal systems. Moreover, governments at all levels have systematically pumped subsidies into housing. Almost three new homes have been built for every four households since 1949—over 18 million dwellings in all—to transform a situation in which one family in four was without a regular home into one with more dwellings than households in the country as a whole. Public assistance has included outright grants, low-cost loans, accelerated depreciation on homes, savings bonuses for future home-owners, and rent subsidies for tenants. The state has subsidized the construction of about 30 percent of all homes built since 1949. From the standpoint of subsidies given, housing has enjoyed the highest priority of any single industry, but housing assistance has also been offset by price supports for food and coal. (A "coal penny" tax on gas and electricity subsidizes the price of coal to power stations, as well as construction of coal-fired stations. On balance, it raises the cost of home heating and electricity.)

Because of the federal nature of West Germany's government, control over social insurance, public investment, and housing is decentralized down to regional and local levels. This allows local preferences and needs to assert themselves more decisively. In state-sponsored vocational education, for example, the land governments and business enterprises have much control over course content. Many of the details of publicly assisted homebuilding—the kinds of homes to be built, layout, design, and so forth—are determined by local authorities, instead of by the central government. Local and land agencies, notably the *Heimstätten* or Home Centers, have been deeply involved in planning, research, and development related to housing.

Government at all levels also engages in community planning, emphasizing the relations between homebuilding, transportation, employment, and leisure activities. According to one observer, "The Federal Republic's most distinctive achievement is probably in the field of housing and town and country planning. The quantity of building is a great accomplishment, but an even greater one is its quality."[28] In recent years, two of every three homes built have been one- or two-family houses. The combination of public and private initiative has also resulted in a greater mixing of social classes than elsewhere in Europe.

Unfortunately, housing has also had its darker side, especially since the mid-1970s. Owing to population density and affluence—as well as to farm price supports, which reduce the supply of nonagricultural land—real-estate values are high, and so are building costs. Housing is expensive on the open market, with the price of a new home running at least six times the annual average income, gross of taxes, in most of the country. One consequence is a high proportion of renters—some 55–60 percent of all households—and payment of housing allowances to more than 2 million low-income families, as of 1985. As a rule, housing costs have been more reasonable for renters than owner-occupiers, but the rental market is also split between a rent-controlled sector and one where rents are set by supply and demand and therefore higher. Most dwellings built with public assistance are rent-controlled and vice versa. In return for his building subsidy, the landlord must charge no more than a "costs-rent." But there is a shortage of rent-controlled housing, and some households can't afford homes whose prices are set by the open market, even with the system of housing allowances.

Since 1974, the building subsidy has been too small to reimburse landlords the difference between the costs rent and the income obtainable from other uses of the buildings and grounds. Completion of publicly assisted rental units therefore fell, from 100,000 per year to 30,000 over 1974–77, and remained low, at least through

1985. This was a time of high unemployment when a baby boom generation was coming of age. If rent-controlled apartments could be found at all in many cities, the landlord often charged several thousand DM for the keys, in addition to the ceiling rent. Some owners have tried to demolish rent-controlled buildings or to convert them to other uses, and an epidemic of squatting began in 1979, often in buildings that were vacant and scheduled for demolition or conversion. The alternative of lifting rent ceilings and expanding subsidies to low-income households encounters political barriers, including pressures to reduce government deficits.

17-4. Industrial Democracy and Labor Relations

A. Representation on the Shop Floor

We have noted that West Germany is the home of a system of partial industrial democracy called codetermination (*mitbestimmung*), also part of its system of labor relations. The basic laws on codetermination date from 1951 and 1952, but limited workers' participation in management has deep historical roots in Germany, dating from the Revolution of 1848. Although they had little power in practice, the works councils of the Weimar era (1919–33) became the basis for the system that emerged after World War II. Following Hitler's defeat, these councils sprang up again at many work places. The Allies, intent on limiting the power of the managerial élite that had supported Hitler, sanctioned the councils and extended them to additional firms. The councils became a permanent feature with passage of the Shop Organization Law in 1952, amended in 1972 to extend their role and to increase the power of unions over their selection and operation. There are now over 150,000 works councils in West Germany.

The Shop Organization Law was one of several passed over 1951–56 that established the basic framework prevailing until 1976. Workers received representation at three levels—on the shop floor through the works council, at the company level through representation on its boards of directors and economic committee, and at the government level through representation in several bodies, notably the eighty-one Chambers of Industry and Commerce and the Federal Institute of Labor.[29] The Institute is like the Bundesbank, in that the Minister of Labor may not give it detailed instructions. Subject to his overall direction, its main decisions are taken by various self-management bodies in which employers, workers, and public authorities are equally represented. Consequently, when the Institute negotiates with a firm over dismissals, retraining, demotion, or any other redeployment of labor, worker representatives can enter the discussions and influence the outcome at both ends—through the works council and through the local or regional labor office of the Institute.

Until 1976, there were two kinds of codetermination—a more extensive version applying to the coal, iron, and steel industries and a less extensive version applying to most other private firms employing over five hundred workers. However, they differ only where employee representation on company boards of directors is concerned. On the factory floor, where codetermination is most effective, firms in all industries receive similar treatment. Thus, every business employing five persons or more must have a works council consisting of from one to thirty-five members, depending on firm size. The council is elected by all employees—and only by employees—in secret ballot for three-year terms. The employer cannot fire works council members while they are in office or for one year afterward. When a company operates more than one production facility, it must have a central works council composed of two members from each plant council. As far as possible, council membership composition must mirror the composition of the work force electing it, in terms of males and females and manual vs. nonmanual workers. Young workers have a special right to be represented. Once every three weeks, the works council must report on its activities to a general meeting of all employees, which the employer or his representative is invited to attend. The meeting may submit resolutions to the council and make comments on its work. Works councils are especially useful for airing small grievances and removing minor irritants before they become major.

Companies with a hundred or more employees must also choose an Economic Committee of four to eight members, half representing the workers (including at least one from the works council) and half representing management. The employer must regularly inform this committee about all aspects of the firm's economic situation and keep it abreast of future plans regarding investment, finance, marketing, production, any reorganization of the enterprise, technological progress, and other changes, taking special care to explain how these will affect the workers. In smaller firms, the employer has a similar obligation to keep his employees up to date. If the works council is not satisfied with the work of the economic committee, it can transfer that committee's tasks to one of its own committees. One goal of the economic committee is to give the personnel a better insight into problems of running the company—as well as to allow the works council an opportunity to discuss issues and to prepare recommendations in advance—but a no less important aim is to feed worker sentiment and reaction back to the employer. (The same could be said for the entire codetermination apparatus.) Management is only obliged to consult with the economic committee, which has no formal right to codetermine any management decisions. Yet, firms have subdivided into smaller legal units in order to avoid formation of an economic committee, as well as to weaken their works councils.

Let us distinguish decisions bearing mainly on personnel relations, wages and benefits, working conditions, hiring and firing, and promotion and demotion from those dealing with production, pricing, investment, finance, marketing, and research and development. The works council's rights to affect enterprise policy begin and end with the first set of issues. If the second set does not lead to dismissals, demotions, or worsened working conditions, the council's rights are to be consulted and to express an opinion, and this only in firms with at least 100 employees. In welfare and personnel matters, however, the employer cannot operate efficiently without council cooperation. The two jointly manage questions of retraining and redeployment of labor, and when jobs become available, the council can insist that applicants first be sought from within the enterprise. As well, it "enjoys parity in deciding . . . hours and allocation of work, work breaks, holidays, internal welfare arrangements, work rules [including such matters as the speed of an assembly line], individual workers' conduct, piece work and bonus rates, and methods of payment."[30]

The council cannot prevent dismissals. However, the employer must consult it before laying a worker off and must give his reasons. The council can object on a number of grounds, including hardship for the individual. If it objects and if the employee files suit with the local labor court, dismissal cannot occur unless and until the court has ruled in favor of the employer (although it does so in over 99 percent of such cases). When the firm plans to lay off a number of employees, the works council has the right to be notified at least a month in advance and to insist that the firm draw up a "social welfare plan" to ease the adjustment burden—e.g., through severance pay and coverage of moving expenses. Thus, the councils have often been able to delay firings, demotions, and wage reductions. Finally, the Labor Relations Act gives works councils the right to negotiate humanization of the workplace.

It is because of their ability to protect jobs, wages, and status that the councils are highly valued by German workers. In contrast to other Western nations, the works council, rather than social legislation, is the main protector of employee interests, and there is much to be said for the flexibility and decentralization that this allows. Where personnel and welfare matters are concerned, a works council can ask for mediation if it is not satisfied. If disagreement persists and both sides are willing, a board of arbitration, consisting of equal numbers of labor and management representatives, decides the issue. Ultimately, a dispute may go to the system of labor courts.

Originally, the Christian Democratic party intended works councils to be independent of the unions and even a rival way of representing labor, based on the workplace, rather than the industry. The question of whether codetermination should be built around the workplace or the union remains a point of contention between the right and left of West Germany's political spectrum. However, the independence of works councils has, in practice, been limited. Although some rivalry has developed between the two, the unions have two kinds of leverage over council activities. First, more than 80 percent of council members are "trusted men" (*vertrauensmänner*) of the unions, even though less than 40 percent of private sector employees belong to a union. Partly as a consequence of labor court decisions, German unions are centralized, with the major decisions being taken at national and regional levels, and the same is even more true of German employers' associations.

Second, works councils have no formal authority to negotiate wages and working conditions, although, in practice, they have played a growing role here, and they are responsible for interpreting agreements applying to their enterprises. Formal collective bargaining takes place between labor unions and employers' associations. West Germany has seventeen major unions bound together in the Federation of German Trade Unions (DGB), in addition to which there is a much smaller Christian Trade Union Federation and two federations for public employees. By and large, each union covers one or more industries, within which it represents white- as well as blue-collar employees (although the workers of a given firm may be represented by more than one union). The forty-three employers' associations are similarly organized, with the Federation of German Employers (BDA) as their peak alliance. About 90 percent of industrial employees work for enterprises belonging to member associations of BDA.

Each spring, collective bargaining takes place between unions and employers' associations, first at the national and then at the regional (land) or local level. Because the autonomy of unions and employers' associations is well established and accepted, the main bargaining is industry-by-industry and not centralized for the whole economy (as in Sweden). Nevertheless, there is general agreement that wage increases should be consistent with satisfactory export performance. Since I. G. Metall, the world's largest union, which organizes the metal workers, is the main union for workers in export industries, it usually negotiates the trend-setting agreement. As a rule, contracts are extended to nonunion workers, so that unions bargain on behalf of 90 percent of all white- and blue-collar employees. As long as an agreement is in force or a dispute is being mediated, a peace obligation binds each side not to start an industrial action over an issue covered by the agreement or mediation. West Germany loses fewer days per thousand employees to labor disputes than virtually any other Western country except Austria. (In recent years, it may also have a better record than Yugoslavia, the only socialist country where strikes are legal and tolerated.) Most strikes are short-term and take place in connection with annual contract negotiations. As a partial offset, West Germany loses more working days to absenteeism, holidays, and time off for personal reasons than does Japan, the United States, or Canada. (During the early 1980s, a Volkswagon employee not involved in work stoppages put in forty to forty-five more days per year in the U.S. than in the Federal Republic.)

Several unions are so powerful that when they call a national strike, the consequences are bound to be dire for the whole economy. Moreover, a local strike will often escalate into a national conflict, because employers are likely to respond by locking out other employees in the same union. The national employers' associations control compulsory strike and lockout funds, from which they may compensate member firms for all expenses resulting from industrial conflicts, including damage claims by customers or suppliers, as well as labor and overhead costs. The associations can also prohibit other members from taking customers away from a firm involved in an industrial action or from hiring its employees or transferring business away from it. National unions can similarly protect their locals. Moreover, the Employment Promotion Law allows employees who are out of work, as an indirect consequence of a strike, to draw unemployment benefits. Unions have taken advantage of this right—by calling strikes only in factories supplying key components—to use unemployment compensation as a strike fund, in effect, although their ability to do so in future is reduced by a 1986 amendment to the Employment Promotion Law.

Still, the likely escalation of local conflicts will probably cause both labor and management to continue to seek to avoid strikes, except as a last resort. Legally, a strike must precede a lockout, and a strike may not be called unless 75 percent of a company's work force have voted to go out—a requirement that explains the high proportion of wildcat strikes, especially when labor relations are tense. The six-week strike in the steel industry at the end of 1978, called by I. G. Metall, was the first official walk-out in industries organized by the metalworkers' union in over fifty years, although the same union then called a seven-week strike in 1984, which became the longest and costliest labor dispute in West German history.[31] In theory, government stays out of labor negotiations, but it has generally expressed its views about desirable wage and benefit increases, and the Council of Experts also gives its opinion. The resulting pressure, particularly on the metalworkers' agreement, acts as a kind of incomes policy.

Formally, works councils enter the picture as joint interpreters, along with management, of the details of agreements already reached. In the process, there is often room for negotiation over wages and working conditions, especially since the collective agreements specify only minimum rates of pay for each industry and region. Despite union control over works council selection, rivalry has developed between the two. Since the early 1970s, the focus of union demands has shifted toward fewer working hours and protection of full-time workers against replacement by capital or by illegal and part-time labor. This has helped to increase the role of works councils, which sometimes go further in making concessions to management—e.g., over rationalization of production—and often win significant concessions. Employers prefer to give piecemeal, revocable concessions to their works councils instead of having these written into a contract. For example, "wage rates in the auto companies appear to run about 20 percent above the contract rate." But unions have also been able to intrude on works councils' prerogatives. "The elaborate nature of the unions' general framework contracts, with their minute details concerning work procedure, job content, and most other aspects of factory life, clearly aims to regain some of the unions' lost shopfloor presence by setting macro-level parameters for the works councils' micro-level existence."[32]

B. Representation in Management

The works councils, in conjunction with the labor unions, also select employee representatives for company supervisory boards of directors. The supervisory board (*Aufsichtsrat*) of a West German corporation sets the firm's broad policy, while the executive board of directors (*Vorstand*) runs the company on a day-to-day basis, the latter being elected by the former. Until 1976, in corporations (and consumer cooperatives) outside the coal, iron, and steel industries, the stockholders (members) elected two-thirds of the supervisory board, while the company's employees elected the remaining one-third.[33] At least two of the latter had to be employees themselves, including one blue-collar and one white-collar worker, but the rest were (and are) normally union officials rather than employees. The device does give employees a voice on the corporate board, and it has sometimes proved a useful feedback mechanism. But complaints have also been aired that labor representatives have grown aloof from their constituents, and their effectiveness within the framework of partial codetermination has been limited. With just a third of the Aufsichtsrat seats, employee representatives have had to accept partial responsibility for policies that they could not effectively oppose.

By contrast, in iron, coal, and steel firms with 1,000 employees or more, the supervisory board usually consists of five representatives of labor, five stockholder representatives, and a neutral eleventh member. The latter is often a civil servant or academic expert in industrial relations, who must receive at least three votes from each side. In larger companies, the Aufsichtsrat may be composed of fifteen or twenty-one members, but labor and shareholder representatives are always of equal numbers, and the neutral member must receive a majority of each side's votes. In this sense, labor has parity, but the number of firms to which full codetermination applies has fallen from one hundred fifteen in 1951 to under thirty, because of mergers, reorganizations, and the decline of the coal and steel industries. A 1956 law allows companies to opt out of full codetermination when their iron, coal, and steel business falls below 50 percent of total sales, and a number of firms have taken advantage of this opportunity. Full codetermination now applies to less than 2 percent of the industrial labor force.

Of the five labor representatives on the supervisory boards of most enterprises under full codetermination, one white-collar and one blue-collar worker are each elected by the works council. Two are union officials, and one must have been neither an employee of the firm nor connected with the relevant union for a year prior to joining the board. Usually, he will be a DGB official. Thus, if labor representatives caucus and vote as a bloc, as is usual, the union rather than the employee view will tend to prevail, when the two are in conflict. By the same token, one stockholder representative must have had no connection with the company for at least a year before joining the board. Stockholder representatives tend to be lawyers, economists, prominent businessmen, and finance specialists. Labor representatives vary more widely as to background, but the unions have set up courses and training sessions to prepare them for their roles.

By law, the Vorstand of each company in the iron, coal, and steel industries consists of three members—a technical, a commercial, and a labor director. The former two represent the owners, while the labor director—usually a former trade unionist—is chosen by the labor representatives on the Supervisory Board. All three directors are jointly responsible for running the firm on a day-to-day basis, but personnel and social affairs are the special province of the labor director. An association of labor directors has been formed to discuss common problems.

Of all employee representatives, the labor director usually finds himself most often torn between his obligations to the workers and to the enterprise—on top of which he must deal with pressure from the union and the DGB. In this respect, he is in a position not unlike that of the director of a Yugoslav firm, who must constantly reconcile the competing claims of the state and his employees. In each case, the individuals involved have sometimes gone through extreme psychological adjustment problems—including identity crises and even alcoholism, refusal to take decisions, and emotional breakdowns. In recessions, the labor director tries to postpone layoffs, hoping to wait out the downturn. Frequently, he has some success.

As on the shop floor, worker representatives on boards of directors have had the most influence over personnel and social decisions, while stockholder representatives retain control over production, pricing, investment, and other economic decisions. This is a natural division of labor, but it has led to charges that labor is really a "junior partner" rather than an equal partner in management, even in the iron, coal, and steel industries.

The two different forms of codetermination established by the 1951 and 1952 laws represent two different traditions in German social and economic thought. Full codetermination has its roots in left-wing syndicalist and social democratic views, which stress that labor should play (at least) an equal role with capital in managing the enterprise and, ultimately, in managing the economy. Partial codetermination has its roots in corporatist Christian views that stress workplace cooperation, consultation, and harmony—buttressed by job security and employee control over conditions of work—but which leave professional management in firm control of the basic direction of the enterprise. The syndicalist view also stresses the union's role as labor's representative, while the Christian version—which is both consistent with social market philosophy and a natural part of the CDU/CSU platform—would effectively substitute the works council for the union.

The 1976 law is a compromise between these two views, which the Free Democrats obliged the Social Democrats to accept, as a condition for continuing their coalition government. This law applies to all firms with over 2,000 employees—some 650 companies and 4.5 million workers, who constitute a fourth of all private-sector employees outside the coal, iron, and steel industries. Enterprises with 500 to 2,000 employees still follow the 1952 law, and many firms have legally subdivided themselves in recent years, to avoid crossing the 2,000-employee threshold. We can understand the 1976 changes by looking at the supervisory board of the giant Bayer Chemical Works. Previously, this board had fifteen members, including five labor representatives. Because of the 1976 law, it has expanded to twenty, of whom ten represent the owners and ten the employees.[34] Instead of a neutral twenty-first member, one stockholder representative acts as chairman and casts two votes in case of a tie. Moreover, one of the employee seats must go to a senior executive, who is more likely to identify with the shareholders than with labor. Nor have the nine "true" labor representatives—three union officials and six employees—yet been able to select the company's labor director. This compromise has been acceptable neither to labor nor to management. The employers' confederation (BDA) challenged its constitutionality, since the West German constitution guarantees the right to own property. Although labor's voice on the supervisory board has been strengthened, owners' solidarity will still carry the day. Often, the shareholder representatives caucus before the board meets and then vote as a bloc at the actual board meeting. The owners' caucus thus becomes the real decision-making forum. The exceptions to this rule tend to be companies, such as Volkswagen, where Social Democratic land governments control blocs of shares. The union view is that real codetermination outside the coal, iron, and steel industries has yet to be won. This portends conflict, because in ruling the 1976 law constitutional, the Constitutional Court also implied that it would strike down a law extending the full codetermination model to all of industry.

C. Codetermination and Efficiency

German unions have long considered themselves the ultimate inheritors of the material means of production, within a society characterized by union-based industrial democracy at each work place. Meanwhile, they rationalize cooperation with management, in a "capitalist" environment, on grounds of protecting their "inheritance"—an attitude codified in the 1963 Düsseldorf Program. The means of production must be kept in good condition and expanded in a way that serves the long run interests of the labor movement. In part, West German prosperity therefore rests on cooperation between social partners (labor and capital) whose long-range goals and expectations are incompatible—a good arrangement in some respects, as long as the incompatible expectations can be sustained. The nature of the future society envisioned by union leaders is vague, but it would at least feature full codetermination at all enterprises of consequence plus participation by the unions as dominant partners in economic councils at the federal and land levels, which would plan and implement the course of economic development. These councils would also include representatives of other socioeconomic groups—traditional management, small business, farmers, etc. By controlling the allocation of investment, they would reduce the allocative role of the market. At present, political (and member) support for this vision is weak, and the next ten to twenty years may reveal to what extent it can be postponed or compromised without raising the militancy or lowering the time horizons of union leaders.

Such considerations aside, efficiency arguments against widespread full codetermination are similar to those raised against the Meidner Plan in Sweden (outlined above in section 15-8). In particular, if labor representatives represent the unions, the result would be to turn one industry after another into a monopoly.[35] The problems that this would create might then lead to further centralization, resulting in a command economy and eventual loss of political democracy. Efficiency in a market economy requires competition, which obliges codetermination to be based on the employees of each enterprise, rather than on industry-wide unions. At present, about 95 percent of employee representatives on supervisory boards are union members, and some 1,700 board seats are controlled by union officials, the vast majority of whom are affiliated with DGB.

Proponents of full codetermination argue that industrial democracy can lead to greater job enrichment, removal of alienation, and a satisfaction derived by workers from being their own bosses. This should make employees more productive, and they would fairly take home higher earnings in consequence. At present, the unions argue, "the worker has little idea of the real point of his employment; he is dominated and surrounded and often replaced by machinery. [He is] a mere number to employers, [and] he rarely knows the suppliers of the company he works for or the purchasers of his output. The worker in large modern factories has no scope for personal initiative, nor has he much influence on the type of work he does. . . ."[36] But if this is so, removal of alienation requires some participation in management by employees at each place of work. Local power sharing (including selection and review of professional managers and participation in solving local work-related problems) is necessary to develop team spirit and intrinsic motivation, based on control by workers of their conditions of work and their identification with the firm and its products. With their version of full codetermination, unions may be in a position to exercise more monopoly power than any German cartel has ever had, but union-appointed decision makers may still be remote from the workers.

Notes

1. G. Denton, M. Forsyth, M. MacLennan, *Economic Planning and Policies in Britain, France, and Germany* (London: Allen & Unwin, 1968), p. 47. See, as well, Walter Eucken, *Grundsätze der Wirtschaftspolitik* (Munich: Rowohlt, 1959); and *The Foundations of Economics* [translated by T. W. Hutchinson] (Edinburgh: Hodge, 1950). The phrase, "social market economy," was first coined in 1946 by Alfred Müller-Armack. See his *Wirtschafts-Ordnung und Wirtschaftspolitik* (Freiburg: Verlag Rombeck, 1966).

2. According to the 1972 Quadrapartite Agreement between the U.S., the USSR, the United Kingdom, and France, West Germany retains the right to represent West Berlin in foreign countries. Representatives of West Berlin also sit in the West German Parliament as nonvoting members. Several West German government bodies, such as the Supreme Administrative Court, have their permanent seats in West Berlin, and the mayor of West Berlin takes a turn, along with the presidents of the ten provinces or laender, as president of the Bundesrat, the upper house of the German Parliament.

3. OECD, *Economic Survey of Germany*, 1985–86, p. 24, and 1987–88, pp. 62–65; as well as H. Klodt, "Industrial Policy and Repressed Structural Change in West Germany," Kiel Institute of World Economics, Working Paper No. 322, Kiel, West Germany, March, 1988. Concessions and cash aid from federal, provincial, and local governments were close to 20 percent of their combined revenues in 1986. In 1980, 31 percent of this assistance went to industry and trade; 28.5 percent went to housing; 13 percent went to promote household saving; 11 percent was channelled to agriculture; about 7 percent went to transport; and 10 percent went into other programs. If we add Germany's contribution to the EEC to support farm prices, agriculture's share jumps to 22 percent, part of which went to farmers in other

EEC countries. More recently, industry's share has fallen.

4. This often requires the Community to buy and store produce—hence the "mountains" of cheese, butter, beef, and powdered milk, and the "lakes" of wine. The EEC also exports significant amounts of farm produce, generally at highly subsidized prices. Farm goods account for nearly 6 percent of total West German exports.

5. G. M. Carter and J. H. Herz, *Major Foreign Powers*, 6th ed. (New York: Harcourt Brace Jovanovitch, 1972), p. 474.

6. The Godesberg Platform also asserted that "free consumer choice and free choice of workplace are important foundations, free competition and free entrepreneurial initiative are important elements of social-democratic policy. . . . Totalitarian economic regimentation destroys freedom. . . ." It called, as well, for vigorous promotion of competition, when necessary.

7. Gustav Stolper, Karl Häuser, Knut Borchardt, *The German Economy: 1870 to the Present* (New York: Harcourt, Brace, and World, 1967), p. 93.

8. Alfred Marshall, *Industry and Trade* (London: Macmillan, 1979), quotes on pp. 347, 358, and 342, respectively. On p. 347, Marshall also notes that "it seems . . . that [in England] prompt and strong assistance is not always to be had for such inventions and other ideas, as are in the minds of men whose financial position is not already strong: and who do not know their way about the city of London."

9. These decisions must be approved by 75 percent of the voting shares in any company incorporated as an Aktiengesellschaft, usually abbreviated AG, as in Volkswagenwerk, AG. This is roughly comparable to (although more restrictive than) the terms, "incorporated" (inc.) in the U.S. and "limited" (ltd.) in the British Commonwealth.

10. All German companies with over five hundred employees have two boards of directors—a supervisory board (*Aufsichtsrat*) elected by the shareholders and an executive board (*Vorstand*) appointed by the supervisory board. No one may serve on both boards. The Vorstand runs the day-to-day affairs of the company, for which it is responsible to the shareholders and to the Aufsichtsrat. When legal documents refer to the company or to its management, they mean the *Vorstand*. A company's supervisory board will at least approve major investment decisions, and it usually plays an advisory role vis-à-vis the Vorstand. In practice, the relative power of the two boards in determining the long-run evolution of the firm varies from company to company. A rule of thumb is that the Vorstand's power is likely to be greatest when the enterprise has no dominant shareholder, such as a bank, the government, a wealthy family, a labor union, or a foreign concern.

11. Charles Wilson, "Economic Conditions," in F. H. Hinsley, ed., *Material Progress and World-wide Problems, 1870–1898*, Vol. 11 of *The New Cambridge Modern History* (Cambridge: Cambridge University Press, 1962), p. 74.

12. J. H. Clapham, *Economic Development of France and Germany, 1815–1914* (Cambridge: Cambridge University Press, 1968), pp. 314, 311.

13. Ibid., pp. 309–10.

14. Wilson, "Economic Conditions," p. 62.

15. Marshall, *Industry and Trade*, p. 563n.

16. Wilson, "Economic Conditions," p. 59.

17. Clapham, *Economic Development*, pp. 363–64.

18. Michael Balfour, *West Germany* (New York: Praeger, 1968), p. 52.

19. Domestic constraints include minimum reserve requirements plus rules which force banks to maintain "adequate" capital and liquidity and to accept only "prudent" risks. In particular, domestic lending may never exceed 18 times a bank's equity. No individual loan may exceed 75 percent of its equity; its five largest loans may not exceed three times its equity, and all large loans together may not exceed eight times its equity, according to a 1976 law. The German banker referred to above is Dieter Hoffman, then a manager of the Bank für Gemeinwirtschaft. See his "German Banks as Financial Department Stores," in the *Federal*

Reserve Bank of St. Louis Review, November 1971. See, as well, Hans-Jacob Krümmel, "German Universal Banking Scrutinized," *Journal of Banking and Finance*, March 1980.

20. Formally this is the ratio of net financial debt to total trading assets, valued at historical cost. Sources for this paragraph and the ones to follow are W. Friedman, D. H. A. Ingram, D. K. Miles, "Business Finance in the United Kingdom and Germany," *Quarterly Bulletin of the Bank of England*, September 1984, and "Financial Flows, Total Financial Assets and Liabilities in the Federal Republic of Germany in 1985," *Deutsche Bundesbank Monthly Report*, May 1986.

21. In fact, Marshall Plan aid consisted of physical goods shipped to Europe, mainly from the U.S. (Canada also provided aid.) The value of each good was assessed in deutsche marks, and a "counterpart fund" of this amount created. The ensemble of these funds became a revolving fund, and the Reconstruction Loan Corporation was created to lend it in line with priorities established by the Ministry of Economics, under Ludwig Erhard. The managers of RLC had the right to determine which specific firms would get the loans, as well as the exact nature of the projects for which they would be used.

22. See John Cable, "Capital Market Information and Industrial Performance: the Role of West German Banks," *Economic Journal*, March 1985, and references cited, especially the reports of the Federal Monopolies Commission.

23. The figures in this paragraph come from E. O. Smith, *The West German Economy* (London: Croom Helm, 1983), pp. 188, 287, and from the 1986–87 report of the Monopolies Commission, whose English summary, *Extending the Framework of Competition* (Baden-Baden, 1988) is available from the Monopolies Commission or the Federal Cartel Office in West Berlin. For a discussion of West German antimonopoly law, see Corwin D. Edwards, "American and German Conduct toward Powerful Enterprises: A Comparison," *Antitrust Bulletin*, Spring 1978.

24. Under flexible exchange rates, a rise in public spending or a fall in taxes, which is financed by borrowing, will tend to push up interest rates. This will lead to an inflow of foreign currencies, taking advantage of the higher interest return, which will raise the value of the domestic currency (deutsche mark). This rise in the exchange rate will reduce exports, by making them more expensive to foreigners, thereby offsetting the expansionary fiscal policy—unless this is financed by expansionary monetary policy (that is, an increase in the money supply). For a more general discussion, see R. A. Mundell, "Capital Mobility and Stabilization Policy Under Fixed and Flexible Exchange Rates," *Canadian Journal of Economics and Political Science*, November 1963.

25. For further discussion of central bank independence, see Joachim Klaus and Hans-Jürgin Falk, "Monetary Policy and Overall Control," *German Economic Review*, No. 2, 1970. See as well *The Deutsche Bundesbank: Its monetary policy instruments and functions*, Deutsche Bundesbank Special Series, no. 7, Frankfurt, October 1982. (This is a booklet published by the Bundesbank.)

26. If the interest rate charged on a loan is 10 percent and both borrower and lender expect an average 6 percent inflation rate over its duration, the expected real interest rate on the loan is 10 percent minus 6 percent = 4 percent. On average, the buying power of the unpaid balance of the loan will fall by 6 percent per year, and this is a cost to the lender.

27. See Toni Pierenkemper, "The Standard of Living and Employment in Germany, 1850–1980: An Overview," *Journal of European Economic History*, Spring 1987, for a summary of most of this evidence, especially, Table 4, p. 60 and Table 11, p. 68. See, as well, the references cited in section 3–5 plus the OECD's *Economic Survey of Germany, 1987–88* (Paris: OECD, 1988), Parts 2 and 3, and Klodt, "Industrial Policy and Repressed Structural Change."

28. Graham Hallett, *The Social Economy of West Germany* (London: Macmillan, 1973), p. 120.

29. Such representation—through the Federal Institute and the Chambers of Industry

and Commerce—gives the unions influence over vocational education. There are also labor representatives in all public corporations (the railways, the central bank, radio and television broadcasting, etc.), as well as in the land governments.

30. Stanley Radcliffe, *Twenty-Five Years on the Two Germanies* (London: Harrap, 1972), p. 80.

31. Both strikes were called in support of an official thirty-five-hour week (in place of the existing forty hours), with no cut in pay to compensate for the reduction in hours. In 1984, the unions argued that they were trying to "spread the work" in order to create more jobs to help relieve high unemployment. But since I. G. Metall and other unions had almost certainly pushed wages and benefits into the elastic portion of the long-run demand for labor, the net effect would have been to reduce the number of jobs in these industries, if union demands had been met.

32. A. S. Markovitz, "The Legacy of Liberalism and Collectivism in the Labour Movement: A Tense But Fruitful Compromise for Model Germany," in Markovitz, ed., *The Political Economy of West Germany* (New York: Praeger, 1982), p. 169. The previous quote is from Trevor Bain, "German Codetermination and Employment Adjustments in the Steel and Auto Industries," *Columbia Journal of World Business*, Summer 1983, p. 40.

33. To give an example of this arrangement, Volkswagenwerk A.G. had a twenty-one-member supervisory board until the 1976 changes, with seven labor representatives, including Eugen Loederer, head of I. G. Metall. Mr. Loederer was also vicechairman of the Aufsichtsrat, and the other labor representatives were the heads of works councils at the main Volkswagen plants. As well, the federal government and the land of Lower Saxony each own 20 percent of VW's shares. Each therefore has the right to nominate representatives to the supervisory board, at least some of whom are usually Social Democrats.

34. Enterprises with 2,000 to 10,000 employees must have six shareholders and six labor representatives. Companies with 10,000 to 20,000 employees must have eight of each, and larger firms must have ten of each. Of the employee representatives, two will be labor unionists in companies with 2,000 to 20,000 employees, and three will be unionists in firms with over 20,000 employees. The other labor representatives must work for the company, and at least one seat must go to each of three categories of employees—blue-collar, white-collar, and executive. Subject to this requirement, the other employee seats will be split among the three categories as closely as possible in proportion to numbers.

35. Neoliberals opposed codetermination if dominated by unions, although not necessarily otherwise. The key paper is Franz Böhm, "Das Wirtschaftliche Mitbestimmungsrecht der Arbeiter im Betrieb," *Ordo*, No. 4, 1951.

36. Frank Vogl, *German Business After the Economic Miracle* (London: Macmillan, 1973), p. 79.

Questions for Review, Discussion, Examination

1. Why do German neoliberals support a competitive market economy? How do they differ from nineteenth-century advocates of laissez faire?

2. What three benchmarks can we identify in the evolution of the postwar West German economy? Briefly indicate why each was important.

*3. In West Germany, prices received by producers of coal and of farm produce are above prices paid by users of these goods, which are, in turn, greater than world market prices. How does West Germany (in common with several other nations) maintain such a price structure? Discuss the efficiency costs of keeping this price structure intact.

4. How may West Germany's use of subsidies over 1973–87 have worked to reduce economic growth and to raise the rate of unemployment, despite the fact

that this assistance was designed, in part, to preserve jobs?

*5. Prior to the customs union (*Zollverein*) of 1834, individual German states tended to overtax commerce, from the standpoint of promoting industrial development. Why do you suppose they did this and what was their incentive to agree on the mutual tariff reductions that constituted the customs union?

*6. Why did the shortage of industrial collateral (or security) lead to ownership ties between banks and firms in nineteenth-century Germany? Why were banks necessary intermediaries between savers and investors and why did they insist on some control over major investment decisions?

*7. Banks often suppressed price competition in nineteenth-century Germany via cartel agreements and other forms of collusion. However, they also fostered competition based on new products and production processes. Why did they have incentives to do both of these things? (*Hint*: Why would their ownership ties to German industry give them an incentive to do both?)

8. Why do you suppose the reduction of trade barriers and growth of international trade since 1960 has gone hand-in-hand with an explosive growth in the number of mergers, in West Germany as in other countries of Western Europe?

9. In what concrete way has German experience with open inflation after World War I, and with repressed inflation after World War II, helped to increase price stability since 1949?

Why did restrictive policy not produce significant unemployment before the 1980s? (See also question 11.)

10. What variables has monetary policy sought to directly influence in West Germany and how has it operated? What major change in monetary policy tools occurred in the early 1980s?

11. The insider-outsider dichotomy discussed at the end of chapter 3 suggests that *un*foreseen shifts in the demand for labor will alter employment levels, while shifts that are foreseen will mainly alter nominal earnings, rather than employment. Moreover, real earnings tend to be rigid, and unforeseen reductions in demand may create long-term unemployment. How may these observations help to explain West Germany's postwar experience with employment and unemployment? What other factors may help to account for high unemployment during the 1980s?

*12. Explain how price supports for food have made housing more expensive in West Germany? (*Note*: At the end of chapter 14, we briefly discussed the same phenomenon in Japan.)

13. At what three levels do employee representatives enjoy codetermination rights in West Germany? At which of these levels are they most effective? At this (most-effective) level, which types of issues do they have the most power to influence? Discuss briefly.

*14. Collective bargaining in West Germany has been more decentralized than in Sweden, with the most important negotiations taking place at the level of the industry.

(a) What feature of West German negotiations helps to ensure that wage-benefit increases do not exceed what export industries are able to pay? What features help to ensure labor peace?

(b) What principal goal of the Swedish union movement is DGB less well equipped to pursue?

(c) What is the *de facto* role of works councils in collective bargaining?

15. Costly strikes were called in 1978 and 1984 to support demands for a thirty-five hour week (in place of the existing forty hours) in West German metalworking industries, with no cut in pay to compensate for the reduction in hours. In 1984, the labor union involved (I. G. Metall) argued that it was trying to "spread the work," in order to create more jobs.

Is it likely that the metalworking industries would have hired more employees, had union aims been realized? Explain briefly. (*Note*: The union finally accepted a smaller reduction in working hours, in combination with an adjustment of work rules favorable to management.)

16. Briefly describe and compare the three types of codetermination in private companies with five hundred employees or more, noting the similarities and differences. How have companies reorganized themselves to change the type of codetermination that applies to them? Why? How do unions rank the three types by order of preference? Why?

*17. Economists' efficiency arguments against widespread full codetermination are similar to those raised against the Meidner Plan in Sweden. Explain briefly what these objections are. Do you share them? Why or why not?

* = more difficult.

Suggested Further Readings

Note: The monthly reports of the Deutsche Bundesbank, which are translated into English, provide much useful information, as well as a good statistical profile of the economy, with emphasis on the financial sector. The annual OECD reports on West Germany provide further information and insight. Finally, most of the August 1976 issue of the *Labour Gazette* (vol. 76), a monthly publication of Canada's Federal Department of Labor, is devoted to a discussion of codetermination from several points of view.

Arndt, Hans-Joachim. *West Germany: The Politics of Non-Planning.* Syracuse, N.Y.: Syracuse University Press, 1966.
Bain, Trevor. "German Co-determination and Employment Adjustments in the Steel and Auto Industries." *Columbia Journal of World Business* 18 (Summer 1983): 40–47.
Balfour, Michael. *West Germany.* New York: Praeger, 1968.
Berghalm, V. R. *Modern Germany: Society, Economy, and Politics in the Twentieth Century.* Cambridge: Cambridge University Press, 1983.
Bhagwati, J. N., Klaus-Werner Schatz, and Kar-Yiu Wong. "The West German Gastarbeiter System of Immigration." *European Economic Review* 26 (1984) 277–294.
Blumenthal, W. H. *Codetermination in the German Steel Industry.* Princeton: Princeton University Press, 1965.
Braunthal, Gerard. *The Federation of German Industry in Politics.* New York: Cornell University Press, 1965.

Cable, John. "Capital Market Information and Industrial Performance: the Role of West German Banks." *Economic Journal* 95 (March 1985): 118–132.

Cable, John, and M. J. Dirrheimer. "Hierarchies and Markets: An Empirical Test of the Multi-divisional Hypothesis in West Germany." *International Journal of Industrial Organization* 1, 1 (1983): 43–62.

Carter, G. H., and J. H. Herz. *Major Foreign Powers*, 6th ed. New York: Harcourt Brace Jovanovich 1972. Part 3.

Crawley, Aidan, *The Rise of Western Germany: 1945–72*. London: Collins, 1973.

Denton, D., M. Forsyth, and M. MacLennan. *Economic Planning and Policies in Britain, France, and Germany*. London: Allen & Unwin, 1968.

Duwendag, D. "The Postwar Economic System in Germany: Creation, Evolution and Reappraisal." *Federal Reserve Bank of St. Louis Review* 57 (October 1975): 16–22.

Dworkin, J., C. Hobson, E. Frieling, and D. Oakes. "How German Workers View Their Jobs." *Columbia Journal of World Business* 18 (Summer 1983): 48–54.

Edwards, Corwin D. "American and German Policy Toward Conduct by Powerful Enterprises: A Comparison." *Antitrust Bulletin* 23 (Spring 1978): 83–146.

Emery, F. E., and E. Thorsrud. *Form and Content in Industrial Democracy*. London: Tavistock, 1969.

Erhard, Ludwig. *Prosperity Through Competition*. London: Thames and Hudson, 1962.

Eucken, Walter. *The Foundations of Economics*. Edinburgh: Hodge, 1950.

Feldman, Gerald. *Iron and Steel in the German Inflation, 1916–1923*. Princeton: Princeton University Press, 1977.

Fels, Gerhard. "Inflation in Germany." In Krause, L. B., and W. S. Salant, eds. *Worldwide Inflation*. Washington, D.C.: Brookings, 1977, pp. 589–622.

Fleming, Gunter, and Klaus-Dieter Schmidt. "West Germany's Balance of Payments Surplus: Causes and Problems." *Three Banks Review* 105 (March 1975): 25–37.

Friedman, Philip. "The Welfare Costs of Bilateralism: German-Hungarian Trade, 1933–1938." *Explorations in Economic History* 13 (January 1976): 113–125.

Friedman, W., D. H. A. Ingram, and D. K. Miles. "Business Finance in the United Kingdom and Germany." *Monthly Report of the Deutsche Bundesbank* 36 (November 1984): 33–42.

Frowen, S. F. et al., eds. *Monetary Policy and Economic Activity in West Germany*. New York: Halsted, 1977.

Fürstenburg, Friedrich. "Workers' Participation in Management in the Federal Republic of West Germany." Bulletin No. 6, Geneva, International Institute for Labor Studies (February 1969): 94–147.

Grosser, Alfred. *Germany in our Time: A Political History of the Post-War Years*. New York: Praeger, 1971.

Hallett, Graham. *The Social Economy of West Germany*. London: Macmillan 1973.

Hamburger, M. J. "The Demand for Money in an Open Economy." *Journal of Monetary Economics* 3 (January 1977): 25–40.

Hanby, V. J., and M. P. Jackson. "An Evaluation of Job Creation in Germany." *International Journal of Social Economics* 6, 2 (1979).

Hartmann, Heinz. *Authority and Organization in German Management*. Princeton: Princeton University Press, 1959.

Hodgman, D. R. *National Monetary Policies and International Monetary Co-operation*. Boston: Little, Brown, and Co., 1974, chapter 4.

Klaus, Joachim, and Hans-Jurgen Falk. "Monetary Policy and Overall Control." *German Economic Review* 8, 2 (1970): 97–114.

Klodt, H. "Industrial Policy and Repressed Structural Change in West Germany." Kiel Institute of World Economics, Working Paper No. 322, Kiel, West Germany (March 1988).

Kloten, Norbert, and Rainer Vollmer. "Stability, Growth, and Economic Policy." *German Economic Review* 13, 2 (1975): 97–116.

Kouri, P. J. K. "The Hypothesis of Offsetting Capital Flows: A Case Study of Germany." *Journal of Monetary Economics* 1 (January 1975): 21–39.

Krümmel, Hans-Jacob. "German Universal Banking Scrutinized." *Journal of Banking and Finance* 4 (March 1980): 33–55.

Leaman, Jeremy. *The Political Economy of West Germany, 1945–1985: An Introduction.* New York: St. Martin's, 1987.

Markovits, Andrei S., ed. *The Political Economy of West Germany: Modell Deutschland.* New York: Praeger, 1982.

Marsh, David. "New Battleground for the Bundesbank." *The Banker* 130 (July 1980): 77–82.

Mendelsohn, M. S. "Tight Money Squeezes the Banks." *The Banker* 130 (July 1980): 85–89.

Mendershausen, Horst. *Two Postwar Recoveries of the German Economy.* Amsterdam: North-Holland, 1955.

Morgan, E. W., R. Harrington, and G. Zis. *Banking Systems and Monetary Policy in the EEC.* London: The Financial Times, 1975, pp. 35–47.

Müller, Jürgin. "The Impact of Mergers on Concentration: A Study of Eleven West German Industries." *Journal of Industrial Economics* 25 (December 1976): 113–132.

Mueller-Armack, Alfred. "The Social Market Economy as an Economic and Social Order." *Review of Social Economy* 36 (December 1978): 325–331.

Neumann, M. J. M. "Offsetting Capital Flows: A Re-examination of the German Case." *Journal of Monetary Economics* 4 (January 1978): 131–142.

Radcliffe, Stanley. *Twenty-Five Years on the Two Germanies, 1970.* London: Harrap, 1972.

Reuss, Frederick. *Fiscal Policy for Growth Without Inflation: The German Experiment.* Baltimore: Johns Hopkins University Press, 1963.

Roskamp, Karl. *Capital Formation in West Germany.* Detroit: Wayne State University Press, 1965.

Schnitzer, Martin. *East and West Germany: A Comparative Analysis.* New York: Praeger, 1972.

Shonfield, Andrew. *Modern Capitalism.* Oxford University Press, 1965, chapters 11, 12.

Sohmen, Egon. "Competition and Growth: The Lesson of West Germany." *American Economic Review* 49 (December 1959): 986–1003.

Sommariva, Andrea, and Giuseppe Tullio. *German Macroeconomic History, 1880–1979: A Study of the Effects of Economic Policy on Inflation, Currency Depreciation, and Growth.* New York: St. Martin's, 1986.

Stein, Jürgin. *The Banking System of the Federal Republic of Germany,* 10th rev. ed. Cologne: Federation of German Banks 1977.

Smith, E. O. *The West German Economy.* London: Croom Helm, 1983.

Stolper, Gustav, Karl Häuser, and Knut Borchardt. *The German Economy: 1870 to the Present.* New York: Harcourt, Brace, and World, 1967.

Tuchtfeldt, Egon. "Social Market Economy and Demand Management—Two Experiments of Economic Policy." *German Economic Review* 12, 2 (1974): 111–133.

Vogl, Frank. *German Business After the Economic Miracle.* London: Macmillan, 1973.

Wallich, Eli. *Mainsprings of the German Economic Revival.* New Haven: Yale University Press, 1955.

Wilkens, Herbert. *The Two German Economies.* London: Gower, 1981.

Zugel, W. "The Banks and Industrial Investment in Germany." In Glyn Davies, ed. *European Finance for Development.* Cardiff: University of Wales, 1974, pp. 77–98.

18

THE RISE AND FALL
OF NATIONAL SOCIALISM
AND GERMAN RENEWAL
AFTER WORLD WAR II

18-1. The Weimar Period, 1919–33[1]

A. Instability of the Weimar Régime

Germany emerged from World War I badly defeated and financially distraught. As a nation, it had only been politically united since the Franco-Prussian War in 1871. In this union, the central government or Reich had relatively weak powers of taxation vis-à-vis the provincial or *land* governments, although the center was able to levy new taxes just prior to and during the war. Whether the Reich ever got enough authority to pay for the war from taxes can be debated, but 80 percent of its cost was, in fact, financed from the printing press. Originally, the government had expected a short war, and the expectation survived for a long time that Germany would win and that the defeated Allies would be made to bear its cost. The amount of money in circulation by war's end was about five times as great as in 1914, although wartime controls prevented much of it from being spent. Thus there was considerable repressed inflation during the war, which became open once the war was over.

The military collapse in November 1918 forced the Kaiser to flee to Holland and brought the monarchy to an end. Coming on top of the hardships endured by Germans during the war, and the apparently unequal distribution of war burdens, it also triggered uprisings of soldiers and workers, and several cities became battlegrounds. The left wing of the Social Democratic party split off to found the Communist party, which hoped to lead a successful socialist revolution, modeled on the one in the USSR. It demanded a dictatorship of the proletariat, with power to be exercised by councils of workers and soldiers that had arisen in factories and units of the armed forces at war's end. However, the Social Democrats refused to go along with this demand. The division of the left ensured that no successful revolution would occur, although the government was under pressure to maintain full employment and (for those days) extensive social programs.[2]

Instead, a parliamentary government emerged with the Social Democrats in power. They enlisted the regular army's support, promising to keep out Communist influence in return. Many officials of the former Imperial Reich assumed important government posts, and the Imperial officer corps remained in command of the armed forces. Walter Rathenau, the organizing genius behind wartime procurement, was Foreign Minister until his assassination in June 1922. As a reaction to Prussian hegemony under Imperial rule and to escape the street fighting in Berlin, the new Parliament (*Reichstag*) first met in Weimar, a town in Thuringia, now part of East Germany. Hence the name "Weimar Republic."

At the outset, pressure from revolutionary elements, including the Communists, forced the SPD to the left. Claiming that "socialism is on the march," the new government declared its goal of nationalizing key industries. It also gave labor unions full collective bargaining powers, raised wages, and instituted an eight-hour day. Finally, it sought to promote the growth of industrial democracy, whose seeds had been planted during the war by the same coalition of unions and moderate business interests that controlled the first Weimar government. The Works Council Act of February 1920 ratified the establishment in 1916 of works councils in firms performing war-related tasks and extended this institution to all of industry. A 1922 law reserved one or two seats on each supervisory board of directors for works council members. The councils were to carry out the mandate of Article 165 of the Weimar Constitution, which stipulated that "Workers . . . are called on to participate with equal rights and in common with employers in the regulation of wages, salaries, and working conditions, and in the entire economic development of productive forces."[3]

However, once the threat from the radical left subsided and the crises of the early 1920s receded, the coalition that had originally formed the government tended to break up. The program of nationalization fizzled, and industry-wide cartels became stronger than ever, forcing the state to constantly intervene to contain price gouging. By 1923, the balance of power had shifted to the employers. Once the Ruhr occupation and hyperinflation of that year had ended, they unilaterally extended the working day, cut real wages, and curtailed the powers of the works councils. Later, in 1934, the Nazis would abolish the councils and repeal labor's right to supervisory board representation.

Although 1924–29 was a period of comparative peace and prosperity, it is probably fair to say that the Weimar régime never really took root. In principle, it had a stronger central government than the monarchy. The center received increased taxing and law-making powers, and took advantage of these by levying dozens of new taxes and thoroughly revising its budgetary system. In addition, the entire rail network—the largest single rail unit in the world—came under its ownership and control. Yet several forces, including the fact that Germany was experimenting with democracy for the first time, acted to undermine and then to destroy the Republic.

Perhaps the most serious internal political factors were the method of electing Parliament, which led to unstable governments, and the constitutional provision for presidential rule by decree during emergencies. The former eventually helped to create the emergencies that led to presidential rule on a continuing basis. The problem was that citizens voted for political parties rather than for candidates, under a strict rule of proportional representation that awarded each party one seat for every 60,000 votes it obtained. There was no provision for excluding parties from the Reichstag when they failed to get 5 percent of the vote. The Weimar system is the only one that treats all parties alike and makes the legislative strength of each solely a function of its share of the popular vote.

But it is also a system that potentially fragments the political spectrum into many distinct parties, each of which is able to elect some representatives. Coalition governments involving several parties are often necessary, and in difficult times, these are constantly threatened with dissolution over some divisive issue. In Weimar, it was harder and harder to form coalitions capable of governing, and this became nearly impossible after the onset of the Great Depression. By 1932, nearly forty different parties were contesting seats in the Reichstag. The present West German method of voting—especially the 5 percent cutoff rule—is a reaction to the frustrations of this era. Over the fourteen years of the Weimar Republic, there were nine elections, the last of which (on March 5, 1933) confirmed Hitler in power, although with just 43.7 percent of the vote. This marked the boundary between Weimar and the Third Reich.

The Nazis probably could not have come to power, if the Reich President was not already ruling by emergency decree. Originally, the Presidency was considered a ceremonial post—the head of state—with little real power, not unlike the King of England. However, he was also popularly elected; he did not derive what power he had from the Reichstag. Under emergency rule, he could name his own Chancellor (in effect, the Prime Minister or head of government). The Reichstag could refuse to support his declaration of emergency, but by dissolving Parliament—several times in succession, if need be—the President could get around this legislative veto. When General von Hindenburg, a conservative war hero, was elected President in 1925, this possibility became a real one. Over 1930–32, no majority capable of governing could be formed in the Reichstag. In effect, Germany had a presidential government, and it was Hindenburg who finally appointed Hitler as Chancellor. The present West German Constitution omits this provision for emergency presidential rule, and the President is no longer popularly elected.

B. Hyperinflation and Economic Policy

The Weimar Republic might still have had a chance, were it not for two overwhelming economic phenomena, which combined to destroy it. First, it inherited a colossal financial burden, which directly and indirectly helped to cause a rapid inflation over 1918–23, culminating in the Hyperinflation of 1923. Second, it was unable to cope, later on, with the Great Depression—partly because it had been willing to destroy the value of the mark during the hyperinflation and to repudiate most of its own interest-bearing debt afterward. These policy choices undermined confidence in the Republic, both at home and abroad, and helped to establish adverse expectations, which made deficit financing of public spending virtually impossible during the Great Depression. The government was therefore helpless in the face of declining output and soaring unemployment. This helped to pave the way for Hitler's rise to power.

The origins of disaster lie in Germany's war debt and, to a greater degree, in the heavy reparations burden which the victorious Allies added to this. Weimar had an incentive to try to avoid this indemnity, which most Germans viewed as unjust. Thanks to the inflation and to large inflows of foreign capital, mainly from the United States, Germany did avoid it. Reparations came to about 6 percent of GNP over 1919–23, and declined thereafter. Depreciation of the value of foreign deposits in German banks—as the mark's value fell more quickly than anticipated against other currencies—nearly covered the entire cost of reparations during the inflation. Moreover, inflows of foreign capital swamped reparations and other capital out-flows over most of 1919–30, enabling Germans to enjoy an average living standard above that justified by domestic productivity.[4] Yet foreigners lost heavily on these investments. Allied efforts to collect reparations did influence German policy making in the early postwar years, and in particular, were a major indirect cause of hyperinflation. When it culminated in November 1923, 10.2 billion marks had the purchasing power of one mark in August 1922. In 1918, the U.S. dollar was worth 4 marks; in 1922, 7,000 marks; and on November 20, 1923, 4.2 billion marks. Many people watched their life savings vanish, and a horror of inflation was implanted in the minds of Germans that probably helped to promote prosperity after World War II.

Hyperinflation came because the government's spending commitments far exceeded its ability to pay, especially after the French-Belgian occupation of the Ruhr (Germany's industrial heartland) in January 1923, which cut it off from the rest of the German economy. The initial policy of passive resistance required payments to workers, civil servants, and industrialists who remained idle, and the government was already deeply involved in redistribution via welfare payments and other transfers. In addition, it was subsidizing many firms, in order to maintain production, especially after mid-1922. Subsidies took the form of loans at increasingly negative real interest rates—eventually amounting to virtual grants—supported by the Reichsbank's rediscount policy. Real interest rates were above 5 percent in early 1922 and below negative 100 percent by end-1922. Such aid was necessary to maintain production and full employment because of the change in foreign attitudes toward the stability of the German government and the future value of the mark in mid-1922. Up to that time, foreign money had poured into Germany to speculate against changes in the mark's value. But Rathenau's assassination plus the refusal of the French to reschedule reparations payments and the rejection by English and American bankers of Germany's application for a long-term loan led to a worsening of expectations. This caused a sudden outflow of funds, threatening banks and industry with a liquidity crisis. To prevent widespread illiquidity and bankruptcy, the Reichsbank flooded the banking system with credit, replacing foreign funds with marks.

If we consider all claims against the Reich—both its own expenditure and the "needs" of German industry for subsidies—these were fixed or rising in real terms, relative to tax revenues, especially after mid-1922. To fill the gap, the state created money. This raised the ratio of money to goods and caused inflation, which, in turn, required a more rapid rate of money creation to cover the same real obligations of the state. The result was a rising and then an accelerating rate of inflation. In the latter half of 1923, prior to the total collapse of the currency, thirty paper mills and two thousand presses were running day and night in a vain effort to fulfill the need for cash. Yet, government expenditures (not including subsidies through the banking system), which had been 2.75 times revenues in 1920–21, rose to over 5.1 times revenues by 1923–24. The hyperinflation was brought to an end by a currency reform (the "Miracle" of the Rentenmark) which vastly deflated the volume of money in circulation. The reform was accompanied by higher taxes, stronger restraints on credit creation, and expectations that Allied pressure on reparations would ease, while the areas cut off from the German economy would be reintegrated. (The hyperinflation also lowered Allied expectations of collectible reparations.) To compensate for lost subsidies, employers were allowed to reduce real labor costs.

Some economists view the great inflation as rational policy, and in the short run, it may have been. In effect, Germany did make foreigners pay her reparations obligations and finance a living standard beyond her means to boot. Until mid-1922, the inflow of speculative funds also played a major role in financing reconstruction. Yet inflation ruined many Germans financially, and left the banking system in a vulnerable state. While the economy was booming over 1919–22, industry expanded irrationally. By 1924, there was overcapacity in heavy industry, with good political ties and access to funds, but the growth industries of this era—autos, electronics, aircraft, aluminum—were short of capital. Worse, adverse expectations built up during this era made the Great Depression more severe.

Germany was eventually able to negotiate a reduction of the reparations burden to about 28 percent of its original level and to lengthen the payment period. This relief permitted six relatively prosperous years, 1924–29, but an enormous debt remained, and a government able to repudiate it, to restore German honor and sovereignty, and to rebuild military power could mobilize substantial support. The Great Depression raised the potential support for a government able to restore full employment. Even over 1924–29, moreover, exports were rather low, owing to continuing cost pressures on German exporters. The latter can be traced to income demands of wage and salary earners, who feared a renewal of inflation, right up to the onset of the Great Depression. Since the government was under pressure to maintain confidence in the mark, both at home and abroad, it also refused to devalue and followed a restrictive credit policy. (Relaxation of the latter might have caused a disastrous deterioration of expectations.) Tight credit raised interest rates and caused an inflow of funds on capital account, which offset the current account deficit and reparations outflow. As noted, this inflow benefitted Germany, but much of it consisted of short-term loans, which could be quickly withdrawn.

There was also a lack of confidence in Weimar's bonds. Originally, the hyper-inflation made these worthless, although confidence might have been restored, had they subsequently been revalued reasonably, in terms of gold. But in 1925, they were given new values, which averaged less than 10 percent of their original gold prices, and some were as low as 2.5 percent. Henceforward, borrowers would perceive the Reich's bonds as risky assets. The government was forced to borrow mainly at short term, and by the eve of the Great Depression, it could scarcely borrow at all, giving it no alternative to tight monetary and fiscal policies. Over 1929–32, public investment fell by more than 60 percent and the Reich's budget deficit by more than 80 percent, while unemployment soared.

Two further measures, taken at the behest of Reichsbank President Hjalmar Schacht, made matters worse. First, at end-1926, the Reich withdrew from foreign bondholders their exemption from German taxes, which made most of them subject to double taxation. Then, in May 1927, the Reichsbank threatened to refuse to rediscount loans to commercial banks, who were lending "excessively" to finance buying on the stock market. Schacht believed that speculation in stocks was diverting money from investment. As a result, securities prices fell, and these two measures caused a withdrawal of foreign funds from Germany. In June 1927, the government restored the tax exemption on new foreign purchases of German bonds, but permanent damage in terms of their perceived attractiveness had been done. Although Schacht had played a major role in ending the hyperinflation and stabilizing the mark, his subsequent policies helped to undermine Weimar. Later, Schacht would design the machinery (described below) that enabled Hitler to run massive budget deficits, financed by creation of new money, without which he would have been unable to pay for rearmament and war. Yet, there was no crisis of confidence in the Nazi régime until military defeat began to take its toll.

The Weimar era is known for its intellectual freedom and its artistic and scientific creativity. It also introduced the beginnings of industrial democracy and extended the social welfare system. In particular, the first unemployment insurance appeared in 1927, although the scheme could not withstand the massive unemployment of the Great Depression. Finally, the government recognized collective bargaining and provided for mediation in labor disputes. However, the breakdown of cooperation between labor and management over 1923–24 undid most of the original gains in labor relations. It forced the state to arbitrate disputes and to extend existing labor contracts to employees and employers who had not participated in the bargaining on which these agreements were based. The result tended to be a system of administered or "political" wages, which only by chance would clear markets for different kinds of labor in different geographical regions. The government thereby antagonized both business and labor and may have aggravated unemployment, once the Great Depression was underway. In housing, the accumulated excess demand after World War I prevented the removal of wartime rent controls—which would have caused rents to soar—and the government embarked on an ambitious construction program, while subsidizing private home building, in an effort to remove the shortage.

The first anticartel law in German history also passed in 1923, but it was ineffective. Cartels were stronger during the Weimar era than before, notably in coal, potash, chemicals, and iron and steel. An official estimate put the number of cartels at 2,500 in 1925, eight times the number estimated in 1905. In addition, close ties between banks and firms carried over from the Imperial era, along with the high percentage of long-term loans, but the Reichsbank had much less control over the commercial banking system. Herein lay the origins of the Banking Crisis of 1931, the beginning of the end for Weimar.

C. Crisis and Rise of the Nazis

As a matter of customary practice, German banks converted deposits that could be withdrawn on short notice into medium- and long-term loans. Thus, they were always potentially vulnerable to a crisis that would cause depositors to withdraw large amounts of money, and this vulnerability rose during the Weimar era. They had always converted their own capital, as well as deposits, to long-term loans, but under Imperial rule, the ratio of own funds to deposits in long-term loans was around one-to-four. Being net creditors, the banks lost heavily during the hyperinflation. They did not rebuild their own funds afterwards, and by the early 1930s, the ratio of own capital to depositors' funds in long-term loans had fallen to about one-to-fifteen. Moreover, 40–50 percent of these deposits came from abroad. The Reichsbank was unable to restrain bank enthusiasm for lending, and prior to the 1929–30 crash, some banks seemed to think that prosperity would last forever. Of course, the Great Depression burst this bubble, but two specific events started the rush of foreign depositors to withdraw their funds.

The first was the spectacular gain by the National Socialists in the September 1930 elections. Their Reichstag strength climbed to 107 seats from 12, on the promise of jobs, bread, land, and restoration of German pride and honor. They were still a decided minority in an assembly with 577 seats, and to make themselves more effective, they tacitly combined with the far left in efforts to bring about an end to the Republic (virtually the only concrete goal shared by the two groups).

This problem would have been surmounted, had not the worldwide depression continued to deepen and had it not been for the Austrian banking crisis of May 1931, the second event referred to above. It led to the bankruptcy of one of Europe's largest banks and caused a run on German banks that could only be contained by a moratorium on German war debts (the Hoover moratorium of July 1, 1931) plus foreign credits granted to the Reichsbank.

Nevertheless, in July 1931, the Darmstädter und Nationalbank, one of Germany's Big Four commercial banks, was forced to stop payment on withdrawals, after a textile firm in which it had invested heavily went bankrupt. The bank's losses exceeded its total assets. Ultimately, the Darmstädter Bank had to be absorbed by the Dresdner Bank, but there was mounting danger that much of the commercial banking system would go under. Consequently, the government declared a bank holiday, guaranteed all deposits in the Darmstädter Bank, and effectively nationalized the remaining big banks. Coupled with a moratorium on payment of short-term debt plus foreign-exchange controls, this kept the outflow of foreign currencies from reaching crisis proportions. But by now, the government's ability to cover a budget or trade deficit was nearly at an end.

Consequently, it cut public investment and raised taxes, even as unemployment was rising to record levels, industrial output was collapsing, and net investment was becoming negative. The régime also cut social benefits, especially unemployment compensation, and reduced wages and prices by decree, while extending wage and price controls. In 1932, unemployment stood at 44 percent of the labor force, nearly the highest level in the Western world. The economy was a disaster area, and hostility toward the government was growing. Communists and Nazi storm troopers were clashing daily in the streets, and it was only a question of which extreme would come to rule and when. To some, Hitler appeared the safer alternative, and to others, the only one who could restore Germany to her "rightful place." Then there was the view in some quarters that he ought to be given enough rope to hang himself. On January 30, 1933, Hitler became Reich Chancellor and on March 5, in coalition with the Nationalist party, he gained control of the Reichstag. Soon after, he acquired dictatorial powers by legal means:

> When the Assembly met [after the elections of March 5] . . . the Deputies were presented with an Enabling Bill which would for four years authorize the Chancellor . . . irrespective of the Constitution, to issue laws on any subject he chose . . . only the Social Democrats voted against it . . . henceforward, [the Reichstag] only met at intervals to be harangued.[5]

Thus did Hitler silence his political opposition. By getting rid of parliamentary investigation and enquiry—and then giving similar treatment to the press—Hitler gained more leeway than Weimar had to finance recovery from the Great Depression. He also used this freedom to brutalize his opponents and to prepare for war, in violation of the Versailles Treaty.

18-2. The Germany Economy During the Nazi Era, 1933–45

A. *Evolution of the Nazi Economy*

The German economy under National Socialism has been called a capitalist command economy, but this is misleading. The Nazis did not control the economy until 1936 or 1937, and it was only in 1942, after the Soviet army had turned back the drive on Moscow, that comprehensive control over supplies of important materials came under a single head—in this case, the new Minister of Armaments, Albert Speer. Even then, allocation of labor remained outside Speer's control, and his ministry did not take over aircraft production or key aspects of the civilian economy until mid-1944. Prior to 1942, there was no real central authority besides Hitler himself, whose Führer-commands could cut through red tape quickly. Otherwise, the National Socialist chain of command, above the industry or geographic region, was more like a bureaucratic maze, with overlapping jurisdictions and less than clearcut lines of authority and responsibility.

With some oversimplification, we can identify three stages in the evolution of the German economy under Nazi control. The first, lasting to the end of 1936, saw the leadership of the Nazi party under Hitler sharing power with other groups inside and outside the party. The growing power of Hitler's "oligarchic clique" was, in part, consolidated by murdering the leaders of the paramilitary storm troopers (the Brown Shirts or SA) and of the party's left wing during and after the Night of the Long Knives, June 30, 1934. By early 1934, all free trade unions had been suppressed and replaced by the German Labor Front, a party organization that included managers, as well as workers, at each work place. This allowed the Nazis to freeze wages, a key part of their program to recover from the Great Depression and prepare for war.

The Nazis also suppressed small business in favor of big business, despite campaign promises to do the reverse. (Both nationalization of large corporations and profit sharing within them were part of the original "unalterable" party program, but neither was carried out.) By the mid-1930s, there were four main poles of power in Germany—the Nazi élite military organization (or SS), the Nazi party élite, big business, and the military élite of the regular army. Each pole dominated its respective sphere, although there were also other powers to be reckoned with, including lower level Nazi officials.[6] Each of the four groups was trying to defend and to enlarge its sphere of influence, but by 1937, the party élite was coming out on top.

From early 1937 to early 1942, Germany was a mixed economy under the Nazi élite, although the latter had to make its programs reasonably attractive to the other groups. For example, prices were fixed to provide "reasonable" profits to cartels and large business firms, and government contracts with industry contained what were called "profitability guarantee" clauses, ensuring minimum sales volumes and "reasonable" profit margins. Although the banking system was an important tool in mobilizing the economy for rearmament and war, the government returned the shares of commercial banks taken over by the Weimar Republic to their original owners in 1937, at a handsome profit to the latter.

From early 1942, until the downfall of the régime in 1945, the Nazis ran a quasi-command economy. Even then, many overlapping jurisdictions remained, resulting in duplication and wasteful competition, although the ensuing standoff could sometimes be manipulated by Hitler and his entourage to get their way more quickly. Thus

> it was a regular part of National Socialist administrative practice, when something really important needed to be done, to appoint an *ad hoc* administrative committee to do the job. . . . [Once the urgent task had been accomplished], the individual [who headed the committee] would create his own machine and then cast around for some sphere of responsibility to take over. His "own" administrative machine might then be filling much the same sort of role as the ministries had done in the Weimar Republic. In fact, many surviving ministries were left to compete in a similar way with such essentially "private" organizations.[7]

Industries were fairly tightly organized after 1936, as an extension of the cartel-plus-bank principle. There was a fair amount of investment planning, as well as planning for research and development, and "rationalization," in the sense of forcing firms to specialize within particular product lines. When the various centers of power could agree on priorities, the banking system was a ready means to channel funds to firms and to enforce their use for ends desired by the régime. Although bureaucratic entrepreneurship and muddled lines of authority often made priorities impossible to agree on or to implement, Hitler was able to impart a sense of direction and purpose to Germany. He was successful, partly because of his audacity and cunning, partly because he was able to disguise much of what he was doing, and partly because he was willing and able to inflict enormous costs on some groups, while sharing benefits with supporters.

In particular, the Nazi economy was based to no small extent on plunder, principally of the Jews and of other peoples who came under German hegemony, beginning in 1938. Ordinary workers and soldiers were also exploited, and workers imported from Eastern Europe during the war were effectively slaves. Without a basic reform, the system could not have survived, once the opportunities for plunder had run out, even if Germany had won the war. By engaging in massive, deficit-financed government spending, Hitler did restore full employment by end-1937, thereby gaining the support of many who were able to go back to work. But his accumulated budget deficits were disastrous for postwar Germany.

Prior to World War II, only 75 percent of the Reich's expenditures were covered by revenues from all sources. The other 25 percent ultimately came from the printing press. After 1939, government revenues from all sources covered less than half of government spending. Some of this revenue took the form, not of taxes or social insurance contributions (which, in the full-employment economy prevailing after 1936, greatly exceeded outlays), but of expropriations from Jews and enemies of the régime, of deliberate depreciation of German debts to foreigners, and of war booty. But Germany did not plunder the countries it captured in World War II very efficiently. Neither did it organize a rational division of labor or specialization according to comparative advantage within the territory under its control. Germany did bring in skilled labor from France and unskilled workers from Eastern Europe to man its industries, and without this help, it probably could not have continued to fight a two-front war. Moreover, Germany solved potentially critical food shortages with imports from France.

B. Organization of the Nazi Economy

Hitler's approach to mobilizing the economy, insofar as he had a coherent strategy, rested on five pillars. The first was to break the bargaining power of labor and subsequently to freeze wages. To pave the way for these actions, the Nazis appropriated May Day (May 1, 1933) as an occasion to celebrate their rise to power. Traditionally, only labor unionists and socialists marched in parades on that day, but the Nazis required businessmen to march as well, generally at the rear of parades led by their workers. This put the National Socialists on good terms with labor. The next day, storm troopers arrested union leaders, closed union offices, and seized union property. In January 1934, the government dissolved the unions, along with the works councils, replacing these with the German Labor Front. This allowed it to raise aggregate demand and to put people back to work without having to worry about raising wages and prices. Over 1933–38, national income grew by over 80 percent, but the wage and salary share fell from 63 percent to 57 percent.[8] By 1939, unemployment was under 1 percent, a level that would not be reached again in post-World War II West Germany until the building of the Berlin Wall (in August 1961) stopped the flow of refugees from the East. Table 18.1 shows the evolution of real wages and unemployment in Germany from 1924 to 1939.

The Nazis expanded aggregate demand through a massive, semisecret rearmament program and a small, highly publicized program of public works—including construction of Germany's first super highway—plus easy credit for homebuilding. This became Hitler's second pillar. Often, public works proved an excellent way to train and toughen young people physically in advance of actual conscription into the armed forces. The latter began in March 1935, in violation of the Versailles Treaty. Spending on armaments rose from two billion Reichsmarks (RM) in 1933–34 to 16 billion in 1938–39, not including some outlays by civilian agencies. By offering guaranteed markets, the government also subsidized those industries making major direct and indirect contributions to the military effort. By 1938–39, armaments production had expanded to over seven times its low 1933–34 level. The Nazis also achieved direct control over imports and partly direct, partly indirect control over exports by the mid-1930s. This was necessary for self-sufficiency, again desirable on military grounds, and was the third pillar of economic mobilization. Control over financial markets became the fourth pillar. Both of the latter were brainchildren

Table 18.1

Unemployment and Average Real Wages in Germany, 1924–39

Year	Unemployment (as % of the labor force)	Real wages (1924=100)
1924	13.1%	100
1926	18.0	118
1927	8.8	120
1928	8.6	127
1929	13.3	133
1930	22.7	140
1932	43.8	136
1934	20.5	132
1936	12.0	135
1938	3.2	145
1939	0.9	150

Source: Toni Pierenkemper, "The Standard of Living and Employment in Germany, 1850–1980: An Overview," *Journal of European Economic History*, Spring, 1987, Table 3, p. 59 (Galenson-Zeller figures) and Table 10, p. 67 (Brumback-König figures).

of Hjalmar Schacht, whom we have already met.[9]

The Reichsbank had begun exchange control during the banking crisis of 1931 to protect the balance of payments, as well as the banking system. This was the first step, as it turned out, toward direct control over imports. In 1931, the central bank was trying to limit the amounts of foreign currencies that could be taken out of Germany. To this end, foreign exchange derived from selling goods abroad and from long and short-term investment by foreigners in Germany was not freely sold to anyone who wanted it, but was instead rationed among would-be users. The total amount rationed out was always small enough to keep Germany's foreign currency reserves from becoming depleted. When Britain devalued the pound soon afterward, Germany had to extend its foreign-exchange controls because investors, expecting Germany to devalue, were again threatening to withdraw short-term capital. The controls prevented a flight of currency from Germany, and German exports exceeded imports in 1931, 1932, and 1933, although trade had sunk to half its already depressed 1930 level by 1933.

Until 1934, these controls were not systematically used to alter the mix of goods produced in Germany, although this could have been done, by giving high import quotas to firms producing outputs with a high state priority. In 1934, another exchange crisis arose out of German efforts to rearm. "While most public works could be realized through the use of domestic resources, armament orders called for specific industrial raw materials that could be obtained only from foreign countries."[10] To offset the trade deficit resulting from armament import needs,

Germany declared a moratorium on payment of foreign-held debts in June 1934. Then, in September, it announced a "New Plan," which sought to harness foreign trade and payments to the pursuit of Nazi goals. The New Plan set import quotas that were high for inputs into armaments and heavy industry and low or negligible for consumer goods or inputs into production of consumer goods. Each branch of industry was placed under a supervisory board which reported, in turn, to the Ministry of Economics. In some cases the government also compelled German companies to buy minimum percentages of their inputs from domestic sources. The New Plan also used export subsidies, bilateral clearing and barter arrangements— such as are common to modern command economies—and selective depreciation of the large debt owed by Germany and Germans to foreigners.

Barter meant exchanging specific German exports—usually goods with a low domestic priority—directly for high-priority imports, without compensating flows of money in either direction. Bilateral clearing agreements, each signed between Germany and another country, were a more complex form of barter. Once again, trade took place without causing a flow of funds across international frontiers. Two countries—Germany and a trading partner—would agree to buy the same values from each other over the course of a year. If the agreement held, German importers would pay marks to a clearing office in Berlin, which would use the proceeds to pay German exporters to the country in question. The same would happen in the other nation.

Economists say that the disadvantage of bilateral barter and clearing arrangements is that they do not allow participating countries to realize all their potential gains from trade, because they do not allow each country to fully specialize according to comparative advantage. With such specialization, trade might not balance between any two nations, even when it balanced between each country and the rest of the world. But in the 1930s, specialization by comparative advantage was nearly impossible, and it did not suit Germany's political goals, which stressed reducing vulnerability to blockade in the event of war. Following the Great Depression, the world monetary system broke down, as each country joined the rush to export its own unemployment and "beggar her neighbors," by erecting barriers to imports and subsidizing exports. As part of the latter effort, most countries devalued their currencies—some more than once—to make their exports cheaper on world markets. Germany did not devalue explicitly, for reasons to be explained. Instead, it used the chaotic conditions to further Nazi goals.

In particular, the six nations of southeastern Europe—Hungary, Bulgaria, Greece, Austria, Yugoslavia, and Romania—were finding it nearly impossible to trade with England or France. The southeastern countries had incurred debts in connection with World War I reparations or postwar reconstruction, which they could not continue to pay, once the Great Depression was underway. When they tried to trade with France or England, some of their payments for imports were arbitrarily assigned to debt service. Consequently, they turned to Germany as the main market for their export surpluses, and the Nazis took the opportunity to tie these countries closer to Germany, both politically and economically.

In part, this was done by overissuing export licenses to German firms. Thus, if Germany had agreed to import and export 100 million marks' worth of goods from Hungary, it would deliberately issue 110 million marks' worth of licenses. This forced Hungary to buy more German goods than had been agreed to—in order to balance trade between the two—or else to effectively lend money to Germany on generous terms. Consequently, Germany was able to expand its imports of essential goods, whereas exports were limited to a list of goods considered "nonessential" by the government.[11] Most western countries refused to make bilateral agreements with Germany, forcing the Nazis to subsidize exports to western markets with the proceeds of a secret domestic sales tax enacted in June 1935. Subsidies allowed German exporters to cut their prices by up to 35 percent, and over half of all exports were subsidized in this way. Private cartels set export prices high enough to yield good profits, once subsidies were taken into account; acceptance of these prices became a condition for receiving the subsidies.

A country devalues by reducing the value of its currency in terms of other currencies or of gold. (An example would be Britain lowering the value of the pound from $2.00 to $1.50 U.S.) It is also possible to devalue implicitly by raising barriers to imports and subsidizing exports, and this was the route chosen by Germany. The advantage of implicit devaluation is that a country can effectively devalue its currency by more for some purposes than for others. It can price-discriminate against its weaker trading partners or else use trade to further economic domination, as was the case for Germany vis-à-vis the countries of southeastern Europe.

However, the main targets of Nazi price discrimination were foreign holders of German debt. After the foreign debt moratorium of June 1934, German citizens and companies owing money to foreigners had to pay the principal and interest on these loans into blocked accounts at a special government bank. Generally, the full sum borrowed had to be repaid in marks. The Nazis would have preferred to expropriate all repayments and use the money for their own purposes (largely rearmament). However, such a drastic move would have brought retaliation by countries owing money to Germany (who would have refused to pay) and, perhaps, even an economic blockade, for which it was not yet ready.

Consequently, when a foreigner applied to withdraw funds from the blocked accounts, he was paid, not in money, but in coupons or "scrips." These scrips had a face value in marks equal to the sum withdrawn, but they could only be spent in Germany for goods on a restricted list prepared by the government. These goods were overpriced in terms of the face value of the scrip. Before long, a market arose outside Germany, on which importers and prospective visitors to Germany bought the scrip from Germany's creditors. Because of its limited use and deflated buying power, the exchange value of the scrip fell below its face value. When Germany exporters presented the scrip to the Reichsbank for redemption, the latter deducted an amount (usually 30 percent) from its face value as the government's share of debt depreciation.

Over 1933–39, the Reich treasury profited from this operation by at least 5 billion marks—the difference between the value of principal and interest paid into the blocked accounts and the value of scrips redeemed to German exporters—even as the total value of Germany's foreign debt was being cut in half.[12]

The effort to remold German foreign trade into the handmaiden of rearmament was successful. Over 1933–38, total imports did not rise much in real terms, while imports of food and textiles declined. However, raw materials imports rose, especially for basic inputs used by the armaments industry. Germany's trade was also reoriented, away from traditional partners in Western Europe and North America and toward South America, the Balkans, and the Middle East. The share of these areas approximately doubled, partly for political reasons and partly because bilateral clearing agreements could be used there.

A second handmaiden of the rearmament effort was the drive to reach self-sufficiency. Here, the main goal was to produce synthetically from domestic resources key materials that would not be available in the event of war and naval blockade, including efforts to raise the outputs of key foodstuffs and to reduce reliance on food imports. The Reich also tried to make better use of other domestic resources, such as low-grade iron ore. Thus, the Nazis began crash programs to produce gasoline from coal and to turn out synthetic rubber, dyestuffs, wool, silk, rayon, and acetate. Many of these activities were not close to being cost effective, including the famous hydrogenation processes for making synthetic gasoline. The Third Reich built twelve hydrogenation plants over 1936–43, which produced about 4 million tons of synthetic oil and gas from coal in 1943–44, the peak period of operation. (Later, this would be less than two days' U.S. consumption during peacetime.)

The Nazis also introduced more comprehensive planning into agriculture. Virtually every producer connected with the food chain, from farmers and their suppliers, to food processors, wholesalers, retailers, etc., were organized into an all-embracing national cartel, The Reich Food Estate, under the Minister of Food and Agriculture. Farmers and food processors received input and output targets designed to raise production, as well as to make them rely more heavily on domestic inputs than cost considerations alone would have dictated. The Food Estate tried to set all prices and profit margins. Although there was some rationing of key foodstuffs, farmers generally received better prices, backed by stronger protection from import competition, than under the Weimar Régime.

In finance, the state soon dominated credit markets, thanks to control over the banking system bequeathed by the Weimar Republic and to the wizardry of Schacht. During the 1931 banking crisis, Weimar had barred local governments from selling bonds, and this ban was later extended to mortgage bonds. Its intent was to forestall possible default and contain the banking crisis. In 1933–34, the Nazis expanded these controls. All new issues of stocks and bonds had to be approved by special supervisory boards, which often refused offerings despite the initially high unemployment. The number of securities markets was greatly reduced, and those remaining came under close government scrutiny.

These measures reduced the demand for loanable funds, putting downward pressure on interest rates, which the government tried to intensify as a means of helping small businessmen and farmers who were key Nazi supporters. (Breaking the bonds of "interest slavery" had been a Nazi campaign slogan.) The Weimar régime had set a precedent for such pressure. In December 1931, rates on all outstanding loans were set at a maximum of 6 percent, meaning that borrowers had to pay no more than this, regardless of what the loan contract said. Subsequently, farm mortgage rates were forced down to 4 percent, requiring government subsidies to keep some credit institutions out of bankruptcy. Then, in 1933, Hitler reduced by decree both interest rates and the principals to be repaid on some outstanding loans to farmers and municipal governments. In most cases, the state paid subsidies to ease the blow on creditors, although this was not done if the latter were Jewish or considered unfriendly to the régime. In 1935, an interest ceiling of 4.5 percent was put on all long-term loans, except for industrial bonds issued by manufacturing corporations. Subsequently, interest ceilings were applied to most other types of loans.[13]

This allowed the Reich to enter both the demand and the supply side of the loanable funds market. Over 1933–34, more than 60 percent of all new issues of stocks and bonds were by private firms. Over 1935–38, only 12 percent were private, because of government restrictions, while 88 percent were public. By 1938, new government bond issues were one hundred times as great as during the low year of 1933 and 4.7 times as great as in 1935, when rearmament had already begun. Such a huge demand for loanable funds would normally have put tremendous pressure on the 4.5 percent interest ceiling, despite the forced reduction of private and municipal demand. To alleviate this pressure, the Reich placed a ceiling on dividends, giving firms more retained earnings to invest and to buy government bonds with. Undistributed profits soared to nearly twenty times their low 1933 level by 1938. Moreover, since the most profitable firms tended to be those supporting the military effort, this is where most of the increased investment out of retained earnings took place.

Still, the Reich's appetite for loanable funds was so insatiable that it was ultimately forced to create much of the money that it borrowed. Its ability to do this was crucial to rearmament and recovery from the Great Depression, but the operation had to be disguised, since rapid expansion of the money supply would otherwise have evoked images of 1923 and undermined confidence in both the currency and the régime. To this end, a new enterprise called the Metallurgical Research (or "Mefo") Company came into being. It was founded by the Reichsbank, the Defense Ministry, and four armaments producers, notably Krupp—not to do metallurgical research, but to serve as a front, disguising effective creation of new money.

When state procurement agencies bought arms, they often paid suppliers with short-term government bonds called "mefo-bills." These had a six-month maturity, renewable for up to five years. Once endorsed by the Mefo Company, they were guaranteed by the government and readily accepted by the Reichsbank as collateral for short-term loans to banks. They could also be used as part of the reserve necessary to meet banks' liquidity requirements. Both savings and commercial banks had to invest a portion of their deposits in mefo-bills or similar short-term bonds, but most banks accepted these bills willingly. Thus, they were soon circulating as money. When deposited with the banking system, they became reserve backing for new demand deposits or else were exchanged with the Reichsbank for currency. Either way, they ultimately resulted in new money, and the money supply rose by a third between 1933 and 1938. Over 1933–39, they also helped to raise the domestic debt of the central government from 12 to 43 billion marks.

To absorb some of the currency being exchanged by the Reichsbank for mefo-bills, the central bank offered to sell other short-term bonds—sola bills or promissory notes—to banks only, at prices that gave them relatively attractive yields. Sales of these bonds recovered 6 billion marks for the treasury, or about half the 12 billion marks paid out for mefo-bills that were returned to the Reichsbank. Ultimately, that is to say, many of the mefo-bills were replaced by sola bills. However, many mefo-bills were also replaced by money or were not replaced and continued to circulate as money.

By World War II, banks, firms, and individuals had gorged themselves on government scrip and bonds yielding, at most, 4.5 percent. During the war, they would swallow or be forced to swallow a good deal more. Yet, demand plus savings deposits rose by 18 billion marks over 1933–38, and the overflow of funds into the stock market, where new issues were sharply curtailed, was so great that stock prices had to be fixed by decree in 1942. The economy had, by then, a huge monetary overhang that would normally have taken it on an inflationary binge. That the régime could prevent this right up to its collapse was due in part to its success in enforcing price controls, in selling bonds, in raising taxes, in suppressing dividends, in providing tax abatements for funds invested in projects favored by the régime, and in maintaining ceilings on wages. The latter concentrated excess liquidity in the hands of banks, firms, and the upper half of the income distribution, who were sometimes frustrated in finding ways to spend their wealth. Black market trading could be severely punished, however, even by death, and since Nazi rearmament enriched these people they tended to go along.[14]

The final pillar of Hitler's mobilization was the organization of industry. As we have seen, the Nazis extended and strengthened the cartel system. Cartels that had been voluntary now became compulsory for all firms in a given industry and region, and the state extended its enforcement of minimum cartel-set prices, along with its prohibition of competition from firms who were not cartel members. During the first four years of Nazi rule, 1,600 new cartel agreements were signed and 120 compulsory cartels were formed.

The middle and lower-middle classes, including many small farmers, were originally the backbone of the Nazi party—at the polls, in the streets, and in their grassroots organizations. These people had lost heavily, first during the hyperinflation and later during the Great Depression. They felt they had not shared commensurately with big business and labor in the 1924–29 prosperity. They were embittered against labor unions for inflicting what they considered to be high labor costs and social insurance charges on them, against big business for profiteering during the inflation and for taking markets away from small business during the depression (due to the lower costs and better access to finance of the former), and against the Allied victors for the harsh peace of World War I. Thus, the Nazis depicted the Versailles Treaty as the main cause of Germany's woes and the Weimar government as the tool of the victors. Besides nationalization of big business, they promised profit sharing, suppression of labor unions, a house for every family, and glorification of the peasantry, plus restoration of Germany's national pride. Finally, they promised to "break the bonds of interest slavery," using this to justify much of the financial scheme outlined above, along with persecution and robbery of the Jews.

While the Nazis did suppress labor unions, "break the bonds of interest slavery," and glorify the peasantry, they carried out other promises only for a time. Small businessmen, farmers, and white-collar workers were numerous and, thus, necessary in the voting booth, at rallies, and in building party strength. But military might required the support of big business, and there was always risk of an alliance between big business and the military against the Nazis. (Moreover, to mobilize agriculture for greater self sufficiency in food, the Nazis had to rely on the larger, more efficient farms and especially on the Prussian landed aristocracy or Junkers.) Many small businessmen, artisans, and farmers wanted an organization for each industry and region that was a kind of cross between a medieval guild and a union of employers and workers, modeled on fascist unions in Mussolini's Italy.[15] The small firms of any given industry and region would be united in a guild or group, whose membership would include managers, as well as white- and blue-collar employees. Large enterprises and cartels were to be kept out, or admitted only with provision for small business control. The government was also supposed to protect small firms from "excessive" competition by large enterprises, and the guilds were to have power to control prices and entry of new competitors, as well as vocational training. Wages were to be kept low.

The Nazi economy was partitioned by branch of industry into groups and sub-groups, but in practice, the group structure was blended into the cartel structure. The cartels grew stronger and were dominated by big business. Theoretically, a wage and price freeze prevailed, beginning in 1936. In fact, prices were allowed to rise; there was better enforcement of minimum prices set by cartels. Workers received labor books into which were entered all pertinent facts about their present and past employment. Individuals were increasingly unable to move from job to job without permission and could be assigned to tasks deemed crucial to the war effort.[16]

C. The War Economy

Despite the military buildup, the average German consumer appears to have been better off in 1938 than in 1932, although income inequality also rose. The 1938 standard even compares with the peak of predepression prosperity. During the early war years, Germany was sometimes represented as straining under the war effort, with its arms-production capability near its peak. Instead, it was operating with substantial reserves. This explains why Germany could achieve a production "miracle" under Albert Speer, who brought armaments output in 1943 to over 2.25 times its 1941 level. (Thereafter, Allied bombing caused it to decline.) This required only a 5–10 percent drop in consumer-goods output, thanks to more efficient and intensive utilization of available resources.

It was the planning genius of Fritz Todt and the organizational genius of Albert Speer, the successive Ministers of Armaments and Munitions, that finally transformed the German economy into one mobilized for all-out war. But such a transformation did not come until the first half of 1942, when the war had already been going on for over two and a half years. Supplies of most key materials then came under control of Speer's ministry, which rationed them according to priorities handed down in broad outline from above, but worked out in detail by Speer and his associates with representatives of the military and industries concerned. Speer's ministry also received the power to decide how production capacity was to be utilized. He succeeded in reducing duplication of effort and crisscrossing jurisdictions and was able to rationalize and to standardize production to a much greater degree.

One economic historian (A. S. Milward) argues that Germany had a *blitzkrieg* war economy from 1939 to mid-1942, to go with its famous blitzkrieg military tactics that brought spectacular success in Poland, France, and the early Soviet campaigns. Blitzkrieg means "lightning-war," or a combined attack by infantry, artillery, air, and motorized forces to deliver a quick knockout blow against the enemy from a position of strength. Thus, the term conjures up surprise, flexibility, daring, even bluff, but not necessarily all-out mobilization or in-depth preparation. Roughly the same is true of "blitzkrieg economy." Prior to 1942, organization of the German war economy was largely ineffective. However, because the central government was based to a large extent on personal loyalty to Hitler, his Führer-commands could cut quickly through the red tape to concentrate resources on achieving a target, provided the required commitment was not too great. According to Milward:

> [The Führer-commands called forth] no far-reaching changes in the economy, only changes of emphasis from one section of armaments production to another, to suit the needs of each particular [military] campaign. Many economic crises arose, but . . . the presence of reserves of manpower, floorspace, machines, and raw materials meant that economic factors did not impose limits on military, naval or air strategy. . . . There is no doubt that agencies responsible for war production wasted much time and paper competing with each other. But the flexibility of the [administrative] machinery to some degree compensated for this, and the large safety margin . . . permitted quick transfers of men and materials to eliminate any bottlenecks.[17]

Not every historian agrees with Milward. Although Hitler provoked World War II in Europe, his long-term plans for converting the economy foresaw a major war no sooner than 1943. In addition, this conversion was incompetently managed over 1938–42 by Göhring and, ultimately, by Hitler himself. Thus, the apparent blitz-kreig economy may really have been an *ad hoc* response to an unforeseen crisis, which worked during the early campaigns, but failed before the resistance of Britain and the Soviet Union. Many Germans were not devoted to Hitler's goals. Local Nazi officials were often reluctant to impose sacrifices, and the people were reluctant to accept them unless they were clearly necessary. The same officials were jealous of their power and resisted efforts by higher level authorities to move workers, machinery, and materials or to directly control production within their jurisdictions. Before Germany could be efficiently mobilized for total war, a drastic change in military fortunes was necessary. This came in December 1941, when the Red Army stopped the Germans at the gates of Moscow and launched successful counterattacks, retaking Rostov-on-Don in the South. As it turned out, this was also the beginning of the end, although few Nazis were then prepared to contemplate such a possibility.

18-3. War Aftermath, Currency Reform, and the Start of the Economic Miracle

A. The End of the Third Reich

The destruction of Germany, first by air and then by land and air over 1943–45, is unimaginable. Over one billion tons of Allied bombs rained down on it between May 1943 and May 1945, destroying 20 percent of all homes (only half escaped some sort of war damage), killing over two million people and maiming several hundred thousand, and putting about 30 percent of all industrial capacity out of operation. The cities of Germany came to resemble the landscape of the moon.[19] Early estimates of the cost of the war put the number of civilian and military dead at nearly 7 million, the number of maimed at 1.5 million, and the destruction of national wealth at two-thirds of the total existing in 1935. In all likelihood, the material cost of the war and its aftermath exceeded total income and output produced during the twelve years of National Socialist rule, but it is also true that the early estimates of wealth loss proved to be exaggerations.

Thus, about a third of national wealth was destroyed forever, and irretrievable damage to production capacity was only on the order of 20 percent, since much of it could eventually be reassembled and put back into operation, with the addition of a few parts. Allied strategic bombing often had little effect on Germany's capacity to wage war, but it did finally paralyze the Third Reich, largely by destroying the transport system and, in particular, by isolating the Ruhr from the rest of Germany.[19] By early 1949, despite postwar dismantling of factories by the victors and the low level of new construction over 1945–48, West German industrial capacity had recovered its 1936 level in the corresponding part of the Third Reich. During the Allied occupation, output was not held back by shortage of capacity (except in a few bottleneck sectors) as much as by shortages of raw materials, poor organization, and the devastation of transport, which remained a constraint until 1948. Yet, by 1951, production in West Germany had surpassed the highest prewar level within the same territory.

Nevertheless, Germany was the last West European nation to recover from the ravages of war. While physical and psychological exhaustion was extreme all over Europe, Germany was the only country to emerge without an indigenous government. As a political entity, it ceased to exist after her unconditional surrender on May 9, 1945. The main Allied victors—the U.S., the USSR, the U.K., and France—were agreed that all traces of National Socialism in Germany should be forever destroyed. All Germans who had participated more than nominally in Nazi party activities were barred from political office, a decree that ruled out 20 percent of the population. Because the Nazis had suppressed all political opposition, there was no alternative German government acceptable to the Allies. In addition, many Germans were reluctant to assume political responsibility when the full extent of Nazi atrocities was just becoming known, and there was German resentment at some of the policies of the victors.

The Allies therefore had to govern Germany, and an Allied Control Commission came into being for this purpose. In principle, Germany was to be governed as a single unit, and all parts were to receive uniform treatment, although it was also to lose nearly 25 percent of its prewar territory to Poland and the Soviet Union. The country was carved into four zones—one for each of the main Allies—a move that ensured, as it turned out, its long-term division into West and East German states. The Allies also agreed to exact $20 billion in reparations, of which the Soviet share would be half, since the Soviets had suffered most from Nazi aggression. Reparations were to be paid in kind, largely by dismantling German factories and railroads, by diverting part of German output to the homelands of the victors, and by using German conscript labor in Allied countries. These had been the policies adopted by the Nazis in their occupied territories, and they harmonized with the Allied goal of destroying the German war machine, while preventing another evasion of reparations. However, the will to extract payment varied directly with the extent of suffering at German hands, being greatest for the Soviets and least for the Americans.

Thus, while eastern Germany had suffered much less war damage than the west, the USSR dismantled nearly half of industrial capacity in its zone, whereas just 8 percent of capacity was dismantled in western zones. These factories proved to be far less productive outside Germany than they would have been as part of a program of German reconstruction. (In this sense, the cost of dismantling to Germany was several times the victors' gain from the program.) Consequently, both the USSR and France soon shifted their emphasis toward taking raw materials and current output from Germany. As late as 1947, moreover, up to 5 million German prisoners of war were still doing forced labor in Allied countries (out of an original 12 million at war's end), including over 3.5 million in the USSR.

Nevertheless, by late 1946, it was clear that Western Europe could not rebuild and grow without German participation. Germany had traditionally been a major supplier of coal and key industrial goods, and a major market as well, something overlooked by those who advocated keeping Germany permanently poor. By early 1947, the Marshall Plan was already a gleam in the eyes of U.S. leaders, and by February, the Hoover mission to Germany and Austria had enquired into ways of reviving German industry. Thus, the emphasis was shifting from dismantling to rebuilding. Between mid-1945 and mid-1948, net investment in the western zones was negative. Over the following year and a half, total net investment was at least three times the value of assets lost through dismantling.

B. Breakdown of the Economy

The early postwar years in both West and East Germany saw poverty, famine, and even starvation. The problems were that exchange broke down within what had been prewar Germany, and that the shrunken state (all four zones of occupation) became the destination of 12 million refugees—ethnic Germans expelled from Czechoslovakia, Poland, the USSR, and other lands annexed or occupied by Hitler. By end-1949, one West German in every five was a refugee. Yet, there were not enough semihabitable homes for the indigenous population, with the result that many wound up living in ruins, in railway stations, or in the streets, often paying a rent for the privilege. The miseries of famine came on top of these other woes. In August 1945, over half the babies born in Berlin died, largely from causes traceable to malnutrition. Food consumption over 1945–47 usually averaged 1,250 to 1,750 calories per day in the three western zones and in the summer of 1947 fell to no more than 900 calories among the nonfarm population vs. a normal minimum of 2,400 to 3,000 calories, depending on occupation.

Before the war as well, the eastern part of Germany—areas now in the Soviet zone or no longer part of Germany—had been its breadbasket. They were regions of substantial agricultural surplus. But now, the Soviet zone had no surpluses to export, thanks partly to the destruction and dislocation of war (including the removal of Germans for forced labor in the USSR) and to the land reform introduced there in August 1945. This broke up the large semifeudal estates operated by the Junker nobility into some 400,000 plots of twelve to twenty-one acres, which were given to refugees. More than a third of all agricultural land area was affected by the reform, including some of the most productive farms of prewar Europe. No one was permitted to use hired labor on his farm. As well, there was a shortage of fertilizer (a problem also plaguing the Western zones), and farm equipment, although generally in poor condition, could not be replaced. Food production remained at 50–60 percent of prewar normal well into 1948—it did not recover the 1934–38 average until 1957—and the Soviets responded by trying to force farmers to deliver large quantities of produce at low prices. This caused many farms to be abandoned.

The disruption of east-west intra-German trade went hand-in-hand with a breakdown in trade within the Western zones. To an extent, these were split into regional cells, each controlled by a local Allied commander. These officials often had empire-building tendencies and were reluctant to allow goods to leave their zones—an inclination reinforced by the massive disruption of the transport network. Finally, France took all exports from its zone and effectively annexed the Saar, a move ratified by plebescite in 1947. The Saar did not become part of the Federal Republic until 1955; in the meantime, most of its natural resources were unavailable to Germany.

On top of this, the currency became nearly worthless soon after Germany's military collapse. We recall that the Nazis directly and indirectly financed much of rearmament and war from the printing press. By war's end, the supply of money and near money was about five times as great as in 1938, while industrial and farm output were, respectively, one-third and 60 percent of 1938 levels.[20] The result would have been rapid inflation, had it not been for the wage and price freeze of 1936—which remained officially in effect through the collapse of the Third Reich—and the measures outlined earlier, which successfully reduced the velocity of circulation of money and built up liquidity. To prevent a rapid upsurge of prices, the Allies continued this freeze. The official cost of living index was up just 12 percent in October 1945, and 31 percent in May 1948 over 1938. But whereas the Nazis had resorted to increasingly severe penalties for violating wage and price controls, the Allies were lax in enforcement, and punishment was light. A black market mushroomed, on which prices of goods like coffee, butter, milk, eggs, and cigarettes could be up to 150 times their legal levels. One author estimates that average prices were 50 times their legal ceilings. While only 10 percent of all transactions by quantity traded went through this market, it absorbed 80 percent of all circulating money.[21]

However, there was another black market that worked far less efficiently and which absorbed perhaps half of all transactions by volume. This was largely a barter market, although American cigarettes did function as a partial medium of exchange when they were available—which wasn't often, as far as the average German was concerned. As a rule, cigarette "prices" were much closer to RM prices on the first black market than to official price ceilings. Often, there was no usable medium of exchange. Although complex barter exchanges often took place, many trades that would have been routine in normal times failed to occur—because of the need for a double coincidence of wants—or else were consummated only after one or more parties had borne high transactions costs.

This disrupted production and consumption and made shortages worse. In the cities, it was especially hard to obtain food. Farmers were in a favorable bargaining position—because the eastern zone was cut off and agricultural output in the western zones was only about two-thirds of prewar levels—while urban dwellers had trouble finding something to trade for food unless they happened to work in a suitable light industry. (Farmers were reluctant to take cash, which might be hard to dispose of, although they did trade on the first black market.) Firms producing consumer goods often paid their workers in kind—even though this was illegal—and some factories took up production of light industrial products for this purpose. For many, it was then necessary to make regular pilgrimages to the countryside:

> Grotesque conditions resulted . . . vast hordes of people trekked out to the country to barter [for] food. . . . In dilapidated railway cars from which everything pilfer-able had long since disappeared, on the roofs and on running boards, hungry people travelled, sometimes hundreds of miles at a snail's pace, to where they hoped to find something to eat. They took their wares—personal effects, old clothes, sticks of furniture, whatever bombed-out remnants they had—and came back with grain or potatoes for a week or two. Many . . . succumbed to their hardships.[22]

The only lasting remedy for these conditions was a currency reform—that is, a new money issued in small enough amounts to permit supply and demand to balance without too great an average increase in prices. The need for such a reform was obvious, but it would have political implications, since the division of Germany into East and West was not yet finalized. A new currency could not be issued for just a part of Germany unless that part was going to remain economically and, presumably, politically separate from the rest. Ideally, one new currency would be issued for the whole of Germany. But this, in turn, would require a central bank, with a monopoly on note issue, and a single banking system for the entire nation. The kind of banking system that would emerge would necessarily be different for a command than for a market economy. Here, the Soviet Union and the United States could not agree on Germany's future, and neither was willing to make significant concessions. There was also disagreement over how a currency reform should penalize or reward different socioeconomic groups.

Nevertheless, pressure on the U.S. and the U.K. to do something came from their respective taxpayers, as well as from Germans. By 1947, the occupation of Germany was costing them around $700 million per year. Moreover, the need for a general recovery in Europe had been brought to a crisis level by the winter of 1946–47, the harshest on record, which caused suffering throughout the continent, but especially in Germany. Low European living standards were making the ''Communist alternative'' more attractive, and to official U.S. eyes, raising the urgency of economic assistance. On June 5, 1947, U.S. Secretary of State George Marshall outlined what came to be known as the ''Marshall Plan,'' which would play a decisive role in launching Europe onto a path of sustained growth. Germany was included in the program, but this meant that a stable currency would have to establish itself, at least in the Western zones.[23]

Therefore, a currency reform was announced for June 1948, and political union between the three Western zones took place the same month. This was the economic formation of West Germany. To keep their zone from being flooded with the new West German money, the Soviets launched their own currency reform in East Germany. On the political level, they responded with the Berlin blockade, the "official" start of the cold war. In October 1949 they established the German Democratic Republic, in response to the formal founding of the Federal Republic earlier that year.

C. Currency Reform and Regeneration

The currency reform triggered a period of uninterrupted growth that would last for eighteen years and then resume for another six, after a year's pause. Thus, the reform is said to have launched an "economic miracle" and was a minor miracle in and of itself. The index of industrial production, which had been 29 percent of the 1938 level in 1946, 33 percent in 1947, and 47 percent in June 1948, rose to 67 percent in December of that year—a net gain of over 40 percent in six months. The reform took place on June 20. On June 21, "goods reappeared in the stores, money resumed its normal function, black and grey markets reverted to a minor role, foraging trips to the country ceased, labor productivity rose, and output took off on its great upward surge. The spirit of the country changed overnight."[24]

The mechanics of the reform were basically as follows. A new currency, the deutsche mark (DM), was introduced and exchanged for the old Reichsmark. On average, West Germans received just over 6.5 DM for every 100 RM that they held. Thus, the money supply fell to slightly more than 6.5 percent of its original volume—a more realistic ratio between money and goods—and at the outset, official RM prices were simply requoted in DM. Not every 100 RM was worth 6.5 DM, however. Each person had the right to exchange up to 60 of his or her RM, a sum that nearly everyone had, for 60 DM. Forty DM were handed out on the day of the reform, together with the regular ration allotment, and the remaining 20 DM two months later. All additional RM, except for small coins, had to be placed in bank accounts. Small coins continued to circulate, at 10 percent of original value, and were gradually replaced. Originally, bank accounts were to be exchanged ten-for-one, but, in fact, 35 percent of their value was liquidated, and the rest exchanged ten-for-one. Thus, for each 100 RM in the hands of private individuals beyond the first 60, about 6.5 DM were issued. Accounts of private firms received similar treatment, and businesses got, in addition, 60 DM per employee on a ten-for-one basis.

All debts were reduced to 10 percent of their original amounts, except for the internal debt of the Third Reich, which was cancelled altogether. Where this debt was in the hands of banks and insurance companies, however, something had to be done to ensure their solvency. These institutions therefore received low-interest, illiquid bonds, issued as debts of the land governments. Public authorities also received initial quotas of deutsche marks. In all, just 10 billion DM were issued, to give the public confidence in the new money.

The Allies also intensified measures to promote competition by breaking up cartels and other concentrations of economic power. (Previously, these measures had been part of the program to destroy Germany's war potential and to reduce its industrial might; now, they were represented as crucial to rebuilding Germany as a democratic, free-enterprise society.) The income tax, which had been raised to confiscatory levels in 1946, was lowered in 1948 and again in 1950. All prices, rents, and wages were initially set at their legal RM ceilings, meaning that wage, rental, and profit income was effectively exchanged at a rate of 1 RM = 1 DM. In November 1948, the wage freeze was abolished, after more than twelve years, and free collective bargaining was restored.

Clearly, many legal ceiling prices would not balance supply and demand after the reform. Some could be expected to rise and some to fall, but labor unionists and Social Democrats feared that, on the whole, prices would rise and wages would fall, owing to an excess labor supply, which was fed by a continuing inflow of refugees. There was sentiment for retaining most controls, not only among Germans, but also within the Allies, who still ran the price control boards. But the western zones of Germany were represented by Ludwig Erhard, a believer in the neoliberal philosophy of Walter Eucken and thus fundamentally opposed to controls. He also noted that, by removing price controls and ration quotas, he could greatly reduce the opportunity for Allied interference in the German economy.

When Erhard proposed to the American General Clay that rationing and price controls be removed from all goods except "essentials"—housing, bread, milk, meat, electricity, coal, iron, and steel—Clay reportedly replied, "My advisors tell me they are much opposed to this." "Never mind, general," said Erhard, "mine are telling me the same thing." With the economic advisors in rare agreement, the economic miracle was launched by doing the opposite of what they recommended. In fact, prices tended to decline, on balance, in the years following the reform. It was 1955 before the official cost of living index rose permanently above the level prevailing in June 1948. By this time, hourly wages were over 80 percent higher. Since the average industrial work week expanded from forty to forty-nine hours during the same period, weekly take-home pay was on the order of 2.2 times the 1948 level.

Over 1948–58, real consumption per head grew by more than 6 percent per year. National income and output rose even faster, as Marshall Plan aid flowed in, as industrial bottlenecks were alleviated, as the housing shortage was reduced, and as a better allocation of labor between industries and regions was realized—thanks partly to smaller housing shortages. After years of poverty, the will to earn was strong, and overtime earnings bore virtually no income tax. Since unemployment was fairly high, this aspect of taxation benefitted workers with good seniority or strong union backing, at the expense of refugees and others with relatively small bargaining power, who bore the brunt of unemployment. There were also technological gains, as destroyed or dismantled plants were replaced by the latest equipment, and as initiative and ingenuity went back to work. Profits were good after the reform, and they improved over the next several years, partly because of special tax exemptions. Thus, the incentive to invest was also strong, and West Germany's investment share of GNP over 1950–57 was one of the highest in the Western world.

Not all price controls were removed. In particular, most rent ceilings did not come off until the 1960s. Controls on many dwellings remain to this day, and housing is still one of Germany's most regulated industries. However, the 1963 Housing Assistance Law replaced some ceilings with subsidies for tenants and owner-occupiers whose housing costs were considered excessive, relative to income. To have allowed food and housing costs to soar, in the early days of the Federal Republic, would have been to force many people to continue to live in ruins or on poor diets—although these conditions were inflicted for a time on many of West Germany's 12 million refugees, who had the poorest access to housing. It would also have made labor unions bargain harder for higher wages. Thus, decontrol of some sectors was gradual. As a rule, remaining price ceilings were lifted as it became probable that resulting increases would not be excessive. The excess demand for housing was estimated as a function of the number of households in a given area divided by the number of dwellings. When this ratio fell below 103 percent, rent control was lifted.

In addition, the deutsche mark did not become a convertible currency until 1958. At first, foreign currencies were rationed among would-be users, and goods could not be imported without licenses, which were given more freely to firms in basic heavy and export industries than to other firms. Stringent controls also existed on the movement of currency out of the country. West Germany had bilateral clearing agreements with most of its trading partners, although those with other European countries were replaced in 1950 by the European Payments Union, a multilateral clearing-house which Germany joined and promptly became indebted to. In 1949, imports were nearly double exports, with foreign aid making up most of the difference. Thus, the DM had to be devalued from 3.3 to the dollar—a rate set by the Allies—to 4.2. The West German balance of payments was in various stages of crisis until about mid-1951, when it finally made a decisive turn into surplus, aided by a demand stimulus resulting from the Korean War. The Federal Republic also owed a large foreign debt, mostly from the Nazi era. Because of the balance-of-payments crisis, this debt was at first held in blocked accounts. Gradually, however, all controls in the area of foreign trade and payments were removed, along with most of those on the domestic economy.

The currency reform and the associated freeing of markets removed the major obstacles to recovery and long-run growth in West Germany. These were immensely beneficial moves, and some observers now view Germany's removal of controls as a potential model for reforms of Soviet-type economies. In both cases (Germany in 1948, the socialist countries in 1980), there was considerable excess demand for goods and services prior to reform, including a large pent-up demand. Although the currency reform deflated demand in Germany, enough purchasing power remained to launch the period of rapid economic growth. In addition, West Germany had surplus labor in 1948 and received a further influx of refugees over the next thirteen years. Soviet-type economies also have labor surpluses, in the form of underemployed workers. The major difference between the two cases is that the incentives to expand production in a cost-effective manner and in response to demand signals were strong in West Germany. The difficulties of reproducing these incentives in socialist economies (owing to unwanted distribution effects and to other problems outlined in section 5-1) have so far limited the success of reforms there.

As the West German reform was anticipated, there was considerable hoarding of goods, including food, in advance. If we look at prices on legitimate markets, savings embodied in goods rather than money were exchanged approximately one-for-one. Over the year following the reform, DM prices were about the same, on the average, as legal price ceilings in RM had been. However, prior to the reform, it was possible at some cost to sell goods at prices many times their RM ceilings on black or barter markets. The fact that businessmen and farmers preferred to hoard in anticipation of the reform meant that costs of transacting on black markets were usually so high as to make selling there not worth the higher prices obtainable. By eliminating excessive transaction costs, the reform benefitted hoarders, but also those who eventually bought their goods. Everyone shared to some extent in the gains from trade, and with normal channels restored, plus a usable medium of exchange, businessmen could count on regular flows of supplies and predictable levels of demand. Thus, their time horizons expanded.

Still, the reform imposed burdens—since many savings were wiped out—which fell unequally on different segments of the population. The reform worked against refugees and others with little bargaining power, against those who held bonds of the Third Reich—by no means all of whom were relatively well-to-do—against those whose savings were in the form of money, and against net debtors, unless their debts were backed by equities or tangible assets. It also worked against pensioners and other inactive persons, although they did benefit to some degree from the existing social insurance system inherited from the Weimar Republic.

Another apparent consequence of the reform was rising unemployment, although this may have been an illusion. Before the reform, there was continual excess demand for goods, owing to the vast overhang of money and near money, which was in excess supply. Many employers had more Reichsmarks than they could spend or wanted to save. Thus, they were willing to hire more than the profit-maximizing amounts of labor. Indeed, to have a job was a requirement for obtaining a ration card, and, thus, for survival. Many people listed as employed were really without work, but able to find an employer who would certify them as his employees. After the reform removed both the excess supply of money and the excess demand for goods—and given the continuing influx of refugees—official unemployment grew, from 3.2 percent of the labor force in June 1948 to 5.3 percent in December, to a 7.7 percent average in 1949, and to 8.7 percent in 1950, before declining. But this is statistical illusion, owing to the 30 percent or more of the labor force listed as employed before June 1948 but really without work.

Finally, there was the question of unequal distribution of war burdens. While many Germans had lost their assets as a result of the war, many others had gotten off comparatively lightly. Provided its beneficiaries were not Nazi collaborators or war criminals, sentiment was strong for a tax on property owners to compensate victims who had been left property-less by the war. Many Germans, with a variety of political views, wanted such an "equalization of war burdens" tax to be combined with the currency reform. However, negotiation of such a combination among the Allies would have delayed and complicated the reform. The United States, in particular, insisted that redistribution be carried out by the Germans themselves after they had formed a government. Thus, the currency reform was divorced from the Equalization of Burdens Law, which did not pass in definitive form until 1952, and even then fell far short of the goal implied by its title. But by the same token, postwar prosperity far surpassed anyone's expectations in early 1948, and its benefits were widely shared.

D. The Start of the Economic Miracle

Once the currency reform removed the major roadblock, many factors contributed to West Germany's recovery and long postwar expansion. Aid from the United States and other Western nations—and their assumption of most of the Federal Republic's defense burden—augmented its savings and freed them for productive investment in industry. By 1952, the DM was probably an undervalued currency, and it remained undervalued over most of the 1950s and 1960s. The 1953 London Debt Agreements helped, by fixing West Germany's total foreign debt at 14 billion DM—a sum well within its ability to pay—which mildly stimulated the economy without troubling the balance of payments. (In addition, the Federal Republic agreed to pay Israel 3.45 billion DM, as compensation for Jews driven out of Europe by the Nazis.)

The refugees, who at first appeared to be an unsolvable problem, became an economic windfall once growth was underway. Many of them had valuable skills, and most were prepared to work for low wages. This made it possible for production to expand rapidly all through the 1950s without any increase in wage costs (once productivity gains were taken into account). To reduce union pressure on wages and to establish confidence in the new government, it was also necessary to have a tight monetary policy. This kept down domestic prices and motivated German entrepreneurs to seek export markets for their goods, which they established in this era and never lost. Much has been made of German capacity for hard work, thrift, and ingenuity, which could come into play, once people were able to foresee rewards for their efforts, in the form of higher living standards.

For West Germany's leaders, it was equally important to gain for their country a place of status and dignity among the nations of the world. A chance to begin the road back came in the form of an opportunity to join the International Ruhr Authority—an agency to regulate the production and distribution of Ruhr coal, coke, and steel—which came into being in April 1949. As the Ruhr lay wholly within West Germany, the fact that it was only one signatory among seven nations to this treaty was viewed by some Germans as a humiliation. However, West Germany had previously had no say in the use of Ruhr resources, and its Chancellor, Konrad Adenauer, realized that German participation in the Authority would constitute a crucial step forward in international acceptability.

The Ruhr Authority gave way in 1952 to the European Coal and Steel Community (ECSC). The ECSC established free trade in coal and steel products among its member countries—France, Belgium, Luxembourg, Italy, the Netherlands, and West Germany—along with an international authority to coordinate production of coal and steel. By virtue of its leading position as a coal and steel producer, West Germany was able to join ECSC as an equal partner, which meant that the other member nations submitted their industries to the same international coordination and control as West Germany had been doing. Moreover, ECSC turned out to be the forerunner of the European Economic Community (EEC), in which the Federal Republic became a charter member. Another factor in postwar prosperity has been codetermination, whose legal foundation was set out in laws passed in 1951 and 1952, and which fundamentally remolded German labor relations, as described in section 17-4. The 1951 law was a major political victory for the union movement and also removed a strike threat in the bottleneck sectors that could have delayed launching of the economic miracle.

A final factor in West Germany's recovery and prolonged expansion was that it made good use of what investment funds were available, concentrating its resources in bottleneck sectors so that the additional output created by each DM invested would be high. This, in turn, was made possible by selective incentives. The Allies refused to allow West German officials to lower overall tax rates as much as the latter wanted to at the time of the currency reform, but did agree to a variety of special concessions. High overall rates were maintained for the next few years by the Minister of Finance, Fritz Schäffer, whose main goal was to balance the budget. However, a number of tax loopholes and other special exemptions were fashioned in the Economics Ministry under Erhard, which were designed to raise investment. Speaking generally, the tax laws favored saving and investment over current consumption, and reinvestment of profits, as opposed to paying them out as dividends.

Monetary policy was restrictive, since it was charged with preserving the value of the currency, although the money supply did grow fast enough to help fuel the expansion. Capital markets continued to be suppressed by interest rate ceilings. We have seen how these markets were taken over by the Third Reich, and they all but disappeared with Hitler's demise. After the currency reform, the government's urgent priority for housing limited their revival. An interest rate ceiling was put on mortgage bonds to keep the cost of mortgages down to a level commensurate with rents, which were controlled. Consequently, an interest ceiling also had to be placed on industrial bonds to keep them from becoming too attractive to buyers, relative to mortgage bonds.[25] The upshot was that firms could not sell their bonds. Less than 7 percent of total gross investment, over 1950-53, was financed through capital markets, and a slightly smaller share came from long-term bank loans. Another 25 percent came from public budgets and special public funds, such as the ERP Special Fund, formed with the Marshall Plan endowment.

Most of the remaining 61 percent came from firms' own funds—retained profits plus depreciation allowances—which were especially favored by tax concessions. The biggest single stimulus was the right of business enterprises to set arbitrarily high values on their assets at the time of the currency reform. This was discouraged by high taxes on capital, but encouraged even more by the generous depreciation allowances that could then be deducted from taxable profits. In addition, accelerated depreciation could be claimed on new factories, on repairs to war damage, and on new residential property. Firms could write off small investments (less than 600 DM) in one year. Exports and, indirectly, investments to expand West Germany's export capability benefitted from rebate of the sales tax and from the right of each enterprise to deduct 3 percent of its export sales from its taxable profits.[26] Moreover, the government insured exports at low rates and, until May 1953, exporters could retain part of the foreign currency they earned from sales abroad; this did not go into the central pool from which most foreign exchange was rationed to importers.

Extra tax credit was also given for savings invested in housing and shipbuilding, and the latter played a major role in West Germany's recovery, after its merchant marine had been drastically reduced by dismantling. Loans to these industries could be entirely written off in one year from taxable income, and the same later became true for loans to the Equalization of Burdens Fund. The result of subsidies for homebuilding, which had the highest single priority during these years, was construction of about 1.4 million dwellings over 1949–52 and another 1.1 million over 1953–54. On a per capita basis, this led the world, and most of the new housing was low cost. Nevertheless, in 1950, a fourth of all West German families had no regular home; as late as 1954, 500,000 people were still living in camps. An influx of nearly 325,000 refugees per year made this problem impossible to overcome in the short term.

The German entrepreneurial drive was strong in the years following the currency reform, and the central bank—then the Bank Deutscher Länder—absorbed its share of risk by rediscounting (or covering) some commercial bank loans when the credit-worthiness of the ultimate borrower was questionable. In this connection, a number of stories are told. For example, one hundred technicians of the world-famous Zeiss optical works were rounded up in a British prison camp after the war. The company's plant and equipment were in the Soviet zone and therefore had to be written off. The men had no money and few personal belongings beyond the clothes they were wearing. At the suggestion of a leading banker, the Deutsche Bank agreed to lend them 120 million DM to set up a new factory with only their technical competence as collateral. The enterprise soon regained its international standing.

The Pittler Machine Tool Works had been located in Leipzig and were also confiscated by the Soviets. In June 1945, eighteen Pittler engineers and their families arrived penniless, as refugees, in the U.S. zone. At first, they received neither rations nor aid from the Americans, and were resented by the natives because of the shortages of food and housing. Gradually, however, they made themselves useful by repairing Pittler machines in the district, and they succeeded in borrowing a small sum to set up a repair shop in a local factory, where they earned the equivalent of about 25¢ U.S. per day. As their work became known, similar arrangements were made in other plants in different parts of West Germany, and contacts were established with bankers and former clients. After the currency reform, the Hesse Land government made them a loan, and the Reconstruction Loan Corporation gave them a grant. "Even before the new factory was finished in 1953, Pittler machine tools were being shown in the trade fairs of Europe, and orders were pouring in. . . . [By 1962, there were] 40,000 square meters of factory space, 17,000 employees, most from East Germany or Eastern Europe, and a turnover of 60 million DM per year."[27]

Before West Germany was permanently launched on a path of long-run expansion, it also had to survive a crisis in the "bottleneck" sectors. These were key basic industries—iron and steel, coal, electric power, railways, and other public utilities—whose production capabilities had been sharply reduced by war damage, dismantling, and the partition of Germany. Because the outputs of these industries were used directly and indirectly by virtually all others, their recovery and expansion was vital to the rest of the economy. We recall that their prices were controlled—both to limit the financial burden on direct and indirect users and to prevent their earning excess profits—and quota systems were used to allocate their outputs. The government also subsidized these industries in an effort to eliminate the shortages. When investments made with the help of Marshall Plan funds proved inadequate to this task—especially after the Korean War demand explosion—the federal government passed the Investment Assistance Act of 1952.

This law forced firms that were the largest users of bottleneck sector outputs to contribute to a fund of 1 billion DM, which was collected like a tax and lent on attractive terms to bottleneck sector producers for expansion. The resulting capacity increases prevented prices from rising unduly when price ceilings were removed (which might have discouraged expansion in other sectors), and in particular, allowed exports to grow rapidly. Although it was not then evident, West Germany had turned the corner by end-1951. The immediate problems were resolved, and a long-run path was charted toward eliminating the more intractable shortages of homes and jobs. As this became apparent through the early and mid-1950s, the support and respect of the West German people for their government and leaders grew. In retrospect, Allied occupation authorities made many mistakes and often operated on an *ad hoc* basis, without a master plan for Germany's future, in contrast to the Soviet Union. But the Allies also took several hard political decisions, notably relating to the currency reform. When West German sovereignty was restored, the new country started with a clean slate. Several prerequisites for future growth had been created, and the most reactionary political forces of previous eras (the East Prussian landed aristocracy, the military, a number of industrial barons) were either eliminated or at least temporarily discredited. These were advantages Weimar never had, and they helped to ensure that the chances for a successful German experiment with democracy would be better than ever.

Notes

1. Standard references for the material covered in this chapter include Gustav Stolper, Karl Häuser, Knut Borchardt, *The German Economy: 1870 to the Present* (New York: Harcourt, Brace, and World, 1967), chs. 3–7; and Michael Balfour, *West Germany* (New York: Praeger, 1968), chs. 2–8.

2. Several uprisings by the extreme left occurred over the early postwar period, and extremists held power in Bavaria until May 1919. The army had to put down a revolt by Berlin workers over January 5–15, 1919, and the Social Democrats, who were then in power, did not stop the murders of Communist Leaders, Rosa Luxembourg and Karl Liebknecht, by right-wing death squads. Left-wing terrorists also roamed the streets, and there was a Communist-led uprising in 1920.

3. In order to mobilize labor's support for the shift to "total war" in the fall of 1916—particularly in view of a 25 percent average real wage cut and other sacrifices that the war had already imposed on workers—the Imperial government passed the Auxiliary Service Law of December 1916, which set up works councils in firms with 50 employees or more. These were to become the vehicle for employee codetermination of working conditions and (to a minor degree) of wages and salaries with management.

The quote below comes from W. M. Blumenthal, *Codetermination in the German Steel Industry* (Princeton: Princeton University Press, 1956), p. 17.

4. See Carl-Ludwig Holtfrerich, "Internationale Verteilungsfolgen der Deutschen Inflation, 1918–1923," *Kyklos*, Fasc. 2, 1977. Regarding the discussion below, see, in particular, the articles by T. Balderston: "The Origins of Economic Instability in Germany, 1924–30: Market Forces vs. Economic Policy," *Vierteljahrschrift für Sozial und Wirtschaftsgeschichte*, Vol. 69 (1982), No. 4; and "The Beginning of the Depression in Germany, 1927–30: Investment and the Capital Market," *Economic History Review*, August 1983. Finally, see Stephen A. Schuker, *American "Reparations" to Germany, 1919–33: Implications for the Third-World Debt Crisis*, Princeton Studies in International Finance No. 61, Princeton: July 1988.

5. Balfour, *West Germany*, pp. 96–97.

6. The four-way division of power just described is outlined by Arthur Schweitzer in *Big Business in the Third Reich* (Bloomington: Indiana University Press, 1964), especially ch. 6. The "oligarchic clique" (Schweitzer's term) of the party comprised the circle around Hitler, who were willing to put power above principle, in contrast to the "intransigent" Nazis, who took a much more literal view of the party's platform. Ultimately, the intransigent Nazis were suppressed. The paragraphs below rely on Schweitzer, as well as Balfour, *West Germany*; Stolper, Häuser, and Borchardt, *The German Economy*; and Alan Milward, *The German Economy at War* (London: Athlone Press, 1965).

7. Milward, *The German Economy at War*, p. 9.

8. See Stolper, Häuser, and Borchardt, *The German Economy*, p. 151, Table 17. Part 5 of this volume plus Schweitzer, *Big Business in the Third Reich*, are the most important sources for the discussion of Nazi economic organization below.

9. Schacht writes about this period in his *Confessions of "The Old Wizard"* (Boston: Houghton, 1956).

10. Schweitzer, *Big Business in the Third Reich*, p. 437.

11. In the strict economic sense, Germany apparently did not exploit the countries with whom it had bilateral clearing agreements. That is, it apparently offered terms of trade that were better than those prevailing on world markets, although it is impossible to be sure. The offered terms were also better for Germany than producing the imported goods itself, but they represented, as well, a comparatively inexpensive means through which its trading partners were able to expand output and recover from the worst ravages of the Great Depression. The cost was greater economic dependence on Germany. See Larry Neal, "The Economics and Finance of Bilateral Clearing Agreements: Germany, 1934–38," *Economic History Review*, August 1979.

12. The total gain from depreciation of Germany's foreign debt was usually shared between the Reich, the exporting firm, and the foreign buyer of German goods. This total equalled the difference between the face value of the scrip and its exchange value outside Germany. The face value indicated the amounts paid into blocked accounts by Germans owing money abroad. The exchange value gave the amount paid by the foreign buyer for the scrip, who then bought German goods at inflated prices. When the German exporter presented the scrip to the Reichsbank for redemption, the government took its share.

13. Schweitzer, *Big Business in the Third Reich*, p. 424.

14. In addition, by spending selectively the 35 percent of national income that it controlled, the Reich could selectively reward or punish firms according to their support for Nazi policies.

15. More specifically, they wanted a form of corporatism. This is a loose concept stressing cooperation between employers and employees in organizations based on kind of occupation or place of work. An economy with worker-managed firms would qualify as corporatist, but so would economies in which workers are organized in labor unions and employers in employers' associations, as long as a framework exists within which these elements can cooperate to their mutual benefit and settle disputes "peacefully and constructively." (Both Sweden and West Germany could be described as modern corporatist states.) In Mussolini's Italy, the corporatist organizations were fascist unions of employers and workers that served in practice as instruments of state control over the economy. The same was true of the German Labor Front.

16. At first, if a worker left his job without permission, he was denied unemployment insurance. Later, the penalties became harsher and could even amount to death. Nazi party representatives, who were generally at each place of work, gained more control over hiring and firing, and dismissal became increasingly likely to occur on political grounds.

17. Milward, *The German Economy at War*, pp. 31–32. The alternative view (indicated below) is due to R. J. Overy. See his "Hitler's War and the German Economy: A Re-interpretation," *Economic History Review*, May 1982.

18. For descriptions, see Aidan Crawley, *The Rise of Western Germany, 1945–72* (London: Collins, 1973), chs. 2–4; Alfred Grosser, *Germany in Our Time: A Political History of the Postwar Years* (New York: Praeger, 1971), ch. 2; and Richard Hiscocks, *Germany Revived: An Appraisal of the Adenauer Era* (London: Gallancz, 1966), ch. 2.

19. During the war, production to meet military needs had gone on amid the rubble—in caves, in isolated areas, and underground. Industrial capacity created and brought back into production during the war exceeded the amount destroyed or temporarily knocked out.

20. See Karl Roskamp, *Capital Formation in West Germany* (Detroit: Wayne State University Press, 1965), pp. 39–40; and Nicholas Balabkins, *Germany Under Direct Controls* (New Brunswick: Rutgers University Press, 1964), p. 143. See, as well, Horst Mendershausen, *Two Postwar Recoveries of the German Economy* (Amsterdam: North-Holland, 1955), ch. II.

21. Roskamp, *Capital Formation in West Germany*, pp. 39–40. Estimates of black market prices vary from source to source, and such prices were not necessarily uniform within a given geographical area.

22. Eli Wallich, *Mainsprings of the German Economic Revival* (New Haven: Yale University Press, 1955), p. 65. When firms were caught paying their workers with goods, the Allied authorities cut legal rations, thereby forcing the workers to obtain even more of their necessities on the black market.

23. To keep matters in perspective, we note that Marshall Plan aid to West Germany came to about $1.3 billion. When all official aid to West Germany, in the form of long-term loans and nonmilitary grants, came to an end in 1955, it totalled $3.9 billion, but the Marshall Plan provided capital goods that served as a catalyst for German revival.

24. Stolper, Häuser, Borchardt, *The German Economy*, p. 71.

25. Ceilings on mortgage and industrial bond interest rates were 5 percent and 6.5 percent, respectively. The resulting black market discounted mortgage bond prices by 10 percent to 12 percent (Wallich, *Mainsprings of the German Economic Revival*, p. 185), giving an interest yield of 5.5 percent to 5.7 percent. This market might have been more active and black-market yields might have been higher, had not public investors, including social insurance funds, been willing to buy mortgage bonds with low yields, in order to help out low-cost housing.

26. There were other deductions as well, described in Wallich, *Mainsprings of the German Economic Revival*, pp. 244–251.

27. Crawley, *The Rise of Western Germany*, p. 179.

Questions for Review, Discussion, Examination

1. In what way was the Weimar Republic politically unstable? How does the Federal Republic (West Germany) seek to avoid the danger of this kind of instability?

2. What caused the Hyperinflation of 1923? Did hyperinflation result from rational economic policy on the part of the Weimar government? How did Weimar avoid much of Germany's World War I reparations burden?

3. How did the German banking system become more vulnerable during and after the Hyperinflation of 1923?

*4. The economic causes of Hitler's rise to power are rooted in the Great Depression, but also in the 1923 hyperinflation, brought about, in part, by the war debt and reparations burdens with which the Weimar government was saddled in 1919. Show how the hyperinflation, in combination with the Great Depression and the political system of the Weimar Republic, helped to create conditions favorable to Hitler's rise to power. How did the revaluation of Weimar bonds after the hyperinflation also contribute? (*Hint*: How did the hyperinflation and bond revaluation help to make the Great Depression worse in Germany?)

5. What three stages can we identify in the evolution of the German economy under Nazi control? Explain briefly. Why did the Nazis increasingly follow policies favorable to big business, whereas they had relied initially on small businessmen, farmers, shopkeepers, and even labor to gain and consolidate their power?

6. How did Hitler "solve" the economic crisis of the Great Depression by ending unemployment and renewing economic growth after his rise to power? Why was such a solution unavailable to the Weimar government? How did the massive unemployment of the Great Depression actually make it easier for the Nazis to pursue their goals?

*7. Hitler's approach to mobilizing the German economy (insofar as he had a coherent strategy) rested on five pillars. Explain any four of these. Show how they contributed to Nazi goals.

*8. Confining yourself to purely economic reasons, why do you suppose the Nazis wanted to break the bargaining power of labor, at the outset of their rule? With unemployment running around 40 percent, was organized labor not already weak? (*Hint*: In answering, you may again want to take the insider-outsider discussion at the end of chapter 3 into account.)

*9. Discuss Hitler's harnessing of foreign trade and payments to the pursuit of economic recovery (from the Great Depression) and to Germany's preparation for war. Have any methods used by the Nazis found systematic use since World War II? Explain how the Third Reich "taxed" foreign holders of German debt.

*10. Discuss Hitler's harnessing of financial markets to the pursuit of economic recovery, full employment, and Germany's preparation for war.

What was the post-World War II cost of Hitler's method of financing government expenditure?

11. What does the term, "*blitzkrieg* war economy," mean? What was the major strength and the major weakness of the German war economy from September, 1939 to mid-1942?

*12. "The currency reform took place on June 20. On June 21, goods reappeared in the stores, money resumed its normal function, black and grey markets reverted to a minor role, foraging trips to the country ceased, labor productivity rose, and output took off on its great upward surge. The spirit of the country changed overnight."

(a) Why did the economies of the three Western zones work so poorly under Allied occupation over 1945–48?

(b) What were the basic provisions of the currency reform of June, 1948, and why did it "restart" Germany's economic engine (in effect, launching the economic miracle)? Explain why such a beneficial move was delayed for so long.

13. How did government policies in the early years of the Federal Republic help to promote savings, investment, and expansion of exports?

Briefly describe the Investment Assistance Act of 1952. How did it contribute to growth?

* = more difficult.

INDEX

Hoffman, Dieter, 649*n.19*
Höglund, Elisabet, 565*n.26*
Holland. *See* Netherlands, The
Hollerman, Leon, 518*n.21*
Holmlund, Bertil, 564*n.23*
Holtfrerich, Carl-Ludwig, 688*n.4*
Holtzer, L., 249*n.25*
homebuilding. *See* housing
Honda, 453, 465, 482*n.8*, 505, 517*n.12*
Honda, S., 447
Hong Kong, 301, 302, 303, 307
Hopkins, Sheila V., 148*n.33*, 150*n.48*
horizons. *See* time horizons
horizontal supervision, 74
Horvat, Branko, 401*n.25*
hours of work. *See also* work hours
    in Germany, during the Weimar period,
        657
    in Hungary, 228
    in Japan, 450
    in Sweden, 534, 598
    in West Germany, 642, 644, 681
housing
    in China, 270, 271–72, 282, 283
    in France, 608*n.19*
    in Germany
        during the Nazi period, 666, 673
        during the Weimar period, 662
        during World War II, 675
        during World War II aftermath,
            677, 681
    in Hungary, 212, 214–15, 228, 230,
        247
    in Japan, 430–31, 432, 433, 458, 459,
        472, 480, 608*n.19*
    in Sweden, 528, 550, 568, 575
        assistance, 546, 549, 604
        building, 608*n.19*, 609*n.38*
        cooperatives, 595, 599–600
        and rent control, 578, 582–86
        shortages, 608*n.18*
    in the U.S., 608*n.19*
    in the USSR, 216
    in West Germany, 608*n.19*, 619, 620,
        638–40, 648*n.3*, 681, 682, 685,
        686, 687
    in Yugoslavia, 376, 382
HSB. *See* National Association of
    Tenants' Savings and Building Socie-
    ties in Sweden
HSWP. *See* Hungarian Socialist Workers'
    party

Hua, Guofeng, 264, 265, 279, 345
Huang Hsiao, Katherine H.Y., 287*n.10*
Huang, Wenjun, 320*n.15*
human bondage, 103. *See also* serfdom;
    slavery
    and population growth, 108, 109, 121
    and technological change, 121
human capital, investment in, as major
    source of income, 142
Hungarian Socialist Workers' party, 162,
    211, 213–14, 219, 223, 225, 226,
    341, 343
Hungarian uprising, 209–10
Hungary, 50–51*n.12*, 160, 418. *See also*
    under specific subjects
    demographics, geography and history,
        210
    economic growth, 242–46
    economic reform attempts, 46–47
    economy, 209–47
    evolution of socialist system, 164–65
    growth rates, 171
    infrastructure, 233
    New Direction, 332
        prospects, 341–44
        since 1979, 335–41
    New Economic Mechanism (NEM),
        210, 217–19, 222–23, 240, 241
        aftermath, 330–35
    Prices and Materials Board (PMB),
        211, 216, 332
    reform attempts, 176–77
    reform, main task of, 217
    reforms, 172, 175, 176, 193, 222, 224,
        330–44
    State Economic Commission (SEC),
        211, 216, 337
    trade, 218, 231, 334–35, 335–36, 341,
        342, 343
        within COMECON, 236–42
        decline, after 1979, 341
        decline, in the 1970s, 334–35
        import substitution, 342
        under the New Direction, 335–36
        organization of, 236–42
        during the 1930s, 668
        with the USSR, 239, 240, 334, 336
        with the West, 240
        with West Germany, 357*n.13*
Huntford, R., 609–10*nn.53, 54*
Huo, Bolin, 320*n.24*, 321*n.36*
hydraulic states, 124–26, 148*n.28*

subsidies (*continued*)
in Germany
during the Nazi period, 668, 669, 671
during the Weimar period, 659, 660
in Hungary, 214, 215, 229, 238, 333, 334
and inflation, 181
in Japan, 459, 472, 477, 495, 497
to agriculture, 432, 435, 445n.10, 507, 512, 513, 515
and postwar reconstruction, 442, 507
to priority industries, 457, 494, 498, 507, 508, 510, 516n.3
in Sweden, 525, 531, 538, 549, 573, 575
for housing, 582–83
to industries, 528, 567–69, 575
and labor market policies, 526, 549, 552, 591–92
for wages, 568
in the USSR, under *perestroika*, 189
in West Germany, 619–21, 627, 631, 633, 637–38, 639, 686
in Yugoslavia, 352, 363, 391, 392, 397, 413, 414, 415, 416
success indicators, 20, 61, 64–65, 67, 225, 597. *See also* profits and profitability—as success indicators
Sudan, 302
suffrage, 158. *See also* voting
Sumitomo, 439, 464
Sumitomo Bank, 453
Sumitomo Shoji, 465, 468
Summers, L. H., 150n.49
Sunding, David, 288n.20
supervision
and coordination, 61–67
horizontal, 74
and independent judgment, 121
and rewards, 76
supervisory scale economies, 60
supply and demand. *See also* elastic supply responses; excess demand; excess supply
in command economies, 56
and controls, 583
in Lange-Lerner model of socialism, 166n.6
and prices, 15–18, 50n.3
and quotas, 9–11, 15

Supreme Soviet of the USSR (SSU), 31
survival of the fittest thesis, 102
Suzuki, Yukio, 518nn.25, 26
Suzumura, Kotaro, 518n.25
Svenska Riksbyggen (SR), 600, 609n.44
Sweden, 44, 47, 637, 689n.15. *See also under specific subjects*
geography, 529
government expenditure, 229
population, 529, 532
public-sector growth, 44
ratio of public spending to GNP, 45
trade, 45, 564n.19
decline of exports in the 1970s, 527, 545, 570
dependence on, 542
export specialization, 239
free trade advocated by LO, 536
impact of oil crisis, 542–44
with Japan, 542
with OECD countries, 542
trade barriers, 524, 537
Swedish Building Workers' Union, 600
Swedish Communal Industries, 592
Swedish Employers' Confederation. *See* SAF
Swedish Institute, The, 607n.11, 609n.47
Swedish Labour Market Administration, 608n.28
Swedish Ministry of Economic Affairs and the Ministry of the Budget, 607n.8
Swedish Ministry of Finance, 563n.13
Switzerland, 239, 532, 583, 616
trade barriers, 435
Szalai, E., 356n.9, 357n.15
Szikra Falus, K., 249nn.24, 25. *See also* Falus-Szikra, K.

Tabori, Andras, 247n.7
Taft-Morris, Cynthia, 321n.30
Taiwan, 47, 298, 301, 471, 513
Tanaka, Kakuei, 445n.8
TANEP construction company, Hungary, 343
Tardos, Marton, 248n.15, 248n.18, 356n.7
targets. *See* output targets; production targets
tariffs. *See* trade barriers
Tarjan, D., 249n.24
taxation, 579
in China, 281, 282, 301, 308, 348

Union of Soviet Socialist Republics. *See*
USSR
unions. *See* labor unions
United Kingdom, 47, 231, 462, 562*n.5*.
See also England; Great Britain
cartels, 626
gross national product, 48, 49, 430
income distribution, 244
oligopoly, 462
trade, 307, 516*n.8*
wages, 473
work days lost to industrial disputes,
480, 539
United States International Trade Commission, 457, 99*n.24*
United States Occupation authorities in
Japan (SCAP), 436–40, 443, 444,
445*n.13*, 454, 476, 517*n.14*
United States of America, 47, 468, 530,
562*n.5*, 676. *See also under specific
subjects*
ratio of public spending to GNP, 45
trade, 499, 619
with China, 307, 320*n.11*
with Japan, 429, 457, 493, 511,
516*n.8*
trade barriers, 513
universal suffrage, considered crucial by
Marx and Engels, 158
unofficial economy. *See* second economy
use rights
and alienation, 155
in China, 291, 297
and communal property, 5
defined, 4
and income rights, 7, 15
and ownership, 7
and private property, 5
and private property rights, 6
and state control, 6
and state property, 5
and state property rights, 6
transfer of, in a socialist market economy, 23
in the USSR, under *perestroika*, 189
in Yugoslavia, 7, 24
USSR, 39, 47, 231, 236, 361, 417,
518*n.28*, 674, 676. *See also under
specific subjects*
Central Committee (CC), 30
and China, 258, 280
Council of Ministers, 29, 31

USSR (*continued*)
Gosplan, 287*n.5*
industrial espionage, 173
in the Middle Ages, 126
New Economic Policy Era, 162, 163
per capita growth rates, 171
Presidium of the Council of Ministers,
31
Presidium of the Supreme Soviet, 31
reform attempts, 176–77
reforms, 166, 168–98
regional economic councils, 287*n.5*
and Soyuz natural gas pipeline, 50–
51*n.12*
trade, 236, 237, 421*n.10*
with China, 302, 307, 308–12
with Hungary, 239, 240, 334, 336
under *perestroika*, 190–91
utopian views of communal property
rights, 11–12

vacations, in Sweden, 546
Vanek, Jaroslav, 394, 400*n.20*, 401*n.28*
vanguard elite, 158
Varga, G., 356*n.9*
venture capital, in capitalist economies, 24
Vietnam, 162, 236
Viklund, Birger, 563*n.13*
Vinde, Pierre, 607*n.7*
vocational training. *See* job training
Vogl, Frank, 651*n.36*
Volkswagenwerk A. G., 647, 651*n.33*
Volvo, 552, 554, 555, 564*n.25*, 570
voting, 78–82, 110. *See also* elections
VVBs (industrial associations in East Ger-
many), 174–76, 193
VW Shanghai, 344

Wachtel, Howard M., 399*n.12*, 401*n.35*
wage control
in Germany, 673, 678, 681
in Hungary, 334
in the USSR, 226–27
wage determination, Marxian view of,
135–38
wage differentials
in France, 473
in Italy, 473
in Japan, 472–73, 477–78
in Sweden. *See* wages—in Sweden
in the U.K., 473
in West Germany, 473

ABOUT THE AUTHOR

Richard L. Carson received an M.A. in journalism from the University of Minnesota and a Ph.D. in economics from Indiana University. He is presently associate professor of economics at Carleton University in Ottawa, Canada, where he teaches courses in comparative economic systems and economic theory. He has also published extensively in these areas, including articles in the *Canadian Journal of Economics*, the *American Economic Review*, the *ACES Bulletin*, the *Journal of Economics and Businesss*, and the *Eastern Economic Journal*.